THE MAKING OF THE EAST LONDON MOSQUE, 1910–1951

MINUTES OF THE LONDON MOSQUE FUND AND EAST LONDON MOSQUE TRUST LTD.

THE MAKING OF THE EAST LONDON MOSQUE, 1910–1951

MINUTES OF THE LONDON MOSQUE FUND AND EAST LONDON MOSQUE TRUST LTD.

edited by
HUMAYUN ANSARI

CAMDEN FIFTH SERIES
Volume 38

CAMBRIDGE
UNIVERSITY PRESS

FOR THE ROYAL HISTORICAL SOCIETY
University College London, Gower Street,
London WC1 6BT
2011

Published by the Press Syndicate of the University of Cambridge
The Edinburgh Building, Cambridge CB2 8RU, United Kingdom
32 Avenue of the Americas, New York, NY 10013-2473, USA
477 Williamstown Road, Port Melbourne, VIC 3207, Australia
C/Orense, 4, Planta 13, 28020 Madrid, Spain
Lower Ground Floor, Nautica Building, The Water Club,
Beach Road, Granger Bay, 8005 Cape Town, South Africa

First published 2011

A catalogue record for this book is available from the British Library

ISBN 9781107014923 hardback

SUBSCRIPTIONS. The serial publications of the Royal Historical Society, *Royal Historical Society Transactions* (ISSN 0080–4401) and Camden Fifth Series (ISSN 0960–1163) volumes, may be purchased together on annual subscription. The 2011 subscription price, which includes print and electronic access (but not VAT), is £121 (US $203 in the USA, Canada, and Mexico) and includes Camden Fifth Series, volumes 38, 39, and 40 (published in April, July, and December) and Transactions Sixth Series, volume 21 (published in December). Japanese prices are available from Kinokuniya Company Ltd, P.O. Box 55, Chitose, Tokyo 156, Japan. EU subscribers (outside the UK) who are not registered for VAT should add VAT at their country's rate. VAT registered subscribers should provide their VAT registration number. Prices include delivery by air.

Subscription orders, which must be accompanied by payment, may be sent to a bookseller, subscription agent, or direct to the publisher: Cambridge University Press, The Edinburgh Building, Shaftesbury Road, Cambridge CB2 8RU, UK; or in the USA, Canada, and Mexico: Cambridge University Press, Journals Fulfillment Department, 100 Brook Hill Drive, West Nyack, New York, 10994–2133, USA.

SINGLE VOLUMES AND BACK VOLUMES. A list of Royal Historical Society volumes available from Cambridge University Press may be obtained from the Humanities Marketing Department at the address above.

Printed and bound in the United Kingdom at the University Press, Cambridge

CONTENTS

PREFACE

These Minutes are currently held in the East London Mosque Archives, East London Mosque & London Muslim Centre, 46–92 Whitechapel Road, London, E1 1JX. They consist of a series of papers, bound together with occasional additional documents, in one large file.

The range of alternative spellings of personal names as well as of terms used in the Minutes has been retained for authenticity. This inconsistency is due in part to contemporary inconsistencies in transliteration and changes in spelling of words over time. For example, 'Mussulman' is used at some points, as are 'Moslim', 'Moslem', and 'Muslim'. Likewise, 'Sayyid', 'Sayed', 'Sayyed', and 'Syed' are all variations on the same title. While this kind of usage of language has been left as it was in the original documents, readers can find variant spellings in the Index, which will direct them to the correct biographical entry where applicable. Similarly, any small grammatical or spelling errors have been left as in the original documents.

Biographical details for major figures related to the development of the East London Mosque are contained in Appendix I. These vary in length, depending on the availability of information of relevance to the subject. The first mention in the Minutes of anyone whose details are contained in Appendix I is marked with an asterisk. Unfortunately, it has not been possible to identify all those individuals mentioned in the Minutes. Appendix II contains the complete text of the 1948 Articles of Association of the East London Mosque Trust Limited. It, along with the selection of documents included in Appendix III, have not been annotated, as they are primarily intended to supplement the information contained in the Minutes themselves.

Some references annotated in the footnotes are spelled out in detail if they are hard to find. For others that are more easily accessible, for example via a link to a website or a readily available text, just the reference to the source is provided.

This annotated record ends with the Minutes of December 1951. This date marks the end of the first collection of minutes preserved at the Mosque, at a time when the 'old guard' of Trustees was still largely in charge of the project, despite the fact that by then India and Pakistan had attained independence. There is no obvious later cut-off point that, first, would have excluded material that might still be regarded as confidential or lacking a suitable historical context, and, secondly, would have avoided the edition becoming too large for publication in this form.

I have had generous assistance from many people in preparing this edited collection. In particular, Hamzah Foreman gave liberally of his time, facilitated access to the archival material, and provided much useful information. Thanks must also go to Mohammad Shakir, Mueenuddin Chowdhery, and Dr Muhammad Abdul Bari. Many others at the East London Mosque answered my questions and allowed me access to background information. Gail Boxwell and June Jackson meticulously transcribed the Minutes and appendix material, and both Gail and Farhaan Wali helped to research additional material for the Introduction. Finally, I am extremely grateful to the Marc Fitch Fund for its support for this project.

Humayun Ansari
Royal Holloway University of London

LIST OF ABBREVIATIONS

BL, IOR	British Library, India Office Records
EDL	English Defence League
ELM	East London Mosque
ELMT	East London Mosque Trust
GLC	Greater London Council
IFE	Islamic Forum of Europe
JI	Jamaat-i-Islami
LMC	London Muslim Centre
LMF	London Mosque Fund
ODNB	H.C.G. Matthew and Brian Harrison (eds), *The Oxford Dictionary of National Biography*, 60 vols (Oxford, 2004) (http://www.oxforddnb.com)
TJ	Tablighi Jamaat
YMO	Young Muslim Organisation

INTRODUCTION

In November 2010, the East London Mosque celebrated its centenary. One hundred years earlier, the Aga Khan[1] and Syed Ameer Ali[2] convened a public meeting at the salubrious Ritz Hotel where, with support from some sympathetic members of the British establishment, they set about putting in place a strategy for the construction of a mosque in London, one that would be 'worthy of the capital of the British Empire'.[3] The London Mosque Fund was founded to finance its construction. Often regarded as the first mosque in London,[4] the ELM, like many other mosques in the UK, took a long time to materialize. As with other mosques, the ELM also had to move several times during its long history. From the three converted houses in Commercial Road in the East End of London in which it had finally been set up in 1941, following a compulsory purchase order in 1969, it first moved to a prefabricated structure in Fieldgate Street in 1975 and then on to the present purpose-built one in Whitechapel Road in 1985.[5] This in turn was extended to incorporate the London Muslim Centre in 2004 to meet the needs of the locality's fast-growing Muslim community. The story of its journey enables us to throw fresh light on the changing nature of interactions with wider society

[1]See Appendix I.

[2]See Appendix I.

[3]'On November 9th 1910, a public meeting was convened by [Rt. Hon. Syed Ameer Ali . . .] under the chairmanship of the Rt. Hon. Aga Khan. Following a resolution passed at the meeting, funds were raised for the purpose of "providing a Mosque in London worthy of the traditions of Islam and worthy of the capital of the British Empire".' See ELM Archives, report by Sir Ernest Hotson, Honorary Secretary, contained in the brochure of the Opening Ceremony of the East London Mosque and Islamic Culture Centre, Friday, 1 August 1941; BL, IOR, L/P&J/12/468, fo. 40.

[4]This is open to historical challenge. The Fazl Mosque, built by the Ahmadiyya community in 1926, was reported by *The Times* as 'the first building erected in London for Islamic worship' (*The Times*, 2 October 1926). However, the Ahmadiyya movement has been subject to religious controversy from its inception in the late nineteenth century because, while Ahmadiyyas consider themselves to be Muslim, they are regarded as outside the fold of Islam by orthodox Muslims. See Simon Ross Valentine, *Islam and the Ahmadiyya Jama'at: history, belief, practice* (New York, 2008).

[5]The opening ceremony of the East London Mosque in its Whitechapel Road premises took place on 12 July 1985.

and the relationships between London's Muslim community and the institutions of the British state; the latter's expedient character was starkly reflected, for instance, during the Second World War when Churchill and his government sought Muslim support in a global conflict in which the loyalties of Muslims throughout the British Empire could prove crucial.

The ELM's Minute Books record the debates and dilemmas of meetings of the Trustees of the LMF and the East London Mosque Trust from the first one, held in 1910.[6] They offer a detailed, intimate account of the process of mosque-making, the financial and organizational management of the LMF/ELMT, and its role in building London's Muslim community and its institutions. Drawing on these materials as well as the archives at the East London Mosque and the British Library, this introduction to the context in which these Minute Books were compiled will show how religious activity was shaped by local, national, and international developments. Through this story of mosque-building, we can trace not just a history of immigration but also its connections with empire, trade, and war, and the contours of the process through which the 'Muslim' community in London's East End become established.

Considering later minutes alongside more contemporary records, it is also possible in this introduction to explore the role of the ELM/LMC in the evolution of the Muslim community to the end of the first decade of the twenty-first century, in the process revealing complex interactions between the mosque, local communities, and the wider society that has come to exist in London's East End since 1951. We can thus explore the changing symbolic and political dynamics of communities and their identities as reflected in the controversies, debates, and tensions generated by such culturally inscribed, visual appropriations of the built environment – mosques as sites for building a sense of community, 'belonging', and identity; as sites for resisting what was thought to be discrimination against Islam and Muslims and for their empowerment through assertion of cultural rights; and as sites that are viewed as aesthetically and socially disruptive, posing threats to Britain's heritage and to 'the British way of life'.

The history of the London Mosque Fund together with that of the East London Mosque Trust is worth telling, not only because it records the early presence of the Muslim faith and Muslim communities in Britain – something that is not widely appreciated – but because

[6] This annotated edition reproduces the Minute Books that cover the period 1910–1951, and that are currently housed in the ELM Archives. The Minute Books, however, continue until 1982, and these later recordings of developments have also been drawn upon extensively in the writing of this introduction.

its establishment and use was often marked by conflict around sets of issues that continue to exist to this day. Issues concerning the so-called 'Islamization of space' and the reactions against such incursions into autochthonous space are crucial in understanding the contested history of many mosques established in Britain. By locating the history of the LMF and Muslim places of worship in London within the context of imperial and global forces, and by examining the long, and often fraught, struggles about how a Muslim sacred space is created, represented, and used, a politics of identity is teased out as increasing pluralization of Britain's religious make-up has gathered momentum.

In the wake of the 9/11 and 7/7 terrorist attacks, the mosque, as a socially dynamic and influential multi-purpose community institution, has come under increasing scrutiny as academic and political debates surrounding identity and belonging, the radicalization of young Muslims, struggles for power within and beyond Muslim communities, and policies on integration and social cohesion reach a new pitch. For a Muslim to feel at home, or for a non-Muslim to recognize a Muslim 'space', the presence of certain Islamic symbols is important. In Britain, the physical construction of mosques has been part of a process of identity formation, something that has become embroiled with non-Muslim concerns over visible and audible Muslim presence. By exploring historically the dynamic interplay between Muslim experience and the institutions of British society with regard to the struggle for a mosque in London, this introduction seeks to deepen our understanding of how Muslims have sought to establish themselves as an integral part of British society, through a specific kind of place-making.

Here questions are addressed that can potentially provide new insights into a central aspect of an arguably misunderstood minority faith community: what is the symbolic significance of the mosque in Britain for identity formation among 'diasporic' Muslims? How does the mosque interact with its local environment – physically, socio-culturally, and politically – and with the communities and institutions surrounding it? Thirdly, and importantly, what functions do mosques and the struggle for their establishment serve? Did they/do they, for instance, reinforce a sense of community belonging and act as 'a potential bridge to non-Muslim communities', or did they/do they also represent a site of contestation and social divisions within and between communities? Through a historical exploration of the effort for the establishment of a mosque in London as a religious, community, and social institution, we can gain a better understanding of the relations of power vis-à-vis wider society and within the Muslim community, the sources of inclusion and exclusion of particular groups, and the struggles that were waged to overcome their marginalization.

Wherever Muslims have established relatively permanent communities in the non-Muslim world, history demonstrates that they have sought to form structures that, they have hoped, will enable them to sustain their religious traditions and practices. While mosques have been perceived primarily as spaces for religious rituals, it is accepted that these do not require dedicated physical space. Traditionally, mosques were not places merely for purposes of worship; they also functioned as centres for religious learning and for the propagation of Islam; this was where believers interacted socially, culturally, and, indeed, politically. It is therefore not surprising that this would be the institution to which they would turn when they began to make new homes in Britain. When we look at mosque-building in Britain, however, what we find is that its significance has changed in the diasporic context as it is recreated and re-imagined in new settings.

The London Mosque Fund and the East London Mosque: 1910–1941

In Britain, the earliest examples of attempts to create dedicated 'Muslim space' go back to the nineteenth century. Congregations were organized by embryonic Muslim communities, primarily in boarding-houses or converted buildings: in Manchester, for instance, Levantine and Moroccan Muslim merchants held Friday prayers regularly in an ordinary house.[7] Similarly, boarding-houses catering for Arabs and Somalis in South Shields and Cardiff had rooms reserved for prayers. Abdullah Quilliam (1856–1932), a convert to Islam, set up a mosque, first, in 1887, in a house in Mount Vernon Place in Liverpool, and then, when evicted from there, in West Derby Road in 1891. In 1889, the Shah Jahan Mosque in Woking, an initiative of an Orientalist, G.W. Leitner (1840–1899) and sponsored by the Begum of Bhopal (Shah Jahan was at the time the female ruler of the princely state of Bhopal in India), was opened on the former's private estate. Though a 'Muslim space', the fact that it was created by an 'agent' of British authority in India (Leitner had worked for years in the Punjab) meant that it reflected colonial relations of power. Rather patronizingly, Leitner declared the mosque to be 'proof of British toleration', to be 'used in that [same] grateful and reverential spirit'. Indeed, his facilities were to be narrowly limited to Islamic religious practices as he understood them, which meant that he was certainly not prepared to permit their use for the conversion of 'Englishmen to Islam, or to introduce new doctrines into that faith, or to promote any religious and political

[7] H. Ansari, *'The Infidel Within': Muslims in Britain since 1800* (London, 2004), p. 70.

propaganda, or to celebrate [what he regarded as] the generally unhappy marriages between Mahommedans and Englishwomen': in short, only those of whom he approved – Muslims of 'good family' background and gentlemanly conduct – were acceptable.[8] Clearly, this was how social distance between the dominant and subject people and the status quo could be most effectively maintained. Operating under such strictures, the Woking Mosque was never in regular or widespread Muslim use during Leitner's lifetime. After his death in 1899, the mosque was closed down by his family and remained practically empty, and more-or-less unused, until 1912. Contrast this, however, with what happened after Khwaja Kamal-ud-din[9] (1870–1932) took it over just before the First World War. Within a few years it became a vibrant centre for Muslims in Britain, a well-attended venue for religious and social festivals alike. Later, during the inter-war decades, a number of Muslim leaders based in London became its Trustees and contributed to its wide range of activities,[10] while visits by high personages from different parts of the Muslim world enhanced its symbolic importance.[11]

In the absence of a mosque in London, congregations and celebrations of Muslim festivals were organized in an ad hoc fashion. Hence, *The Times* reported on 22 December 1903 that 'members of the Moslem [*sic*] colony in London assembled, under the auspices of the Pan-Islamic Society, in Caxton-hall [. . .] to celebrate Eed-ul-Fitr (The Feast After the Fast). The gathering was thoroughly representative, Persians, Turks, Indians, Moors, Egyptians, Dutch, &c., being present in their national costumes'. The service was conducted by Redjai Effendi, Imam of the Imperial Ottoman Embassy. Joy was expressed at 'the true Islamic spirit of unity and brotherhood prevailing among Moslems from all parts of the world now residing in the British Isles', and an appeal was made to the Muslims to contribute towards the Mosque Fund.[12] Around 1905, Khalid Sheldrake,[13] a proactive Muslim

[8] K. H. Ansari, 'The Woking Mosque: a case study of Muslim engagement with British society since 1889', *Immigrants & Minorities*, 21, no. 3 (November 2002), pp. 6–7.

[9] See Appendix I.

[10] Sir Abbas Ali Baig (d. 1933), Syed Ameer Ali, and Sir T.W. Arnold were founders of the Woking Mosque Trust in 1915. See M.P. Salamat, *A Miracle At Woking: a history of the Shahjahan Mosque* (Andover, 2008), pp. 97–99. The latter two were also Trustees of the London Mosque Fund. Others who took close interest in its activities included the Aga Khan, Marmaduke Pickthall, and Lord Headley.

[11] These included the then Begum of Bhopal, the Shah of Persia, the Sultan of Zanzibar, Prince Amir Saud and Amir Faisal of the Saudi royal family, M.A. Jinnah, the 'founder' of Pakistan, King Farouk of Egypt, and Princess Saniyya of Albania. See the various issues of *Islamic Review* for relevant details.

[12] *The Times*, 22 December 1903.

[13] See Appendix I.

convert, began conducting prayers at a house in Peckham,[14] and the Pan-Islamic Society also organized Muslim congregations in rented London halls.[15] So here we see religious space being created – albeit temporarily – often but not always by 'diasporic' Muslims continuing practices belonging to the communities they had left behind. The sense of contrast with the rest of society, and the difficulties of sustaining normative religious practices that were different from those of the majority population, seemed to heighten its merit and the desire for a 'space' where such activities could be conducted.

The need for a dedicated place of Muslim worship in London was felt with added urgency in the early twentieth century. The initiative for a mosque came from a significant cluster of Muslim activists in London who had become increasingly self-conscious and possessed the capacity to articulate the concerns and discontents of their co-religionists. Syed Ameer Ali called public attention to the subject as early as May 1908: as he put it,

> It does not require great imagination or political grasp to perceive the enormous advantages that would accrue to the empire itself were a Moslem place of worship founded in London, the hold it would give on the sentiments of the people or the addition to prestige and influence that would be gained thereby.[16]

In October 1910, *The Times* reported further developments:

> A movement has been started by Mr Halil Halid[17] for the erection of a mosque in London. Subscriptions are already being received by the Ottoman Bank at Constantinople from Turkish sympathisers of the movement and the support of all who are interested in Mahomedans in India, Egypt and Turkey in Great Britain will be enlisted.[18]

In the following month, a meeting, presided over by the Aga Khan, was convened at the Ritz Hotel in London, and a committee was formed, with Syed Ameer Ali (the driving force behind the Fund's creation) as its chairman, to collect funds for the construction of a mosque in London.[19] The fund was opened at the Bank of England, with the Aga Khan promising an initial subscription of £5,000.[20]

[14] M. Everest-Phillips, 'The suburban king of Tartary', *Asian Affairs*, 21, no. 3 (October 1990), p. 325.

[15] Sheldrake remembered the *namaz* (prayer) held at Caxton Hall (London), 'and the worshippers were Ottomans, Indians and Egyptians, myself the only Englishman': see *Islamic Review and Modern India*, April 1917, p. 83.

[16] *The Times*, 5 January 1911.

[17] See Appendix I, under 'Bey, Halil Halid'.

[18] *The Times*, 28 October 1910.

[19] See above, n. 3.

[20] By the end of 1917, donations amounting to about £5,000 had been received and invested in Inscribed Securities held by the Bank of England. The securities stood in the

The Turkish Ambassador, the Persian Minister, the Turkish Minister at Brussels, Lords Lamington, Ampthill, Avebury, and Ronaldshay, Sir Seymour King, Sir William Bull MP, and three members of the Council of India – Sir Theodore Morison, Sir James La Touche, and Mr Abbas Ali Baig – also joined the Committee. The joint secretaries were Mr C.A. Latif, Major Syud Hasan Bilgrami, and Professor T.W. Arnold, with Mr A.S.M. Anik as treasurer and Mr M.T. Kaderbhoy as assistant secretary. Mr Halil Halid was also a member of the Executive Committee.[21] For the Muslims involved in this venture, who hailed primarily from Western-educated classes of Indian society – namely, administrators, merchants, and professionals – a mosque in London formed part of a wider set of strategies designed to advance their individual interests as well as the interests of their community. They were certainly receptive to some 'British' values and ideas, but awareness of the shortcomings of British society also confirmed them in their Islamic faith and many of their own traditions. While conscious of the contempt and rudeness that they experienced in their encounters with many English people, they attributed these attitudes to an unfortunate lack of understanding. Such Muslims, then, while they accepted the hegemony of existing British values, wanted to push at the boundaries of social and political discourse in order to create more space for Muslim concerns. Take Syed Ameer Ali, for instance.[22] He had deliberately adopted English as 'the language of culture and civilised progress'. He regarded himself as a 'bridge-builder' and a 'mediator' – a key member of the group that saw itself as leading the campaign for Muslim representation in Britain, and that believed that a mosque in London would be an appropriate site through which religious needs could be satisfied, misconceptions about Islam removed, and Muslim interests promoted. As suggested in *The Times* soon after the formation of the Fund,

> To devout Musalmans [. . .] the project will be the more attractive from the anticipation that a place of worship in the metropolis of the Empire for the performance of simple devotions of Islam will tend to secure a larger measure of sympathy from observers in the country not familiar with the tenets of the Muslim faith. Moreover, as the scheme includes the provision of a library of Islamic literature to be attached to the mosque, it will aid the work of scholarly research into the history and theology of Muslim people.[23]

names of seven Trustees, five of whom were Muslims and two English noblemen 'whose sympathy with Moslems is well-known, Lord Ampthill and Lord Lamington' (*Westminster Gazette*, 20 December 1917).

[21] *The Times*, 5 January 1911.

[22] See Appendix I.

[23] *The Times*, 5 January 1911.

However, their plans faced a number of hurdles, both historic and contemporary. First, towards the end of the nineteenth century, rising political tensions in Europe together with imperial competition meant that attitudes as well as policy in Britain showed increasing hostility towards Islam and Muslims. For instance, the former prime minister William Gladstone, a committed Christian, who had earlier denounced the Qur'an as 'that accursed book'[24] and Ottoman 'atrocities' in putting down the Bulgarian rebellion in 1876,[25] gave full vent in 1896 to rising popular indignation against the Ottomans in reaction to their allegedly brutal treatment of Armenians, launching a scathing attack on 'that wretched Sultan, whom God has given as a curse to mankind'.[26] Such antagonism towards Islam, perhaps not surprisingly, began to galvanize opinion among Muslims in Britain in defence of the Sultan-Caliph as the key symbol of the *umma*, or worldwide Muslim community. At the same time, as British foreign policy moved away from support for the Ottomans at the turn of the century, several strands of pan-Islam emerged.[27] Quilliam, upon whom the Ottoman Sultan had earlier conferred the title of Sheikh al-Islam of the British Isles, defended him against Gladstone's tirade. Muslims in London, too, expressed concern for the *umma*. Religious festivals became occasions when Pan-Islamic solidarity was vigorously displayed, and British handling of Muslim issues came under thinly veiled criticism. For instance, in 1907, at a dinner celebrating Eid-ul-zuha,[28] M.H Kidwai, the honorary secretary of the Pan-Islamic Society, referring to 'the Musalmans [. . .] groaning under the despotism of Lord Cromer' in the British protectorate in Egypt, called for the Khedive[29] to be given a free hand in ruling his country. He challenged appeals to Christendom to crush Pan-Islamism – that fight, he declared would be in vain; and he restated that the objects of his Society were very peaceful, that its members were loyal subjects of King Edward VII, and that the Society wanted 'perfect

[24] N. Daniel, *Islam, Europe and Empire* (Edinburgh, 1966), p. 37.

[25] See W.E. Gladstone, *Bulgarian Horrors and the Question of the East* (London, 1876), reproduced at http://www.archive.org/stream/bulgarianhorrorsoogladrich/bulgarianhorrorsoogladrich_djvu.txt (accessed 8 May 2010).

[26] Ansari, *'The Infidel Within'*, p. 81.

[27] See H. Ansari, 'Making transnational connections: Muslim networks in early twentieth-century Britain', in Nathalie Clayer and Eric Germain (eds), *Islam in Inter-War Europe* (London, 2008), pp. 31–63.

[28] The Feast of Sacrifice at the end of Ramadan, the Muslim month of fasting.

[29] Abbas II (1892–1914) reigned over Egypt at the time that Lord Cromer (1841–1917) exercised executive power as the Consul-General. His repressive policies were criticized in both Egypt and Britain. See A. Sonbol (ed. and trans.), *The Last Khedive of Egypt: memoirs of Abbas Hilmi II* (Reading, 1998).

friendship' between Great Britain and Muslim sovereigns.[30] Even the older generation of 'empire-loyalists', such as Syed Ameer Ali, could not remain unaffected and strove to influence British policy in favour of the Muslim world through constitutional means, albeit within the framework of the empire. Hence, Ali inaugurated the London branch of the All-India Muslim League on 6 May 1908 at Caxton Hall, with the aim of preserving Indian Muslims from disintegration and pauperization, and, in particular, of seeking equitable representation in the political sphere.[31]

With the Italian invasion of Tripolitania in 1911, pan-Islamic sentiment, simmering away since 1908, boiled over. A spate of memorials, newspaper articles, petitions, and manifestos poured out of London. Agitation was mounted and protest meetings organized with the help and support of prominent British men. At the fifth annual general meeting of the London All-India Muslim League, the Aga Khan said that 'the recent Turkish war had demonstrated the solidity of [. . .] Moslems [. . .] their interest in each other's welfare [. . .] the trials and tribulations of Turkey had absorbed Indian Moslems [. . .] The currents of feeling were very strong'.[32] Much disappointment was expressed at the British unwillingness to intervene against the Italian military invasion. These empire-loyalists argued that Islamic feeling towards Britain, especially among Indian Muslims, was changing for the worse, and that this would prove harmful to British interests. While some operating in the ruling circles of the empire expressed sympathy for such views, others within the British establishment, undoubtedly imbued with a mixture of racism, uncertainty, fear, and paranoia, were never confident about the 'clever Native'. King Edward VII himself epitomized this attitude: when opposing Syed Ameer Ali's nomination for membership of the Privy Council in 1909, he wrote that 'you never could be certain that he might not prove to be a very dangerous element'.[33] Nor, given his elitist disposition, did Syed Ameer Ali inspire much confidence even among his own core constituency of Westernized Muslims. While many in the British establishment accused him of 'rocking the imperial boat' thanks to his 'continued attempts to stir up against the British Government in connexion with their Turkish Policy sentiments of hostility and hatred among his

[30] *The Times*, 28 January 1907.

[31] *The Times*, 5 May 1908; 17 November 1908; 24 February 1909; 25 June 1909.

[32] *The Times*, 15 July 1913.

[33] M. Forward, 'Syed Ameer Ali: a bridge-builder?', *Islam and Christian–Muslim Relations*, 6, no. 1 (1995), pp. 50–51.

co-religionists',[34] the emerging Muslim leadership in India also criticized him for 'selling our community'.[35]

Given the nature of the suspicions surrounding Syed Ameer Ali and other Muslim Trustees of the London Mosque Fund, their relative lack of success in generating adequate sponsorship for the mosque becomes more understandable. The initial enthusiasm evident for the project in different parts of the Muslim world, and its concrete manifestation in the subscription of £7,000 by the Begum of Bhopal[36] and £1,000 each by the Ottoman Sultan[37] and the Shah of Persia,[38] receded quickly, partly because of the internal troubles in what was still known as Persia and the urgent need to divert funds to relieve distress and suffering caused by the Tripolitan and Balkan conflicts.[39]

As the First World War erupted, the scheme for building a mosque in London suffered a further setback. Ottoman involvement on the side of Germany created hostility towards Muslims at all levels of British society and immediate doubts about the loyalty of all classes of Muslims living within the British Empire. This antipathy was further exacerbated by the Sultan-Caliph's proclamation ordering Muslims who were being ruled by 'enemy' governments to engage in a *jihad* against them.[40] Not surprisingly, leading politicians such as the Prime Minister, David Lloyd George, unleashed in retaliation a barrage of vituperative rhetoric against Islam and the Turks. Lloyd George described the fight against Turkey as a great civilizing duty that would emancipate people from under the shadow of great tyranny, and called the military operations in Palestine 'the British crusade'.[41]

Nevertheless, despite the deeply negative circumstances, Muslims in Britain continued to pursue the mosque project optimistically. The sources for funding that they could consider were threefold: the wealthier class of Muslims based in Britain; Muslim governments,

[34] *Ibid.*, p. 51.

[35] *The Times*, 31 October 1913.

[36] *The Times*, 4 December 1912.

[37] *The Times*, 28 March 1911.

[38] *The Times*, 11 April 1911.

[39] Towards the end of 1911, Syed Ameer Ali, undeterred by the lack of official response, set up the Red Crescent Society, through which funds could be gathered and provisions sent to help the Turks. '[T]he Indian Moslems in London decided yesterday evening to establish a Red Crescent Fund for the relief of the wounded Turks and Tripolitans. The Fund is to be under the joint management of the All-India Muslim League and the Islamic Society and has been headed by a first donation of £400 from the Aga Khan' (*The Times*, 3 November 1911). On 8 November 1911, *The Times* reported that the Red Crescent Society was collecting contributions for the relief of sickly Turks, widows, and orphans in Tripoli.

[40] See 'A universal proclamation to all the people of Islam', in J.M. Landau, *The Politics of Pan-Islam: ideology and organization* (Oxford, 1994), p. 351.

[41] *Muslim Outlook*, 30 October 1919; 6 October 1919.

rulers, and communities elsewhere; and the British government itself. Having largely failed to attract funding from the first two, it was the last source that they decided to explore, with some expectation of a positive outcome. They argued that, contrary to British suspicions regarding Muslim loyalties, thousands of Muslims were in practice fighting for king and country against Britain's enemies, including the Ottoman Caliphate, the paramount symbol of the *umma*. As Lord Headley, a leading convert, and Maulvi Sadr-ud-din, Imam of the Woking Mosque, jointly declared, by 'freely pouring out their life blood in defence of honour and for the love of truth and justice', these Muslims were demonstrating their unequivocal identification with, and commitment to, the British war effort.[42] Muslim soldiers were therefore entitled to an honourable place in the land for which they were fighting (and often dying). Indeed, they argued that recognition – in culturally appropriate ways – would help to create a bond, as well as mark their acceptance as equal stakeholders in the British imperial polity.

Setting out his case in this way, in 1916 Lord Headley wrote to Austin Chamberlain, the Secretary of State for India, recommending building in London

> at the country's expense, a [handsome] mosque in memory of the Muslim soldiers who have died fighting for the Empire [. . .] Just now it would be most politic to mark our appreciation of Muslim loyalty and devotion [. . . It] would have a magical effect [. . .] a gracious and spontaneous act of this kind would be returned to us an hundredfold.[43]

None of this, however, cut much ice with junior and senior officials, who, reflecting accurately the wider mentality of the time, remained generally unsympathetic if not overtly hostile to this project. As Sir Arthur Hirtzel commented: 'I am dead against it – on grounds of both policy and religion [. . . that] a Christian Government should be party to erecting one [a mosque] in a Christian country is to me unthinkable'.[44]

The extent of negative feelings in Britain towards Ottoman Turkey in particular and Muslims more generally intensified as the war grew increasingly bloody. The British government decided that, rather than

[42] *Islamic Review*, October 1914, p. 421. 'By Armistice Day, 400,000 Muslims had enlisted', and had fought on the Western Front in Europe, in Mesopotamia, and in Africa. 'In total approximately 60,000 men perished, 13,000 medals and 12 Victoria Crosses were awarded to Indians for valour and courage.' See Jahan Mahmood, 'The stories of Muslim soldiers on the Western Front; WWI', http://www.britainsmuslimsoldiers.co.uk/images/w1.pdf (accessed 8 May 2010).

[43] BL, IOR, L/MIL/7/18861, Lord Headley to Austin Chamberlain, 23 March 1916.

[44] *Ibid.*, A. Hirtzel's note, 31 March 1916.

address pan-Islamic sensitivities or offer assistance in the building of a mosque in London in fulfilment of Muslim religious needs, even at a time when religion possessed considerable potency, it would adopt a different approach to counter the Turkish threat. On balance, the two-pronged strategy of fomenting an Arab revolt and of recognizing Sharif Husayn of Mecca as the rightful Arab Caliph was considered a more effective option, even though it was acknowledged that Husayn was perceived by non-Arab Muslims as having betrayed pan-Islam and as being manipulated as a puppet by the British. Chamberlain accepted Hirtzel's view and instructed his office that a reply to Headley should ignore the question of a mosque, and tell him instead that 'the most appropriate form of memorial [...] a cemetery with a [...] gateway on which might be inscribed the names of the fallen [... was] under consideration'.[45]

Matters improved little after the war ended. Muslims such as Syed Ameer Ali, together with the Aga Khan, continued desperately to urge the British government to assure the Caliphate's preservation, even after its defeat.[46] With the Allies occupying Istanbul and Greek forces, with British backing, penetrating deep into Turkey in 1920, it seemed that the British government was in no mood to countenance Indian sentiments in respect of any revision of the Turkish peace treaty, even though, as the Aga Khan recalled, 'The Prime Minister [had] told the House of Commons in 1920 that we could not have won the war

[45] *Ibid.*, Austin Chamberlain's note. Indeed, arrangements were made by the Secretary of State for India, in consultation with the War Office, to preserve the graves of Muslim soldiers who died while under treatment in this country at Brookwood near the Woking Mosque and in an enclosed area in Horsell Common. See *The Times*, 18 April 1916. Designed by an India Office surveyor and architect, a Muslim burial ground with arches, minarets, and domed gateway was built by a local firm in 1917; the cemetery received nineteen burials of Indian Army Muslim soldiers during the First World War, and a further five during the Second. The graves were set at an angle to the normal position in a British cemetery so as to allow the body to lie in the correct direction towards Mecca. All the costs were borne by the government. In 1921, the War Graves Commission took over its upkeep. See H. Ansari, '"Burying the dead": making Muslim space in Britain', *Historical Research*, 8, no. 210 (November 2007), p. 561.

[46] In a letter to the editor of *The Times*, Syed Ameer Ali and the Aga Khan, drawing attention to 'the anguish and pain which the threatened dismemberment of Turkey has created among Musalmans', pleaded for the maintenance of the Turkish Empire (*The Times*, 6 June 1919). Later that same year, a memorandum to the Prime Minister from a number of leading figures, including British Indians – for example, the Aga Khan, Lord Ampthill, Syed Ameer Ali, and Marmaduke Pickthall – reminded him of the insult to religious feeling and alienation that would be caused in the Muslim world if Turkey was stripped of its sovereignty. They 'urged upon the Government the imperative necessity of a Policy towards Turkey that would lead to appeasement of the ferment and unrest among the Moslems of the world mainly due to apprehension that it is proposed to further dismember the Turkish Empire and completely to destroy the free life and political power of the remaining Moslem States' (*The Times*, 24 December 1919).

without the aid of Indian troops'. To the large proportion of the Indian soldiery belonging to the Islamic faith, fighting against their 'brother Moslems' had imposed a great sacrifice for which just recompense was due. Hence, the Indian Muslim view was that, in the case of Turkey, the principles of liberty and self-determination of nations proclaimed by the Allies should be scrupulously upheld.[47]

In view of Britain's hostility towards Turkey, antipathy in Britain towards Muslims remained high. This only resulted in further heightening their identification and solidarity with fellow Muslims. Pan-Islamic networks in London became even more resolute in their challenging of the negative perceptions circulating in British society and in their defence of Islam against widespread misrepresentations. Alongside resistance to attacks on the *umma* through a range of lobbying groups, a desire also grew to construct bonds through collective religious observance. With the number of Muslims in the capital rising steadily, the pressure for a mosque mounted. The Trustees of the LMF at this stage decided to take two measures to secure a dedicated space for a congregation in London. First, they started to conduct Friday prayers at Lindsey Hall, Notting Hill Gate, in central London.[48] Then they established a *namaz-gah* (prayer-room) in rented accommodation in Campden Hill Road. Called the 'London Muslim Prayer House', it attracted significant numbers of worshippers and audiences to its services after the First World War.[49] It continued to function as a mosque and a literary meeting place, with the imam of the Woking Mosque (and in his absence Marmaduke Pickthall) conducting congregations there on a regular basis, until 1927, when, with attendances declining, the tenancy was terminated.[50] Second, the Trustees also renewed their appeal for donations to the Fund. In 1923, Lord Headley and Khwaja Kamal-ud-din, Imam of the Woking Mosque, went on pilgrimage together to Mecca, but while the former was decorated by King Hussein, the Sharif of Mecca,[51]

[47] *The Times*, 14 March 1921.

[48] As early as March 1914, a grant of £120 a year was approved to rent a building in London. See below, p. 107.

[49] For instance, in October 1919, 350 officers and privates of the Indian Peace Celebration contingent came to attend 'the Friday Sabbath Prayers. But the Muslim prayer House could not hold them. Arrangements were therefore made at Hyde park for the Cathedral Service' (*Islamic Review*, October 1919, p. 354).

[50] See below, pp. 135–136.

[51] Sayyid Hussein bin Ali (1853–1931) became Sharif (ruler) of Mecca in 1908. He proclaimed himself 'king of the Arab lands' in October 1916. Soon after, Britain recognized him as 'king of the Hejaz' (now part of Saudi Arabia). He initiated the Arab Revolt in 1916 against the Ottoman Empire. In 1924, he further proclaimed himself Caliph of all Muslims. He ruled the Hejaz until 1924, when, defeated by Abdul Aziz al Saud, he abdicated the kingdom in favour of his eldest son, Ali. He is buried in Jerusalem.

no financial assistance for the mosque proved to be forthcoming.[52] With the Ottoman Empire abolished in 1924, the Trustees resolved, in 1925, to invite King Fuad of Egypt, the Amir of Afghanistan, and the Nizam of Hyderabad to become patrons of the Fund in conjunction with the Shah of Persia, in the hope of obtaining financial help.[53] The expediency of approaching the British government for the grant of a site for the proposed mosque was also considered. But, by 1926, while the LMF had grown to a sizeable amount, it was not nearly sufficient for the Trustees to countenance the construction of a fitting mosque.[54]

Consequently, Syed Ameer Ali launched a fresh appeal in April 1927, reminding 'the Mahommedan subjects of the King [. . .] and the Moslem nations in friendly relations with England of the crying necessity for a suitable mosque worthy of the position of Islam as a world religion in the metropolis of Great Britain'. According to him, 'The small mosque at Woking does not serve as the symbol of the dignity of the Muslim faith'. With the opening of the Great Mosque in Paris in July 1926, accompanied by 'great pomp and ceremony', he hoped that the

> wealthy princes and magnates of India and the countries within the ambit of Great Britain's cultural influence would realise their pious duty, and that his Majesty's Government would give to our efforts the same support and sympathy which has been extended by the French Government to the Mosque in Paris.[55]

Efforts to collect funds in India were accordingly redoubled. Headley went to India and came back with a donation of £60,000 from the Nizam of Hyderabad,[56] albeit with the proviso that a new trust – its name, the 'Nizamiah Mosque' – be created for these funds, with Headley a co-trustee.[57] In 1928, the 'London Nizamiah Mosque Trust Fund' was duly established, a site was purchased for £28,000 in West Kensington, and a well-known English architect was even commissioned to produce the design for a mosque.[58] However, with the onset of the Great Depression, the chances of adequate sponsorship

See *ODNB*, http://www.oxforddnb.com/view/article/75900?docPos=4 (accessed on 10 November 2010).

[52] On Lord Headley's reception by King Hussein, see *The Times*, 30 August 1923.

[53] See ELM Archives, LMF Executive Committee Minutes, 24 June 1924.

[54] *The Times*, 6 October 1926.

[55] *The Times*, 26 April 1927.

[56] This was Asaf Jah VII (Osman Ali Khan Bahadur) (1886–1967), whose reign lasted from 1911 until the annexation of the state of Hyderabad by India in 1948. In 1937 he was reported as the wealthiest man in the world (*Time Magazine*, 22 February 1937).

[57] See below, pp. 137–138, for copies of the telegraphic correspondence between Sir Amin Jung in Hyderabad-Deccan, and Syed Ameer Ali.

[58] *The Times*, 5 June 1937.

materializing receded. While, in June 1937, the foundation stone of 'The Nizamiah Mosque' was laid by Nizam's heir-apparent, the Prince Berar, Azam Jah Bahadur, in a public ceremony attended by many Muslim and non-Muslim dignitaries,[59] the mosque itself literally never got off the ground, and the balance of the Fund – which had reached around £77,000 – remained dormant, with the Nizam refusing to make it available for any other mosque projects.[60]

However, the changing context in the 1930s prevented the London Mosque project from fading away permanently. In the run up to the Second World War, fascist states such as Italy and Germany, in pursuit of their imperial objectives, increased their efforts to woo Muslims in the Middle East. The proposals for the partition of Palestine stirred Muslims in Britain as elsewhere in equal measure. Within the empire, as the struggle for Home Rule in India gathered momentum, increased Muslim self-consciousness led to more assertive political demands, first raised in Britain in 1933, for separate communal space.[61] Through the 1930s, as the key promoters of the project slowly began to die away, the quest for a London mosque was taken up by those who had lobbied energetically for Muslim interests, even though these efforts did not produce any significant outcomes, at least in the short run. For instance, at the end of 1933, Margaret Farquharson, President of the National League, a London-based organization that concerned 'itself with Moslem and particularly Arab interests',[62] wrote to R.A. Butler

[59] *Ibid.*; see also ELM Archives, 'Address of Welcome' presented to the Prince by the following Board of Trustees of the Nizamiah Mosque Trust: Abdul Qadir, Hafiz Wahba, Dr. Mohemadi Aqil Jung, and Al Haj Ali Raza.

[60] BL, IOR, L/P&J/12/468, fos 373–374, G.H. Hall of the Colonial Office to Lord Pethick-Lawrence, 24 August 1945.

[61] In January 1933, Chaudhary Rahmat Ali, an Indian Muslim student at Cambridge University, issued a declaration entitled 'Now or never', in which he called for a separate 'homeland' – 'Pakistan' – for India's Muslims. See K.K. Aziz, *Rahmat Ali: a biography* (Stuttgart, 1987), p. 87.

[62] The National League, with premises in St James Street, London, was, as described in its own words, a 'non-Party organisation founded in 1912 by Mary Adelaide Broadhurst and Margaret Milne Farquharson. It has an appeal to all classes, and is organised to maintain the patriotic and pioneer spirit by constructive Policy and Action. It believes in the unity of the British Race. From 1918 to 1922 the League pioneered the struggle to wake the Nation to the dangers of Bolshevism through meetings and the national press'. Between 1921 and 1936, the National League brought together Members of both Houses of Parliament and delegations from Palestine in conferences and receptions. In 1933 it organized several debates and held influential meetings 'to win a just basis for Palestine'. Apparently, its efforts in bringing about greater understanding between Britain and the Muslim world were publicly much appreciated by reputable Muslim figures such as the Aga Khan, Sir Mohammed Iqbal, Hajj Amin Husseini (Grand Mufti of Palestine), Hajee Abdoola Haroon, and the Nawab of Chhatari (India). See BL, IOR, L/P&J/12/468, fos 226–227. Reports of these events appeared, from time to time, in *The Times*: see, for example, 2 October 1931, 30 June 1933,

MP setting out a proposal to build a Muslim Centre in London.[63] Echoing Lord Headley's earlier request, she stressed that the

> spontaneous gesture from the Government of the granting of a Site together with a Parliamentary Grant [. . .] would have a most favourable influence at a critical time, throughout the Moslem World [. . .] the news of such a Grant would create a wave of friendly feeling to the Muslim World through a time of change in a constant, spontaneous, and firm relation to the British Crown, and to the British Government [. . .].[64]

Government officials, however, were dismissive of Farquharson, regarded her as a nuisance and as a person of little consequence, whose requests were unworthy of serious consideration.[65] Butler responded negatively – he was

24 November 1933, 7 November 1934, 6 March 1935, 16 July 1935. The British government viewed the National League as 'a bit of a nuisance': see BL, IOR, P&J (S)/607, 14 June 1933, fo. 256. Anti-Zionist and critical of the mandatory regime in Palestine and the activities of the Zionist organizations, it was regarded by the government as 'a partisan propagandist concern', with which it was inappropriate for Cabinet ministers to associate. A detailed secret official note on the National League stated that, as an 'ill-advised critic of British administration and champion of the Arab malcontent, it is held in unfavourable light by the Home Office' (BL, IOR, L/P&J/12/468, fo. 226). Its supporters included British 'die-hard' politicians such as Lord Lloyd and Sir Alfred Knox (see BL, IOR, P&J (S)/916, 12 July 1934, fos 239–240). According to one government report, it first came to prominence in 1927, when it was conducting propaganda in England and America on behalf of Arabs. From 1929 it was in close touch with the Muslim–Christian Alliance of Palestine, and it was concerned with endeavours to effect a revision of the 1917 Balfour Declaration regarding the Jewish National Home in Palestine, in order (apparently) 'to placate the Muslims'. At a meeting on 7 June 1931 at the Hyde Park Hotel 'to enable British and Muslim leaders to make a united stand for a clear policy on Palestine', it was reported that Lord and Lady Headley and Abdul Majid, Imam of Woking, were present, with Waris Ameer Ali among the speakers. A farewell reception to the Muslim delegation to the Round Table Conference took place on 23 November 1932, at which Lord Lamington took the chair and the Aga Khan was one of the speakers. In a memorandum enclosed with a letter to R.A. Butler, Farquharson 'proposed to consolidate friendship [between Great Britain and the Muslim World] by the building of a Muslim Centre in London'. The League appealed 'to the Crown for a site to be granted in St. James's [together with a Parliamentary Grant] upon which to build a Muslim Centre'. This project, it claimed, commanded the support of 'all the eminent Moslem Leaders [. . .] as well as rank and file [. . .] which also unites all shades of influential British opinion'. Mr Baldwin, however, was advised not to give 'his patronage to the proposal [. . .] In our experience the League is a rather dangerous body and we try to have as little to do with it as possible'. See BL, IOR, P&J (S)/916, 15 June 1934, fo. 245.

[63] Lord Ampthill, writing to A.S.M. Anik, referred to this scheme 'for building not only a Mosque but also a Social Club for Moslems'. See below, p. 164.

[64] See BL, IOR, L/P&J/12/468, fo. 273, Memorandum.

[65] Sir Samuel Hoare advised Lord Willingdon 'to take no notice of the lady. She inundates me with circulars and I never pay the least attention to them'. BL, IOR, L/P&J/12/468, fo. 242, extract from private letter from Sir Samuel Hoare to Lord Willingdon, 7 July 1933. Nevertheless, government intelligence kept an eye on her. An 'Extract from New Scotland Yard', 3 November 1937, reported that 'Miss Margaret Milne Farquharson [was] obtaining money from affluent Indians and Arabs in this country, for the purpose of supporting her

> reluctant to suggest fresh expenditure of such a nature at the present time when every effort must be strained to achieve economy in State expenditure. You will also appreciate that if the concession for which you ask were granted, it would be difficult to resist similar requests made on behalf of other religious communities.[66]

In January 1938, the baton was picked up by an Egyptian merchant, Ibrahim Mougy,[67] who met with officials at the Foreign Office to discuss 'a proposal to found a Moslem Institute in London'. This institute, he was determined, would exclude politics altogether from its scope and function, being nothing more than 'a religious and social centre for Moslems living in or visiting England'. In contrast to the Woking Mosque, which he claimed was in the hands of the Ahmadiyya sect, his institute would preserve a universal Muslim character, 'entirely unsectarian and open to Moslems of all shades of religious belief and of all nationalities'.[68] Yet again, the British government was approached with a request for resources, reminding it that 'the British Empire comprised the greatest number of Moslems in any Empire in the world, and that British relations with the independent Moslem countries were close and important'.[69] By offering to found an institute which would be purely religious, social, and apolitical, Mougy hoped that the authorities would find his proposal more appealing than those already on the table. At the same time, he also went public and presented his project of a mosque for London to an audience of distinguished Muslims at an Eid gathering at the Royal Egyptian Club.[70] But government officials remained sceptical and thought it 'unwise for [them] to depart in any way from an attitude of strict neutrality or commit [themselves] to giving a blessing to any such scheme as proposed until [they] know more about it and particularly whether it has the backing of influential Indian Moslems'.[71]

Meanwhile, the growth of the Muslim community in the East End of London brought into sharp focus the need for a more local religious space. This was recognized by the Trustees of both Trusts. When, in

Pan-Islamist movement. She is devoting the funds so obtained to furthering the Arab cause in Palestine' (see BL, IOR, L/P&J/12/468, fo. 222).

[66]BL, IOR, L/P&J/12/468, fo. 268.

[67]G.W. Randel of the Foreign Office described Mougy as 'at best [...] a somewhat irresponsible adventurer, obviously lacking in balance and judgement' (BL, IOR, L/P&J/12/468, fo. 220, G.W. Randel, memorandum, 24 January 1938).

[68]See BL, IOR, L/P&J/12/468, fos 216–217, L. Baggallay, memorandum recording a conversation with Mougy at the Foreign Office, 14 January 1938.

[69]*Ibid.*, fo. 216.

[70]At the 'Id-ul Azha' congregation, he spoke of the need for a 'Moslem Centre' in London. See *The Times*, 31 January 1938.

[71]BL, IOR, L/P&J/12/468, p. 196, letter to H.L. Baggallay, 29 July 1939.

1930, Syed Hashimi, the Nizam's emissary, visited London to gauge the situation, he reported to the LMF that

> It is, as you know, the East End parts of London where a number of poor Muslims have permanently settled [. . .] these are the people who need most to have a Mosque and some provision for the religious instruction of their children who shall other wise inevitably drift towards irreligion.[72]

He suggested that the LMF should consider building a mosque in the East End from their funds, leaving 'the project of constructing a grand building' in central London to the Nizamia Mosque.[73] The LMF Trustees accepted Hashimi's proposal, but when the LMF requested 'pecuniary assistance' for running the proposed mosque, the Nizam excused himself on account of 'the present widespread financial depression and the many demands on [the] resources within the State itself'.[74]

As the British economy began to pick up after the Great Depression, the lure of London became stronger and 'jumping ship' by non-British sailors came back into fashion; this increased steadily until just after the Second World War and with it grew a sizeable Muslim community. As the community expanded, so did their cultural and religious needs and concerns. In 1934, Jamiat-ul-Muslimin was founded[75] with the objective of serving 'the cause of Islam truly by creating facilities for the observance of its principles'.[76] Its creation reflected the extent to which, over the course of the inter-war period, a number of Indian Muslims had come to London's East End from farming backgrounds in the Punjab and Bengal – merchants, peddlers, seamen, students, and professionals. I.I. Kazi, its first president, from the province of Sind (now in Pakistan), was a barrister. Others had worked up enough resources to set up cafés and lodging-houses to service the maritime workers who frequented the port. Some also ventured into trading and commercial enterprises (apparently, not always lawful[77]) more widely: 'There were quite a few Punjabis in Backchurch Lane (Stepney) – they had scent and clothing factories'.[78] Sahibdad Khan,[79] for instance,

[72] See below, pp. 148–150, letter from Syed Hashimi to A.S.N. Anik, August 1930.

[73] *Ibid.*

[74] ELM Archives, Mahdi Yar Jung, political member of HEH the Nizam's government, to Lord Lamington, 22 March 1933.

[75] ELM Archives, Minutes of the first meeting on 29 March 1934 in the 'Register of proceedings of the Managing Board, Jamiat-ul-Muslimin'. I.I. Kazi was elected its first president, Said Amir its secretary, and Noor Mohamad Sangha its treasurer.

[76] ELM Archives, Jamiat-ul-Muslimin, Rules and Regulations, August 1938, p. 2.

[77] BL, IOR, L/P&J/12/468, fo. 75.

[78] See C. Adams (coll. and ed.), *Across Seven Seas and Thirteen Rivers: life stories of pioneer Sylhetti settlers in Britain* (London, 1986), p. 84.

[79] BL, IOR, L/P&J/12/468, fo. 78.

a Trustee of the London Mosque Fund, ran a perfumery business; Ahmad Din Qureshi,[80] a Jamiat-ul-Muslimin president, was a silk merchant; Said Amir Shah,[81] treasurer in 1943, was reported to have 'in his time run Indian boarding houses in the East End, and also had a shop at 36 Old Montague Street'. He was a member of 'Shah Brothers, Silk Merchants and Warehousemen'.[82] Such men also helped those who jumped ship with accommodation and advice regarding job opportunities. They were the pioneers who became active leaders of the Jamiat-ul-Muslimin, and in time were at the heart of running the East London Mosque on a daily basis.

The Jamiat-ul-Muslimin's broader objectives, which these men helped to formulate, called for stringency of religious practice, 'insisting upon members to observe all the tenets of Islam', and advocating pan-Islamic interaction 'to promote the preservation of a permanent union between Muslims of different nationalities [. . .] to provide and maintain a comfortable place to bring together, and promote social intercourse between the resident Muslims, thus creating unity, amity and general brotherhood'.[83] An address of welcome presented to the Crown Prince of Saudi Arabia, Amir Sa'ud, stated that its main effort was directed towards 'union and organization of all Muslims over these islands'. It noted that the community of Muslims in London – which it estimated at 300, 'excluding students and occasional visitors' – lacked a place for regular prayers and hoped that it would be able to 'procure means for the building and maintenance of a suitable, conveniently located mosque'.[84]

In the next few years, before the Second World War broke out, the activities of the Jamiat-ul-Muslimin began to give organizational shape to the local Muslim community. The organization challenged those who, it felt, had behaved in ways that were harmful to Muslim interests. Denigration of Islam and the Qur'an, and attacks on aspects of Muslim identity, were passionately resisted. A significant example of this was the Jamiat-ul-Muslimin's reaction to passages in H.G. Wells's *A Short History of the World* (first published in 1922) that they felt had insulted the Prophet Muhammad and disparaged the Qur'an.[85] In response, its leaders decided to mount a strong protest;

[80] *Ibid.*, fo. 71.
[81] *Ibid.*, fo. 75.
[82] *Ibid.*
[83] *Ibid.*
[84] See ELM Archives, 'An address of welcome' presented at the Savoy Hotel on 18 July 1935.
[85] The passages that they found particularly offensive included one about the Prophet Muhammad and another about the Qur'an. Wells wrote, 'He [Muhammad] seems to have

'a party of Indian Mohammedans' in London's East End ceremonially committed a copy of Wells's book 'to the flames'.[86] The *Manchester Guardian* reported that a march was being organized to visit the India Office demanding the book's 'proscription'. The Joint Secretary of the Jamiat wrote to the High Commissioner for India, Sir Firoz Khan Noon,[87] who was also an ex-officio trustee of the London Mosque Fund at the time, that a march would take place from Bank to India House on 18 August 1938.[88] A leaflet, entitled *The Most Cowardly Attack on the Holy Prophet and the Holy Quran*, exhorted 'every Muslim to do his duty towards Islam by joining the march and [. . .] bringing pressure on the author to withdraw his remarks from the book'.[89] Noon met Muhammad Buksh and Fazal Shah, both leaders of the Jamiat-ul-Muslimin, and sought to dissuade them from marching. He argued that the exposure of Wells's book was mischief-making on the part of a Hindu journalist, Mr. Rau, and told them that the protest was 'useless', since they were

> not rendering any service to Islam by falling into the trap of this Hindu, and the best thing they could do was to keep quiet and live peacefully in the East End. After all they were a very small minority and it would do them no good to try and be mischievous in this country, no matter how genuine their grievances were.

He went on that 'it was no use bringing a delegation of 500 people to [him] or to the Secretary of State, because in a matter like this [they] were helpless'. The 'freedom of expression' principles enshrined in British law precluded any useful intervention. Nor could the publishers of the book be persuaded to withdraw it. 'This is a country', Noon said, 'in which there are people who criticise the Christian religion and Jesus Christ'. In a letter from his office he again advised against the organization of the protest march. While he was willing to receive

been a man compounded of very considerable vanity, greed, cunning and self-deception, and quite sincere religious passion [. . .] And then, regarded as literature or philosophy, the Koran is certainly unworthy of its Divine authorship' (H.G. Wells, *A Short History of the World* (place unknown, limited edition published 1 May 2008), p. 144).

[86] *Manchester Guardian*, 13 August 1938. According to British intelligence, it was at King's Hall, 85 Commercial Road, where the Jamiat-ul-Muslimin met every Friday for prayer, that the book was burnt. See BL, IOR, P&J (S)/716, fo. 1, IOR. However, the report rejected articles 'that have appeared in the Press of the Association's intention to burn an effigy of Mr. Wells [. . .] neither does it intend, at present, to approach Mr. Wells with regard to this attack on the Prophet Mohammed, nor act in any way that would bring discredit on the Association' (*ibid.*, fo. 3). On 14 January 1989, Muslims in Bradford burned a copy of Salman Rushdie's novel, *The Satanic Verses*, which they found equally offensive.

[87] See Appendix I.

[88] BL, IOR, P&J (S)/723, fo. 12, letter from A.D. Khan, 16 August 1938.

[89] BL, IOR, P&J (S)/723, fo. 13.

'not more than six leading gentlemen' of the Jamiat-ul-Muslimin, he strongly deprecated 'any demonstration whatsoever outside India House'.[90]

All the same, it seems that the Jamiat-ul-Muslimin disregarded Sir Noon's opposition and, since the authorities could invoke 'no power to prohibit a procession of this sort', the demonstration went ahead as planned on 18 August 1938. 'Cries of "Down with ignorant Wells!" and "Allah is Great" could be heard when between 300 and 400 Moslems marched through the City of London' demanding the banning of the book.[91] The High Commissioner received a deputation of six men, representing the Jamiat-ul-Muslimin's executive committee, who presented a written petition to him against a passage in Wells's book. The petition,[92] with 136 signatures, 'strongly, vehemently and angerly [*sic*] protested against the false, cowardly and maliciously slanderous statement by H.G. Wells [...] against our revered, respected and honoured prophet Mohammed (peace be upon Him) and our holy Quran'. It demanded 'an immediate public apology' from Wells. The High Commissioner agreed that the passage in question was offensive and he felt it very much as a Muslim. If there was anything that he could do to get it withdrawn he would be only too glad to help. But in England only obscene or blasphemous books could be proscribed, and blasphemy was only against the Christian religion. Proceedings could, of course, be taken in a court of law by individuals or a society if there was any defamation, but on this the best course would be to consult some of the Muslim lawyers who were practising in London. The High Commissioner 'would gladly bring to the notice of His Majesty's Government [...] the fact that the passage had offended Muslim sentiment very strongly and that every effort should be made to get it withdrawn'.[93] In fulfilment of his promise to the Jamiat-ul-Muslimin deputation, Noon then met the Marquess of Zetland, Secretary of State for India, and discussed with him what further steps could be taken. It was agreed that a carefully drafted letter would go from Zetland to Noon that would then be conveyed by the latter to the deputation.[94] For Zetland, it was 'a matter of deep regret [...] that offence had been given to the members of the deputation

[90] BL, IOR, P&J (S)/723, fo. 14, High Commissioner of India's Office to the Joint Secretary of the Jamiat-ul-Muslimin, 17 August 1938.

[91] *Manchester Guardian*, 19 August 1938. The High Commissioner's Office reported that '500 Indian Musulmans of London marched from the East End to India House' (BL, IOR, P&J (S)/723, fo. 17).

[92] For the petition see BL, IOR, P&J (S)/723, fos 18–24.

[93] See BL, IOR, P&J (S)/723, fos 15–16, note prepared by the High Commissioner's Office, 1 August 1938.

[94] BL, IOR, P&J (S)/723, fos 25–26.

and those whom they represent, on a matter concerning their Faith. But having regard to the freedom permitted to the expression of views in this country', he said that he had 'no power to secure a modification to the passage to which exception had been taken'.[95] Noon, on receiving Zetland's letter, communicated the Secretary of State's remarks to the deputation.[96] Copies of it were also sent to the original publisher of Wells's book, William Heinemann, and to Penguin Books, who had published it in a Pelican edition. While the former in acknowledgement merely noted its contents, the latter intimated that they had 'no authority to alter an author's work without his express permission' and that nothing could be done 'in connection with the passage complained of'.[97] What this episode reveals is that the Jamiat-ul-Muslimin, from its base in the East End of London, was already in a position to be able to mobilize Muslims in London collectively to make demands that the British state could not ignore. As we shall see later, the East London Mosque was involved in similar campaigns in the following decades.

In these early years of its existence, the Jamiat-ul-Muslimin also strove hard to achieve its other key objective: 'to raise funds for building a Mosque in the East End of London' and 'By creating an endowment to provide for the maintenance and upkeep of the Mosque'.[98] Concretely, this meant having a space in which 'such festivals [and rituals] as the Birthday of Prophet Mohammad, 'Ashura, Idan [*sic*] and Friday Prayers' could be performed. In 1933, the LMF felt sufficiently persuaded to approve expenditure for 'a Moslem Preacher and Prayer Room in the East End of London'.[99] The Jamiat-ul-Muslimin's first annual report, in 1934–1935, noted that 'Friday prayers along with conversazione have been held regularly throughout the last year at King's Hall, Commercial Road'.[100] Not satisfied with being entrusted with the temporary arrangement of the various religious functions involved, it urged both the LMF and the

[95] BL, IOR, P&J (S)/723, fo. 28, Lord Zetland to Sir Firozkhan Noon, 24 August 1938.

[96] BL, IOR, P&J (S)/723, fo. 29, Sir Firozkhan Noon to Lord Zetland, 31 August 1938.

[97] BL, IOR, P&J (S)/723, fo. 33, letter from William Heinemann Ltd., 9 September 1938; fo. 34, letter from Penguin Books Limited, 12 September 1938.

[98] ELM Archives, Jamiat-ul-Muslimin Rules and Regulations, August 1938, p. 2.

[99] See below, p. 165. The Jamiat-ul-Muslimin Minutes of 7 May 1934 (ELM Archives) record the association's 'sincere thanks' to A.S.M. Anik Esq and Sayed Waris Ali Esq for 'their sympathetic and kind gesture for the association, out of the mosque fund, a contribution towards the cost of hiring a hall for congregational prayer [. . .] The association, however adds that it would be glad if the Trustees could kindly see their way to provide the association with a permanent place that could be used as a Sunday school and a lecture room'.

[100] See below, p. 186, for the reference to 'the dance hall at 85–87 Commercial Road for the holding of prayers and religious observances'.

Nizamia Mosque Trust to 'build a mosque in the East End of London', which it claimed had become 'the centre of Muslim population and the resort of seamen from abroad'.[101]

The search for suitable premises to house the mosque on a more permanent basis continued over the next five years and in 1940, at a cost of £2,800, the Trustees purchased a freehold property in Commercial Road; the first Juma prayer was offered in the new mosque on 23 May 1941. Repaired and remodelled, it was formally inaugurated as the East London Mosque by the Egyptian Ambassador on 1 August 1941.[102] The Jamiat-ul-Muslimin's Eighth Annual Report, 1941–1942, recorded the opening ceremony, the provision of a library, a medical service, and, with the co-operation of the Indigent Moslems Burial Fund that had been set up by some of the LMF Trustees in 1927, a burial service.[103] The Jamiat-ul-Muslimin, now based at the same address as the East London Mosque, supervised all these functions. Its influence and representative character, and its crucial role in the organization of the new mosque's activities, were recognized in its appointment as the LMF's agent, with its office in the same premises. This, then, after thirty years, was the culmination of the LMF's efforts. The Fund, which stood at just over £10, 687 on 31 December 1939, could not afford anything on a grander scale.[104]

However, by the time that Hassan Nachat Pasha, the Egyptian Ambassador, announced his plan for a central mosque in London in January 1940,[105] the British government's position had become

[101] ELM Archives, Jamiat-ul-Muslimin First Annual Report, 1934–1935, p. 4.

[102] See ELM Archives, brochure of the Opening Ceremony of the East London Mosque and Islamic Culture Centre, Friday, 1 August 1941.

[103] ELM Archives, Jamiat-ul-Muslimin Eighth Annual Report, 1941–1942, pp. 3–5. *The Times* on 14 April 1925 reported: 'A fund is being raised to make provision for the proper burial of indigent Moslems dying in this country, in accordance with the rites of Islam. The president of the committee, the Aga Khan, donated £200, A.S.M. Anik, the secretary and treasurer, £100 and Syed Ameer Ali, the chairman, 50 guineas'. The founding Trustees of The Indigent Moslems Burial Fund, A.S.M. Anik and Syed Ameer Ali, were both Trustees of the LMF: see ELM Archives, 'Declaration of Trust', 19 December 1927.

[104] See the Report by Sir Ernest Hotson, Honorary Secretary, contained in the brochure of the Opening Ceremony of the East London Mosque. See also BL, IOR, L/P&J/12/468, fo. 267, 'Extract from Metropolitan Police Report', 14 October 1943. In 1940 the assets of the LMF amounted to £10,417 ('The London Mosque', *Royal Central Asian Journal*, 27, pt. 2 (1940) pp. 221–223). By March 1941 the total assets had risen to just over £11,489 (BL, IOR, L/P&J/12/468, fo. 139).

[105] On 29 January 1940, at a meeting of the Royal Central Asian Society's Dinner Club, the ambassador made a statement on the provision of an adequate and worthy religious centre for Muslims of all nationalities living in or visiting London. He drew attention to the significant fact that the Islamic world was supporting the Allied cause in the war, explaining that 'this was to be expected from the fact that Islam is a democratic religion, and could not hesitate in the choice between the democratic and the aggressive totalitarian conceptions.

more sympathetic. The 'Arab Revolt' in Palestine that took place between 1936 and 1939 under the leadership of the Grand Mufti of Jerusalem, Haj Amin Al-Husseini, protesting against British support for Jewish demands in Palestine, had caused widespread anxiety (and sympathy) among Muslims worldwide. The British Government, with war looming, was keen to reduce any growing antagonism. With the Axis powers wooing Muslims in the Middle East (indeed, there is some evidence to suggest that the German SS helped finance the Revolt), the exigencies of the war quickly converted earlier hostility and the present neutrality into active support.[106] 'Experts' canvassed in both the Middle East and India were broadly supportive of 'the proposal to provide a site for the establishment of a Mosque in London'.[107] In Sir Harold Satow's opinion, 'as a tribute to the loyalty of the Moslems of the Empire, the proposed expenditure would be justified'.[108] Most thought that such support would help to improve relations with the Muslim world. Firoz Khan Noon, still the High Commissioner for India and ex officio a member of the London Mosque Fund, felt that

> The idea of a mosque in London is as excellent as it is opportune [. . .] If an appeal were to issue over your signature to all offices in charge of territory where Moslems reside and if the scheme were also backed by Moslem ambassadors and ministers in London I feel you would get sufficient funds to build and endow a good mosque.[109]

Headley's arguments that had been rejected in 1916 were now unabashedly re-invoked in favour of the project. In a memorandum to Churchill, George Lloyd, the Colonial Secretary, pointed out that it was 'anomalous and inappropriate' that in London, which 'contains more Moslems than any other European capital, there should be no central place of worship for Mussalmans'.[110] In his letter to the Secretary of State for India, Leo Amery, Lloyd was even more scathing:

He felt that the provision of a worthy centre of Moslem culture in London was long overdue. He had submitted certain proposals to King Farouk who had fully accepted them and was pleased to give his high patronage'. Sir Hassan Suhrawardy, chairman of the LMF readily expressed his support. See *The Times*, 1 February 1940.

[106] In a letter dated 8 February 1940 to the Viceroy of India, the Marquess of Linlithgow, Lord Lloyd said that 'Quite apart from the intrinsic need of such a mosque, which is great, one cannot be blind to the political and propaganda importance of such a step at the present time' (BL, IOR, L/P&J/12/468, fo. 116).

[107] BL, IOR, L/P&J/12/468, fo. 130, 'Opinions regarding the proposal to provide a site for the establishment of a mosque in London'.

[108] *Ibid.*

[109] BL, IOR, L/P&J/12/468, fo. 139, Firoz Khan Noon to Secretary of State for India, 24 September 1940.

[110] The co-signatories of the memorandum, dated 10 October 1940, were Lord Halifax, the Secretary of State for Foreign Affairs, and Leo Amery, the Secretary of State for India (BL, IOR, L/P&J/12/468, fo. 151).

'It is really a scandal that an Empire which has more Muslims in it than Christians should not have in its capital a place of worship for Mohammedans worthy of the Empire'.[111] The announcement that such a mosque was now to be built and that the authorities had provided a site, would, in his view, 'serve as a tribute to the loyalty of the Moslems of the Empire'[112] and 'make a good impression in the Moslem world to-day'.[113] Surely, he said, the support for the mosque project would further reinforce 'the cooperation in the present war by the world of Islam in friendly interest and sympathy with the British Commonwealth of nations'.[114]

Convinced of the political efficacy of the project, Lloyd, shortly after he became Secretary of State for the Colonies, persuaded Halifax (the Foreign Secretary), along with Amery, to join him in submitting a memorandum to the War Cabinet entitled 'Proposals that His Majesty's Government should provide a site for a mosque in London'. The memorandum, stating the, by now well-rehearsed, arguments in support of the project, was approved on 18 October 1940;[115] financial assistance up to £100,000, announced in the House of Commons soon after, was to be a gift or tribute to the thousands of Indian Muslim soldiers who had died defending the British Empire – the form of recognition that, it might be recalled, had been explicitly rejected in 1916.[116]

Following protracted discussions and negotiations[117] between the Central Mosque Committee and the government regarding not only the selection and purchase of a suitable site but also the collection

[111] BL, IOR, L/P&J/12/468, fo. 134, Lord George Lloyd to Rt. Hon. L.S. Amery, 16 September 1940.

[112] BL, IOR, L/P&J/12/468, fo. 151.

[113] BL, IOR, L/P&J/12/468, fo. 134.

[114] Commenting on the gift by the British government of a site in London for a mosque and a Muslim cultural centre entirely under Muslim control, *The Times* of 14 November 1940 said that the 'gift is the more welcome since in the struggle in which Britain and the British Empire are engaged the Muslim communities of the Empire had clearly shown where their sympathies lie. In India, in East and West Africa, Arabia and Malaya there must be over 120,000,000 Muslim subjects of the Crown and Government's gift recognises the value of the support, moral and material, which this great community is giving us in the struggle for civilization. [...] Nor must it be forgotten that our Allies in the Near and Middle East are Muslim nations [...] and have given abundant proofs of their attachment to our cause'.

[115] BL, IOR, L/P&J/12/468, fo. 151.

[116] G. Hall, Under-Secretary, Colonial Office, in his reply to a Supplementary Question by Creech Jones MP, made the announcement on 13 November 1940. See *The Times*, 14 November 1940. See the full reply in *Parliamentary Debates* (House of Commons), CCCLXV, pp. 1710–1711.

[117] Disheartened by the slow progress in the acquisition of a site by the British government, the Egyptian Ambassador threatened resignation from the Mosque Committee. See BL, IOR, L/P&J/12/468, fo. 224, Lord Moyne to Lord Reith, 29 January 1942.

of sufficient funds for the construction of the mosque, Regents Lodge – Lady Ribblesdale's property with substantial lands in Regents Park – was acquired at a cost of £60,000.[118] For the construction of a new mosque, Lloyd had already written to Ali Maher Pasha, the Prime Minister of Egypt, to take the lead, hoping that other Muslim leaders would follow suit.[119] With the Mosque Committee's requests going unheeded, Amery wrote to Linlithgow, the Viceroy in India, asking him to persuade the Nizam of Hyderabad to transfer his fund to this project.[120] The Nizam refused.[121] Realizing that the ongoing efforts were unlikely to bear fruit any time soon, the Mosque Committee decided to make alterations to the existing premises so that they could be put to proper use as a cultural centre as well as a mosque. The property was then transferred to the Mosque Committee, and the Islamic Cultural Centre, which included the so-called 'Central London Mosque', was opened, ceremonially marked by King George VI's visit on 21 November 1944.[122] However, a full three decades were to pass before a building for this Central London Mosque was actually constructed.

Since the property for the Central London Mosque was purchased for £60,000 out of the sanctioned amount of £100,000, Suhrawardy, chairman of the LMF, wrote to Amery at the India Office asking him to consider diverting the residual money from the grant 'to acquire the land contiguous to the present East London Mosque and Islamic Culture Centre'. It would then be possible 'to erect buildings in every way suitable for a mosque [. . .] after the War'.[123] While this particular request was not met,[124] the British government was aware of the significant role that this particular mosque was beginning to play in shaping the attitudes of an important layer of London's Muslim population towards the war effort, as well as regarding political developments in India. For instance, a secret report recorded that Indian soldiers were 'frequenting the East London Mosque, attending daily congregations to observe the Ramdan fast', and that 'The Pakistan Movement [is] propagating among the troops

[118] BL, IOR, L/P&J/12/468, fo. 243, Sir Hassan Suhrawardy to the Rt Hon. L.S. Amery, 5 August 1942.

[119] BL, IOR, L/P&J/12/468, fo. 117, Lord Lloyd to Ali Maher Pasha, 23 February 1940.

[120] BL, IOR, L/P&J/12/468, fo. 166, Paragraph for Secretary of State's letter for Viceroy, 29/10–4/11/40.

[121] BL, IOR, L/P&J/12/468, fo. 143, extract from private letter from Lord Linlithgow to Mr Amery, 21 March 1941.

[122] *The Times*, 22 November 1944.

[123] BL, IOR, L/P&J/12/468, fo. 237, Sir Hassan Suhrawardy to the Rt Hon. L.S. Amery, 27 July 1942.

[124] BL, IOR, L/P&J/12/468, fo. 92.

of the Indian Army in this country and when soldiers visit the Mosque they hear about the scheme whereby Northern India, Bengal and Hyderabad could be federated into an independent Muslim State'.[125] While the British government had now committed itself primarily to the Central London Mosque project, it did feel that some support for the East London Mosque, with a view to developing understanding of British culture among local Muslims, would help to dispose them more positively towards Britain, especially at this critical time. So, with the approval of the India Office, in the autumn of 1941, the British Council started making monetary grants, as well as providing a variety of literature, to the cultural centre affiliated to the East London Mosque.[126]

The project for which the London Mosque Fund had originally been established – to build 'a mosque in London worthy of the tradition of Islam and worthy of the capital of the British Empire' – had still not come to fruition, at least not through the resources mobilized by the Fund itself. What the early promoters of the project had initially envisioned was no ordinary space along the lines of the premises in Commercial Road. Moreover, the congregation that they had had in mind was less the working-class seafaring community of the East End of London and much more the cosmopolitan community of students, merchants, and princes who visited London regularly. The space for which they had lobbied was intended, above all, to stand as a grand symbol of the dignity of Islam and of the power of the worldwide Muslim community – 'the great "cathedral" [...] in the centre of London, of stately dimensions, with domes and minarets in graceful Saracenic style of architecture in a conspicuous position'.[127] It was obvious, however, that such an ambitious undertaking was unlikely ever to be successful unless wealthy donors were prepared to commit substantial resources. A committee with the right kind of credentials was constituted with this aim in mind. With connections among the educated upper social classes, the higher echelons of Muslim governments, and the British establishment, it comprised men representing a number of Muslim states, headed by the Egyptian Ambassador. King Farouk of Egypt was invited to take a lead and give the project his 'august patronage [...] such a lead [it was hoped]

[125] BL, IOR, L/P&J/12/468, fo. 218.

[126] BL, IOR, L/P&J/12/468, fo. 197, J.P. Gibson to A.W.G. Randall of the Foreign Office, 4 June 1941. The LMF Minutes of 23 July 1941 recorded the acceptance of 'the offer of a capital grant of £100 and a recurring grant of £75 for this year and if possible subsequent years' (see below, p. 189).

[127] See BL, IOR, L/P&J/12/468, fo. 39, welcome speech by Sir Hassan Suhrawardy, Chairman of the Executive Committee of the LMF, at the inauguration of the East London Mosque.

would be a catalyst for the deriving of the resources for the project from the vast Muslim wealth that was there in the British Empire and in friendly foreign Muslim countries'.[128] But all this was to no avail. Adequate sponsorship for a grand Central London Mosque failed to materialize. Attempts to amalgamate the three existing Mosque funds,[129] which would have been a huge step towards making available sufficient finances for the project, floundered despite the fact that many of the same Muslim notables in London served on all three trusts. The Nizam could not be persuaded to transfer his funds even when the Saudi Minister personally made the request. He declined because he disliked this new project encroaching upon the one that he had started some years ago; in effect, his refusal stemmed from his reluctance to see the prestige of promoting this project pass from himself to one dominated by Arab interests.[130] Mougy and the Arabs, on the other hand, did not wish the project to be monopolized by Indian Muslims. Sectarian issues were another obstacle, given that the LMF had been initiated by Syed Ameer Ali, a Shia, and the Aga Khan, an Ismaili. The project for the creation of space to house a non-sectarian universal Islam was holed below the water line by considerations of power and influence.

Indeed, this examination reveals how far the quest for Muslim space was shaped by the institutions of wider society. The British state became engaged in the project for several reasons, among which maintaining hegemonic power over colonial people and social control over what was viewed as a potentially unstable section of the population were probably significant. To achieve this, it sought to ensure that control of the management of mosque committees lay in the hands of men who were either government officials or very closely allied with the government; men who were on the whole operating on the same political wavelength as the rest of the British establishment. But these Muslims were also striving to gain a greater share of power in the imperial domain, and mosque initiatives were one of a number of ways of achieving that objective. Recognizing that the meagre resources available to them within Britain would be inadequate to fulfil their purposes, they sought leverage from other parts of the Muslim world. Hence their identification with pan-Islam was not only a way of increasing their own power in negotiations with the British state but also represented a political strategy for gaining practical support for the realization of their mosque project.

[128] BL, IOR, L/P&J/12/468, fo. 118, Lord Lloyd to Ali Maher Pasha, 23 February 1940.
[129] See Appendix III.
[130] See Appendix III.

The East London Mosque, as has been the case with some of the more recent mosque projects in Britain, also became a site of contestation with regard to identity and power within London's emerging Muslim communities. This Muslim space was a resource whose use was envisaged differently by various individuals and groups, and thus its control was crucial to the shaping of the activities that took place within it. Such control was exercised through ownership of the premises, combined with a firm hold on the finances. Hence, representation on the various committees and trust boards was hard fought. This is evident in the struggle that began to unroll between the Jamiat-ul-Muslimin (which had only a minority representation on the Trust Board) and the rest of the Trustees of the LMF after the inauguration of the East London Mosque in 1941; we will see how that struggle for control was really about shaping the character of this Muslim space.

The London Mosque Fund and the East London Mosque: 1941–1951

After its establishment in Commercial Road in 1941, the East London Mosque quickly became a site where religious activity overlapped with politics. Since different Trustees represented widely varying views and political interests, there arose considerable tension among them. A comment in a New Scotland Yard report suggested that the British authorities disapproved of politics in the mosque; indeed, they viewed as 'unsatisfactory' the use of the East London Mosque 'as a Pakistan propagandist centre' for Indian Muslim soldiers who frequented it when observing the Ramadan fast.[131] However, the chairman of the Mosque's Executive Committee, Sir Hassan Suhrawardy, advisor at the India Office and 'a sympathiser of the Pakistan National Movement', allowed its material to be distributed. Nevertheless, when the Jamiat-ul-Muslimin began initiating activities at these premises that were seen as running counter to, or not broadly in line with, those of more 'establishment' Muslims, sanctions were swiftly applied. Hence, while a Pakistan Movement pamphlet was freely circulated at the ELM's opening in 1941 under Sir Hassan Suhrawardy's benevolent eye,[132] pro-Congress members of the Jamiat-ul-Muslimin such as Said

[131] BL, IOR, L/P&J/12/468, fo. 116, extract from New Scotland Yard report, 15 October 1941.

[132] 'Copies of a booklet entitled "The Millat of Islam and the Menace of 'Indianism'", written by C. Rahmat Ali, founder of the Pakistan National Movement, were distributed among the audience by an unidentified "Mohammedan". This pamphlet, which was

Amir Shah (whose 'Muslim Committee was [. . .] violently opposed to the Muslim League and the Pakistan Plan'[133]) were asked to call a halt to activities that were not construed to be strictly in the religious domain. When this instruction was ignored, the Jamiat-ul-Muslimin was given notice terminating its agency status.[134]

There then ensued a ferocious battle between the Jamiat-ul-Muslimin and the LMF's Executive Committee. The Jamiat-ul-Muslimin refused to accept this termination on the grounds that, as the Board and the Executive Committee of the LMF 'were not wholly Islamic bodies', they did not have authority with regard to how the Mosque's affairs should be conducted.[135] Posters were circulated bearing the caption 'Hands off the East London Mosque and the

violently opposed to the inclusion of the Moslem people in a federated India [. . .] was the subject of considerable discussion and argument. It was said to have been distributed at the ceremony with the approval of Sir Hassan Suhrawardy, who is friendly with the author and a sympathiser of the Pakistan National Movement' (BL, IOR, L/P&J/12/468, fos 205–206, extract from New Scotland Yard report no. 199, 6 August 1941).

[133]BL, IOR, L/P&J/12/468, fo. 72. Indeed, later on, at one Friday congregation led by Sir Hassan Suhrawardy, he loudly prayed for the victory of the Allies. This invited rebuke from some of the members of the Jamiat-ul-Muslimin (according to Majid Qureshi, one of the congregants, Amir Shah asked, 'Why did you pray for the British? We have come for a religious function not to pray for the British' (see Adams, *Across Seven Seas and Thirteen Rivers*, p. 162)), who at the time supported the Indian National Congress as the party fighting for India's independence and denounced the All-India Muslim League as not only 'a traitorous organisation in the pay of Great Britain' but also divisive and elitist. See BL, IOR, L/P&J/12/468, fo. 76.

[134]The Jamiat-ul-Muslimin had been appointed as the agents for 'arranging prayers, supervising the buildings, and doing work for the Indigent Muslims Burial Fund'. A room had been given to them to use as an office. See ELM Archives, Sir Hassan Suhrawardy to the Hon. Secretary of the Jamiat-ul-Muslimin, 8 July 1941. Earlier, Firozkhan Noon had written to Suhrawardy: 'we do not wish the mosque to be mixed up with a political body [. . .] I think it is best to keep it entirely as a religious place of worship, a mosque, in possession of the Jamiat, and for this purpose' (ELM Archives, Firozkhan Noon to Hassan Suhrawardy, 11 December 1940). A little later he suggested that a clause be added to the agency agreement 'to the effect that no political meetings or speeches will be allowed'. He thought it was 'useful to have this clause in order to protect ourselves against any future controversies arising amongst the congregation' (see ELM Archives, Firozkhan Noon to Suhrawardy, 21 February 1941). Such a clause was added to the agency agreement: according to Clause 4, 'You are to see that [. . .] the said premises are used only for the religious purposes aforesaid and for no other purpose and in particular you are not to allow any meetings or speeches of a political nature to be held or take place on any of the premises' (ELM Archives, Sir Ernest Hotson, Hon. Secretary, London Mosque Fund to the Jamiat-ul-Muslimin, 20 May 1941). The notice, dated 23 September 1943, to terminate the agency agreement with the Jamiat-ul-Muslimin was served, but the Jamiat refused to accept the termination, stating it to be in violation of the 'word and spirit of the Quran'. While the LMF's solicitors threatened legal proceedings if the mosque was not vacated, as the Minutes reveal (see below, pp. 241–242), this action was postponed as further discussions with the representatives ensued. See BL, IOR, L/P&J/12/468, fo. 270.

[135]BL, IOR, L/P&J/12/468, fo. 270.

Trust Fund'.[136] At a protest meeting attended by some 400 people – primarily Punjabi and Bengali Muslims – Allah Dad Khan on behalf of the Jamiat-ul-Muslimin stated that the Trustees were not 'good Muslims': they put the interests of the British government before their duty to Islam; similarly, they never came merely to pray, but always had sinister or ulterior motives for their casual visits.[137] He alleged, with some justification, that it was the India Office that ran the affairs of the East London Mosque through its representatives such as Sir Hassan Suhrawardy and Sayeedulla (who combined the role of Secretary with that of Indian Seamen Welfare Officer for the London area, appointed by the High Commissioner) and that these were the type of Muslims on the LMF whom the Jamiat-ul-Muslimin wished to replace with more 'conscientious' and 'trustworthy' Muslims.[138] Jamiat-ul-Muslimin leaders accordingly demanded that a majority of the Trustees and the members of the Executive Committee should be drawn from their organization. Their argument, it must be stressed, did not go unchallenged from other delegates present at the meeting. For instance, the delegate from Newcastle said that

> the board of Trustees of the London Mosque Fund had not suddenly become an un-Islamic body. There had always been Trustees on the Board who were not Muslims, and if the Jamiat saw fit to conclude an agreement with the Board in the first place, then the Jamiat could not now legally refuse to accept a notice terminating that agreement on the ground that the Board was not an entire Muslim body.[139]

This was certainly not what the British government wanted, given that the Jamiat-ul-Muslimin leaders were viewed as unreliable figures – political opportunists, active in Indian nationalist agitation, seeking to obtain control of the East London Mosque and the Mosque Fund.[140] Additionally, in the political context of the Congress-led Quit India movement of 1942, the Jamiat-ul-Muslimin's bid for power in relation to the East London Mosque was a genuine cause for concern, even though officials conceded that 'certain of its members had worked hard in the interests of Islam and have assisted in many ways indigent Muslims and others who have suffered misfortune. The Jamiat was a live and efficient organisation', and that, 'whatever may be said to their discredit, Khan and Shah [Jamiat leaders] commanded far greater support in Muslim circles in East London than the distinguished Muslim Trustees of the London

[136] BL, IOR, L/P&J/12/468, fo. 83.
[137] BL, IOR, L/P&J/12/468, fo. 271.
[138] *Ibid.*
[139] *Ibid.*, fos 271–272.
[140] BL, IOR, L/P&J/12/468, fo. 268 and fos 71–74.

Mosque Fund'.[141] As correspondence within government circles reveals, Sir John Woodhead, the LMF's secretary, felt strongly that the Jamiat-ul-Muslimin 'not merely because of its political complexion but also [. . . because] it was made up largely of East End profiteers, ought not to be given a preponderating voice on the Trust or the Executive Committee if that can be avoided'.[142] The Jamiat's drive for control of the mosque was seen as questioning the status quo and the hegemonic power of the British imperial state. That would not do. Rather, the British authorities wanted 'their men' to continue to run the mosque, keeping their objectives and interests paramount.[143] Muslims such as Suhrawardy and Noon were reliable loyalists, culturally assimilated, cosmopolitan men. The leading members of the Jamiat-ul-Muslimin, on the other hand, were described in a police report as 'bigoted Muslims who, on a religious issue, would not hesitate to subordinate all their other interests to the cause of Islam'.[144] Regarded as rigid in their religious beliefs and practices, they were deemed to be more inflexibly committed to 'traditional' Islam and its prescriptions that they had imbibed from their parents and in Indian mosques and *madrassas* (Islamic schools).

Herein lay the crux of the conflict between the Jamiat-ul-Muslimin and the majority of the LMF Trustees. The chairman of the LMF was authorized to remove misleading impressions caused by the action taken by the Jamiat.[145] While Sir John Woodhead, taking note of the Jamiat's objections to non-Muslims being on the Management Committee, was happy to hand over the LMF's treasurership to a Muslim, the Trustees hoped that 'it would be possible for Sir John Woodhead not to resign'.[146] Given the difficulties that the mosque was then experiencing, the chairman, Dr Hassan Nachat Pasha

[141] BL, IOR, L/P&J/12/468, fo. 268.

[142] See BL, IOR, L/P&J/12/468, fo. 85, Mr Silver's secret report. Sir John Woodhead accepted the post of Hon. Treasurer of the London Mosque Fund in succession to Sir Ernest Hotson in 1941. He was the sole non-Muslim member of the LMF's Executive Committee (see BL, IOR, L/P&J/12/468, fo. 84).

[143] As Mr Silver reported, 'The Jamiat have for some time been making themselves difficult having got into the hands of Congress-minded Moslems [. . .] demanding a predominant share in the appointments both of the Trustees and on the Executive Committee [. . .] They are also objecting [. . .] to the presence of non-Moslems on these bodies (Lord Winterton and Sir J. Woodhead) and are strongly critical of Sir H. Suhrawardy's policy [. . .]. The question arises whether he and Lord Winterton should tender their resignations. If this happens in Sir H. Suhrawardy's absence [on leave in India] there will be no-one to keep an eye on developments from the official angle [. . .] It is obviously undesirable [. . .] and this has kept Sir J. Woodhead from resigning up to now' (BL, IOR, L/P&J/12/468, fo. 84).

[144] BL, IOR, L/P&J/12/468, fo. 268, extract from Metropolitan Police report, 14 October 1943.

[145] See below, p. 242.

[146] *Ibid.*

(the Egyptian Ambassador), who had also led the scheme for the Central London Mosque, suggested at the December 1943 meeting of the Trustees that the management of the East London Mosque be transferred to the committee of the Central London Mosque.[147] Even though friction between the Trustees and the Jamiat-ul-Muslimin continued, legal action by the former against the latter was avoided. By 1948, Sir John Woodhead, who was still honorary secretary of the LMF, had changed his view somewhat regarding the suitability of Jamiat-ul-Muslimin leaders to be Trustees of the LMF. Writing to Hassan Nachat Pasha, he explained 'that the trouble with the Jamiat-ul-Muslimin has disappeared and that relations between the Trustees and myself on the one hand and the Jamiat-ul-Muslimin on the other have been satisfactory for about three years'.[148]

Nevertheless, during the late 1940s the locus of power was gradually shifting from cosmopolitan London Muslims to local East End community leaders. With India's independence achieved in August 1947, Sir Torick Ameer Ali, who had replaced Sir Hassan Suhrawardy as 'the Moslem Adviser to the Secretary of State for India' in November 1944 and in that capacity had taken over the chairmanship of the LMF, relinquished this role. Three long-standing, leading members of the Jamiat-ul-Muslimin – Hatim Attari, Fazal Shah, and Ghulam Mohammad – were elected as Trustees instead.[149] In many ways, the Jamiat-ul-Muslimin, using the ELM as its focus, had already given East End Muslims a more organized sense of community, both through its rudimentary set of religious services and through regular gatherings at religious events in the trying circumstances of the Second World War. It had turned itself into an established conduit for the negotiation of Muslim needs with various government bodies and the institutions of wider society, particularly with regard to what many of those whom it represented considered the proper fulfilment of religious prescriptions.[150] Accordingly, it financed funeral services for Indigent Muslims and co-ordinated burial arrangements with the London Necropolis Company for their burials at the Brookwood Cemetery in Woking.[151] In February 1943, the East London Mosque

[147] See below, pp. 248–249.

[148] ELM Archives, Sir John Woodhead to Hassan Nachat Pasha, 14 February 1948.

[149] ELM Archives, LMF Minutes, 5 February 1948.

[150] ELM Archives, letter from S. Jafferji to the Secretary of the Jamiat-ul-Muslimin, 10 June 1947, regarding the post-mortem of his child that was conducted without his permission (which he would not have given on religious grounds), and the explanation provided by the Jamiat-ul-Muslimin of 'the circumstances and the objection of the Muslim Society to the attitude adopted by the Authorities'.

[151] ELM Archives, Managing Director, Necropolis Company Limited to the Secretary of the Jamiat-ul-Muslimin, 10 May 1947.

was registered for 'solemnizing Marriages'.[152] The Jamiat successfully lobbied the Ministry of Food for the provision to Muslims, along with Jews, of 'Kosher margarine' on the surrender of their bacon coupons for 'cooking fat allocation'.[153] It protested against what it perceived to be offensive material in the press, such as the 'publication of the Prophet's picture which along with its caption is misleading, incorrect and mischievous'.[154] On such occasions as Eid-al-Adha and Milad-un-Nabi, it obtained official authorization for rationed foods such as rice, butter, and sugar, as well as slaughter of a sheep.[155] It even secured permission from the town clerk of the local council for the use of the council's baths by its members before Eid congregational prayers.[156]

After the end of the Second World War, growing communal conflict in India brought about a sharp rise in Indian Muslim political self-consciousness. Many became disillusioned with the Indian National Congress, which was increasingly perceived by Indian Muslims as an organization that was promoting Hindu interests and nationalism. The two-nation concept – one Muslim, the other Hindu – gathered momentum. In London, Abbas Ali, who had arrived from Bengal to study law, threw himself fervently into the Pakistan Movement, declaring that 'India is a problem of two rival ideologies', Hindu and Muslim.[157] His view was that 'The Muslim demand for a separate State is just the demand for freedom and peace [. . .] Muslims are against Hindu imperialism as the Indians as a whole are against foreign rule, and are determined "to take control of their own affairs"'.[158] Such views resonated with many other Muslim settlers in London, including a large number of those residing in the East End. For Shah Abdul Majid Qureshi, a Sylheti and previously sympathetic to the Indian National Congress, the idea of 'a majority Muslim state where Muslims would be free to perform their religious duties [. . .] a *real* Islamic state'[159] now became emotionally very appealing. Demonstrations were organized, and resolutions were passed. Slogans such as 'Pakistan or we perish' and 'Muslims call to arms'[160] struck a chord; and Friday prayers at the

[152] ELM Archives, 'Superintendent Registrar's certificate of the registry of a building for the solemnization of marriages therein', 11 February 1943.

[153] ELM Archives, Hon. Secretary of the Jamiat-ul-Muslimin to the Ministry of Food, 11 February 1943, and the Ministry of Food's reply, 4 March 1943.

[154] See ELM Archives, telegram, 10 February 1943.

[155] ELM Archives, F.J. Adams of the High Commission for India to Suleman Jetha, 18 September 1944.

[156] ELM Archives, letter of confirmation, Town Clerk, Metropolitan Borough of Stepney, 21 March 1960.

[157] K. Hunter, *History of Pakistanis in Britain* (Oxford, 1962), p. 97.

[158] *Ibid.*, p. 98.

[159] Adams, *Across Seven Seas and Thirteen Rivers*, p. 172.

[160] See Hunter, *History of Pakistanis*, pl. 17.

East London Mosque became a focus for the British branch of the All-India Muslim League.[161]

In the period between the partition of British India in August 1947 and the beginning of the 1950s, the Muslim community in the East End grew further as maritime workers began to 'jump ship' in greater numbers. The vast majority hailed from Sylhet, a district of Assam that, after a referendum in July 1947, became part of East Pakistan. These included many Bengali Muslim peasants from adjoining Assamese areas who had arrived in Sylhet as 'refugees' after Partition and, lacking any means of subsistence, took the opportunity to come to Britain. By 1951, when the Minutes reproduced in this annotated edition end, 'the community [. . .] from Sylhet living in London had grown to about 300'.[162] They were generally single and male. Most had had little education. They survived by eking out a living from factory, hotel, and restaurant work or seafaring. Few cared overtly for religion – their attendance at the mosque was sparse, not many fasted during the month of Ramadan, and little consideration was given to the consumption of *halal* food. Many co-habited with or married English women.[163] The beginning of the 1950s therefore marked the beginning of a new era in Commonwealth immigration that eventually drew ever growing numbers of Bengalis to London.

The East London Mosque from 1951 onwards

I now turn my focus to developments concerning the East London Mosque's evolution after 1951, when the Minutes reproduced here conclude. Drawing on the later minutes of the ELM Trust it is possible to trace the subsequent history of the mosque as it faced the challenge of ministering to the religious needs of an expanding Muslim community.

As more and more immigrants arrived, their welfare demanded attention. Given its guidance and material support to the community, the Jamiat-ul-Muslimin, which (as noted above) had been actively engaged in the running of the East London Mosque since its opening in 1941, became increasingly influential in shaping the religious behaviour of many local Muslims. At the same time, its

[161] Adams, *Across Seven Seas and Thirteen Rivers*, p. 54.

[162] *Ibid.*

[163] *Ibid.*, p. 160. Majid Qureshi's oral testimony is supported by Stephen Barton, who, when researching the position of post-Second World War Bengali Muslims in Bradford, observed that the original Bangladeshi migrants 'suffered an almost total lapse of religious observance'. See *The Bengali Muslims of Bradford: a study of their observance of Islam with special reference to the function of the mosque and the work of the imam* (Leeds, 1986), p. 177.

leading members also contributed to the more secular community organizations, such as the Indian Seamen's Welfare Association, which had been set up in 1943 but which was superseded by the Pakistan Welfare Association (PWA) in 1952. Apart from acting as an interlocutor vis-à-vis the relevant British public institutions, such as the social services, given the discriminatory behaviour that East Pakistanis perceived from the West Pakistani-dominated state institutions, the Jamiat-ul-Muslimin also carried out a lobbying function on the former's behalf in bureaucratic dealings with the Pakistan High Commission. Thus, as demand for unskilled and semi-skilled labour in Britain rocketed in the early post-war years, many East Pakistanis wanted to migrate but were concerned that they were being denied opportunities by the Pakistan government's imposition of restrictions over issuing passports to them. In 1954, at a meeting in the packed Grand Palais Hall in Commercial Road, Bengali PWA leaders (including the Sylheti trade unionist Aftab Ali) called for the lifting of curbs on granting passports to East Pakistanis. As pressure continued to mount, the newly installed Bengali Prime Minister of Pakistan, Hussain Shaheed Suhrawardy, agreed in 1956 'to grant one thousand passports to "distressed seamen", their survivors or nominated dependents'.[164] Subsequently, rules were further relaxed, allowing men other than ex-seamen to proceed to Britain for employment purposes. Over the next couple of years, two to three thousand men from East Pakistan joined the existing settlers in London's East End.[165] The ensuing steady stream of East Bengali migrants meant that, by 1962, a community of about 5,000 had become established in Spitalfields and its surrounds.[166]

A number of community organizations emerged to meet these East Pakistani migrants' social, cultural, religious, and welfare needs. The Pakistan Caterers' Association was formed in 1960.[167] Its leaders, who included Shah Abdul Majid Qureshi, Ayub Ali, and Taslim Ali,[168] owned restaurants, boarding-houses, cafés, general stores, and funeral

[164] *Ibid.*, p. 62.

[165] *Ibid.*, p. 64.

[166] Sir John Woodhead in his letter to M.A.H. Ispahani, 2 March 1954 (ELM Archives), gave this number as an estimate.

[167] Adams, *Across Seven Seas and Thirteen Rivers*, p. 177.

[168] Taslim Ali, from East Bengal and married to an English woman who converted to Islam, opened a boarding-house/restaurant/café and a *halal* butcher's shop (a fish and chip shop according to Salahudeen Haleem, one of the present Trustees) in East London in the 1940s, and became increasingly active in mosque affairs from the 1950s. In 1950 he established a firm of undertakers, Haji Taslim Funerals (see below, n. 189).

parlours.[169] Since the 1962 Commonwealth Immigrants Act[170] meant that migrant labourers were allowed entry into Britain only if they had jobs to go to, the Association – by operating as a sponsoring vehicle – facilitated the granting of work vouchers for Bengali cooks and students who doubled up as waiters in the growing catering industry. Many of these 'caterers' were also active in local religious and welfare organizations such as the Jamiat-ul-Muslimin, the ELM, and the Indigent Moslems Burial Fund.

Reflecting these broader trends, by the mid-1950s control of the ELM Board of Trustees continued to pass from the more Westernized 'pro-establishment' Muslims and those non-Muslims who were closely connected with the British authorities to members who were more deeply committed to encouraging the practice of an Islamic way of life among London's Muslims. The influence of the former was also weakening as the result of the shifting of interest on the part of the ambassador-Trustees from Saudi Arabia and Egypt to an ambitious scheme initiated by the Egyptian Ambassador for the establishment of a grand central mosque in the heart of London's West End. Indeed, the latter did not attended trustee meetings after 1955, while the former no longer took part after 1958.[171] Along with a number of other Muslim ambassadors, they became Trustees of the Central London Mosque Trust instead. The High Commissioner for Pakistan, while he remained the chairman of the Council of Management, also adopted an increasingly 'hands-off' approach. Consequently, local representatives of the East London Muslim community, comprising primarily Jamiat-ul-Muslimin leaders, were now the prime movers in the Council of Management's decision-making processes.

Interestingly, there seems to have been little resistance to the shift in power away from the existing Trustees. Indeed, they were content to make changes in the constitution of the London Mosque Fund that enabled its Council of Management to 'be drawn largely from residents of the East end of London where the Mosque is situated'.[172] For Sir John Woodhead, the long-serving honorary treasurer and secretary of the Trust, this was a move in the right direction, as he claimed that he had 'always considered it right and proper that the Moslems who worship at the East London Mosque, should be actively

[169] For Majid Qureshi, see Adams, *Across Seven Seas and Thirteen Rivers*, pp. 141–178; for Taslim Ali, see *ibid.*, pp. 53, 87, 160–161, 163; for Ayub Ali, see *ibid.*, pp. 39, 41–44, 62, 85, 161, 163, 174.

[170] See Z. Layton-Henry, *The Politics of Immigration: immigration, 'race' and 'race' relations in post-war Britain* (Oxford, 1992), pp. 75–76.

[171] See ELM Archives, East London Mosque Trust Council of Management Minutes, 27 May 1970.

[172] ELM Archives, Sir John Woodhead to Dr Hassan Nachat Pacha, 14 February 1948.

associated with the management of the "trust"'.[173] As early as 1948, when seeking approval for the appointment of Fazal Shah and Ghulam Mohammed as LMF Trustees, one of the reasons he gave was that they 'live in the East End of London and are connected with the Jamiat-ul-Muslimin'.[174] When, in June 1949, the London Mosque Fund had become a trust corporation, both these men were included among its first Trustees, together with the ambassadors of Egypt, Saudi Arabia, and Pakistan, Sir Torick Ameer Ali, and three other leading members of Jamiat-ul-Muslimin.[175]

However, while the Jamiat-ul-Muslimin continued to emphasize the necessity of organizing Muslim lives in line with Islamic principles and values in a non-Muslim environment, its increasing influence in the 1950s on the East London Mosque Trust, which had formally replaced the London Mosque Fund in 1949,[176] did not necessarily mean a strong move towards stringency in religious outlook or practice. The Trust's objectives in 1954 were set out in relatively ecumenical terms – they were concerned with those matters of the Muslim faith that could be conveniently and properly undertaken by the Jamiat-ul-Muslimin Trust. The most important of these were the establishment in London of a religious and cultural centre for Muslims 'from all parts of the world', the provision of 'accommodation for Muslim students with a view to guiding their activities and helping them to live their lives in accordance with the tenets of Islam', and to 'inculcate tolerance and liberal outlook in general'.[177] The social, educational, and occupational backgrounds of the fifteen Trustees of the Jamiat-ul-Muslimin Trust in 1954 seemed to reflect the liberality and broadness of their vision. Apart from the High Commissioner for Pakistan, the Trust membership comprised a former lecturer at the School of Oriental and African Studies, a barrister, three doctors, two students, five merchants, a boarding-house keeper, and, interestingly, a so-called 'housewife'.[178]

Nevertheless, those who actively ran the Jamiat-ul-Muslimin projected themselves as committed to the ideal of pan-Islamism and to the embedding and promotion of Islamic practices among Muslims in Britain through their activities. While uneasy about the unravelling political crisis in Pakistan, these Jamiat-ul-Muslimin activists from East Bengal seemed, throughout the 1950s and 1960s, to remain wedded

[173] *Ibid.*
[174] *Ibid.*
[175] See Appendix II.
[176] *Ibid.*
[177] See ELM Archives, 'Memorandum and articles of association of Jamiat-ul-Muslimin Musjid [*sic*] and Students' Residential Centre Trust (London) Ltd.', 1954, p. 1.
[178] *Ibid.*, p. 14.

to the hope of Pakistan becoming an Islamic state, despite their fellow Bengalis receiving what was often perceived to be discriminatory treatment at the hands of the West Pakistani ruling elite. It would appear that in retaining this vision they were ideologically influenced by two religio-political organizations with which they developed close connections: Tablighi Jamaat[179] and the Jamaat-i-Islami.[180] Indeed, members of the Tablighi Jamaat, on their periodic visits to Britain, would stay at the ELM premises,[181] and the JI-inspired UK Islamic Mission, when first founded in 1962, was also initially located there.[182] Taslim Ali, who emerged as one of the key figures in the East London Mosque for several decades after the Second World War, had already been a member of the Tablighi Jamaat for several years.[183] In 1960, he was given the title of 'Honorary Welfare Officer of the Muslim Community of London',[184] and four years later he was appointed Superintendent of the ELM.[185]

The provision of welfare services to the Muslim community remained one of the key objectives of the Jamiat-ul-Muslimin Trust, though, in this early period, the orientation of all its activities was overwhelmingly religious.[186] Nevertheless, as the Muslim community in the East End expanded in size, the leaders of the Jamiat-ul-Muslimin, together with the Trustees of the East London Mosque, became acutely aware of the lack of provision for meeting the needs of their

[179] Tablighi Jamaat (literally, the preaching party), is a revivalist, missionary, non-political Islamic movement founded by Maulana Ilyas (1885–1944), who received his religious training at Dar-ul-Uloom, Deoband. For further details about its ideology and practice, see Barbara D. Metcalf, 'The Tablighi Jama'at in America and Europe', in Barbara D. Metcalf (ed.), *Making Muslim Space in North America and Europe* (Berkeley, 1996), pp. 110–127.

[180] Jamaat-i-Islami (literally, the Islamic party), was founded in 1941 by Maulana Abul A'la Maududi (1903–1979), who, educated by Deobandi *ulama* in Delhi (see below, n. 273), qualified in 1926 as a teacher of religious sciences. An Islamist reformist movement, the Jamaat-i-Islami was, ideologically and in its political practice, strongly influenced by Egypt's Muslim Brotherhood. For details, see Philip Lewis, *Islamic Britain: religion, politics and identity among British Muslims* (London, 2002), pp. 40–43 and R. Bonney, *Jihad: from Qur'an to Bin Laden* (Basingstoke, 2004), p. 201.

[181] For instance, 'Tablighi Jamat brethren', while on tour in England, had stayed at the mosque 'from end of November 1956 to 31 March 1957 and beyond' (see ELM Archives, Ishrat Hussain to S.M. Jetha, 6 March 1959); and 'Tablighi Jamats from Pakistan, India (and provinces) [. . .] visit this country at intervals and make their head quarters at the East London Mosque' (ELM Archives, Jetha's report as Hon. Secretary of the ELMT presented at the Committee of Management meeting, 7 October 1964, and attached to ELMT Minutes of that date).

[182] Sarah Glynn, 'Bengali Muslims: the new East End radicals?', *Ethnic and Racial Studies*, 25, no. 6 (November 2002), p. 971.

[183] Metcalf, *Making Muslim Space in North America and Europe*, p. 226.

[184] ELM Archives, certificate prepared by S.M. Jetha, 17 June 1960.

[185] ELM Archives, ELMT Minutes, 15 January 1964.

[186] *Ibid.*, p. 2.

Muslim compatriots. In 1954, explaining the need for a paid welfare officer to combine with the social work that was being conducted voluntarily by members of Jamiat-ul-Muslimin, Sir John Woodhead, as ELMT Secretary, wrote to Mirza Abul Hassan Ispahani,[187] its then chairman, that the majority of Muslims in the area were poor and

> in need of help and guidance in many matters [. . .] In some homes children are neglected and require assistance as regards food and clothing [. . .] not infrequently, hospitals approach the Jamiat for assistance in regard to Muslim patients, and at similar times requests are received from Authorities of prisons in which Muslims are serving sentences of imprisonment.[188]

Leading Jamiat-ul-Muslimin members, such as S.M. Jetha, S.M Hosain, Nawab Ali, and Taslim Ali, who were themselves relatively devout Muslims, established mechanisms (in association with the Jamiat-ul-Muslimin and the ELMT) that would enable Muslims to carry out their religious duties properly. For instance, in 1950, Taslim Ali, with his English wife assisting, was given permission to start a mortuary and funeral service from the ELM premises.[189] He, Nawab Ali, and their two English wives together founded the first *halal* butcheries in Britain.[190] Through the ELM and partly funded by it, they also arranged for the religious education of Muslim children in the local community.

A factor that was to have serious implications for the future evolution of the East London Mosque, however, was the increasing political tension between the two 'wings' of Pakistan that had quickly emerged after the country's foundation in 1947. While many Bengali Muslims had been fervently in favour of the Pakistan Movement, they were soon disillusioned by what they perceived as being at the receiving end of cultural condescension, economic exploitation, and political oppression meted out by the dominant West Pakistanis. Resentment at the attempted imposition of Urdu as the national language at the expense of Bengali resulted in violent protests in 1952.[191] Tensions again rose sharply with the dismissal of East Pakistan's Bengali-led United

[187] Ispahani was Pakistan's High Commissioner to the United Kingdom from 1952 to 1954. He was also a Trustee of the Jamiat-ul-Muslimin in 1954.

[188] Sir John Woodhead to M.A.H. Ispahani, 2 March 1954, ELM Archives.

[189] Taslim Ali 'was the first one who organized the Muslim mortuary – he rented a room near the mosque. He used to pick up the dead bodies from the hospital, wash the body, and give the funeral service according to the Muslim rites'. His wife was also fully trained to conduct Muslim funerals for Muslim women. See Adams, *Across Seven Seas and Thirteen Rivers*, p. 161.

[190] *Ibid.*, pp. 86–87.

[191] Willem van Schendel, *A History of Bangladesh* (Cambridge, 2009), p. 113.

Front government in 1954.[192] Relations between East and West Pakistan worsened still further with the onset of Punjabi-dominated military rule in October 1958,[193] eventually culminating in the establishment on 16 December 1971 of an independent Bangladesh, following a war of independence.[194] Not surprisingly, East Pakistanis in London also felt aggrieved at these developments. As one influential Bengali resident, Majid Qureshi, put it, 'the big posts were all held by West Pakistani people. In the Military, in all the Government posts, there was some unfairness'.[195] More specifically, he had witnessed the '[dismissive] treatment of Bengalis by the West Pakistani Officers, in the Pakistan Embassy itself', where 'the [West] Pakistanis were all the *burra sahibs* ("big shots"), and they had Bengalis to serve them only in clerical jobs'.[196] Newspaper reports in the late 1960s suggest a great deal of dissatisfaction at what appeared to be the High Commission's lack of assistance in dealing with Bengalis' problems, especially with regard to attacks against them as immigrants in the British press.[197] The Trustees of the East London Mosque, still under the chairmanship of the High Commissioner for Pakistan, sensed simmering discontent and the growing politicization of the East Pakistani community in London along nationalist lines, and accordingly advised that the 'Mosque premises be solely used for religious purposes and no political agitation meeting be allowed there'.[198]

While the Trustees of the ELM were successfully able to 'keep politics out of the organisation'[199] as far as the struggle for Bengali self-determination was concerned, serious divisions among the Jamiat-ul-Muslimin's leading members, vying to wrest control of the ELM's resources, had surfaced in 1959 and thereafter caused acute controversies and tensions within the mosque, seriously affecting its administration and strategic direction. Complaints regarding representation on the LMF and malpractices at the mosque, including irregularities in its administration, proliferated in 1959; these continued for several years, with individuals from both factions making accusations against each other.[200] Two rival groups claimed

[192] *Ibid.*, pp. 116–117; see also Charles Peter O'Donnell, *Bangladesh: a biography of a nation* (London, 1984), pp. 49–50.

[193] Schendel, *A History of Bangladesh*, p. 117.

[194] *Ibid.*, p. 172.

[195] Adams, *Across Seven Seas and Thirteen Rivers*, p. 173.

[196] *Ibid.*, pp. 172–173.

[197] *The Times*, 15 February 1968.

[198] ELM Archives, ELMT Minutes, 30 March 1967.

[199] ELM Archives, ELMT Minutes, 2 May 1968.

[200] According to S.M. Jetha, interested persons were making 'illegal claims to hold posts on the Trust and in the Jamiat. They had also written to the Trust's bank, misleading

representation on the Council of Management of the East London Mosque Trust.[201] The Deputy High Commissioner for Pakistan then called a special meeting of the Jamiat-ul-Muslimin at the Grand Palais Hall in Commercial Road to resolve the issue. A meeting attended by 200 people unanimously confirmed Zafar Iqbal Qureshi as president.[202] This vote of confidence did not end the dispute, however, as the ELM Trustees were not fully satisfied that the office-bearers of either of the two factions had been properly elected.[203] The dispute escalated to a point where abuse was hurled and violence threatened.[204] Both the factions turned up at the Council of Management meeting in December 1959, though its chairman had ruled, in the absence of 'proof' of their 'true' representativeness, that neither would be invited.[205] However, when, as director and secretary of the Council of Management, S.M. Jetha sought legal advice as to which of the two factions should be recognized as the 'true representative', it was suggested that the Jamiat-ul-Muslimin should be notified at its registered address of the next Council of Management meeting.[206] As the two factions operated from separate addresses, the Trust's solicitors informed both that the Council of Management '[could] not recognise representatives of Jamiat-ul-Muslimin until it [was] fully satisfied that they were the accredited officers'.[207] This dispute remained unresolved for years, with the Council of Management appearing content to

the manager' (ELM Archives, Jetha's letter, 13 October 1959). Likewise, in Jetha's view, 'I am afraid the seed of dissensions and disunity amongst East End Muslims are sown, and bitter fruits will have to be reaped' (ELM Archives, S.M. Jetha to Sir John Woodhead, 15 November 1959).

[201] ELM Archives, Ghulam Mohammed, Secretary, to Ouvry & Co. (the ELMT solicitors), 25 October 1959.

[202] *The Times*, 17 August 1959.

[203] ELM Archives, ELMT to M. Arshidullah, 23 September 1959.

[204] S.M. Jetha reported to the Council of Management that certain persons 'have not only created "false rival trust" but also they have forcibly taken possession of the upper parts of the Mosque premises [. . .] on Friday last i.e. on 13th the congregation had hardly finished their prayer when [xxxx] suddenly started shouting and threatening Mr Ghulam Mohammad and myself [. . .] he rushed to attack and hit me' (ELM Archives, Jetha to the High Commissioner for Pakistan, 15 November 1959; see also ELM Archives, Jetha to Officer-in-Charge, Arbour Square Police Station, 13 November 1959). Jamil Fazal Dean, superintendent of the East London Mosque, asked for police protection against the alleged threat of violence at a meeting of the Jamiat-ul-Muslimin in the congregation hall of the mosque (see ELM Archives, Jamil Fazal Dean to Superintendent of Police, Arbour Square Station, 19 May 1959).

[205] ELM Archives, Director and Hon. Secretary ELMT to Newbury, 5 December 1959.

[206] ELM Archives, Newbury to Jetha, 8 December 1959.

[207] ELM Archives, undated memorandum from Messrs. Ouvry & Co., solicitors for the Trust.

admit to its meetings the faction that had represented the Jamiat-ul-Muslimin until 1963.[208]

As the 1960s advanced, the East London Mosque Trust, while unable to establish a unified leadership, became increasingly preoccupied with the practical needs and concerns of its growing congregation. A combination of factors – the deteriorating political situation in Pakistan, the introduction of tougher immigration controls, and the continuing availability of economic opportunities in Britain – meant that the vast majority of the migrants opted to settle in their new surroundings. They were soon being joined in large numbers by their families, relatives, kin, and friends.[209] As they put down local roots, they faced resentment, hostility, and racial discrimination from wider society and its white-dominated institutions. The attacks on migrants were spearheaded by opportunistic politicians, such as the former Conservative minister and subsequently shadow spokesperson Enoch Powell. His 'rivers of blood' speech in April 1968 is credited with bringing out 1,000 dockers and 600 Smithfield Market porters to march past Parliament in protest against his 'victimization' and in support of his opposition to immigration.[210]

With the emergence of political uncertainties and economic turmoil created by a bloody 'civil war', from 1971 the volume of Bangladeshi migrants to Britain, both educated and illiterate/semi-literate, rose sharply, as did the flow of their dependants. During the 1970s, this immigration led to considerable demands being made on schools, health, and welfare services. There emerged a broad separation between whites and Bangladeshis in housing, education, and employment in London's East End – the latter became concentrated in the local garment industry, catering trade, and small shop-keeping sectors. Their lifestyles contrasted sharply. Extreme right-wing organizations such as the National Front took advantage of the rising tide of popular racist sentiments and mobilized significant numbers of mainly white working-class young people against 'coloured' immigrant communities, particularly in the East End of London.[211] Seen as a threat, Asians (predominantly Bangladeshis) in Tower Hamlets were increasingly targeted by teenage 'skinheads' and aggressive white juvenile males – their attacks turned

[208] ELM Archives, ELMT Minutes, 27 February 1977.

[209] For instance, Abdul Mahmud from Talukpur, Sylhet District, taking advantage of the relatively open labour voucher system in the 1960s, brought eleven Talukpur men to Britain on restaurant work permits on one trip. K. Gardner, *Global Migrants Local Lives: travel and transformations in rural Bangladesh* (Oxford, 1995), p. 55.

[210] *The Times*, 23, 24, and 25 April 1968.

[211] A.J. Kershen, *Strangers, Aliens and Asians: Huguenots, Jews and Bangladeshis in Spitalfields 1600–2000* (London, 2005), pp. 212–213.

sporadically into violent assaults, popularly called 'Paki-bashing'.[212] The National Front, which had established a significant presence in Tower Hamlets, was instrumental in instigating these attacks by 'skinheads' on Pakistanis.[213] By early 1970, according to both the *Observer* and the *Sunday Times*, they had become a regular occurrence.[214] In April of that year, *The Times* reported that Gulam Taslim, 'son of the Imam at the East London Mosque [Taslim Ali]', had documented thirty-eight attacks that had occurred in the previous few months.[215] 'The Imam', it stated, 'had hospital treatment after being kicked in the mouth and hit with an iron bar. The windows of the Muslim parlour next door to the mosque were broken five times in one week. Bottles had been thrown at mourners'.[216] This racial violence escalated further later in the year. Two Asian employees of the London Chest Hospital in Bethnal Green were physically attacked, and Tausir Ali, a fifty-year-old Pakistani kitchen porter, was murdered by a white youth in Bow, East London.[217] The violence peaked in July, when 150 white youths ran amok through Brick Lane, injuring five Bengalis.[218] The *East London Advertiser* reported the sentencing of a youth from Poplar, East London, convicted of manslaughter of a Pakistani;[219] in November 1970 it reported an attack on a Pakistani by two teenage youths.[220]

The East London Mosque, identified as probably the most distinctly visible symbol of the Muslim immigrant communities' presence in the vicinity, not surprisingly attracted the attention of local racist groups. A letter, signed 'Anglo-Saxon', which was delivered to the mosque on 27 April 1970, warned that

[212] See *Daily Telegraph*, 7 April 1970. Here is a graphic newspaper account of 'Paki-bashing' in *The Sun*, 9 April 1970: 'Tonight the boys will be out again. Along Brick Lane, Stepney, and at nearby Mile End underground station, where the skinheads meet up to plan the "sport" for the evening. "What about a chunter dahn the Brick?" The pattern is set. One helpless man runs for his life, a 10-strong pack on his heels. The boot or knife goes in. The game's over.' Three youths likewise openly boasted on the Thames Television programme *Today* about 'Pakistani bashing' in the East End: see *The Times*, 9 April 1970.

[213] The National Front, formed in 1967, represented various strands of 'revisionist neo-fascist and radical populist politics'. R. Thurlow, *Fascism in Britain: a history, 1918–1985* (Oxford, 1987), p. 275. Riding the crest of the anti-immigrant wave, it attracted considerable support from the white working-class populations in England's inner city areas and mobilized groups of disaffected white youth in direct action against the anti-racist left and 'coloured immigrants'.

[214] See *The Observer*, 5 April 1970; *Sunday Times*, 19 April 1970.

[215] *The Times*, 7 April 1970.

[216] *Ibid.*

[217] *East London Advertiser*, 24 July 1970.

[218] Kershen, *Strangers, Aliens and Asians*, p. 213.

[219] *East London Advertiser*, 24 April 1970.

[220] *East London Advertiser*, 6 November 1970.

> it would be wise for 6,000 of you who have crowded into the East End of our capital city, to know that we are not going to tolerate this. You will go home of your own free will [...] or we will bomb you out [...] Indians and Pakistanis are the creeping scourge of the earth. Get out or die.[221]

Anti-immigrant feelings shared by large sections of the Tower Hamlets white population continued to rise during the 1970s, as did the incidence of racist attacks on Asians. In September 1978, a report compiled by the Bethnal Green and Stepney Trades Council documented 105 specific assaults, stressing that these cases 'appear only to skim the surface of what has been happening'.[222] In those housing estates where they were in a minority, Bengali families suffered violent assaults not just on the streets in their neighbourhoods, where women and children were the easiest targets, but also in their homes, as stones were thrown through their windows, and excrement and petrol bombs pushed through their letter boxes.[223] Articles in newspapers, which negatively portrayed London's East End Asian immigrants as 'backward, fearful, and disliked', actively fuelled antagonism towards them, provoking racist assaults, particularly against the Bengalis. These became a very ugly feature of East End life through the 1970s, 1980s, and 1990s: 'in total five Bengalis died in racial violence in London's East End in 1976'.[224] In June 1978, *The Times* reported that a mob of youths had rampaged through a Bengali area in the East End of London: 'they smashed windows, hurled bottles and lumps of concrete and shouted insults as they charged through the street [Brick Lane]. They damaged five shops and a car. And an Asian man whose face was cut by flying glass [...] received hospital treatment.'[225] The National Front gained in strength as it focused its racist literature – and its leaders their speeches around the Brick Lane area – on the growing Bengali community, mobilizing the locality's 'disillusioned, frustrated and alienated youth'.[226] Anti-immigration marches were organized through Asian neighbourhoods, and, faced with daily incidents of violence, community leaders such as the Reverend Dr Clifford Hill of the Interdenominational Newham Community Renewal programme warned of the growing danger of the 'outbreak of a race war'.[227] As *The Times* reported, 'From their pitches [market stalls] they would swear and spit at any Bengalis that walked past'.[228]

[221] The letter is available at the ELM Archives.
[222] *The Times*, 25 September 1978.
[223] Kershen, *Strangers, Aliens and Asians*, p. 214.
[224] *Ibid.*
[225] *The Times*, 12 June 1978.
[226] *The Times*, 14 June 1978.
[227] *The Times*, 13 June 1976.
[228] *Ibid.*

The East London Mosque was vandalized on a number of occasions.[229] In November 1973, Taslim Ali, its superintendent, informed S.M. Jetha, its honorary secretary, that 'a gang of youths broke windows and a fanlight'.[230] Jetha reported the harassment experienced by the worshippers to the local police. 'For some time', he wrote, 'we have been disturbed constantly whilst saying our prayers by young people who have been throwing stones at the windows of the Trust's premises.' Could the police, he asked, not increase their 'vigilance'?[231] However, the police force's indifferent response, its apparent lack of sympathy to their plight, and its inability to deal effectively with racial crime engendered frustration and resentment.[232] The feeling in the community was that there was not much point in reporting such matters. Public statements by police officers on why racial crime was not a priority caused further disenchantment and anger, and confirmed perceptions of police attitudes towards such attacks: for instance, after the April 1970 murder of Tausir Ali, the reasoning offered by a detective belonging to the local police for its lack of effort was as follows:

> This could escalate to a civil war in the East End. We don't want it. We're not even sure we could handle it. Regrettably, it's safer in the long run if an occasional coloured man gets beaten up than to have two sides facing each other with all sorts of weapons.[233]

A report by the Pakistan Workers' Union insisted that the police were unable to give them adequate protection.[234] Others in the community offered examples of the police's unsatisfactory response. When Taslim Ali, who combined his role of superintendent with that of imam of the East London Mosque, was assaulted from behind by a gang of skinheads while fastening the shutters on a friend's shop in Commercial Road, he reported the incident three times and claimed that nothing was done.[235] As 'race-hate attacks' continued, immigrant businessmen in Forest Gate, East London, accused police

[229] ELM Archives, Jetha to the Guardian Royal Exchange Assurance Group, 17 November 1973, regarding insurance for damage to windows of the mosque caused by stone-throwing youths. In a reply, dated 20 November 1973, the company refused to pay out unless the 'incident be accepted as a Riot'. See also *East London Advertiser*, 1 February 1974.

[230] ELM Archives, letter from Taslim Ali to Jetha, 14 November 1973.

[231] ELM Archives, Honorary Secretary of the ELMT to Chief Superintendent of Police, Arbour Square Police Station, 17 November 1973.

[232] The report from the Bethnal Green and Stepney Trades Council criticized the police severely for lack of action in investigating cases reported to them, and said that the Bengali community had virtually no confidence in the police. See *The Times*, 25 September 1978.

[233] *The Sun*, 9 April 1970.

[234] *Daily Telegraph*, 7 April 1970.

[235] *The Sun*, 9 April 1970.

of 'inefficiency' in responding to emergency calls for help as white youths provoked violent confrontation, shouting and swearing, and smashing windows of a restaurant with bottles.[236]

What caused a deterioration in relations between these immigrants and local and national institutions was the latter's lack of willingness to treat the former's concerns in ways that would infuse trust. Influenced to some degree by the negative portrayal of Asian immigrants, particularly in London's East End, public representatives and government officials refused to accept that the police's attitude towards attacks on the local Bengali community was in the least bit questionable. Even Peter Shore, the Labour MP for Stepney and Poplar, who had praised 'the people from Sylhet' (a significant and rapidly growing population in his constituency) for showing 'great initiative, and courage as well as adaptability in making the immense change from village life [. . .] to that of a great modern city', and had criticized the media's depiction of Asian immigrants in his area as 'backward, fearful, and disliked' for causing offence and upset to the Asian community, nevertheless insisted that the police had made a special and very thorough investigation of the twenty-two incidents that immigrant organizations had highlighted to him. Perhaps even more dismaying for the East End's immigrant community was the dismissive refusal of the Home Secretary to recognize the racial nature of the assaults on Pakistanis. In a letter to Peter Shore, Reginald Maudling declared that, while he accepted that 'assaults, some of a fairly serious nature had been committed against Pakistanis', that the robberies had occurred, that windows of immigrants had been broken, and that children had made themselves a nuisance outside their homes, all these occurrences were typical of what went on generally in this part of London. In his view, crime figures did not support the claim that 'Pakistanis' were being exclusively singled out and, for him, 'the situation as a whole had been greatly exaggerated'.[237]

As racial attacks mounted, the East London Mosque's leadership struggled to develop an effective strategy to protect the communities that the institution represented. As a Pakistani welfare worker put it, 'we told people to keep quiet, not to go out at night unless really necessary, and to stick together when coming home from work'.[238] The mosque was acutely aware of the hostility that the community was experiencing. Suleman Jetha, secretary of the ELMT, had brought it up in his report at one of the Council of Management meetings, referring to it as 'the present hardships and suffering [that are being]

[236] *East London Advertiser*, 18 September 1970.
[237] *East London Advertiser*, 31 July 1970.
[238] *The Times*, 9 April 1970.

inflicted on our brethren especially in East London, where a handful – commonly known as skinheads – are committing these cowardly acts on lonely law-abiding Indians and Pakistanis'. 'On one occasion', he continued, '30 to 40 hooligans tried to damage their shops'. Apparently, only 'the timely arrival of a few brethren' saved the situation. But aside from this ad hoc 'fire-fighting', all that Jetha was able to suggest was for the Pakistan High Commissioner, still the Council of Management's chairman, 'to take this matter to a higher level to the Home Office and to see that these vagabonds and thugs are properly punished and due vigilance and protection is given by the Metropolitan Police to these innocent victims'.[239] That the ELMT had thus far been unable to develop a coherent plan of action was reflected in the speech that Salman Ali, the Pakistani High Commissioner, gave when he visited the East End of London after the murder of Tausir Ali. At a meeting attended by over a hundred local Muslims (including victims of attacks), he was unable to offer anything more than an expression of his concern about the increasing frequency of attacks on life and property.[240] The Trustees argued that they did not want to provide the skinheads and the National Front with 'the oxygen of publicity' that they craved. Instead the mosque, perhaps a bit naively, wanted to 'open up a dialogue so that they could come to know it better'.[241]

The community and ELM leaders continued to work with representatives of the police, the church, and other relevant institutions. But reporting racial incidents to the police had not, it seemed, improved the situation significantly. Realizing that the police were still failing to protect the victims of racial attacks, the leaders initiated independent community action. Street patrols, along the lines that had proved successful 'in the Euston area where the [Pakistani Workers' Union] had four or five groups standing by to rescue Pakistanis or hit back at attackers', were formed in East London. In the Brick Lane area they were supported by the Anti-Nazi League in organizing their self-defence.[242] As the problem worsened, they combined with the largely white Anti-Nazi League[243] to combat the

[239] ELM Archives, Jetha's report to the Council of Management, 29 April 1970. In the meeting with the East End's Pakistani community after the murder of Tausir Ali, Salman Ali said he had been assured in his discussion with the Commonwealth Office 'that the matter would be put before the Home Office and the authorities concerned'. See *The Times*, 9 April 1970.

[240] *The Times*, 9 April 1970.

[241] Author's interview with one of the Trustees at this time, Mueenuddin Chowdhury.

[242] *The Times*, 1 November 1978.

[243] The Anti-Nazi League was a broad-based pressure group set up in November 1977 to oppose the anti-immigrant racist activities of the far-right groups in Britain. It was at its

National Front, which had become increasingly active and aggressive in Brick Lane. For instance, in June 1978, in a demonstration organized by the Anti-Nazi League, some 2,000 people marched through Brick Lane in protest against violent anti-Bengali disturbances of the week before.[244] A month later, another demonstration occupied the site habitually used by the National Front to sell their party newspaper and other inflammatory literature.[245] When Altab Ali, a young Bangladeshi machinist was murdered in May 1978, the community was outraged. A mass rally was planned. More than 5,000 Asians marched peacefully in protest against what they regarded as the racial killing of a Bangladeshi. Starting in St Mary's Churchyard off Whitechapel Road, where Ali had been repeatedly stabbed, the procession made its way to Hyde Park and then on to 10 Downing Street where a petition was handed in.[246] The Anti-Nazi League joined the march, along with trade unionists. Dissatisfied with the way police were dealing with racist attacks in Tower Hamlets and Newham, Bengalis in London's East End called for a Home Office inquiry on policing;[247] an action committee against racist attacks, reported in the local press as 'the first move towards Asian vigilante patrols in the East End', was set up soon after the news of Ali's murder,[248] and, while a conference of immigrant organizations supported 'the formation of multiracial community self-defence groups in immigrant areas "to complement and assist the efforts of the police"', it decisively rejected a suggestion to form vigilante groups.[249] In July 1978, responding to an Anti-Nazi League call, Asian traders and factory workers in the Brick Lane area struck for a day against 'racialism'.[250] In September 1978, the East London Anti-Nazi League, in response to the National Front march into the East End of London, decided to 'occupy' Brick Lane.[251]

During this period, the East London Mosque remained on the sidelines and preferred to play a calming role behind the scenes. While the Trust showed its support for the Anti-Nazi League's efforts

height between 1977 and 1979. It organized several well-supported protest marches, public meetings, and rock music concerts. It joined the march protesting at Altab Ali's murder, which, it was reported, 'happened in a week of rising frustration for racists and fascists, with the anti-Nazi carnival attracting 80,000 people and the National Front defeated at the polls'. See *East Ender*, 13 May 1978. Its decline followed that of the National Front after the 1979 general elections. See S. Saggar, *Race and Politics in Britain* (London, 1992), pp. 183–185.

[244] *The Times*, 19 June 1978.

[245] *The Times*, 17 July 1978.

[246] *The Times*, 15 May 1978.

[247] *The Times*, 27 June 1978.

[248] *East Ender*, 13 May 1978.

[249] *The Times*, 31 July 1978.

[250] *The Times*, 18 July 1978.

[251] *The Times*, 23 September 1978.

by making a donation of £25,[252] there is little evidence to suggest that the mosque officially participated actively in its campaigns. Similarly, three years later, in a spate of racist incidents in East London (including Poplar and Spitalfields)[253] that included Mrs Baris Khan and her three children being burnt to death in Walthamstow in what was suspected to be a racially motivated arson attack,[254] while a protest march organized by the Khan Massacre Action Committee took place locally,[255] the mosque, while it recognized the racially violent nature of the deaths, confined itself simply to offering prayers for the four victims.[256]

Based on this cumulative experience, a perception emerged among London's East End Pakistani/Bangladeshi community in the 1970s that the institutions of wider society could not be trusted to take up their concerns in a fair way and that the only strategy open to them if they wanted their issues addressed (in particular the problem of racial attacks) was to form their own community organizations that would represent them more robustly and effectively. Given that the East London Mosque had not been able to offer any credible approach or leadership for the defence of the local Muslim community, a viable alternative seemed to be to organize actions on the basis of common ethnic and cultural distinctiveness and interests. In this process, in the 1970s and the 1980s, community groups in Tower Hamlets were helped by a number of policy developments at the governmental level. In order to regenerate the declining local economy and improve the environmental and housing conditions of an area where the proportion of the Bangladeshi population was increasing rapidly, and in recognition of its 'special needs', Bangladeshi pressure groups, especially tenants' associations and youth groups, were encouraged with allocation of resources. Government-funded centres were established to help Bangladeshis in respect of housing, education, employment, health, women's rights, recreation, and community relations. Consequently, Bangladeshi voluntary organizations in the area expanded quickly, though this did not happen without conflicts among various sections of the community. Of the 112 organizations in the Borough of Tower Hamlets, a substantial proportion were run by Bangladeshis.[257] For instance, the Kobi Nazrul Centre, named in

[252] ELM Archives, Minutes of the emergency meeting of the Council of Management of the ELMT, 25 April 1979.

[253] *East London Advertiser*, 10 July 1981.

[254] *The Times*, 4 July 1981.

[255] *East End News*, 10 July 1981.

[256] ELM Archives, Minutes of the 23rd Annual General Meeting of the ELMT, 11 July 1981.

[257] J. Eade, *The Politics of Community: the Bangladeshi community in East London* (Aldershot, 1989), pp. 31–32.

honour of a famous Bengali Muslim poet, opened in October 1982 with the remit to organize Bengali cultural events. The Bangladeshi Youth Programme offered advice and guidance to Bangladeshis in areas of housing, employment, and social and welfare services – it also organized recreational activities. The Bangladeshi Educational Needs in Tower Hamlets was likewise set up to co-ordinate the improvement of educational resources for Bangladeshis, especially in Spitalfields.[258]

While still trailing the secular voluntary bodies in attracting community support and recognition from the institutions of wider society, given the Greater London Council's commitment to addressing the specific cultural (including religious) needs of its hard-pressed minority ethnic communities in the context of urban regeneration, the mosque leaders conducted tough negotiations with the GLC between 1969 and 1982 that enabled them to make a relatively successful transition from what were by now rather dilapidated premises in Commercial Road to the grand building in Whitechapel Road. It is worth looking in detail at this process through which the East London Mosque was able to articulate the particular interests of some layers of the local Muslim community and arrive at the threshold of being accepted as a significant representative for them.

As part of its plan for the redevelopment of the Commercial Road area for social housing, in December 1969 the GLC had made a Compulsory Purchase Order (CPO) to acquire the premises in which the mosque was located, but with the proviso that the Trustees of the mosque should not be required to vacate it until an alternative site had been found.[259] From the Trustees' perspective, this decision had not taken their needs sufficiently into account and they immediately protested against the order. Major E.W. McArthur (in whom the mosque found a doughty ally), secretary of the East London Federation of Industry and Commerce (of which Jetha had opportunistically become a member[260]), argued that Muslims were being 'ignored and ridden over roughshod', with the result that the needs of local Muslims were being 'disregarded just to fit in with the plans of the GLC'.[261] He asked why, when 'considerable attention' was normally given to the retention of religious buildings in redevelopment and planning, no such consideration was being afforded in this case. He urged

[258] *Ibid.*, p. 32.

[259] ELM Archives, Greater London Council, 'Report on relocation of East London Mosque by Controller of Planning and Transportation, Director of Housing and Director of the Valuation and Estate Department'.

[260] ELM Archives, Jetha's report to the ELM Trust, 29 April 1970.

[261] *Hackney Gazette & North London Advertiser*, 17 July 1970.

that the mosque, which now served an estimated 12,000 Muslims in the area, should be excluded from the CPO. The GLC officials, while agreeing that 'most places of worship were left undisturbed', argued that in this particular case it was not possible to do so for practical reasons. In their view, Muslims were not entitled to special consideration where 'the greater good of the greater number' was concerned – as in the re-housing of people in good accommodation.[262] Proposals for offering them alternative accommodation were under consideration, and a synagogue in Brick Lane, Bethnal Green, had been offered.[263] Indeed, Jetha, accompanied by other members of the ELMT, visited the synagogue but rejected it on the grounds that it was 'too big'.[264] McArthur, on the other hand reasoned that, given that 'the two religions were "virtually at war" negotiations between them would be impossible'.[265] Despite the Trustees' spokesman pressing their case robustly, the Secretary of State for the Environment confirmed the CPO.[266] That left the Trustees seeking the maximum amount of compensation possible. They showed great tenacity in the ensuing negotiations, which finally ended in an agreement between the GLC and the ELMT in November 1982.[267] This stipulated the permanent relocation of the mosque to a site held by the Planning Committee on the south side of Whitechapel Road, Tower Hamlets. When the temporary relocation of the mosque to Christian Scott School was deemed unsuitable, the Council agreed in May 1974 to erect a temporary mosque – at a cost of £45,000 – in Fieldgate Street, to the south of the proposed permanent site, to which the Trust moved in May 1975.[268] Lengthy discussions then took place between the Trust and the Council in its role as planning authority, with the Trust wishing to construct a building that could accommodate the expanding Muslim community and hence required a much larger site than that occupied by the original mosque. In 1982, in the final settlement, £192,000 was paid to the Trust in compensation for the

[262] *Ibid.*

[263] This refers to the negotiations to buy the synagogue on the corner of Fourier Street and Brick Lane. See ELM Archives, E.W. McArthur to Jetha, 27 November 1970.

[264] See ELM Archives, Minutes of the Extraordinary General Meeting of the Council of Management of the ELMT, 29 April 1970.

[265] *Hackney Gazette and North London Advertiser*, 17 July 1970.

[266] ELM Archives, McArthur to Jetha, 21 September 1971.

[267] See ELM Archives, Greater London Council, 'Completion of purchase' form, 30 November 1982. Purchase money, or compensation, was stated here to be £192,000.

[268] *East London Advertiser*, 4 July 1975. The keys of this mosque were handed to S.M. Jetha on 9 May 1975. See ELM Archives, Jetha's speech on the occasion of the foundation-stone-laying ceremony, 23 September 1982.

Commercial Road premises and a further site was allocated, costing the Trust £25,000.[269]

The East London Mosque and increasing Islamic observance

In the 1980s, the East London Mosque emerged as one of the more influential institutions of London's East End Muslim community. Its increasingly important role was shaped by a number of internal and external social, cultural, and political developments. First, the 'civil war' in East Pakistan in 1970–1971 meant that, given its devastating impact, those migrants who might have thought of returning to Bangladesh under normal circumstances decided to settle permanently in Britain – sojourners had turned settlers. The passing of the 1971 Immigration Act effectively put a stop to Bengali primary immigration and the vast majority of those who were allowed to enter were family members. As families reunited and settled on a more permanent basis, the communities that they formed began to change in their attitude to life in Britain, to its people and its institutions. The arrival of families had broadened the scope of interaction with wider society, especially over matters concerning education, health, and social welfare. At the same time 'chain migration'[270] had brought along distinct ethnic, linguistic, and regional residential clustering, leading to the establishment of communal organizations as effective channels for conducting business in areas of need. Segregation ensued along village-kinship, ethnic, and sectarian lines. These Muslim immigrants became anxious about the fate of their cultures, traditions, and values. They wanted to create the best possible conditions for practising their faith as they understood it, and they also wanted to ensure that it would survive through its effective transmission to future generations. With this further growth and consolidation of the Bangladeshi immigrant community in East London, bodies with a distinct Muslim identity, such as mosques, were able to gather substantial resources through contributions from individuals and groups within the communities, which, in turn, enabled them to grow and become firmly established.

[269] See ELM Archives, report submitted by Controller of Planning and Transportation, Director of Housing and Director of the Valuation and Estates Department; see also the purchase order of the GLC, 2 November 1982.

[270] Chain migration is a 'movement in which prospective migrants learn of opportunities, are provided with transportation, and have initial accommodation and employment arranged by means of primary social relationships with previous migrants' (J.S. MacDonald and L.D. MacDonald, 'Chain migration ethnic neighborhood formation and social networks', *The Milbank Memorial Fund Quarterly*, 42, no. 1 (January 1964), p. 82).

Community identity began to be defined relatively more strongly in religious than in ethnic terms. Mosques took on many of the services that had previously been offered by the minority ethnic organizations that had received the overwhelming share of the public funding disbursed during the 1970s.

The Conservative Party's victory in the 1979 general election prompted a substantial dismantling of the policy of multiculturalism that had been at the heart of previous government policy, as far as ethnic minorities were concerned, since the 1960s. The policy changes wrought by Margaret Thatcher's government during the 1980s, especially its restrictions on local government support of community organizations, had a radical impact on the development of Muslim organizations. This was further exacerbated by the abolition of the Greater London Council in 1986. With the sidelining of the minority ethnic groups in the East End, the balance of power shifted increasingly to those groups who saw Bangladeshi concerns primarily through an Islamic prism. Mosques – the ELM perhaps rather more than the Jamme Mosque in Brick Lane – became an important form of self-organization for Tower Hamlets' Muslim community. Never having relied on public resources, they appeared relatively more independent and less compromised, though it soon became clear that their dependence on funding from the Middle East was bound to have some effect on the shaping of their perspectives and strategies. With funds drastically reduced for secular community groups, bodies with a distinct Muslim identity (which, in the past, had received few resources from the state and so had had to rely largely on contributions from individuals and groups within their communities) survived the Conservative government's onslaught on sources of support for the voluntary sector relatively well, and emerged with an enhanced profile in the eyes of the authorities.

As the role and influence of the East London Mosque increased from the 1970s, its Trust witnessed vigorous debates about what the mosque did or should do. Its chairman, still – rather anomalously, bearing in mind the Trust's Bangladeshi links – the High Commissioner for Pakistan, suggested that the mosque, apart from being a place of worship, should also act as 'a cultural and meeting centre for the community'.[271] As a centre for families, 'womenfolk and children', it should offer religious instruction for adults and children.[272] The Council of Management accordingly discussed issues such as the accrual and disbursement of financial resources; the provision of welfare services such as funeral arrangements, marriage facilities,

[271] ELM Archives, ELMT Minutes, 29 April 1970.
[272] *Ibid.*

donations, and loans; and the performance of other forms of ritual. The ideological influence of the Deobandi tendency emerged in a range of areas of the mosque's policies and functions.[273] This could be seen, for instance, in discussions about the role of the imam and the qualifications required for the performance of his duties. Indeed, the appointment of a qualified imam became part of a 'prolonged discussion'.[274] Eventually, it was agreed that the selection criteria for such an appointment would be based on the *Shariat*.[275] In this regard, a sub-committee of the Trust was 'appointed to go into the question of Shariat'.[276] After much deliberation it suggested the appointment of

> a Sanadyafta Aalim Maulvi[277] and [...] Hafiz[278] who should have [...] knowledge of Arabic & Urdu and if possible English and Bengali languages, and who should give daily classes to children, Guide Adults in their day to day Masails[279] and lead Five Times Prayers as well as Juma Prayers with Sermon according to practice and traditions.[280]

That the Sub-Committee held a particular doctrinal view regarding what it considered to be the *Shariat* with regard to the qualifications for an imam is made clear in the following note:

[273] Deobandis are followers of a Sunni Islamic reform movement that originated in the Islamic seminary in the town of Deoband in northern India in 1866/1867. It emphasizes a scripturalist approach to Muslim life and the use of Islamic law as central to societal interactions. As such, it rejects the separation between the religious and political spheres. For more information about the founding of this movement, see B.D. Metcalf, *Islamic Revival in British India: Deoband 1860–1900* (Princeton, 1982). Both the Tablighi Jamaat and the Jamaat-i-Islami were founded by Deobandi-trained scholars, and the ethos, interpretations, and programmes of these organizations, while displaying some significant differences in practical terms, evolved out of Deobandi thinking and principles.

[274] ELM Archives, ELMT Minutes, 27 May 1970.

[275] Islamic law: 'It was unanimously decided to have a "Pesh-Imam" for the East London Mosque with qualification laid down by the *Shariat*' (ELM Archives, ELMT Minutes, 14 June 1975).

[276] ELM Archives, ELMT Minutes, 27 May 1970. This sub-committee met on 26 June 1970. It found that there was no imam at the East London Mosque with the appropriate qualifications, and that the existing imam did not fulfil the required conditions for the position as laid down in the *Shariat* and the Traditions of the Prophet. See ELM Archives, 'Report of the sub-committee on the appointment of the imam of the East London Mosque', 24 July 1970. The sub-committee strongly urged the appointment of a qualified imam, who should not be a 'disputive [*sic*] figure'.

[277] Religious scholar who has been awarded a certificate of qualification from a recognized Islamic seminary.

[278] A person who has learnt the Qur'an by heart.

[279] Matters that require religious advice and/or guidance/opinion.

[280] See 'Report of the sub-committee on the appointment of the imam'.

> growing the beard to the required length according to the Sharriyat-e-Muhammadi S.A.W.,[281] and to do such act as trimming or cutting shorter the hairs or shaving the beard is Entirely Haraam[282] [. . .] for which there is no Ikhtilaaf[283] or differences of Interpretation by Muftiyanul Ummat[284] of India and Pakistan. An Imam who does not have a proper length of beard [. . .] and still performed the Prayers, then such prayers are Makrooh-Tehreemi which is very near Haram.[285]

Later, when Isa Mansuri was appointed as the Pesh Imam[286] he soon attracted criticism from some members of the Trust. However, it was unanimously decided that if he were to be replaced, the candidate would have to meet the qualifications laid down by the *Shariat*[287] – he would be assessed by the Trustees on the quality of his delivery of the sermon (*khutba*) and how he led the Friday prayer.[288] The criteria for the selection of the mosque's imam formulated by the sub-committee and the authority invested in its report clearly reflected the growing ideological hold by Deobandis over the mosque's affairs.

This growing Deobandi control, which could trace its influence there back to very soon after the Second World War, began to create unease among many Muslims arriving from East Bengal, who traditionally had tended to be of the Barelwi persuasion.[289] Doctrinal cleavages within the West Pakistani–East Pakistani communities in

[281] *Sharrayat-e-Muhammadi* literally means the *Shariat of* Muhammmad; S.A.W. is the abbreviation for *Sallallahu Alehe Wassalam* (Arabic for 'Blessings and peace be upon him', that is, the Prophet Muhammad).

[282] Arabic word for 'forbidden'.

[283] Arabic word for 'dispute' or, in this context, 'difference of opinion'.

[284] Reference to the *muftis* (jurists) (who provide *fatawas*, 'legal opinions') of the *ummat*, the Muslim community.

[285] According to Mufti Taqi Usmani, 'It is mentioned in the Hanafi books that the jurists are unanimous on the ruling that a Muslim is obligated to grow his beard to the extent of one fist'. See http://www.albalagh.net/qa/beard_hanafi_deobandi.shtml (accessed 20 November 2010). *Makrooh* in Arabic means 'disliked', 'detested', or 'hated'. *Tehreemi* is a derivartion of *haram*, which means 'forbidden'. See 'Report of the sub-committee on the appointment of the imam'.

[286] See ELM Archives, Minutes, 29 November 1975.

[287] See ELM Archives, Minutes, 14 June 1975. Presumably, this meant *Shariat* as understood by the sub-committee.

[288] See ELM Archives, Minutes, 1 May 1976.

[289] The majority of Bangladeshis in Britain hail from the district of Sylhet. There, local Muslims broadly followed 'Barelwi' Islam, which emphasized the role of custom, shrines, and *pirs* ('sufi' or mystical saints); for instance, Shah Jalal's shrine remains a very popular centre of pilgrimage and devotional singing in this part of Bangladesh (see Adams, *Across Seven Seas and Thirteen Rivers*, pp. 4–5). This partially sufistic strand of popular South Asian Islam takes its name from Rae Bareilly, the home town in India of its founder, Ahmad Raza Khan (1856–1921). Barelwis believe the Prophet Muhammad to be imbued with superhuman qualities, such as knowledge of the unseen. Upholding the legitimacy of intercession by holy Muslims (living or dead), custom, and devotion around sufi shrines all play an important

London's East End were further widened by the political crisis into which East Pakistan/Bangladesh was plunged from the beginning of the 1970s. During the 'civil war' in 1971, the Jamaat-i-Islami, given its pan-Islamic vision and political ambitions, had supported the Pakistani state's efforts to retain 'East Pakistan' as part of the Muslim realm.[290] Those who ran the East London Mosque at the time, irrespective of their ethnic affiliations (Punjabi, Gujarati, or Bengali), saw themselves as Muslims *and* Pakistanis. While the Bangladeshi proportion of the East End's Muslim community was increasing rapidly, the membership of the Council of Management of the ELMT in the 1970s remained ethnically very mixed – Punjabi, Bengali, and Gujarati. It seems that these leading men at the ELM could not let go of the sympathies that they had acquired through a close association with TJ/JI ideologies and personnel; these sympathies had deeply penetrated their consciousness over the years and had come to guide their practice. On a more practical level, continuity with the past was reflected in that many of the Committee of Management's meetings were still held at the Pakistan High Commissioner's offices. While many other political issues, especially those of direct concern to Muslims, were considered at the ELMT meetings, curiously there is not a single record in the Minutes of that time regarding the catastrophic events of the war and their impact in Bangladesh, even though tensions among Pakistani immigrants had been running high and had erupted into violent clashes, leading *The Express* to note that a 'civil war' was breaking out in the East End 'among Pakistani loyalists and supporters of the East Bengal separatists'. Petrol bombs were reported to have been hurled at 'West Pakistani traders by militant Bangli Desh [*sic*] extremists'.[291]

Clearly, as mentioned earlier, the political upheaval in what became Bangladesh caused many people there to move to Britain. These new arrivals included people who had either been involved in the struggle for Bangladesh's liberation or who had opposed East Pakistan's secession. However, the majority of the Bengali Muslims making Britain their home at this time considered themselves as victims of ruthless West Pakistani actions. Furthermore, perhaps the majority of Bangladeshis, especially those belonging to the first generation,

part in their religious life. These theological positions are totally rejected by Deobandis. See Lewis, *Islamic Britain*, p. 40.

[290] This conflict has come to be viewed as a complex struggle 'between Bengalis and non-Bengalis, and among Bengalis themselves, who were bitterly divided between those who favoured independence for Bangladesh [the majority] and those who supported the unity and integrity of Pakistan' (Sarmila Bose, 'Anatomy of civil war in East Pakistan in 1971', *Economic and Political Weekly*, 40, no. 41 (8–14 October 2005), pp. 4463–4470).

[291] *The Express*, 14 May 1971.

were coming to find the East London Mosque's style and its rejection of Barelwi practices as *bid'a* ('heretical innovation') indigestible. The widening doctrinal cleavages in the congregation of the East London Mosque gradually led to a substantial proportion of these Bangladeshis seeking the establishment of a mosque in which they felt more at ease. In 1976, some worshippers broke away, purchased the synagogue in Brick Lane, and converted it into a mosque, leaving the East London Mosque even more firmly in the Deobandi camp.[292]

This split did not, however, mean the end of conflict in Fieldgate Street. The struggle between the two factions of the Jamiat-ul-Muslimin for representation on the Council of Management of the Trust that had taken place at the end of the 1950s re-ignited in 1976. The faction of which Mohammad Irshad Baig was now the president, and that had thus far been excluded from the ELMT, renewed its request to be admitted.[293] Again, when this group, led by Messrs Baig, Aslam, and Malik arrived at an 'ordinary' meeting of the Trust on 1 August 1976 in the hope of obtaining entry, emotions became charged;[294] they were allegedly 'insulted and thrown out'[295] of the meeting.[296] In November 1976, it yet again unsuccessfully sought representation on the Trust, something for which, it claimed, it had been 'fighting' since 1964.[297] Feeling frustrated, this group arrived in full strength at the 'extraordinary' meeting of the Council of Management on 2 February 1977 to plead its case; but again there was uproar.[298] The decision regarding who should represent the

[292] The Jamme Masjid Mosque in Brick Lane claims to be able to accommodate up to 4,000 worshippers. It was originally built as a Protestant chapel, along with a small school, by the Huguenots (refugees fleeing French Catholic persecution) in 1742. In 1898, with the arrival of a large number of Jews escaping pogroms in eastern Europe, it became the Great Spitalfields Synagogue. See http://www.portcities.org.uk/london/server/show/conMediaFile.6057/The-Great-London-Mosque-on-Brick-Lane.html (accessed 10 January 2010).

[293] At the meeting of the Council of Management held on 29 November 1975, M.A. Farooqi asserted that he was the rightful representative of the Jamiat-ul-Muslimin – the faction that had not been allowed entry since 1964. This claim was rejected and those who had been representing the Jamiat-ul-Muslimin 'for the last about 11 years' were declared as 'truly the office bearers of the present Jamiat-ul-Muslimin. M.A. Farooqi was therefore asked to leave the room, which he did' (ELM Archives, ELMT Minutes, 29 November 1975).

[294] Apparently, this group was a delegation sent by '100 members of the East London Muslim Community [. . .] with various complaints' (ELM Archives, P. Bawa to the Hon. Secretary of the ELMT Ltd., 5 January 1977).

[295] ELM Archives, M.I. Baig to the Trust's Secretary, letter received 15 November 1976.

[296] ELM Archives, Minutes of ELMT ordinary meeting held on 1 August 1976 in the Library room of the Mosque, under the chairmanship of Dr Ali Mohammad Khan, contain the following phrase 'Messrs. Mohd. Aslam, I.A. Malik and Irshad Beg left the meeting', though this can be seen to be struck out.

[297] ELM Archives, M.I. Baig to the Secretary, ELMT, 10 November 1976.

[298] ELM Archives, ELMT Minutes, 2 February 1977.

Jamiat-ul-Muslimin on the Trust was, on the suggestion of Illahi Bakhsh Somroo (Minister at the Pakistan Embassy and Council of Management chairman at this meeting) deferred to a future public meeting of the Muslim community. At the Trust's next meeting it was decided that, as the present members representing Jamiat-ul-Muslimin had been participating for the previous fourteen years, they would be allowed to continue.[299] Thus, by the beginning of 1978, the control of the mosque was firmly in Deobandi hands. The Pakistan Ambassador was dispensed with as chair of the Council of Management, and 'an active' chairman, A.T.M. Abdullah (a barrister), was elected instead.[300] This move marked a watershed in the mosque's administration, with the Trustees seeking to put it on a more professional footing.[301]

At the same time as the local Muslim population of the East End began to pay greater attention to their religious practices, the mosque's guidance in its daily affairs increased. Among its activities, it issued fatwas on *halal* meat and certified *halal* butchers.[302] For those who wished religious recognition of their marriages, the mosque could provide *nikah* certificates on the presentation of the registrar's certificate.[303] It provided a mortuary and made arrangements for funerals and burials.[304] It offered guidance in respect of inheritance and, certainly in terms of donations to the mosque, it ignored English law in favour of the Islamic law of inheritance. An important example of this was when Syed Monawer Hossain, a long-time Trustee died

[299] ELM Archives, ELMT Minutes, 27 February 1977.

[300] ELM Archives, ELMT Minutes, 6 July 1978.

[301] In December 1979, Abdullah was appointed chairman cum managing director of the ELMT, to work three days a week for a period of four years, on a salary of £6,000 per annum. His responsibilities included the planning of mosque activities and running its day-to-day administration, public relations and contact with business communities, Islamic organizations, and missions, 'and all related matters regarding the project of new mosque building'. See ELM Archives, letter of appointment from S.M. Jetha, Hon. Secretary to A.T.M. Abdullah, 7 December 1979.

[302] 'Mr Rupa Miah [...] in my opinion [...] carries out animal slaughter as per Moslem rites and I therefore feel that his slaughtering will be acceptable to all Muslims' (ELM Archives, Director and Hon. Secretary, ELMT, to Messrs Barnard & Harbott of Romford, Essex, 28 March 1960).

[303] 'The certificate must be given on the Mosque's letter heads' and 'must be countersigned by the Hon Secretary and the marriage parties must hand over a duplicate copy of the marriage certificate issued by the Registrar for the Trust's records. No "nikah" (Islamic formal wedding ceremony) is to be performed before making sure that the marriage has been first registered in the Registrar's office and a proper certificate is produced' (ELM Archives, ELMT Minutes, 14 June 1975).

[304] Taslim Ali, appointed as Superintendent of the East London Mosque, applied to the Trust for the use of the business premises at the mosque as a funeral undertaker parlour for the 'Goosal (washing of the corpse), Kafan (shrouding), and burials etc. of deceased Muslims' (ELM Archives, Taslim Ali to S.M. Jetha, 4 July 1964).

in 1973, leaving two-thirds of his property as a gift to the mosque in his will.[305] This move would certainly have been valid under English law. However, the Mosque Trustees decided to apply *Sharia* law, as they understood it, and to keep only one-third, disbursing the rest to his nephew Mahmud Hossain and other heirs.[306] All these functions increased the mosque's influence among sections of the local Muslim community. As its influence increased, so did the tussle for control of the substantial and growing resources that it was accumulating.

While the dispute about who should represent the Jamiat-ul-Muslimin on the ELMT faded in the next few years, concerns about the running of the mosque's affairs simmered within the congregation.[307] On 24 December 1981, the discontent became manifest. Over 100 *Mukthadis* ('prayer performers') of the East London Mosque signed and sent a petition to its secretary in which they articulated a number of their complaints. The petition accused the secretary of misuse of mosque funds, as well as the mismanagement of *fitra*[308] donations and loan distribution. It complained that the imam did not lead all the daily prayers[309] (as he should have been required to do),[310] that the *fitra* money was not being distributed fairly and equitably to the deserving, that tens of thousands of pounds of loans were being approved to those who were either themselves members of the Trust or closely connected with the Trustees, and that 'the proper teaching of children was not being done as the imam was not available'.[311] At a well-publicized General Public Meeting held on 7 February 1982, many of these questions were addressed by the chairman and the secretary of the ELMT,[312] and the *Mukhtadis*' challenge was seen off for the time being.

[305] See ELM Archives, ELMT Minutes, 13 September 1973.

[306] See ELM Archives, ELMT Minutes, 17 November 1979.

[307] See for instance, ELM Archives, ELMT Minutes, 1 June 1978 and 6 July 1978. In 1980, it was decided that 'from now on loan giving should be stopped and no committee member should be allotted a loan. If there is any needy and really deserving applicant then the amount of help should not be more than £500.00' (ELM Archives, ELMT Minutes, 24 May 1980).

[308] A type of alms-giving that is obligatory for anyone who is not poor. It is due before or at Eid-ul-Fitr, i.e. the celebration marking the end of the month of Ramadan.

[309] See ELM Archives, A.T.M. Abdullah's Memorandum, 8 October 1979, and ELMT Minutes, 17 November 1979.

[310] This allegation was incorrect, as can be seen by looking at Abdullah's Memorandum, in which he had suggested that the imam 'should lead prayer whenever he is present in the mosque at the time of the prayer'.

[311] ELM Archives, letter from the *Mukhtadis* to the Secretary of the ELMT, 24 December 1981.

[312] ELM Archives, report of the General Public Meeting held at the East London Mosque on 7 February 1982.

It should be noted that, while it is true that some of the challenges mounted against the mosque's leadership in the 1980s stemmed from 'grievances between the large Bengali community and the mosque's ruling committee', this was not essentially a sectarian tussle between JI/Deobandi and Barelwi rivals within the mosque. Rather, it represented a conflict that was instigated by personality clashes, ethnic divisions, and ambitions of power, at the heart of which lay the drive to secure control of the mosque's substantial resources and decision-making apparatus. By the end of the 1980s, the struggle for power had descended into an unprecedented level of bitterness and violence. In 1987, local newspapers reported that the police had been called to intervene in fights between rival factions within the mosque.[313] The following year, a feud between rival Muslims erupted into violence there on New Year's Day, when youths armed with staves and iron bars clashed with scores of worshippers during the Friday lunchtime prayer service and had to be separated by the police. The fighting, 'the worst in a series of incidents' at the mosque over the previous six months, was thought to have started when a notice appeared on the mosque building that fifteen Muslims were banned from entering by a High Court injunction. Among those banned was the sacked imam, whose expulsion had become one of the chief causes of the dispute between part of the congregation and the mosque's management committee.[314] His defiant holding of Friday congregations, apparently under police guard outside the mosque over several weeks, helped to provoke the clashes.

A further bone of contention at this time was who controlled the very substantial financial resources accumulated by the mosque. As the congregation grew, so did the mosque's wealth, with donations through *zakat*[315] and *fitra* and income from investments running into thousands of pounds. Those who sat on the Trust had full control over decisions about the disbursements – inevitably, loans were approved to other like-minded religious establishments and mosques, such as Dawat-ul-Islam, Glasgow, the Waltham Forest Muslim Association in East London,[316] and the Talim-ul-Islam Madrassa, Dewsbury,[317] while the loan application of the predominantly Bengali Tawakkulia Society of Bradford,[318] which belonged to the Barelwi persuasion, was

[313] *East London Advertiser*, 22 May 1987.

[314] *Docklands Recorder*, 7 January 1988.

[315] Islamic alms – the giving of a percentage of one's income to the poor. See ELM Archives, ELMT Minutes, 6 January 1978.

[316] ELM Archives, ELMT Minutes, 8 August 1981 and 20 June 1981.

[317] ELM Archives, EMLT Minutes, 10 May 1975.

[318] For the Tawakkulia Society of Bradford, see Barton, *The Bengali Muslims of Bradford*.

deferred.[319] The Trustees' awareness of the concerns of the *umma*, combined with their pan-Islamic sympathies, meant that they were also prepared to provide financial help to those in need internationally – for example, the 'Iranian victims of war' with Iraq, and the 'Afghan Mujahideen' (fighting against the Soviet-backed Afghan regime).[320] Support was demanded for the Palestine Liberation Organization and the Lebanese upon Israel's invasion of the latter's territory in 1982.[321] Relief was provided for the victims of the cyclone disaster in Bangladesh and, interestingly, for the earthquake victims of Italy, showing empathy for humanity at large.[322] In the disbursement of loans to individuals in the Muslim community – to start up businesses, for hard-up students, and for distressed women – the decisions seemed to be based on an ad hoc consideration of each case, reflecting the client–patron relationship that seemed to be at work here.

As early as the mid-1960s, there had also emerged concerns regarding the religious legitimacy of the Trust's investments and the incomes derived from them. Government stocks and bonds, into which funds had been invested in order to generate income to meet the Trust's expenditure right from the inception of the LMF in 1910, had begun to cause much unease among the leading members because of their interest-bearing character.[323] As a source of income, these were felt to be Islamically unlawful.[324] Alternative

[319] ELM Archives, ELMT Minutes, 14 October 1982.

[320] ELM Archives, ELMT Minutes, 18 February 1981.

[321] In an undated letter written by Jetha to the Council of Management, he said, 'As you are aware that the present Israeli regime with premeditated and planned design ruthlessly invaded Lebanese territory resulting in thousands of deaths of men, women and children, cities and villages demolished and over a half a million people homeless, with a view to destroy the P.L.O. Zionists are committing the same barbarous acts which were met out to them by the Nazis. In my humble opinion Jihad [various literal Arabic meanings include 'exertion', 'effort', and 'armed struggle'] has a very wide meaning appropriate for all occasions when Muslims are in trouble. While we are unable to go and fight shoulder to shoulder with the Palestinians, we could at least offer a reasonably substantial financial assistance to the P.L.O and the Lebanese in their dire need.' See ELM Archives, letter attached to ELMT Minutes, 19 June 1982 (since Israel invaded Lebanon on 6 June 1982, this attached letter must have been written after that date).

[322] ELM Archives, ELMT Minutes, 18 February 1981.

[323] For instance, Jetha (not long after his appointment in 1963) reported in October 1964 that 'Some Muslims have been making objections on the grounds that an income is being derived by way of "interest"'. See ELM Archives, Jetha's report attached to ELMT Minutes, 7 October 1964. A committee was set up 'to discuss [. . .] Interest matters' (ELM Archives, ELMT Minutes, 1 September 1971).

[324] When the audited accounts were presented at the Council of Management in 1973, 'the question of interest was raised by one of the Trustees Mr Abdul Salam'. It was decided to defer the matter to the next meeting, when 'some useful ways could be found to spend this sum for welfare and other appropriate works according to the Islamic Sharia'. See ELM Archives, ELMT Minutes, 13 September 1973. In 1982, when some members of the East

methods of Islam-compliant income generation were suggested. For instance, in 1970 the honorary secretary, Jetha, suggested investment in equities and offered his own property, a house, for sale to the Trust. This investment, he argued, could generate rental income, a religiously legitimate source, instead of earning interest.[325] A finance sub-committee was set up to investigate the matter[326] and, after its meeting in May 1970,[327] its recommendation to the Council of Management to purchase the property was unanimously accepted in September 1971.[328] Examination of 'ways and means of utilising interest money'[329] that would be ideologically acceptable did not stop. Soon afterwards, it was agreed that monies derived from interest-bearing investments[330] should only be used for social welfare purposes and not for the purposes of the mosque.[331] So, a separate welfare fund[332] was opened, from which nothing could be spent on mosque expenses.[333] The Memorandum of Association was amended to stipulate that any income from interest-bearing funds would 'not be spent towards the promotion of the objects of the trust not being in conformity with the Sharia Law and [that] such funds shall be spent for the care and upliftment of poor and needy Muslims'.[334]

From the early 1980s, the vision of what the mosque represented was largely shaped by men such as Suleman Jetha, Taslim Ali, and Mueenuddin Chowdhury. Their ideas regarding its structure and activities continued to be influenced by TJ or JI strategies. Because of these TJ/JI connections, both ideological and programmatic, with

London Mosque's congregation accused its administration of the unlawful disbursement of sums of money by way of loans, Jetha, who was chairman at the time, while denying the charge, explained that the help to needy and distressed Muslims was provided from the interest on bank deposits that could not be spent on 'the mosque causes' owing to religious prohibition, and was therefore collected in a separate 'Welfare Fund' for this purpose. See ELM Archives, T.V. Edwards & Company to The Secretary of the East London Mosque, 15 October 1982, and S.M. Jetha's reply, 9 November 1982.

325 See ELM Archives, Jetha's letter to the Trustees, 8 May 1970.

326 ELM Archives, ELMT Minutes, 12 September 1970.

327 ELM Archives, Report of the Finance Sub-Committee, 22 May 1970.

328 ELM Archives, ELMT Minutes, 1 September 1971.

329 ELM Archives, ELMT Minutes, 1 June 1978.

330 For instance, the interest of £2043.49 on deposits of £221,000 at Barclays Bank: see ELM Archives, Barclays Bank to Jetha, 13 September 1982.

331 ELM Archives, ELMT Minutes, 1 June 1978.

332 'It was finally decided to open a separate Welfare Fund account and all the interest money so far accumulated be transferred into this account and also future interest money earned be put in this account. These amounts should NOT be spent on Mosque expenses' (ELM Archives, ELMT Minutes, 6 July 1978).

333 *Ibid.*

334 The amendments to the Memorandum of the Articles of the Association of East London Mosque Trust Ltd. were approved in the meeting of the Council of Management on 3 January 1979. See ELM Archives, ELMT Minutes, 3 January 1979.

similar formations in Saudi Arabia and other parts of the Middle East, when it came to the next stage of the mosque's development – the construction of the new mosque to replace the temporary, government-financed building in Fieldgate Street – the Trustees looked to potential sources in those quarters for financial support. Apart from the Trustee Tariq Rafique's suggestions to the mosque's building committee for fundraising such as house-to-house collections, sponsorship from founder members and other influential persons and organizations, and donations from Muslim businessmen, banks, and insurance companies, their ambitious multi-pronged plans for the new East London Mosque (the likely cost had mounted to £1.5 million[335]) included fundraising trips to Jeddah, Abu Dhabi, Kuwait, and Cairo. The Trustees also sought help from the governments of Pakistan and Bangladesh. In their negotiations for compensation from the GLC, they again enlisted the support of the Muslim trustee-ambassadors. Hence, the election of Khurram Murad of the Islamic Foundation (closely associated with the Jamaat-i-Islami in Pakistan) as one of the new Trustees may well have obtained the mosque project a sympathetic hearing from potential benefactors in the Middle East.[336]

The strategy paid off. While the Mosque was able to negotiate compensation of around £200,000 from the GLC and to accumulate some £700,000–800,000 through individual donations from local congregants, it was the generous donations from the Middle East, from wealthy Muslims, and, in particular, £1.1 million from King Fahd of Saudi Arabia that enabled the achievement of the £2 million needed for the completion of the new mosque building.[337]

[335] David Rolfe Associates, Chartered Quantity Surveyors, estimated the cost of the project to be £1,436,000. See ELM Archives, David Rolfe Associates to A.T.M. Abdulla, chairman of Council of Management of the ELM Trust, 6 April 1979. 'The Chairman of the ELMT reported on this discussions with the architect and quantity surveyor in regard to the erection of the new Mosque and said that it had been conveyed to him that the estimated cost had now risen to £1 ½ million.' See also ELM Archives, Minutes of the Emergency Meeting of the CoM [Committee of Management] of the ELMT, 25 April 1979.

[336] According to the Minutes, Khurram Jah Murad 'was connected with the Middle East, and was the Director-General of the Islamic Foundation. He was a Mid-east civil engineer and was responsible for the construction of the *Haram sharif*' (ELM Archives, ELMT Minutes, 18 August 1979). *Haram sharif* is the 'noble sanctuary' in Mecca, surrounding the *Kaaba*. The *Kaaba* (meaning a 'cube-shaped room' in Arabic) is a stone structure built in the middle of the Sacred Mosque. Muslims believe that it was built by the Prophet Abraham as a landmark for the House of God, for the sole purpose of worshipping of God alone. It is also the centre of the circumambulations performed during the pilgrimage (*Hajj*), and it is towards the *Kaaba* that Muslims face in their prayers (*salat*).

[337] For a list of the most generous donors, see ELM Archives, brochure prepared for the Opening Ceremony of the East London Mosque, dated 12 July 1985. Apart from King Fahd bin Abdul Aziz of Saudi Arabia, the list of donors included Sheikh Muhammad Akbar Ali Safat, Kuwait (£100,000); Rabitul Alam Al-Islami, Saudi Arabia (£85,000); M/S

However, this also meant that the mosque remained firmly within the Deobandi/JI/Wahabi ideological nexus.

Over time, the more the mosque succeeded, the more its influence in the community grew, bending community practice to its religious prescriptions. Those who disagreed had already left to join other mosques, such as the one in Brick Lane. While it is undoubtedly the case that the East London Mosque's authority came to be disputed by substantial sections of the East End's Muslim population – its ideological position and religious guidance is by no means hegemonic – nevertheless, it has continued to exercise considerable influence over significant sections of this population and acts as an interlocutor vis-à-vis many institutions of wider society, locally and nationally. Through its interactions with influential people in a wide range of Muslim countries, it has gained a measure of recognition as a representative of particular layers of British Muslims. When the new building was inaugurated in 1985, its symbolic importance was demonstrated by the cosmopolitan character of those who were assembled on that occasion – the Ambassador of Saudi Arabia and the Imam of *Kaaba*, local MPs and the Mayor of the Borough of Tower Hamlets, and Muslim and non-Muslim dignitaries from around London and other British cities. That had also been the case at the Foundation Stone-laying ceremony in September 1982,[338] when Akbar Ali from Kuwait, who had initially anonymously donated £100,000 towards the mosque building fund, had been the chief guest.[339] It seems that the mosque leadership also tried to show that it genuinely wished to engage with the process of integration in the evolving multicultural and multi-faith community that the East End of London had become, and of which Muslims were now an integral part. Indeed, Suleman Jetha, who was the chairman of the Trust in 1982, hailed the construction of the mosque, adjacent to the synagogue and a nearby church, as the building of 'a new Jerusalem!'[340]

From the time of its 1985 opening in Whitechapel Road, the East London Mosque steadily deepened its role in the affairs of the

Zahed Tractors, Jeddah, Saudi Arabia (£28,000); H.H. The Aga Khan, Paris (£25,000); Islamic Solidarity Fund, Jeddah, Saudi Arabia (£12,000); Ministry of Awqaf, Government of Kuwait (£11,000); Sudan Embassy, London (£10,000); the Government of Pakistan through the Embassy in London (£5,000); and the Government of Bangladesh (£1,000).

[338] The conditional permission for the construction of the mosque was granted on 19 May 1981. See ELM Archives, undated letter from the Director of Development, London Borough of Tower Hamlets. Planning approval was also reported in the local press: *Hackney Gazette*, 19 May 1981; *New Standard*, 1 June 1981.

[339] See ELM Archives, Jetha's speech on the occasion of the foundation-stone-laying ceremony, 23 September 1982.

[340] *Impact International*, 8–21 October 1982, p. 2.

local Muslim community as the politics and discourses of identity changed their orientation from ethnicity to religion. One influential factor that strengthened the ELM's hand was its association with Islamism,[341] whose global appeal had risen rapidly. With secular radicalism retreating under attack from the new Right, Islamism seemed to offer persuasive solutions to the needs and concerns of many young Muslims, most powerfully with regard to matters of their identity and self-esteem. After the 1986 local election, the Liberal/SDP alliance's reintroduction of housing policies in Tower Hamlets, differential entitlements and allocation that had favoured white families at the expense of their Bangladeshi counterparts, and that had been shelved in the early 1980s as inherently racist, resulted in further disillusionment with the mainstream political parties among large sections of the Bangladeshi community. With their secular community groups increasingly sidelined, local Bangladeshis saw greater possibilities of being more effectively represented by such entities as the mosque even though it viewed their concerns through the Islamic prism. Not having relied on public funding, it (along with other mosques) appeared relatively more independent and less compromised, though it soon became clear that dependence on funding from the Middle East was bound to have some effect on the shaping of perspectives and strategies. Moreover, having survived the Conservative government's onslaught on sources of support for the voluntary sector rather well, bodies with a distinct Muslim identity (which, in the past, had received few resources from the state and so had had to rely largely on contributions from individuals and groups within their communities) emerged with an enhanced profile in the eyes of the authorities.

The position of those who wished to emphasize Islamic needs was strengthened in schools, and also in mosques, prayer halls, and *madrassas*. Community identity began to be articulated relatively more strongly through religious institutions, where Muslim solidarity could be publicly celebrated, and rather less so on the basis of ethnic affiliations, family, village, and class. Indeed, between 1986

[341] An Islamist is a Muslim who 'believes' that 'Islam as a body of faith has something important to say about how politics and society should be ordered in the contemporary world and who seeks to implement this idea in some fashion': Graham E. Fuller, *The Future of Political Islam* (Basingstoke, 2003). According to Bobby Sayyid, writing on Islamism from a British Muslim perspective, 'an Islamist is someone who places her or his Muslim identity at the centre of her or his political practice. That is, Islamists are people who use the language of Islamic metaphors to think through their political destinies, those who see in Islam their political future.' For him, Islamism is not some kind of monolithic edifice without variation or internal differences. See Bobby Sayyid, *A Fundamental Fear: Eurocentrism and the emergence of Islamism* (London, 1997).

and 1990 Islamist groups associated with the East London Mosque intervened on a number of communal issues, including provision of *halal* food and prayer facilities in schools, as well as *The Satanic Verses* protest. The controversy over Salman Rushdie's novel (which was partly set in Brick Lane)[342] that erupted in 1989, was a watershed in the shift from the politics of ethnic identity to those of religious identity. Muslim protesters right across Britain were greatly agitated by the book's perceived attack on the Prophet; 'Cockney Muslims',[343] already feeling embattled by British racism, felt that they had been insulted by Rushdie's satirizing of their religion – he had offended their deepest beliefs and values. The opposition from the British establishment and the public at large, who saw the Muslim agitation as an attack on the principles of free speech, thought, and expression, was equally intemperate and condemnatory. In Britain and the West more generally, it was the core values that produced the fault lines between Muslims and wider society, the liberals arguing that no one 'should be killed or face the threat of being killed, for what they say or write';[344] many committed Muslims countered that no one should be free 'to insult and malign Muslims' by denigrating 'the honour of the Prophet Muhammad'.[345] Instead of sympathy, Muslims found themselves attacked by wider society for their perceived rejection of British values. East End Muslims accordingly vented their anger in public meetings organized both in the Brick Lane and East London Mosques and at large rallies in Hyde Park. The Young Muslim Organisation,[346] which, in alliance with anti-racist groups (Bangladeshi

[342] Rushdie refers to the Brick Lane Mosque thus: 'Jamme Masjid [...] used to be the Machzikel HaDath synagogue which in turn replaced the Huguenots' Calvinist church', (Salman Rushdie, *The Satanic Verses* (London, 1988), pp. 299–300).

[343] C. Douglas, 'A Cockney mosque', *Tower Hamlets News*, September 1986.

[344] Timothy Garton Ash, 'No ifs and no buts', *The Guardian*, 23 June 2007.

[345] See *Aljazeera*, http://english.aljazeera.net/news/asia/2007/06/2008525123146597321.html (accessed 13 October 2010).

[346] The Young Muslim Organisation (YMO), a section of the Islamic Forum of Europe, is a reformist group engaged in practical grassroots programmes. According to its website, 'in October 1978 young Muslim men gathered in a house in London to bring together a dynamic band of youth who would respond to the challenges faced by their community with deep faith, true commitment and a positive and comprehensive work plan [...] Dawah is an essential component of YMO UK's work; indeed it is essential to the Islamic tradition. It is vital simply because without being actively engaged in inviting people to Islam, social change based on Islam cannot be accomplished. YMO UK strives to ensure that its Dawah is comprehensive as well as suited for the specific circumstances of the youth in different parts of Britain. The School Link Project (SLP) and the College Link Project (CLP) working in schools and further/higher educational institutions respectively, organise a wide range of activities from seminars and awards ceremonies to camps and sports activities. Parallel to Dawah work in educational institutions, the YMO UK Community Teams work in neighbourhoods and residential areas across Britain, encouraging the youth

and otherwise), had previously spearheaded the movement against the National Front and racist violence in the East End of London with encouragement from the East London Mosque, participated energetically in the protests against Rushdie. At the rally in Hyde Park in February 1989, 'the chants of their [YMO] leaders could be heard above all others'.[347] Abdal Hussain Choudhury co-ordinated the UK Action Front's demonstration[348] and preceding march from the East London Mosque.[349]

These initiatives dovetailed with wider processes of Islamization, undertaken by groups such as Dawatul Islam[350] and the Tablighi Jamaat among East London's Bangladeshi community, in close association with the East London Mosque, which encouraged a greater conformity with regard to the dress code and religious rituals as defined by Islamist activists. Furthermore, during the 1990s, events in the Middle East (the first Gulf War in 1991), Kashmir, and eastern Europe (especially the plight of Bosnian Muslims) helped create an ever deeper sense of being part of the global Islamic community and of being 'Muslim'. Perceived injustices abroad resonated with discrimination at 'home', creating a powerful sense of Muslim identification. Post 9/11, the coalescence of these factors played a significant role in hastening the move towards Islamization within the Muslim community of Tower Hamlets, especially among the younger generation, most significantly through the growth of Islamist organizations, such as the YMO and the Islamic Forum of Europe,[351] which, with the demise of the Left, were able to present themselves as

to commit their lives to Islam and contribute positively to their society and community. It is our belief that organised collective action; [*sic*] for the sake of Islam is a duty and a necessity.' See http://www.islamicforumeurope.com/live/ife.php?doc=ymo#top (accessed 13 October 2010).

[347] *The Independent*, 20 February 1989.

[348] *The Guardian*, 22 July 1989.

[349] *The Guardian*, 5 May 1989.

[350] In 1977–1978, the Bangladeshi members of the UK Islamic Mission separated from it and formed Dawatul Islam 'to promote work among that community'. All the same, according to Philip Lewis (*Islamic Britain*, pp. 104–105), 'There is considerable overlap between the memberships of the Islamic Foundation, UK Islamic Mission and Dawatul Islam'. The Dawatul Islam website states that it is 'an organisation providing an effective platform to propagate Islam as a balanced and comprehensive way of life'; it aims 'To inform and influence public policy and services in order to achieve better outcomes for British Muslims, their families and communities', and it has 'worked with all sections of society to develop and deliver programmes that deal with education, community cohesion, and respect of other faiths and cultures' (http://www.dawatul-islam.org.uk/index.php?id=37 (accessed 13 October 2010)).

[351] For more information about how the Islamic Forum of Europe presents itself, see its website, http://www.islamicforumeurope.com/live/ife.php (accessed 22 November 2010).

a persuasive political alternative, thereby accentuating the influence of the East London Mosque among local Muslims.[352]

The support for the East London Mosque also increased during this period because, having accumulated considerable experience of dealing with British institutions, its leadership came to be seen as having engaged effectively in the public sphere: it had gained recognition alongside other special interest groups and functioned with similar agendas, its distinctiveness highlighted primarily by its explicit Muslim identity. Local politics provided the main arena in which it developed and exercised influence, negotiating skilfully with various dimensions of local government, seeking compromise, and reaching ad hoc deals in a typically British fashion. By the end of the twentieth century, the East London Mosque was indisputably one of the more influential institutions of London's East End Muslim community. This was reflected when, in November 2001, the Prince of Wales joined in the breaking of the fast during Ramadan.[353] Later that same evening, he spoke at the launch of the construction of the London Muslim Centre, 'congratulating the East London Mosque and London Muslim Centre' on all that it was doing, and promising to 'take the closest personal interest'.[354]

In strengthening its role and influence within this community, the East London Mosque was helped in no small measure by the coming to power of New Labour in 1997. The state's multicultural policies began to move away from the recognition of purely ethnic claims to encouraging faith groups to play a bigger part in civil society and local governance. The government declared that its departments sought 'to ensure that [faith] communities [were] given the opportunity to participate fully in society through voluntary activity and other faith-based projects and that the Government [was] committed to working closely with them to build strong active communities and foster community development and civil renewal'.[355] The East London Mosque and London Muslim Centre (opened in 2004) accordingly declared their commitment to the provision of broad

[352] Writing about Muslims in the East End of London, Sarah Glynn observed that 'Though they may not follow the detailed politics of Jamaat in Pakistan and Bangladesh, most young revivalist Muslims share its ideology and believe that the ultimate ideal would be to live in a world governed by Islamic Law, and that "so far as the teachings of the Quran and the Sunnah [the exemplary practice of the Prophet Muhammad] are concerned, they are eternally binding".' S. Glynn, 'Bengali Muslims: new East End radicals', *Ethnic and Racial Studies*, 25, no. 6 (November 2002), p. 985.

[353] http://news.bbc.co.uk/1/hi/england/1671797.stm (accessed 22 November 2010).

[354] http://www.princeofwales.gov.uk/speechesandarticles/a_speech_by_hrh_the_prince_of_wales_titled_an_example_to_all_243436887.html (accessed 22 November 2010).

[355] Cited in Sarah Glynn, 'Playing the ethnic card: politics and segregation in London's East End', *Urban Studies*, 47, no. 5 (May 2010), p. 1005.

'holistic, culturally sensitive services for the communities of London'.[356] For its part, the Tower Hamlets Borough Council's sympathetic engagement with local Muslim institutions was reflected in its regular communications and dealings with the East London Mosque and its willingness to draw the mosque into their 'partnerships'.[357] The mosque's role in helping the police and the Tower Hamlets Council to put a stop to 'Bangladeshi upon Bangladeshi' gang violence was widely acknowledged.[358]

In 1998, one particular campaign, led by the East London Mosque, 'demonstrated their strengthening position both within the community representation and in the struggle for local resources'.[359] As part of The East London Communities Organisation (TELCO),[360] it waged a determined struggle to prevent the Borough Council giving a property developer permission to build 'luxury flats' next to the mosque. It mobilized thousands, who marched through Whitechapel, demanding that the local Council allow the land adjacent to the mosque to be purchased by the mosque and developed as a community centre. Throughout the year, the mosque continued to lobby the Council for the extension of its premises. When it appeared that the Council was reconsidering the developer's scheme, the mosque mobilized around one hundred worshippers, who 'laid siege to council offices in Bow claiming planners had gone back on a promise over the future of the Whitechapel mosque'.[361] Eventually, after two years of struggle, a solution 'agreeable to everyone concerned, especially the local community was found [. . .] and planning permission was granted for the Mosque to build a community centre and 40 low cost homes on the site in collaboration with the Bethnal Green and Victoria Park and LABO Housing Associations', a solution that met the 'needs of the local residents and worshippers at the mosque',[362] and which was broadcast by the mosque as an example of 'a genuine partnership with the Council'.[363] By the time that the building of the London Muslim Centre began in 2001, the Council 'were fully on board and ready

[356] See East London Mosque and London Muslim centre website, http://www.eastlondonmosque.org.uk/vision (accessed 8 October 2010).

[357] Glynn, 'Playing the ethnic card', p. 1004.

[358] *Independent on Sunday*, 30 August 1998.

[359] J. Eade and D. Garbin, 'Changing narratives of violence, struggle and resistance: Bangladeshis and the competition for resources in the global city', cited in Glynn, 'Playing the ethnic card', p. 1005.

[360] The East London Mosque is a member of TELCO, which includes various faith-based organizations. See http://www.citizensuk.org/about/london-citizens/ (accessed 31 January 2011).

[361] *East London Advertiser*, 5 November 1998.

[362] *East End Life*, 30 November–6 December 1998.

[363] *Ibid.*

to advertise their involvement. Their website described the London Muslim Centre as the result of innovative joint working between the Council and its partners in the Tower Hamlets Partnership, the East London Mosque, the Greater London Authority and the European Development Fund.'[364]

Finally, let us look at this process of Muslim space creation from the vantage point of 2010–2011, the year of the East London Mosque's centenary celebrations. In 1910, the LMF's initiative for a mosque at the heart of imperial Britain was a way of asserting Muslim presence and symbolizing community belonging; it was a relatively modest attempt to embed distinctive cultural values in a new environment. At the same time, by inviting involvement of non-Muslims in the management and activities of the project, a process was started through which social and cultural bridge-building could be carried out and some degree of inclusion in the mainstream attempted. On the other hand, the British establishment and state were prepared to support the mosque project strictly on grounds of political expediency. Post 9/11 and 7/7, growing Islamophobia in wider society, a British foreign policy that is perceived by many British Muslims as inimical to Islam, and the draconian measures introduced by the Labour government to combat Islamist terrorism have tended to alienate significant layers among British Muslims. It should also be remembered, however, that, to counter radicalization especially among young Muslims, the local authorities have viewed the ELM, though not unreservedly, as a relatively 'moderate' religio-political partner. Perhaps the reason why many parts of the British establishment saw the ELM as a moderate mosque was because it openly rejected groups such as Hizb-ut-Tahrir (HT):[365] the period 1992–1995 saw physical confrontations in the prayer area of the mosque, with YMO members ejecting HT activists from the premises;[366] the mosque further attracted heavy criticism from HT and Al Muhajiroon when it took to encouraging the Muslim community to exercise their right to vote in the 1997 elections. Incidents of physical struggle occurred with the Saved Sect in 2007, when the East London Mosque organized a careers day with its mainstream partners such as the London Development Agency and the Job Centre, encouraging careers in the Metropolitan Police and the armed forces. Members

364 Glynn, 'Playing the ethnic card', p. 1005.

365 See, Suha Taji-Farouki, 'Islamists and the threat of Jihad: Hizb al-Tahrir and al-Muhajiroun on Israel and the Jews', *Middle Eastern Studies*, 36, no. 4 (October 2000), pp. 21–46.

366 Ed Hussain, *The Islamist* (London, 2007), pp. 126–127.

of the Saved Sect accused the ELM of 'selling out'.[367] The mosque believed that funnelling resources through its hands enabled it to contribute to its goal of community cohesion in Tower Hamlets. From 2002, initiatives such as ISAP, Way to Work, and Faith in Health were designed to ensure that the whole community would benefit. Particular care was given to ensure that non-Muslims would be comfortable in accessing services that addressed common concerns such as unemployment, health inequality, and school attainment.

That said, in many ways, the community that was being built was increasingly socially encapsulated and separated from local non-Muslims. As Sarah Glynn has pointed out, the ELM and its affiliates now provide 'the means for local Muslims to live in an increasingly separate social sphere, almost from the cradle to the grave' – replacing other ethnic voluntary bodies as a channel for providers of local services. Its ever-expanding programme of activities includes a so-called Islamic playgroup, Islamic summer schemes, sports activities organized in what is described as a 'sound moral atmosphere', gender-segregated youth groups, advice on jobs, and, for Muslim women and the elderly, a wide range of cultural, educational, and recreational activities. At Ramadan, Muslim Community Radio invites listeners to 'tune in with the whole family'.[368]

By the end of the first decade of the twenty-first century, the East London Mosque was clearly an important player in terms of shaping the attitudes and behaviours of substantial sections of the local Muslim community. That it enjoyed a great deal of support within them can be gauged from the hundreds of thousands of pounds of individual and corporate donations that it received for the construction of the mosque in the early 1980s, as well as the millions that it collected to build the London Muslim Centre in the new Millennium. The 15,000 worshippers attending the Friday congregation at the inauguration of this Centre in June 2004, according to the Muslim Council of Britain, symbolized the 'triumph of community spirit',[369] providing ample evidence of the level of popular support commanded by the ELM. The BBC reported that more than 18,000 congregated for Eid prayers there in 2008.[370] Through these developments, the local Muslim population

[367] Information received from Dilowar Khan, Executive Director of the East London Mosque, 17 November 2010.

[368] Glynn 'Playing the ethnic card', p. 1004.

[369] 'Triumph of community spirit: inauguration of western Europe's largest Muslim centre', 19 July 2004, Muslim Council of Britain website, http://www.mcb.org.uk/features/features.php?ann_id=409 (accessed 9 October 2010).

[370] See http://www.bbc.co.uk/london/content/articles/2008/09/30/tower_hamlets_eid_feature.shtml (accessed 8 October 2010).

has become more deeply connected with the mosque and in doing so has 'increased [the latter's] authority as arbiter of all aspects of life'.[371]

More generally, the ELM has been able to present its Islamic prescriptions as the only valid way of life. This has also meant that, from outside its core constituencies, the mosque has recently come to be accused of harbouring extremists and propagating 'jihadism', even though it has been unequivocal in its condemnation of the 9/11 and 7/7 atrocities. Despite its self-proclaimed commitment to 'British' values of democracy, fairness, tolerance, and rule of law, it is still suspected by some observers of aspiring to a radical Islamist transformation of society.

An alternative assessment of the East London Mosque's pronouncements and actions, however, may suggest that it has tried to go as far as it can in coming to terms with the plurality of British society while remaining true to its core values and ideals. Understood in this way, it could be argued that the ELM is not playing any kind of conspiratorial double game, but trying, quite pragmatically, to achieve the best possible outcomes for its constituency, keeping as much as possible to its own frame of reference. This does not necessarily mean that the ELM is not committed to community cohesion as declared in its public pronouncements. But it wishes to promote this cohesion within the framework of its, perhaps inevitably exclusivist, Islamist strategy for attracting people to its standpoint; a strategy based on social activism and civic participation, governed by a religious ethos. Hence, it welcomes an open engagement with non-Muslims[372] (exemplified through the development of the Tower Hamlets Interfaith Forum (THIFF), a multi-faith network that demonstrated unequivocal solidarity in the aftermath of 7/7).[373] But, arguably, it does so primarily as part of its aspiration of creating an Islamic Britain. In practice, this means that, while the ELM has been successful in creating cohesion within layers of the local Muslim population, it has perhaps done so at the expense of its relations with those who are outside its fold.

While there is no official estimate of the number of mosques in Britain, there may now be well over 1,600, with scores in London

[371] Glynn, 'Playing the ethnic card', p. 1005.

[372] For example, see the Lord Chief Justice Lord Phillips's speech, 'Equality before the law', delivered at the London Muslim Centre, 3 July 2008, http://www.eastlondonmosque.org.uk/uploadedImage/pdf/LMC%20Lord%20Chief%20Justice%20booklet.pdf (accessed 22 November 2010). See also the ELM's response, http://www.eastlondonmosque.org.uk/uploadedImage/pdf/ELM-LMC%20PR%20-%20LCJ.pdf (accessed 22 November 2010).

[373] Tower Hamlets Prevent Action Plan, April 2008–March 2011, pp. 13 and 52, http://www.towerhamletsfoi.org.uk/documents/3034/LBTH%20%20Prevent%20Action%20Plan%20June2010.pdf (accessed 21 November 2010).

alone.[374] In carving out this religious space, while Muslims have continued to confront many of the same issues with which they had to grapple before, they have succeeded, through mosque-building, in becoming recognized as significant contributors to the enrichment of Britain's cultural and religious landscape. This has been possible in large part due to the settlement of several million Muslims in a Britain radically different from the one in which the LMF began its campaign in 1910; a Britain in which Muslims as citizens see themselves in a different relationship to wider society and its institutions. With regard to the present-day East London Mosque, one of the largest in Britain, we discover that, as the Muslim community in the East End of London has grown from a few hundred to tens of thousands,[375] so too has power (or control) within the East London Mosque gradually shifted from individuals and institutions far removed from the local community to its direct representatives. The growth of the community has given it greater stature in the eyes of the institutions of wider society, a change that is reflected in its physical and administrative structures and in the character of its activities. That it is able to assert considerable autonomy and authority in institutional decision-making also vouches for the relations of power between the community and the state. And its impressive buildings tell us about the changing relations of power in an increasingly plural Britain. They suggest the increasing capacity of Muslim communities to mobilize resources needed (the

[374] This was the estimate in 2006. See IslamOnline, http://www.islamonline.net/servlet/Satellite?c=Article_C&pagename=Zone-English-News/NWELayout&cid=1162385841442 (accessed 17 January 2011). In 1997, the *British Muslim Monthly Survey* put the figure at around one thousand for registered and unregistered mosques: cited in S. McLoughlin, 'Mosques and the public space: conflict and cooperation in Bradford', *Journal of Ethnic and Migration Studies*, 31, no. 6 (November 2005), p. 1045. In 1963, there were just thirteen mosques recorded with the Registrar General: see J. Nielsen, *Muslims in Western Europe* (Edinburgh, 1992), p. 44.

[375] The London Borough of Tower Hamlets, formed in 1965 through the merger of the three boroughs in the East End of London – Stepney, Bethnal Green, and Bow – has the largest concentration of Bangladeshis in England. By 1981, it was estimated that Bangladeshis formed between 15% and 20% of its population. According to the 2001 Census, it contained 70,000, overwhelmingly Muslim, Bangladeshis. In the borough, historically, Bangladeshis have been concentrated in the four western wards of Spitalfields, St Katherine's, St Mary's, and Weavers. Until recently they were the last in the line of poor migrants to come here, arriving at a time when the local population was declining rapidly. They were confined to council blocks from which white residents had moved. Bangladeshis increasingly occupied space that white people did not want. They experienced some of the worst residential and working conditions in a borough whose population was predominantly working class. They, along with the local white population, suffered from higher than average rates of unemployment. In the 1960s and 1970s, substantial numbers of Bangladeshis, too poor to buy property or ineligible for council housing, occupied privately rented accommodation. Having bought into 'the myth of return', which meant saving as much as they could from their meagre incomes, they lived in overcrowded accommodation.

London Muslim Centre affiliated to the East London Mosque alone cost £10.5 million[376]), not only from within the community but also from the wider Muslim world. Yet, because the construction of the East London Mosque and the London Muslim Centre was funded in considerable measure by the local community itself, this has given it a greater sense of ownership and 'belonging' in the locality in which it is based. The investment needed to put down permanent mosque structures, the establishment of facilities for the religious education of Muslim children, and the appointment of a salaried imam marked the commitment to settle. All of this means that the mosque and its institutional growth have become important markers of community formation. It has become a convenient place for social gatherings and a resource for women, children, and elders, accommodating a crèche, counselling and advisory services, and a library. It has played an educational role for non-Muslims by hosting visits from local schools, and is active in inter-faith dialogue.

The history of the East London Mosque since 1985 has been, in some ways, a narrative of struggle, in which the efforts and sacrifices of Muslims have been met with suspicion and opposition of public authorities and powerful residents' associations. First, there were the prolonged and tortuous negotiations regarding the shift from the Commercial Road premises and then to Whitechapel Road. Soon after, a dispute arose regarding the *azan* (call to prayer): worshippers demanded an increase in the number of calls, while local residents and businesses complained to the Tower Hamlets Council and the Secretary of State for the Environment about the 'noise nuisance'. The local press reported, 'Ritual chants summoning thousands of East End Muslims to worship twice a day hit a sour note with local residents', with Tower Hamlets Council receiving 'a flood of complaints'[377] and considering 'legal action to "pull the plug" on loudspeaker broadcasts [of the *azan*] from the East London Mosque'.[378] Jetha, the long-serving chairman of the Trust, countered by accusing complainants of being 'intolerant' towards other religions: 'I suspect', he remarked, that 'the

[376] 'Over 50% of the building costs for the London Muslim Centre were raised through donations from local worshippers and from around the UK. 23% was derived from public and charitable sources; 10% from international sources including Qatar, Saudi Arabia, Malaysia, Islamic Development Bank; and the balance from the sale of trust assets' (East London Mosque website, http://www.eastlondonmosque.org.uk/?page=faqs (accessed 8 October 2010)).

[377] One complaint noted that: 'My office is adjacent to the minoret, consequently I get the full blast of the tannoy, making it impossible to carry out a phone conversation' (*East London Advertiser*, 2 May 1986).

[378] *East London Advertiser*, 14 April 1986.

real reason behind many of these complaints is racial prejudice'. The complaints to him smacked of double standards, since nobody, he suggested, objected to the ringing of church bells.[379] Local Muslims angered by the dispute urged their religious leaders 'to INCREASE the volume of the prayer calls broadcast', claiming that they could not hear the 'ritual chants'.[380] Eventually, a compromise solution was reached by reducing the volume.[381]

Since the events of 7 July 2005, the ELM/LMC has been targeted more sharply than ever before by the media, politicians, and think-tanks, often with their own axe to grind. Indeed, many of the ELM's detractors view it as a Janus-like organization – they claim that, while its public image is that of a 'moderate' Islamist organization with a 'moderate' message, significant evidence in relation to its internal communication with its members betrays a radical and subversive Islamist hidden agenda. For instance, the Channel 4 *Dispatches* programme, 'Undercover mosque' (broadcast on 15 January 2007), and Denis MacEoin's report, 'The hijacking of British Islam', published in October 2007, for the 'Conservative think-tank' Policy Exchange,[382] suggested that, among other things, the East London Mosque provided a home for extremist, separatist, and sectarian literature. 'This literature', MacEoin declared, 'not only condemns non-Muslim society, but also frequently denigrates other Muslims – those whose standards of Islamic observation are deemed by authors to be insufficiently pure or rigorous'.[383] In 2010, Andrew Gilligan's 'Britain's Islamic republic', shown on 1 March, again on Channel 4, claimed that the 'fundamentalist' Islamic Forum of Europe, based

[379] *Ibid.* One letter to the editor, entitled 'Noisy bells', did complain about the tolling of the bell at the nearby church, defending the *azan* broadcasts: 'I live off Cable Street and am often disturbed by the repetitive sound of church bells from St. George's Church and the church in Wapping. These bell practises [*sic*] sometime go on for an hour or more and can be very annoying but I put up with it [. . .] why can't people here be more tolerant to two or three minutes calling from the mosque?' (*East London Advertiser*, 9 May 1986). A number of local Church of England clerics also thought 'two short periods [of the *Azan* . . .] entirely reasonable' (*East London Advertiser*, 25 April 1986).

[380] *East London Advertiser*, 2 May 1986.

[381] *East London Advertiser*, 14 April 1986 and 2 May 1986. Regarding the complaints, the *London Standard*, on 14 April 1986, reported: 'The ritual chants summoning thousands of East End Moslems to worship twice a day have hit a sour note with residents. Tower Hamlets Council has received many complaints [. . .]'. In reaction to protests over 'excessively loud' prayer calls, a mosque official suspected that the reason for the complaints might be racial prejudice (*The Star*, 14 April 1986).

[382] *The* Times, 30 October 2007, http://www.timesonline.co.uk/tol/comment/faith/article2767252.ece (accessed 17 January 2011).

[383] Denis MacEoin, 'The hijacking of British Islam: how extremist literature is subverting mosques in the UK', Policy Exchange, 2007, http://fliiby.com/file/36648/onr78fia7u.html, p. 7 (accessed 6 October 2010).

in the London Muslim Centre and thought to be closely associated with the East London Mosque, was an organization in possession of an extremist 'Islamist' ideology. Gilligan asserted that it was not the moderate 'social welfare' organization,[384] committed to community cohesion and tolerance, that it claimed to be; on the contrary, he argued that it sought to exploit, through 'deceit',[385] the democratic process, and to 'infiltrate'[386] the local Labour Party (whose secular values were opposed to those of the IFE), so that it could 'subvert the local council' and bend it to its own programme.[387] Gilligan's claims, however, were strongly denied by non-Muslim local activists involved in collaborative work with the ELM. [388]

The fact that Gilligan's report drew on evidence in support of his accusations furnished by individuals in the local Muslim community, as well as IFE documents,[389] suggests that considerable tension still exists between competing interests and ideological positions in the community, who are determined to challenge and undermine the influence that ELM/LMC exercises within it. In a letter to *The Guardian*, a number of community activists representing many 'impeccably non-sectarian Muslims [. . .] who are capable of opposing both racism and fundamentalism', as well as some organizations based in London's East End, while condemning the 'visible rise, in some parts of the country, of anti-Muslim bigotry', also expressed 'legitimate concerns about the leadership of the East London Mosque and the Islamic Forum of Europe', for allowing 'intemperate clerics to speak on its premises, some of whom have promoted values antithetical to

[384] Andrew Gilligan, 'IFE loses its grip on Tower Hamlets', *The Guardian*, 19 May 2010.

[385] Andrew Gilligan, 'IFE: not harmless democrats', *The Guardian*, 4 March 2010.

[386] Andrew Gilligan 'Islamic radicals "infiltrate" the Labour Party', *Daily Telegraph*, 27 February 2010.

[387] Inayat Bunglawala, 'Watch out: democratic Muslims about', *The Guardian*, 3 March 2010.

[388] In a letter to Channel 4 after the broadcast of the *Dispatches* programme, Neil Jameson, lead organizer for London Citizens, commented: 'The recent Dispatches programme: Britain's Islamic Republic broadcasted on Channel 4 on 1st March 2010 gave a very negative and distorted image of two of our members, The East London Mosque and the Tower Hamlets Branch of Islamic Forum of Europe. The East London Mosque was a founding member of The East London Communities Organisation (TELCO) in 1996, joined in 2004 by the London Muslim Centre and in 2009 by The Tower Hamlets Branch of the Islamic Forum Europe. Although IFE formally joined TELCO last year I have known their leadership since 1996 and have been aware of the close relationship and overlap in membership between IFE and East London Mosque. All are thus active and responsible members of LONDON CITIZENS' diverse community alliance' (http://www.eastlondonmosque.org.uk/uploadedImage/pdf/2010_11_15_20_58_56_Letter%20to%20Ch%204%20from%20Neil%20Jameson.pdf (accessed 21 November 2010)).

[389] Gilligan, 'IFE: not harmless democrats'.

those required in a tolerant and progressive society'.[390] These clerics, so the letter claimed, had intimidated and bullied other Muslims into accepting their contested theology as undisputed truth. Similarly, when the English Defence League[391] threatened to march in Tower Hamlets to protest against a meeting organized under the auspices of the Federation of Student and Islamic Societies, a broad-based coalition (including the Brick Lane Mosque), while condemning the 'fascist EDL', also criticized the Islamic Forum of Europe for claiming to 'act as the sole representatives of ordinary Muslims [. . .] operating under the direction of their parent organization Jamaat-e-Islami in Bangladesh'.[392]

It appears that Islamophobic media attacks and anti-Muslim street mobilizations have become part of a 'culture war' in which particular relatively influential anti-Muslim groups and politicians in British society, threatened by the growth of Muslim institutions as embodiments of Islamic power, pursue a range of strategies to weaken them. In this situation, for its congregation at least if not for the Muslim communities more widely, the ELM/LMC represents a fortress to be defended. In a climate fraught with anxieties and threats regarding identity, in an increasingly plural Britain, the contestation of cultural values and rights has become much more politically intense. As opposition to cultural and religious symbols has grown, resistance to this 'backlash' from wider society has resulted in the strengthening of community solidarity. The more that popular concerns about 'militant Islam' and its erosion of 'a British way of life' have risen, the more a sense of being under siege has developed, increasing determination

[390] *The Guardian*, 3 April 2010. Inayat Bunglawala, formerly spokesperson for the Muslim Council of Britain, also felt that 'Gilligan's video clips of events held at the London Muslim Centre – which is largely run by IFE – showing two speakers, albeit from an outside organization that had hired the LMC hall, engaging in deeply offensive rhetoric about gays and women – cannot be easily shrugged off'.

[391] 'The English Defence League emerged from the angry scenes in Luton last March [2009] when a group of Islamist extremists protested as the Royal Anglian Regiment paraded through the town on its return from Afghanistan' (Dominic Casciani, 'Who are the English Defence League?', *BBC News Magazine*, 11 September 2009, http://news.bbc.co.uk/1/hi/8250017.stm (accessed 22 November 2010)). According to Matthew Taylor, 'It has become the most significant far-right street movement in the UK since the National Front in the 1970s' ('English Defence League: inside the violent world of Britain's new far right', *The Guardian*, 28 May 2010). According to John Cruddas, its mobilizations, 'bring[ing] together a dangerous cocktail of football hooligans, far-right activists and pub racists', have focused on popular anti-Muslim sentiment, 'providing a new white nationalist identity' through which its supporters 'can understand an increasingly complex and alienating world and instigating them to defend their Britain against the threat of Islam' ('English Defence League is a bigger threat than the BNP', *The Observer*, 10 October 2010).

[392] 'Tower Hamlets community stands up to fight fascism in all its colours', 19 June 2010, http://www.spittoon.org/archives/6766 (accessed 6 October 2010).

among groups of Muslims to present a united front in the face of this onslaught.

The ELM/LMC, too, has fought back. It denounced, for instance, the Gilligan documentary as a 'distorted and utterly misleading portrayal of the East London Mosque', which, it said, '[t]hrough factual errors, innuendo and an extraordinarily disingenuous selection of commentators, [left] viewers with an entirely false impression of the Mosque'. It reiterated its openness to Muslims and non-Muslims alike, its commitment to the promotion of religious and social tolerance, and its opposition to and condemnation of 'violent extremism in all its forms'. The mosque's representatives, in a lengthy statement in early 2010, declared that it

> actively encourages the congregation to engage in the democratic process, particularly voting during elections, without ever suggesting who to vote for; no organisation or person – and this includes IFE – is allowed to canvass for political parties or candidates in the Mosque or London Muslim Centre. While we try to ensure that those who use our facilities, including for speaking engagements, reflect the values of moderation and tolerance we hold and adhere to, on rare occasion it may be that someone, speaking at an event for which a room or hall has been hired for example, says something we neither agree with nor approve of. It would be very misleading to characterize our Mosque on the basis of these few exceptions, rather the norm of the great diversity of the speakers who maintain the highest standards we aspire to. It is not possible for any organisation in a position such as ours to vet and approve in advance every statement to be made by every speaker addressing audiences at the Mosque and Centre. Intellectual, political, social and religious debate is one of the cornerstones of a democratic society and many organisations (including the ELM and LMC) permit a wide range of speakers who hold varied and often conflicting views. Self-evidently that does not mean that the organisations in questions support or espouse every view expressed by every speaker they host and it would be ludicrous to suggest otherwise.[393]

When the English Defence League marched through central London in March 2010, with placards including the demand 'Close the East London Mosque now', the mosque was able to assemble a powerful coalition of public figures, politicians, and religious and trade union leaders calling for solidarity and support for it.[394]

What has happened in the century-long struggle to build the mosque that now stands on Whitechapel Road has thus depended

[393]East London Mosque 'Response to Channel 4', 2 March 2010, http://www.eastlondonmosque.org.uk/news/231 (accessed 8 October 2010).

[394]'Islamophobia is a threat to democracy', *The Guardian*, 25 March 2010. It is noteworthy that, on 21 June 2010, the leaders of the East London Mosque, together with other community leaders, 'worked hard to discourage disaffected youngsters from getting involved in trouble in Whitechapel after the anti-fascist march in the East End': see http://www.eastlondonadvertiser.co.uk:80/news/community_leaders_worked_for_calm_after_whitechapel_demo_1_672445 (accessed 21 November 2010).

a great deal not only on the size and composition of the Muslim community in London but also on the structure of religious life in British society and the relationship between the state and religion. It was in this nexus that the East London Mosque became a site for cultural negotiation and identity formation for local Muslims. By looking at this particular process of mosque-making, we gain a clearer sense of how particular Muslim spaces (in this case mosques) arose out of negotiations between local and global concerns, competing and conflicting interests, dominant and subaltern loyalties. Indeed, what the unfolding history of the East London Mosque symbolizes, and the Minutes of its Trustees' meetings reveal, is the complex growth of the Muslim presence in Britain as it has become steadily and ineffably woven into the fabric of both local and national British society.

THE LONDON MOSQUE FUND

A Meeting of the Executive Committee of the London Mosque Fund was held at the Caxton Hall[1] on 13 December 1910[2]

Present:

The Chairman [Syed Ameer Ali*]
Sir Theodore Morison K.C.I.E.*[3]
Khalil Khalid Bey*
Hon A.M. Jeevanjee*
Mr C.A. Latif*
Mr A.S.M. Anik*
Mr M.T. Kaderbhoy*

1. The Chairman proposed that His Excellency the Persian Minister[4] be invited to be a Member of the Executive Committee

The Motion was carried unanimously.

2. The Draft of the circular letter proposed to be issued by the Chairman to prominent people in Turkey, Persia, India and British Possessions generally was read and was carried with one amendment proposed by Khalil Khalid Bey, Esq, and seconded by Sir Theodore Morison, to the effect that the words "steps have already been taken

[1]Caxton Hall, located on the corner of Caxton Street and Palmer Street, London SW1, was a venue often used by Muslim groups in London for formal gatherings. Designed by Lee and Smith between 1878 and 1882, it is today listed at Grade II, primarily for its historical associations. Originally built as Westminster Town Hall, it was then used as a registry office until 1979. Its historical associations include the Suffragette movement, speeches delivered by Churchill during the Second World War, and various society weddings.

[2]On 9 November 1910 a public meeting was called by Syed Ameer Ali at the Ritz Hotel in London to discuss the feasibility of constructing a mosque and an Islamic cultural centre in London. Sir Sultan Mohammad Shah Aga Khan took the chair. It was resolved to establish a fund with the purpose of implementing such a project. Sir Ernest Hotson (Hon. Secretary of the LMF) refers to this meeting in his address at the inauguration of the East London Mosque and Islamic Culture Centre on 1 August 1941. See BL, IOR, L/P&J/12/468.

[3]These minutes were recorded at the second meeting of the Executive Committee of the LMF, held on 13 December 1910 under the chairmanship of Sir Theodore Morison.

[4]Official of the Persian Embassy in London. Probably Mirza Mehdi Khan Mushir-ul-Mulk (see n. 5).

to draw attention to the scheme in Constantinople" be inserted in the Draft.

The Chairman was authorized to issue the circular letter under his own signature.

A meeting of the Executive Committee of the London Mosque Fund was held on Monday 20 March 1911, at 17 Hobart Place

Present:

The Rt Hon Syed Ameer Ali (Chairman)
His Excellency the Persian Minister[5]
Sir William Bull, M.P.*
Mirza Abbas Ali Baig Esq.*
Mundji Fikri Bey*
Major Syed Hassan Bilgrami*
Mr C.A. Latif
Reouf Ahmed Bey
Mr A.S.M. Anik
Mirza Abdul Ghuffar Khan[6]
Md. Ali Chewky Bey
Mr M.T. Kaderbhoy

The Minutes of the last meeting were read and confirmed.

The Accounts were submitted, examined and passed.

Sir William Bull suggested that an enquiry might be made from the Russian Embassy as to the exact area of the mosque at St. Petersburg. He also suggested inviting Sir Lawrence Gomme* and Sir Edwin Cornwall* to join the General Committee. It was agreed.

The Chairman brought to the notice of the Committee that a site in Westminster was offered to the Committee for purchase but it was considered as rather too early to go into the matter.

The site proposed by Mr Latif was also considered.

[5]The Persian Minister in London was Mirza Mehdi Khan Mushir-ul-Mulk. See Sir Denis Wright, 'The Iran Society: the first sixty five years: 1935–2000', http://www.iransociety.org/sixtyfive_1.htm (accessed 25 November 2009).

[6]Mirza Abdul Ghuffar Khan was the Persian Consul in London.

Sir William Bull said it would not be a capital site. The site must be in the centre of the Empire.

The County Council would be sympathetic as regards the site near the Kingsway and that a site might be had on the River.

Several other sites were suggested but it was finally resolved that when the Project has made further advance a small Committee should be appointed to go into the question thoroughly as the Mosque was being built for all times and it must be commensurate with the dignity of Islam.

The drafting of the other letters and appeals was left in the hands of the Chairman and Mr Baig.

The letter received from the Bank of England was read by the Chairman.

The Draft rules of procedure for carrying on the work by the Executive Committee were adopted.

The question of the appointment of Trustees was considered – The Chairman said the Ottoman Empire ought to be represented by her Consul-General for the time being. The proposal was unanimously adopted.

His Excellency the Persian Minister proposed His Excellency Sadigh-us-Saltanah* to represent Persia on the Board of Trustees. It was unanimously adopted.

The Chairman proposed Mr Abbas Ali Baig as one of the Trustees for India. It was unanimously adopted.

Mr Abbas Ali Baig proposed The Right Hon Syed Ameer Ali as another Trustee for India. It was unanimously adopted.

The Chairman proposed His Highness the Aga Khan,*[7] Lord Ampthill* and Lord Rothschild* as the remaining Trustees. The resolution was unanimously adopted.

It was further resolved that should Lord Rothschild not accept the office, Sir Ernest Cassel[8] be approached.

It was resolved that at least two thirds of the Trustees must be Mohammadans.

[7] Sir Sultan Mahomed Shah Aga Khan.

[8] The well-known banker, born of Jewish parents, who acted as financial advisor to King Edward VII.

Finally the Committee adopted the following names for the office of Trustees:

1. His Highness the Aga Khan
2. The Rt Hon Lord Ampthill
3. The Rt Hon Lord Rothschild
4. The Rt Hon Syed Ameer Ali
5. Mirza Abbas Ali Baig
6. Mundji Fikri Bey (Imperial Ottoman Consul-General)
7. His Excellency Sadigh-us-Saltanah*[9]

The Secretary to the Board of Trustees to be Mr C.A. Latif

The committee authorized Mr Ameer Ali to invite Lord Rothschild and Lord Ampthill to accept the Trusteeship of the Fund.

It was resolved that the signatures of two Trustees countersigned by the Secretary should be sufficient on Cheques.

Mr Shairani*[10] be made a Joint-Secretary assistant of the Mosque Committee.

That Mr Ameer Ali and Mr Abbas Ali be authorized to draw out an appeal to the nobles and notables of the Moslem world for Funds.

Employment of a clerk on 10/- [shillings] a week was sanctioned for the work of the Mosque Committee.

Confirmed: Ameer Ali Chairman 24 April 1911

A meeting of the Executive Committee of the London Mosque Fund was held at 17 Hobart Place, SW on Friday 7 April 1911

Present:

The Right Hon Syed Ameer Ali (in the Chair)
Sir William Bull, M.P.
Mr M. Abbas Ali Baig
Mirza Abdul Ghuffar Khan
M.A. Chewky Bey

[9] Mirza Abdul Ali Khan.
[10] Hafi Mahmud Khan Shairani.

Mr C.A. Latif
Major Syed Hassan Bilgrami
Mr A.S.M. Anik
Mr M.T. Kaderbhoy

The question of obtaining the gracious assent of His Majesty the King to give his name as Patron of the London Mosque Fund was discussed.

Resolved that the kind offer of Sir William Bull to informally sound the Secretary of State for India[11] whether his Lordship could see his way to advise His Majesty to that effect, be accepted.

Confirmed: Ameer Ali Chairman 24 April 1911

Rules of the Executive Committee

1. At meetings of the Executive Committee the quorum shall consist of five members including the office bearers.

2. Meetings of the Executive Committee shall be convened at the discretion of the Chairman whenever there is any matter of sufficient importance for collective discussion and consideration.

3. Other matters, such as the election of members of the Executive Committee may be dealt with by correspondence.

4. The Executive Committee delegate to the Chairman full power and discretion to elect members on the General Committee, persons living outside London, and report the same at the next meeting of the Executive Committee.

5. All disbursements connected with the printing, typing and postage of letters shall be made by the Treasurer under the direction of the Chairman and the accounts of such disbursements shall be submitted by the Treasurer every three months to the Committee for being passed.

6. Save and except monies received by the Treasurer for preliminary expenses, he shall deposit forthwith on receipt in the Bank of England in the name of the Trustees of the London Mosque Fund, and any [*sic*] contributions or donation received by him for and on behalf of the Fund. The Treasurer shall be at liberty to keep monies received by him for preliminary expenses on his own responsibility at any Bank

[11] Viscount John Morley.*

approved by him and to draw cheques thereon for disbursements connected with the carrying into execution of the Mosque Project.

7. All funds contributed towards the erection, maintenance and permanent endowment of the London Mosque, and any institutions annexed thereto, such as Library and Lecture rooms shall be vested in Trustees of whom at least two-thirds shall be Mussulmans.

Such Trustees shall be nominated at the meeting of the Executive Committee and reported at the next meeting of the General Committee.

A meeting of the Executive Committee of the London Mosque Fund was held on Monday 4 December 1911 at: 17 Hobart Place, Grosvenor Gardens, SW at 4.30 pm

Present:

The Rt Hon Syed Ameer Ali
Sir Theodore Morison
M. Abbas Ali Baig, Esq
Mr W Bullock* (representing Sir William Bull)
Professor T.W. Arnold* (Sec.)
Mr A.S.M. Anik (Treas.)

The minutes of the last meeting were read and confirmed.

The Chairman placed before the Committee a letter received from Her Highness the Begum of Bhopal*[12] regarding the promised donation of £7,000 towards the Mosque Fund.

The money was to be paid in instalments after the Delhi Durbar[13] on the following two conditions:

(a) That sufficient money should be forthcoming for a hostel for students – attached to the Mosque with arrangements for Mohammedan diet.
(b) That all the money required for the mosque be forthcoming.

It was decided after some discussion that the secretary Professor Arnold should draft an answer accepting the conditions with

[12] Sultan Kaikhusrau Jahan Begum.

[13] This *Durbar* (Persian term meaning 'royal court'), attended by King-Emperor George V, was held in Delhi (India) in December 1911 to celebrate his coronation.

reservations, and hoping that Her Highness would send the first instalment at her very early convenience.

The letter to be signed by the Chairman

Confirmed: Ameer Ali 17 April 1912

A meeting of the Executive Committee of the London Mosque Fund was held on Monday 24 April 1911 at the Rooms of the Royal Asiatic Society, 22 Albemarle Street W.

Present:

The Rt. Hon. Sayed Ameer Ali (Chairman)
Mirza Abdul Ghuffar Khan
Reouf Ahmed Bey
Mohammed Ali Chewky Bey
Mr C.A. Latif
Prof. T.W. Arnold
Mr A.S.M. Anik

The minutes of the meeting of 20 March last and 7 April instant were read and confirmed.

The Chairman mentioned to the Committee the circumstances connected with Sir William Bull's approach to Lord Morley and its result.

It was proposed by Mirza Abdul Ghuffar that the subject should be treated as absolutely confidential so that it may not appear that the British Government was lacking in sympathy.[14]

Resolved that the best thanks of the Committee be conveyed to Sir William Bull for his kind trouble in the matter.

Resolved further that the Committee formally appeal for the patronage of His Imperial Majesty the Sultan.*

Mr Reouf Ahmed Bey kindly undertook to obtain His Majesty's gracious permission.

[14]This refers to the request that Lord Morley was asked to make for patronage by the King of the LMF.

The Chairman stated that His Imperial Majesty the Shah* had already telegraphed through his Foreign Minister, that he had been graciously pleased to extend his patronage to the Fund.

The letter from the Persian Minister at Paris was read and the suggestion contained therein that an Advisory Committee – Comité d'Etude – should be formed, was considered.

It was resolved that the suggestion be adopted.

The following gentlemen were appointed to form members of the sub-Committee to consider the question of a site and the models upon which the Mosque is to be built:

Mr Abdul Ghuffar Khan
Syed Mohd. Ali Chewky Bey
Professor Arnold
Mr Latif

The Chairman read the names of the gentlemen who had expressed their assent to join the General Committee.

The Chairman read the letters from Mr W. W. Barnes in reply to his letter inviting him to join the General Committee and asking for names and titles of the Sultans of the Malay Peninsula.[15]

The Chairman placed before the Committee the telegram of Halil Halid Bey.[16]

After some discussion it was resolved that the Secretary (Mr Latif) should write to Mr Halid that his telegram addressed to the Chairman saying that he had formed local committees in Egypt and that he was trying to do the same in Turkey, was considered by the Committee and that he was directed to request Mr Halid to place the secretary in communication with the secretaries of the committees which he had formed, and to inform them that all monies collected on behalf of the London Mosque Fund, should be remitted as soon as collected to the Bank of England, and that the names of the members of the different committees should be furnished to the secretary.

[15]The Malay Peninsula comprised the four Federated Malay States of Selangor, Perak, Negeri Sembilan, and Pahang, established by the British government in 1895, and the five Unfederated Malay States of Johor, Kedah, Kelantan, Perlis, and Terengganu, which came under British protection from 1909 under the Treaty of Bangkok.

[16]Khalil Khalid Bey, first mentioned in the Minutes on p. 81.

The secretary was also requested to inform him that the trustees were appointed at a regularly convened meeting of the Executive Committee.

The Chairman brought before the Committee the letter written to him by Mr Anik (the Treasurer).

At the meeting held on 20 March it was proposed by Sir William Bull that Mr Latif as secretary should countersign the cheques and that Mr Anik should draw only cheques for preliminary expenses.

Mr Anik is of opinion that that makes his position on the Fund anomalous and that he would rather resign – he has all the settling of small accounts, everything is to be done by him. But his name is not to appear in the General Fund – he is, and has been, of great assistance to the committee.

Resolved that the Bank of England be informed that at a meeting of the Executive Committee held on 24 April at 22 Albemarle Street, it was decided that in addition to the counter-signature of the secretary there should be on the cheques drawn for and on behalf of the Fund, the counter-signature of the Honorary treasurer also, and that in the absence of one or other of them from England, one counter-signature should be sufficient.

Professor Arnold promised to give the full titles and designations of:

The Ameer of Afghanistan*[17]
The Sultan of Zanzibar[18]
The Sultan of Lahej
And the names and titles of the Sultans of the Straits Settlements.[19]

Decided that in the appeals to the Princes the paper should have the heading – The London Mosque Fund – the names of Their Imperial Majesties the Sultan and the Shah, the Hon Presidents, the Presidents, the Chairman, the Treasurer and the Secretaries.

Resolved that Mr Shairani be appointed one of the assistant secretaries and be included in the Executive Committee.

[17] Habibullah Khan.

[18] Sultan Sayyid Khalifa bin Harub Al-Busaid became the 9th Sultan of Zanzibar (r. 1911–1960) on the abdication due to illness of his brother-in-law Sayyid Ali bin Hamud Al-Busaid (r. 1902–1911).

[19] The name 'Straits Settlements' was given to the Crown Colony formed by the British possessions on or adjacent to the mainland of the Malay Peninsula. The Sultans were Muslims.

Proposed by Mr Reouf Ahmed Bey that the number of the Executive Committee be limited to eighteen.

Considered desirable that all communications to the press be made by the Chairman.

Confirmed: Ameer Ali 8 May 1911

A Meeting of the Executive Committee of the London Mosque Fund was held on Monday 8 May 1911 at the Rooms of the Royal Asiatic Society, 22 Albermarle Street, at 3.30 p.m

Present:

The Rt Hon Syed Ameer Ali (in the Chair)
Sir Theodore Morison
M. Abbas Ali Baig
Mirza Abdul Ghuffar Khan
Mohammed Ali Chewky Bey
Mundji Fikri Bey
Prof T.W. Arnold
Mr C.A. Latif
Mr A.S.M. Anik
Mr Khaderbhoy
Mr Shairani

The minutes of the last meeting were read and confirmed.

A message was received from Sir William Bull expressing his regret at not being able to be present.

The letter from the Chief Cashier of the Bank of England was placed before the Committee. The suggested form of resolution was considered and approved.

It was unanimously decided that the resolution passed at the meeting of the Executive Committee on 24 April be cancelled and the following substituted:

At a meeting of the Executive Committee of the London Mosque Fund held at 22 Albermarle Street, on Monday 8 May, it was resolved:

"That whenever possible, cheques drawn upon the account of 'The Rt Hon Lord Ampthill and Others' shall be countersigned by the Honorary Treasurer (Abdeali S. M. Anik Esq) as well as by the Honorary Secretary (C. Abdul Latif Esq), and, to provide for the absence of either of them from London, it was further resolved that the Bank of England be authorised to accept at any time the counter-signature of either the Honorary Secretary or the Honorary Treasurer alone".

The Chairman placed before the Committee a letter received from Mr Reouf Ahmed Bey, requesting that he might be authorized (so as to prevent possible misunderstanding) to form local committees in Constantinople.

The Chairman proposed that as Mr Reouf Ahmed Bey was a responsible and reliable person they should give him that authority.

Mundji Fikri Bey informed the Committee that a central committee had already been formed in Constantinople, and that possibly there was no necessity to charge Mr Reouf Ahmed Bey with the authority.

He also reported that Halil Halid Bey had been attacking him personally in reference to the Mosque Fund – It seemed to him most inconsistent, as they were working in the project as a body and not individually.

After some discussion it was unanimously approved that the Committee should authorize Mr Reouf Ahmed Bey to take such steps in conjunction with the Central Committee in Constantinople as may be deemed expedient to form local committees in the Provinces in Turkey.

The Committee also took note of the suggestion of Mr Reouf Ahmed Bey regarding communication to the newspapers that collections should be sent to the Bank of England.

Mundji Fikri Bey informed the Committee that the Central Committee at Constantinople had been formed to receive, in the first place, all contributions from the Provinces, and to send them direct to the Bank of England.

The Committee decided to request Mr Reouf Ahmed Bey to place himself in communication with the Central Committee at Constantinople formed under the Presidency of the Prince Imperial the Heir Apparent,[20] and to act in co-operation with it.

[20]Mehmed VI Wahid ed-din (1861–1926) succeeded Mehmed V Reshad as the 36th and final Sultan of the Ottoman Empire, reigning from 1918 to 1922.

It was approved that Mr Chewky Bey should act as Secretary to the advisory sub-committee.

It was mentioned by the Chairman that the Shah had at once telegraphed his willingness to become a patron of the Fund.

The question of an appeal to the Amir[21] was then discussed. The sense of the Committee was that an appeal should be made to His Majesty the Amir. There was some discussion as to whether he should be asked to extend his patronage along with their Imperial Majesties the Sultan and the Shah.

It was unanimously agreed that that should be deferred.

Decided that it was best not to attach to the Mosque the name of any individual donor.

The Chairman stated that Sir Frank Swettenham* had kindly assented to join the General Committee.

Mr W.W. Barnes the Colonial Secretary at Hong Kong also assented to become a member of the Committee.

Confirmed: Ameer Ali 21 July 1911.

A meeting of the Executive Committee of the London Mosque Fund was held on Thursday 20 July 1911 at 3 pm at 36 Queen's Gate Terrace S.W.

Present:

The Rt Hon Syed Ammer Ali (in the Chair)
Sir William Bull MP
Mirza Abdul Ghuffar Khan
M Abbas Ali Baig
Halil Halid Bey
Professor Arnold
Mr Latif
Mr Anik
Mr Khaderbhoy

[21] Probably Habibullah Khan (1872–1919), the ruler (*Amir*, literally leader/commander/ruler in Arabic) of Afghanistan from 1901 until his assassination in 1919.

The minutes of the last meeting were read and confirmed.

The accounts up to date were submitted:

	£	s	d
The Net Balance at Bank of England	1021	1	5
The Net Balance at London, S. Western Bank	44	19	6
Total expenditure up to date	60	7	6

The accounts were unanimously passed.

The Chairman mentioned under the express condition that the matter should be kept strictly confidential and not to be published until sanction was received from Her Highness, that Her Highness the Begum of Bhopal had promised the sum of £7,000 towards the Fund.

The Chairman informed the Committee that Mr Saiduddin of the Transvaal had written to him to say that collections were being made and that it was proposed to send 1/5 of the total to the Mosque Fund and two thirds to the University Scheme and that they hoped to raise £1,000.

Appeals had been sent to the Malayan Sultans signed both by H H the Aga Khan and the Chairman, through Sir Frank Swettenham. The proposal of the Chairman that he should write to Mr Noordin asking him to visit and interest the Malayan Chiefs and magnates was unanimously approved.

Appeals had been sent to His Majesty the Amir and Their Highnesses the Sultan of Zanzibar, the Bey of Tunis[22] and to Syed Khalifa of Zanzibar.

The Chairman mentioned that Raja Tassaduq Rasul* had remembered the appeal most sympathetically and had asked how much was required for carrying out the Project into execution. The Chairman suggested asking him for Rs. 50,000 – Sir Theodore Morison thought Rs. 100,000 would be better.

It was mentioned by the Chairman that H H the Begum's great desire was to have a hostel annexed to the Mosque for the lodgement of students, and that His Highness the Aga Khan and he had accepted Her Highness' suggestion provided sufficient funds were forthcoming.

[22]Muhammad V an-Nasir (1855–1922) ruled Tunisia between 1906 and 1922.

It was considered advisable to begin to ask for definite sums in the appeals.

Decided to ask Rs. 25,000 from the Divan of Palanpur[23] and the same sum from Wazir Baharuddin Bhai.

Proposed by Mr Baig that the following gentlemen should be written to:

[*in pencil*] list to be inserted

The Chairman mentioned the receipt of a letter from the High Priest of the [*illegible*][24] promising all the support and help in his power in furtherance of the Project but not desiring to appear on the Committee.

He had been asked again and it was mentioned to him that His Highness the Sheikh-ul-Islam[25] and Their Holinesses the Chief Mujtahid of Ndjef and the Chief Mujtahid of Tehran had joined the Committee.[26]

Mr Halil Halid then laid the report of the work he had done in Egypt and Turkey before the Committee.

In the first place he reminded the Committee that at a meeting held at Caxton Hall on the 13 December 1910 previous to his departure he had mentioned his intention of going to Egypt and Turkey for six weeks in order to work for the Fund there.

In Egypt he soon managed to interest and encourage the people by means of the Press. After which a local committee under the presidency of the late Riaz Pasha was formed with Mohamed Bey Salim as its secretary and himself as corresponding member.

It was decided both in Egypt and Turkey that no officials should become members of the committee. The following are the members of the committee in Egypt:

[23] Ruler of the princely state of Palanpur in western India.

[24] The writing in the Minutes here is not clear but it may well be a reference to the High Priest of the Bohras, a Muslim sect to be found in western India.

[25] The highest-ranking Muslim scholar officially appointed by the Caliph; the office of Sheikh-ul-Islam carried the authority to make binding religious pronouncements. For instance, on 14 November 1914 during the First World War, Mustafa Hayri declared *jihad* against the Allies, calling on all Muslims to take up arms against them.

[26] The equivalent of the Sunni office of Sheikh-ul-Islam in the Shia tradition is the Mujtahid, among whom that of Ndjef (in Iraq) and that of Tehran (in Iran) traditionally assumed much authority.

[*no names provided in the Minutes*]

After a period of five weeks they were able to hold a large meeting he himself giving lectures at various places on the Mosque and its great need. The collections at the time amounted to £620. Before he left Egypt the sum had increase by £300.

It had been strongly urged that an Egyptian should be placed on the London Committee.

In Turkey the work was considerably more difficult as the people there were not easily moved or persuaded. He therefore set about to obtain the assent of all the members of the Senate and to obtain an interview with H H the Imperial Heir Apparent whom he begged to become the President of the Committee which they were about to form and he promised to do his best for them.

Mr Halil Halid mentioned that both in Egypt and Turkey the people wished to hold the contributions until the Project was fairly advanced, when they would communicate and then send the result to one of the papers that it might fully take up and explain the matter. The Syrians had taken up the matter and they were going to form local committees in Beirut.[27] The progress was slow but the Project would be taken up later.

The Committee considered Mr Halil Halid's work satisfactory and a vote of thanks was accorded to him.

The Chairman wished to suggest the desirability of asking the secretaries of the different committees to communicate with the secretaries here so that there might be no disunity amongst the parties. It was proposed that their names should be handed to the secretaries here so that communication might be continued whilst Mr H Halid was away. During his absence he would be kept informed of all the proceedings.

Sir William Bull considered that the more the various parties were in touch with each other the better it would be for the prosecution of the work.

In reply to Sir William Bull's question as to his plans Mr Halil Halid said he would be going to Constantinople again but would be in touch with this country.

[27] Beirut was then part of Greater Syria, under Ottoman control. Lebanon eventually achieved independence in 1943.

Sir William Bull considered that as £15,000 were now promised to the Fund the Egyptian committee ought to have no hesitation in making over the contributions collected by them. It was merely necessary to assure them of the extent of the progress.

Regarding the amount now at the Ottoman Bank Mr Halil Halid said the sum was £200[28] and that although he had written about its being transferred to the Bank of England he had heard that nothing could be done until October.

Sir Theodore Morison suggested that the Committee should mention to Mr Halil Halid that he should when he is there – and feels that the opportune time has arrived – inform the local committee that the money should be transferred as soon as possible to the proper Bank of the Fund. Sir Theodore Morison considered that Mr Halil Halid was a better judge of the people he had to deal with and would know exactly when to place the matter before them.

Mr Halil Halid said the people found it difficult to send small sums to the Bank in England.

Mr Abbas Ali Baig suggested that the money might be sent to the Ottoman Bank as a channel as it was a step which would console the people – eventually the monies would have to come to the Bank of England.

Sir William Bull asked in whose name the sum of £200 was – which is at the Ottoman Bank. Mr Halil Halid said the sum was in his name. The remainder being at the disposal of the committee at Constantinople. Mr Halil Halid thought it was in a bank.

The Committee thought it undesirable and most unsafe to keep the collections scattered in so many places.

Mr Halil Halid considered it too soon to communicate with the committees with reference to the money.

It was decided that the name of the secretary in Egypt should be ascertained from Mr Halil Halid and that he should be written to at once, but they should wait with regard to Constantinople.

Secretary of Mosque Fund
Mohammad Bey Salim

[28] There is a note in the margin of the Minutes about this, but its contents are illegible.

19 Shariah Banlak
Cairo

Confirmed: Ameer Ali Chairman 21 Sept 1911

A meeting of the Executive Committee of the London Mosque Fund was held on Thursday 21 September 1911 at 3.30 pm at the Caxton Hall Westminster SW

Present:

The Rt Hon Syed Ameer Ali (Chair)
His Excellency the Persian Minister
Sir William Bull
Mirza Abdul Ghuffar Khan
Reouf Ahmed Bey
Mohammed Ali Chewky Bey
Mr C. A. Latif
Mr A. S. M. Anik

The minutes of the last meeting were read and confirmed.

The Treasurer submitted the accounts:

The total amount up to date	£4273-	9-	4
Total expenditure	£ 75-	9-	10
Amount in Bank of England	£4067-	15-	8
Amount in London South Western Bank	£ 130-	3-	10

The Treasurer pointed out that the money was lying idle at the Bank.

Sir William Bull considered it advisable that a portion of the money say £3,000 should be placed on Deposit at once. He knew that the Bank of England accepted Deposits but he was not sure on what principle it was done.

It was resolved that a letter should be drafted by the Chairman in consultation with the Secretary and the Treasurer and sent to the Chief Cashier of the Bank of England to enquire on what principle the Bank received money on deposit and whether a separate deposit form for every succeeding deposit was used or whether the prior deposit was called in and a fresh receipt issued.

The Chairman then brought to the notice of the Committee that with the exception of £1,000 no money had been received from Turkey whilst Persia had in comparison responded admirably.

India had it was true not done much but the hearts of the people waiting for the Durbar[29] had not yet been touched. It was desirable therefore, and necessary to take some step with regard to Turkey. It was understood that a central committee existed in Constantinople but so far it had made no communication to this committee and except for the information given by Mr Halil Halid nothing was known.

The Secretary in Egypt he understood had been written to on two occasions but no reply had been received.

Mr Reouf Ahmed Bey said that £500 had been collected by the newspaper the "Sabah"[30] in Constantinople.

Mr Halil Halid said that that sum had been collected and that £200 was at the chief office of the Ottoman Bank in Constantinople in the name of the London Mosque Fund.

The "Sabah" held the remainder.

Mr Halil having given the address of the secretary in Constantinople, it was resolved that he should be written to at once on the subject and asked to place the London Committee in communication with the Central Fund.

The Chairman mentioned that local committees had been formed at all centres in Persia by high dignitaries who were in communication with the London Committee and he suggested that the same procedure should be adopted in Turkey and Egypt.

Reouf Ahmed Bey said that he would be going to Constantinople soon and would be glad to do all in his power in promoting the formation of local committees in the European Provinces.

Mr Halil Halid gave the following names of some of the members of the Turkish committee:

His Excellency Prince Said Pacha
His Excellency Ghazi Makhtar Bey (Vice President Senate)
His Excellency Sheriff Haider Bey (Senator)
Rafi Pacha

[29] Another reference to the 1911 Delhi Durbar.

[30] *Peyam-Sabah* (*Morning News*) was a mainstream, Constantinople-based, Ottoman-Turkish, daily newspaper.

Riza Sulh Bey (Deputy for Beyrut)
Mufti Bey (Deputy for [*illegible*], Secretary of Committee)

The Chairman proposed the following gentlemen as members of the General Committee:

Tomail Abaza Pacha and Sounour Bey (Advocate at Cairo)

Approved by the Committee and duly elected.

The Chairman read a letter from Mr B.L Moseley referring to the membership and co-operation of Tomail Abaza Pacha and himself enclosing a cutting from the Egyptian Gazette (19 August 1911)[31] in which a statement made to a representative of the "Near East"[32] by Halil Halid Bey was reproduced.

It was resolved that a letter should be written at once to the secretary of the Egyptian committee welcoming their valuable help as a sub-committee of the London Mosque Fund and telling them that in our judgement it was considered best that all funds collected on behalf of the London Mosque Project should be sent as soon as collected to the proper Bank of the Fund, the Bank of England.

The Chairman requested the sanction of the Committee for the purpose of having the English appeal to the Princes put into Arabic. Mirza Abdul Ghuffar Khan undertook the task.

With reference to the disbursements in Turkey and Egypt by Mr Halil Halid, the Committee considered that they had no right to dispose of money which had been given towards another object.

A letter received from Alladin Devjibhai of Bhavnagar,[33] was read. The sense of the meeting was that the Chairman should reply to the letter personally.

A letter from Mr Zuhudurz Rahim Kalid was considered and the authority therein desired was sanctioned. A letter in reply was to be sent by the Chairman.

[31] The *Egyptian Gazette*, the Middle East's oldest English-language newspaper, first appeared on 26 January 1880. Founded by five Britons, it was produced in Alexandria as a four-page weekly tabloid. See http://213.158.162.45/~egyptian/index.php?action=about_us (accessed 10 January 2011). Its 1911 issues are available at the British Library's Newspaper and Periodicals section, located at Colindale, London.

[32] Past issues of *The Near East* from 1908 to 1925 are available at the British Library's Newspaper and Periodicals section, located at Colindale, London.

[33] The city of Bhavnagar, founded in 1723 CE, was the capital of Bhavnagar State, which was the first princely state to merge with independent India in 1948.

Mirza Abdul Ghuffar Khan undertook to write the letter to the Amir of Afghanistan asking him to become the Patron of the Fund.

Resolved by the Committee that the name of Mr M.T. Kaderbhoy be removed from the Executive Committee of the London Mosque Fund.[34]

A meeting of the Executive Committee of the London Mosque Fund was held on Monday 6 November 1911 at 17 Hobart Place, Grosvenor Gardens, W at 5 pm

Present:

The Rt Hon Syed Ameer Ali
Mohammed Ali Chewky Bey
M. Abbas Ali Baig Esq
A.S.M. Anik Esq
Sir William Bull's representative

Sir William Bull expressed his regret at being unable to be present

The minutes were read and confirmed.

Mr Anik submitted the accounts which were duly passed. The total of donations from the 9 November 1910 to 31 October was £4443-14-2.

Expenditure of £85-8-2.

The question of investing part of the money was discussed. After some consideration the following resolutions were unanimously passed:

1. Resolved that out of the sum of £4273-12-2 standing to the credit of the Trustees of the London Mosque Fund in the Bank of England a sum of £4000 be invested forthwith in the 3 ½ Gold Loan of the Government of India, subject to the sanction of the Trustees.

[34]Most probably because Kaderbhoy had returned to India; it seems that he was still active in Muslim politics and in the All-India Muslim League – for instance, he was present at a meeting of its leaders at the law chambers of Muhammad Ali Jinnah (later first Governor-General of Pakistan) in Bombay on 19 March 1914. See http://www.nihcr.edu.pk/Downloads/Chronology.pdf (accessed 27 November 2009).

2. Resolved further that the Chairman be requested to communicate the resolution to the Trustees and obtain from them the necessary sanction.

Confirmed: Ameer Ali 4 December 1911

A meeting of the Executive Committee of the London Mosque Fund was held on Monday 4 December 1911 at: 17 Hobart Place, Grosvenor Gardens, S.W at 4.30 pm

Present:

The Rt Hon Syed Ameer Ali
Sir Theodore Morison
M. Abbas Ali Baig, Esq
Mr W. Bullock (representing Sir William Bull)
Professor T.W. Arnold (Sec.)
Mr A.S.M. Anik (Treas.)

The minutes of the last meeting were read and confirmed.

The Chairman placed before the Committee a letter received from Her Highness the Begum of Bhopal regarding the promised donation of £7,000 towards the Mosque Fund.

The money was to be paid in instalments after the Delhi Durbar on the following two conditions:

(a) That sufficient money should be forthcoming for a hostel for students – attached to the Mosque with arrangements for Mohammedan diet.
(b) That all the money required for the mosque be forthcoming.

It was decided after some discussion that the secretary Professor Arnold should draft an answer accepting the conditions with reservations, and hoping that Her Highness would send the first instalment at her very early convenience.

The letter to be signed by the Chairman.

Confirmed: Ameer Ali 17 April 1912

A meeting of the Executive Committee of the London Mosque Fund was held on Wednesday April 17 1912 at 3.30 pm at 22 Albermarle Street SW

Present:

The Right Hon Ameer Ali
Sir William Bull
Mr M. Abbas Ali Baig
Syed Mohd. Chewky Bey
Mr Bullock

The minutes of the previous meeting were read and confirmed.

A letter from Her Highness the Begum of Bhopal dated 8 February was read and discussed.[35]

Mr Baig was requested to prepare a draft reply to be approved and signed by the Chairman.

Mr Baig gave a resume of the history of the Woking Mosque Endowment Fund[36] and mentioned that with the consent of Mr Ameer Ali and Mr Arnold they with himself had been appointed Trustees of the Fund and it merely remained for the Committee to decide whether to take over the mosque or not.

Mr Baig stated further that the draft of agreement together with Title Deeds was at the Treasury Office. If the Committee agreed to take it over Mr Baig proposed that Mr Leitner[37] should be asked to join the Committee.

The Chairman proposed that the Committee should take over the Mosque and Institute. Unanimously approved.

Sir William Bull suggested that Trustees should arrange to entrust the Title-Deeds and Agreement to some Bank.

Mr Baig proposed that a tin safety box be purchased and that on it be put the names of the three Trustees and the words "Woking

[35] This letter is not available with the Minutes.

[36] The Woking Mosque Endowment Fund was set up by Gottleib Wilhelm Leitner.* For more details of developments at Woking, see M.P. Salamat, *A Miracle at Woking: a history of the Shahjahan Mosque* (Andover, 2008). See also http://www.wokingmuslim.org/pers/dr_leitner.htm (accessed 27 November 2009).

[37] The reference here is to G.W. Leitner's only son, Henry (1869–1945).

Endowment Trust" and that the same should be reported at the following meeting. Unanimously approved.

Mr Anik was asked to accept the Treasurership which he kindly consented to do.

Mr Leitner was unanimously elected a member of the Executive Committee.

Read and confirmed: Ameer Ali chairman

A meeting of the Executive Committee of the London Mosque Fund was held on Tuesday 16 July 1912 at 3 pm at 21 Cromwell Road, South Kensington

Present:

The Rt Hon Ameer Ali
Professor T.W. Arnold
Mr A.S.M. Anik
Mr Shairani

The minutes of the last meeting were read and confirmed.

The Chairman proposed that Prof Arnold should be asked to undertake the office of Secretary to the Woking Endowment Trust. Unanimously carried.

Prof Arnold as Secretary of the Mosque Fund was requested to enquire from Mr Baig if the deeds of the Trust had been endorsed over by Mr Leitner to the Trustees and what steps still remained to be taken by the Mosque Fund Committee. Also to enquire whether it was not necessary to put someone in charge of the Mosque at Woking.

The President suggested that perhaps a number of gentlemen from the Mosque Committee might be able to visit the spot and decide what was to be done.

The Honorary Treasurer Mr Anik submitted his accounts:

Total amount received	£4969- 7- 9
Balance	£4870-17- 8
Invested	£4000

(Three dividends £104-15)

Balance at date: £955- 9- 9

It was decided that the sum of £700 out of the Balance should be invested.

Mr Anik was requested to enquire from Mr Hayes if he would undertake to audit the Mosque Fund Accounts.

Confirmed: Ameer Ali Chairman

A meeting of the Executive Committee of the London Mosque Fund was held at 41 Sloane Street SW on Wednesday 30 April 1913 at 5 pm

Present:

The Rt Hon Ameer Ali (in the chair)
Mr Abdul Ghufar Khan
Professor T.W. Arnold
Mr C.A. Latif
Mr A.S.M. Anik

The minutes of the previous meeting were read and confirmed.

Woking Mosque: Mr Arnold reported in this connection that as desired he had made the necessary enquiries from Mr Baig who had informed him that no documents had so far been made over but that the matter was still in the hands of the lawyers.

The Treasurer then submitted the Financial Report up to date. This was approved.[38]

The Committee confirmed the investment made by the Treasurer according to the decision arrived at by them at a previous meeting.

It was proposed that in view of the small sum necessary for every day expenses the sum of £300 out of the £417 standing to the credit of the current cash account should be invested.

[38]No details of finances are included here in the Minutes.

This was unanimously approved and Mr Anik was requested to take the matter in hand and he agreed to do so.

Circular letter: The President proposed that a circular letter should be issued explaining why no meetings had been held and no progress made. Professor Arnold undertook to draft the letter which was to be sent to the Trustees and all large subscribers.

Letter from the Begum

On the motion of the President seconded by Mr Abdul Ghaffar Khan it was resolved that Mr Arnold as secretary be requested to communicate with H. H. the Begum in regard to her donation.

A letter was placed before the members from a Mr Michelle containing a request for information regarding the Mosque Fund Project. It was resolved that a copy of the circular letter be sent to him.

Confirmed: Ameer Ali 19 November 1912

A meeting of the Executive Committee of the London Mosque Fund was held on 19 November 1913 at the India Office, Whitehall SW

Present:

The Rt Hon Syed Ameer Ali (in the chair)
Mr C.A. Latif
Mr A.S.M. Anik
Mr Abdul Ghufar Khan
Mr Abbas Ali Baig
Mr T.W. Arnold (Secretary)

Mr Anik reported that £300 had been invested as decided at the last meeting and Mr Arnold reported the issue of letters to H.H. the Begum of Bhopal and other subscribers and to the Trustees setting forth the progress of the Fund.

The Secretary of the Trustees of the Mosque at Woking reported the transactions of a meeting of the Trustees on 20 October as follows:

(i) consideration of a letter dated 10 October 1913 from the Treasury solicitor regarding the deed of transfer and the funds now in the possession of Mr Leitner;

(ii) resolution that the Mosque should be insured as soon as funds are available;

(iii) sanction of the provisional arrangement made by Mr Abbas Ali Baig for the supervision and maintenance of the Mosque by Khwaja Kamaluddin*[39] who was asked to insure the Mosque and the Memorial House, for the present, for £1000;

(iv) resolution that Mr Anik be asked to act as Treasurer of the Trust Funds and Mr Arnold as Secretary of the Board of trustees.

Mr Anik laid before the meeting a statement of the accounts of the London Mosque Fund up to the 15 December 1913 and pointed out that the balance in hand in the banks including securities was £5206-6-0. He was asked to invest £100 now and another £100 after 5 January 1914.

Confirmed: Ameer Ali 22 January 1914

A meeting of the Executive Committee of the London Mosque Fund was held on 22 January 1914 at 141 Sloane Street, SW at 5 pm

Present:

The Rt Hon Ameer Ali (in the Chair)
His Excellency Mundji Fikri Bey
Mr Mirza Abdul Ghaffar Khan
Mr Abbas Ali Baig
Mr C.A. Latif
Mr A.S.M. Anik
Prof T.W. Arnold

Mr Anik reported that he had invested £100 as decided at the last meeting.

Letters from Khuwaja Kamaluddin and Mr Abdul Haq (Secretary of the Islamic Society[40]) were read, asking for a grant of money for the

[39] Khwaja Kamal-ud-Din wrote a large number of books on Islam (and religion more generally), which were published from Woking. Throughout his time in England he worked energetically to institutionalize Islam by mobilizing material and human resources. More specifically, he was committed to establishing a mosque in London, and in the meantime temporarily rented premises in which he regularly led congregational prayers.

[40] *Anjuman-i-Islam* (see *The Times*, 29 January 1896 and 17 November 1897) was a precursor of the Islamic Society; at the Eid celebration held at Caxton Hall under the auspices of the

payment of the rent of a building in London for the purposes of a Mosque.

The Chairman explained that a grant could be made from the Mosque Fund without reference to the Trustees. Proposed by Mr Abbas Ali Baig and seconded by Moh Latif that this committee do recommend to the Trustees to sanction a grant of £120 a year out of the income of the Trust Fund in deposit with the Bank of England to the credit of the Trustees of the London Mosque Fund. The motion was carried.

Proposed by Mr Ameer Ali and seconded by His Excellency Mundji Fikri Bey that the administration of this grant be entrusted to a committee composed of Mr Abbas Ali Baig, Mr Anik and Khawaja Kamaluddin for renting a building or room or rooms for the performance of the Muslim prayers and for expenses incidental thereto; and that this committee submit an annual report as to how the money has been expended. The motion was carried.

Mr Arnold reported that a cheque for £492 was received from Mr Leitner's solicitors by the Woking Mosque Trustees who authorised Mr Anik their Treasurer to invest £490 in India Stock (gold) 3 1/2 per cent, and Mr Anik reported that the investment had been effected and that the Mosque and Memorial House had been insured for £1,000.

Confirmed: Ameer Ali 19 March 1914

A meeting of the Executive Committee of the London Mosque Fund was held on 19 March 1914 at 3 pm at 41 Sloane Street SW

Present:

The Rt Hon Ameer Ali (in the chair)
Mr Abbas Ali Baig
Mr C.A Latif
Mr Willoughby Bullock (representing Sir William Bull)

Pan-Islamic Society (*The Times*, 22 December 1903), an appeal was made for funds to be collected for the building of a mosque in London. There were further newspaper reports of gatherings organized by the Pan-Islamic Society from 1907 onwards (see *The Times*, 28 January 1907 and 13 June 1907).

Professor T.W. Arnold (Secretary)

The minutes of the previous meeting were read and confirmed.

In reference to the resolution passed by the Committee on 22 January 1914 the secretaries reported that they received from the following trustees (Rt Hon Ameer Ali, Lord Ampthill, Moh Abbas Ali Baig, His Excellency Mundji Fikri Bey, Lord Rothschild and Sadigh es Salteneh) letters agreeing to the recommendation of the Committee that a grant of £120 a year out of the income of the Trust Fund be made to a Committee composed of Mr Abbas Ali Baig, Mr A.S.M. Anik and Khawaja Kamaluddin, who will administer the grant for the purpose of renting a building or room for the performance of Muslim prayers.

Lord Ampthill, Lord Rothschild and the Rt Hon Ameer Ali imposed a condition that the Trustees will have the power to withdraw or vary their consent to the grant, whenever it may appear to them desirable to do so. But no answer had yet been received from His Highness Mr Aga Khan.

Mr Bullock stated that he did not consider it expedient to take final action until an answer had been received from him also, as he was one of the Trustees.

Mr Baig therefore proposed that an urgent letter be sent to His Highness informing him that all the other Trustees had given their consent and requesting an early reply.

Resolved (subject to the assent of His Highness the remaining trustee) that the grant should take effect from 1 January 1914 and be paid quarterly to the committee composed of Mr Abbas Ali Baig, Mr A.S.M. Anik and Khawaja Kamaluddin.

Mr Ameer Ali pointed out that the time had come for continuing the appeal for funds for the London Mosque and it was resolved that in reference to the expenditure necessary for such an appeal the balance of quarterly income of the Trust Funds in the Bank of England after payment to the above mentioned committee composed of Mr Abbas Ali Baig, Mr A.S.M. Anik and Khawaja Kamaluddin be utilized for this purpose.

The following form was approved for the cards announcing the Friday prayer:

Allah – O – Akbar[41]
The Jooma Namaz[42] *will be held at the Lindsay Hall, Notting Hill Gate,*[43] *W., regularly every Friday at 12 Noon until further notice.*

Mr Khawaja Kamal-ud-Din of the Mosque, Woking will deliver the sermon and the Dua[44] *will be recited by Haireddin Effindi and Lord Headley* respectively in Arabic and English.*

All Moslems are cordially invited.

The secretary submitted the following statement of the accounts of the London Mosque Fund to 31 December 1913:

Statement of Accounts of the London Mosque Fund

Memo of Receipt:	£	s	d
Donations received	4978	6	5
Library Lecture Room	10		
Dividends on Investments	316	6	8
Total:	**5304**	**13**	**1**
Expenditure	98	7	1
Balance at Banks:			
Bank of England	98	11	1
London South Western Bank (with Mr Anik)	7	14	11
Securities with Bank of England India 3 1/2 % (£5448-5-10)	5100		
Total:	**5206**	**6**	

£316-6-8 Dividends
£ 98-7-1 Expenditure
£217-19-7 still remaining as balance out of Dividends to 31.12.13

The account of the donations is intact.

Confirmed: Ameer Ali 6 June 1916

[41] 'Allah-o-Akbar' (also written 'Allahu Akbar') is the Arabic for 'God is the Greatest' or 'God is Great', and is the first line of the Muslim call to prayer (*Adhan* or *Azan*).
[42] *Jooma Namaz* (often transliterated as *Juma Namaz*) is the Persian/Urdu term for Friday congregational prayers.
[43] Premises rented at this time for Friday congregational prayers.
[44] 'Supplication to God', or prayer.

A meeting of the Executive Committee of the London Mosque Fund was held on Tuesday 6 June 1916 at 5.30 pm at 41 Sloane Street, SW

Present:

The Rt Hon Ameer Ali (in the chair)
Sir William Bull MP
W Abbas Ali Baig
Mirza Abdul Ghaffar Khan
Mr A.S.M. Anik
T.W. Arnold (Secretary)

The minutes of the previous meeting were read and confirmed. With reference to the consent of H H the Agha Khan, the Chairman reported that when H H visited England, he verbally expressed his agreement with the other Trustees.

The Chairman explained the arrangements for the administration of the grant of £120 for a Namaz-gah,[45] and stated that Maulavi Sadrud Din*[46] had taken a room for this purpose in 39 Upper Bedford Place, without however having previously obtained the permission of the sub-committee. The following rules were framed for the management of the Namaz-gah, but Maulavi Sadrud Din had expressed his inability to carry them out:

Rules for the Management of the Namaz-gah in London

1. Any place rented by the London Mosque Fund Committee to serve as a Namaz-gah in London shall be devoted exclusively to Divine Worship and Religious Services.
2. The Namaz-gah shall always remain available for Namaz to every Muslim of any Islamic sect.
3. No society, association or other body shall be permitted to use it for a secular purpose or for holding therein any meeting unconnected with Divine Worship.
4. No person shall be allowed to reside therein or to make any private or secular use thereof.

[45] Persian/Urdu term for a place for prayer or worship.

[46] Maulavi Sadr-ud-Din took the place of Khwaja Kamal-ud-Din as imam of the Woking Mosque when the latter was away from England between 1914 and 1916.

5. The London Mosque Fund Committee or the sub-committee thereof appointed for the control and supervision of the Namaz-gah may, if they think fit, relax the provisions of the Rules 3 and 4 for special reasons consistently [*sic*] with the main object of the Namaz-gah. They may also permit the temporary renting of any extra room or space not used or required for Divine Worship. The rent realised in such cases shall be credited to the Namaz-gah fund.
6. The Pesh Imam[47] for the time being shall be responsible for the proper upkeep of the Namaz-gah and the furniture therein, and also for the due observance of the rules, any breach of which should be forthwith reported to the Secretary to the sub-committee.

Sir William Bull discussed the situation and pointed out that the arrangement with Maulavi Sadrud Din might be terminated at any time, if due notice were given.

A letter dated 1 June from Maulavi Sadrud Din was read. The Chairman stated his opinion that the tone of this letter was reasonable, and it was resolved that the following answer be sent to Maulavi Sadrud Din:

"The Committee of the London Mosque Fund considered your letter of 1 June. They have noted your assurance that the rules are being carried out by you. They do not wish to impose upon you any obligations that are not fair or reasonable, but as you hold the keys, you are bound to be responsible for the rooms and their contents and the maintenance of order. They trust that matters will proceed smoothly in the future and have adjured further consideration of the matter for a period of six months".

It was resolved that in view of the death of Lord Rothschild, the existing trustees should be approached and the name of Lord Lamington* should be suggested to fill up the vacancy.

The Treasurer submitted the account on fol. 19 which the Chairman signed.

It was resolved that a cheque for £25 be handed to the Treasurer to be paid into the L and SW Bank and that £100 be invested in

[47] Urdu/Persian term for the chief leader of prayers at a mosque.

Exchequer Bonds (free of tax) and that after 1 July a further sum of £50 be invested in Exchequer Bonds.

Confirmed: Ameer Ali 23 November 1917

A meeting of the Executive Committee of the London Mosque Fund was held on 23 November 1917 at 3.30 pm at 41 Sloane Street SW

Present:

The Rt Hon Ameer Ali (in the Chair)
Sahibzada Aftab Ahmed Khan*
Mirza Abdul Ghaffar Khan
Mr A.S.M. Anik

The minutes of the previous meeting were read and confirmed.

The Treasurer submitted the accounts up to 23 November 1917 which were passed and signed by the Chairman.

It was resolved that meetings of the Executive Committee shall in future be held once a quarter.

Mr Mirza Hashim Isfahani*[48] was duly elected a member of the Executive Committee.

Resolved that M H Isfahani be appointed to visit periodically on behalf of the Executive Committee the Namaz-gah and report to the Committee as to the conduct of the Namaz-gah.

The Executive Committee confirmed the arrangements made by the Namaz-gah sub-committee in reference to the transfer from Upper Bedford Place to 111 Campden Hill Road[49] and the expenditure connected therewith.

Resolved that Khaja Kamaluddin be requested to furnish a report as to the condition and success of the Namaz-gah from the date of his taking over charge from Maulvi Sadarruddin.

[48] Sometimes spelt 'Ispahani'.

[49] In the absence of a mosque, Lindsay Hall in Notting Hill Gate, supported by the LMF, had been the first building rented for congregational prayers. Referred to as the 'London Muslim Prayer House', it was also used by the Muslim Literary Society and the London Muslim Association for their varied intellectual and cultural activities. Prayers had then been conducted in 39 Upper Bedford Place, before transferring to Campden Hill Road, Notting Hill Gate. See *Islamic Review*, September 1917 and May 1920.

Resolved that £9 a year be granted to the clerk of the British Red Crescent Society[50] and the London All India Moslem League[51] for all clerical work connected with the London Mosque Fund commencing from 1 November 1914.

Resolved that the official habitation of the London Mosque Fund shall be at 41 Sloane Street S.W.1.

Resolved that a fresh letter of appeal inviting influential persons to become members of the General Committee, and asking those who are already members of this Committee to contribute to the funds of the Mosque be drafted.

A communication from the Hon Treasurer of the Islamic Society was read and it was resolved that he should be informed that the accounts will be published in due course.

Resolved that Mr Anik be requested to send a statement of the accounts to the Press for publication.

Confirmed: Ameer Ali 15 March 1918

A meeting of the Executive Committee of the London Mosque Fund was held on 15 March 1918 at 5 pm at 41 Sloane Street SW1

Present:

Rt Hon Ameer Ali (in the chair)
Sahibzada Aftab Ahmed Khan
Mirza Abdul Ghaffar Khan

[50] Ameer Ali was the founder and President of the British Red Crescent Society. During the Turco-Italian War it provided for the relief of the Ottoman sick and wounded and for widows and orphans in Tripoli (now capital of Libya). It also offered medical help. See *The Times*, 8 November 1911; 23 January 1912; 8 April 1912; 5 November 1912. In 1922 it remitted £7,800 to the Ottoman Red Crescent Society for relief in Constantinople. See *The Times*, 13 January 1922; 3 March 1926.

[51] The 'London All-India Moslem League' was founded by Syed Ameer Ali; on 6 May 1908 he delivered its inaugural address at Westminster Palace Hotel (see *The Times*, 7 May 1908). Its objects included 'the advancement and safeguard by all constitutional and loyal methods of the special interests of the Mahomedan subjects of the King [. . .] The London League has been a most valuable exponent of Moslem sentiments and opinion [. . .] by sober, well-reasoned and detailed representations it has made to the India Office, the Colonial Office and other Whitehall departments it has taken the acknowledged lead in formulating and giving expression to Indian Moslem opinion' (see *The Times*, 31 October 1913).

Professor T. W. Arnold
Mr A.S.M. Anik

The minutes of the previous meeting were read and confirmed.

The resolution of the Committee as to the publication of the accounts of the London Mosque Fund was carried into effect by the Hon Treasurer and they were printed in the *Westminster Gazette* of 20 December 1917 among other papers.

The Hon Treasurer submitted the accounts up to 15 March 1918 and they were signed by the Chairman.

A report by Khwaja Kamaluddin on the conduct of the Namazgah was read and it was resolved that this report, together with the accounts of the London Mosque Fund (published in the *Westminster Gazette* of 20 December 1917[52]) be sent to the Editor of *The Islamic Review*.[53]

Confirmed: Ameer Ali 5 November 1919

A meeting of the Executive Committee of the London Mosque fund was held on 5 November 1919 at 4.30 pm at 18 Sloane Street, SW1

Present:

Rt Hon Ameer Ali (in the chair)
Mr A.S.M. Anik
M.H. Isfahani

The minutes of the previous meeting were read and confirmed.

Sir William Bull was prevented by public work from attending. In his letter to the Chairman he wrote as follows:

[52]The accounts were published as part of a letter from Ameer Ali to the editor, which contained details of some of the most prominent donors to the LMF and an implicit appeal for contributions. On 23 November 1917, the balance was £6131–8-6. See *Westminster Gazette*, 20 December 1917.

[53]The original name of the *Islamic Review* when its publication started in February 1913 was *Muslim India and the Islamic Review* but by 1914 it had changed to *The Islamic Review and Muslim India*. In 1921 it was shortened to *The Islamic Review*. For more details about the founding of the journal, see http://www.wokingmuslim.org/history/is-rev/founding.htm (accessed 10 January 2010).

"I have your letter of the 1st instant but regret that I shall be unable to get to the meeting tomorrow. I, however, agree with your view that the London Mosque Fund, the British Red Crescent Society and the London Moslem League should each contribute £40 towards the annual rent of £120 for the premises at 18 Sloane Street".[54]

Proposed by Mr Isfahani seconded by Mr Anik that the London Mosque Fund, the British Red Crescent Society and the London Moslem League should each contribute £40 towards the annual rent of £120 for the premises at 18 Sloane Street.

It was resolved that the Honorary Treasurer be requested to have the lease [*illegible*] in his name as representing the three societies.

Confirmed: Ameer Ali 18 June 1920

A meeting of the Executive Committee of the London Mosque Fund was held on 18 June 1920 at 6 pm at 18 Sloane St, SW1

Present:

The Rt Hon Ameer Ali
Sir Abbas Ali Baig
Mr A.S.M. Anik
Mr M. H. Isfahani
Prof T.W. Arnold (secretary)

The minutes of the previous meeting were read and confirmed.

The accounts of the London Mosque Fund from 9 November 1910 to 18 June 1920 were submitted by Mr A.S.M. Anik and approved. Mr Anik was authorized to invest £121-9-1.

A vote of thanks to Mr Anik was proposed and carried unanimously for his self sacrificing work in keeping the accounts for the last ten years.

Confirmed: Ameer Ali 16 March 1921

[54] Premises rented for the purpose of holding congregational prayers, especially on Fridays.

A meeting of the Executive Committee of the London Mosque Fund was held on 16 March 1921 at 4.45 at 18 Sloane Street

Present:

The Rt Hon Ameer Ali (chairman)
Sahibzada Aftab Ahmed Khan
Mr A.S.M. Anik
Mr M. H. Isfahani
Mr A Yusuf Ali* (after his election)
Prof T.W. Arnold (secretary)

The minutes of the previous meeting were read and confirmed.

The Rt Hon Ameer Ali proposed and Sahibzada Aftab Ahmed Khan seconded the election of Mr Yusuf Ali as a member of the Executive Committee. The proposal was carried unanimously and Mr Yusuf Ali took his seat as a member of the Committee.

The Chairman drew attention to complaints in regard to the Woking Mosque,[55] and as the Committee of the London Mosque Fund is responsible for the management of this mosque, he proposed that a sub-committee (consisting of Mr Anik, Mr Isfahani [convenor] and Mr Yusuf Ali) be appointed to enquire into the occupation, conduct and maintenance of the Woking Mosque together with the Namaz-gah at Campden Hill Road. His Proposal was carried unanimously and the gentlemen nominated consented to act on the sub-committee.

The accounts of the London Mosque Fund from 9 November 1910 to 28 February 1921 were submitted by Mr A.S.M. Anik and were approved. It was decided that in future accounts should be made up yearly by the calendar year.

Confirmed: Ameer Ali 14 October 1921

[55] It is not clear what these complaints were as they are not discussed in detail in the Minutes here.

A meeting of the Executive Committee of the London Mosque Fund was held on 14 October 1921 at 41 Sloane Street SW

Present:

The Rt Hon Ameer Ali (chairman)
Mr A.S.M. Anik
Sir T.W. Arnold (secretary)

The minutes of the last meeting were read and confirmed.

The Chairman reported that Mr Yusuf Ali had resigned from the Committee on the eve of his departure to India to take up his appointment in the service of His exalted Highness the Nizam of Hyderabad.[56]

The Chairman also reported that no report had been received from the sub-committee appointed to enquire into the maintenance of the Woking Mosque and there was no evidence that any action had been taken.

Read a letter from Mrs Gardner,[57] at Campden Hill Road, dated 9 August complaining of her dismissal by Maulvi Mustafa Khan, Imam of the Woking Mosque and also a letter from Maulvi Mustafa Khan in answer to the Chairman's request for an explanation.

Resolved that the Maulvi be asked to inform the Committee whether Mrs Gardner has vacated the house, and who is at present the caretaker in 111 Campden Hill Road, and on what date Khwaja Kamal ud-Din is expected to arrive and resume charge of the Namaz-Gah.

Resolved that all other matters in connection with the Namaz-Gah be reserved until the arrival of Khwaja Kamal ud-Din.

Confirmed: Ameer Ali 8 December 1921

[56] Soon after the signature of the Treaty of Versailles in 1919, Abdullah Yusuf Ali entered the service of the Nizam (ruler) of the state of Hyderabad, India, and in 1921 was appointed as Revenue Member of the Council of the State. See *The Times*, 15 December 1953.

[57] Caretaker at 111 Campden Hill Road.

A meeting of the Executive Committee of the London Mosque Fund was held on 2 December 1921 at 5.15 pm at 18 Sloane Street SW

Present:

The Rt Hon Ameer Ali (chairman)
Mr A.S.M. Anik
Mr Isfahani
Sir T.W. Arnold (secretary)

The Chairman reported that Khwaja Kamal-ud-Din had called upon him that he had found everything in good order back at Woking and in 111 Campden Hill Road, and that Mrs Gardner had left and that no further difficulty has arisen in regard to her.

The proposal was considered to devote a sum of 100 guineas out of the surplus income of the London Mosque Fund for the improvement of the Muslim Burial Ground Brookwood Cemetery.[58] An estimate of the proposed improvement submitted by the Managing Director of the London Necropolis Company was considered and accepted unanimously. It was further resolved that a copy of this resolution be sent to the Trustees of the London Mosque Fund.

The Hon Treasurer submitted a statement of accounts as per attached paper, of the present state of the London Mosque Fund.

Confirmed: Ameer Ali (Chairman)

[58] Known as the London Necropolis, the Brookwood Cemetery was opened in November 1854, with the aim of solving London's burial problem. In time, it became Britain's largest cemetery, catering generously for pauper burials, and more than 240,000 people of all denominations have been buried there. For Muslims, it was a particularly special place since it contained the oldest Muslim burial ground in the country, dating back to the late nineteenth century when a plot reserved for use by the nearby Oriental Institute located in Woking was set aside at the request of G.W. Leitner. During the First World War, Muslim soldiers from the Western Front who died in hospitals in Britain were buried at a dedicated Muslim cemetery on Horsell Common. In the inter-war period, Brookwood was the only public cemetery serving London with a section designated for Muslims, and since there was a mosque nearby at Woking a proper Muslim burial could be ensured. Hence it was chosen as the final resting place by many leading Muslims in Britain at this time. See H. Ansari, '"Burying the dead": making Muslim space in Britain', *Historical Research*, 80, no. 210 (July 2007), pp. 545–566.

A meeting of the Committee of the London Mosque Fund was held on Monday 23 July 1923 at 4.30 pm at 18 Sloane Street SW[59]

Present:

The Rt Hon Ameer Ali (chairman)
Mr A.S.M. Anik
Mr S Aftab Ahmed Khan
Mr G. A. Ardalani[60]
~~Sir T.W. Arnold (secretary)~~[61]

Rt Hon Syed Ameer Ali proposed and Mr Aftab Ahmed Khan seconded that Sir Mohamad Rafique* be elected a member of the Executive Committee of the London Mosque Fund. Mr Anik proposed and Mr Ameer Ali seconded that Mirza Kajim Husain be elected a member of the Executive Committee of the London Mosque Fund. Both these motions were carried unanimously.

The Hon Treasurer submitted the accounts from 9 November 1910 to 21 July 1923 giving full details of receipts and expenditure as per statement of accounts hereto attached. Duly considered and were passed.

Confirmed: Ameer Ali Chairman 24 June 1924

A meeting of the Executive Committee of the London Mosque Fund was held on Tuesday 24 June 1924 at 18 Sloane Street at 4.15 pm

Present:

The Rt Hon Ameer Ali (chairman)
Mr A.S.M. Anik
Sir T.W. Arnold (secretary)

[59] By now these premises contained the offices of the British Red Crescent Society and the London All-India Muslim League.

[60] Gholam Ali Khan Ardalani, Chargé d'Affaires at the Persian Legation in London.

[61] Crossed out in the Minutes.

The Chairman brought to the attention of the members present that Sir Ali Imam Moid-ul-Mulk* had been elected by the agreement of the members obtained by correspondence – this course of action having been adopted in order to obviate delay. The meeting unanimously confirmed the election.

The audited accounts from 9 November 1910 to 31 December 1923 of the London Mosque Fund, audited by Messrs. Hayes chartered accountants, and certified dated 24 January 1924 were placed before the Committee and passed.

Resolved that in the opinion of the Committee the time has arrived for renewing the appeal after the amendment, for the erection of a mosque in London. Further that representatives from the Egyptians and Afghan legations be invited to join the Executive Committee. Resolved further that H H King Fuad[62] of Egypt and H H the King of Afghanistan[63] and that the Nizam of Hyderabad[64] be invited, through the proper channels, to be patrons of the Fund in conjunction with H H the Shah of Persia.

Resolved that the expediency of approaching His Majesty's Government for the Grant of a site for the proposed Mosque should be considered, and that decision in this matter be left in the hands of the Chairman.

The Treasurer moved that as one of the Trustees for the London Mosque Fund is leaving for India in August next, and as his absence is likely to be permanent, investments standing in his name, jointly with the Chairman, should be altered to the name of the Chairman in conjunction with some other Trustee.

Resolved that the Chief Cashier of the Bank of England be requested to alter such investments into the name of the Chairman in conjunction with Lord Lamington.

Confirmed: Ameer Ali 20 May 1925

[62] King Fuad (1868–1936) was king of Egypt from 1917 until his death in 1936.

[63] Amanullah Khan (1892–1960) was *Amir* (ruler) of Afghanistan from 1919 to 1929.

[64] *Nizam*, a shortened version of *Nizam-ul-Mulk*, meaning 'Administrator of the Realm', was the title of the native sovereigns of Hyderabad State, India, which had belonged to the Asaf Jah dynasty since 1719.

A meeting of the Executive Committee of the London Mosque Fund was held on Wednesday 20 May 1925 at 18 Sloane Street at 4.30 pm

Present:

The Rt Hon Ameer Ali (chairman)
Sir Mohammed Rafique
Mr G.A. Ardalani
Sir T.W. Arnold (secretary)

In November 1924 His Highness the Aga Khan urged that a memorial be sent to His Exalted Highness the Nizam on behalf of the London Mosque Fund; and accordingly such a memorial was sent on 26 November 1924 signed by himself and the Right Honourable Ameer Ali. An answer was received dated 30 April 1925 granting a further donation of £1,000 from H E H the Nizam.

The letter was read from H H the Aga Khan urging that H E H the Nizam should be approached again and that it be pointed out to him that the amount of the donation was not in harmony with his exalted position and might damage the success of the project of erecting a mosque in London.

Mr Ameer Ali undertook to carry out this proposal in conjunction with His Highness the Aga Khan.

Confirmed: Ameer Ali Chairman 31 October 1925

A meeting of the Executive Committee of the London Mosque Fund was held on Saturday 31 October 1925 at 18 Sloane Street at 3 pm

Present:

The Rt Hon Ameer Ali (chairman)
Sir Mohammed Rafique
Mr G.A. Ardalani
Mr A.S.M. Anik (treasurer)
Prof A.W. Azzam
Sir T.W. Arnold (secretary)

In connection with the minutes of the last meeting Mr Ameer Ali reported that he had in conjunction with H H the Aga Khan sent a letter to His Exalted Highness the Nizam but that no answer had yet been received by him.

The Chairman read a letter from Mr Anik the Treasurer urging the stabilisation of the London Mosque Fund. In view of the absence of several of the Trustees from this country, it was resolved that Counsel's opinion should be taken as to what steps should be taken for drawing up a deed by which a regular trust may be created in the name of the London Mosque Fund.

The Treasurer reported that there is a balance of £1,209 in the current account at the Bank of England.

Resolved that about £1,000 be invested in some Trust securities.

Resolved that a letter be sent to Khwaja Kamaluddin drawing his attention to the fact that under the Trust Deed the Woking Mosque is placed under the general supervision of the Committee of the London Mosque Fund, and the Committee of the London Mosque Fund would be glad to have particulars as to the proposed enlargement of the Woking Mosque so as to accommodate 2,000 persons as mentioned in the "Sunday Times" of 23 October.[65]

Confirmed: Ameer Ali chairman

A meeting of the Executive Committee of the London Mosque Fund was held at 4 o'clock on Saturday 5 December 1925 at 2 Cadogan Place SW1

Present:

The Rt Hon Ameer Ali (chairman)
Sir Mohammed Rafique
Sir T.W. Arnold (secretary)
Mr A.S.M. Anik (treasurer)

[65]The date recorded for this issue of the *Sunday Times* is incorrect, as 23 October 1925 was a Friday.

Mr Anik reported that £1,000 (face value) were invested in 5% War Loan 1929–47, in the names of the Right Honourable Lord Lamington and the Right Honourable Ameer Ali, registered in Bank of England transferable by deed.

The Secretary reported that he had received from Khwaja Kamaluddin a letter dated 14 November 1925 stating that the contemplated extension to the Woking Mosque is intended to accommodate 200 persons,[66] by adding two wings to the North and South sides of the mosque, and two houses for ablution for ladies and gentlemen and that the work will be carried out under the supervision of Mr Charles Nicholson, who is making a design and estimates.

In reply the Secretary wrote asking for further particulars.

Resolved that the Cashier of the Bank of England be thanked for his communication of 24 November to the Chairman of the Executive Committee relating to the change of the designation of the Fund from the names of Lord Ampthill and others to the name of the "London Mosque Fund" and to the authorisation for drawing cheques on the Fund.

In consequence of the departure from England of Mundji Fikri Bey and Sadik Sultaneh it has become necessary for the due administration of the Trust to fill the place of one or both of them.

It was resolved that Sir Mohammad Rafique, member of the Council of the Secretary of State for India and a member of the Executive Committee be appointed a Trustee in the place of Mundji Fikri Bey.

Resolved further that a copy of this Resolution be forwarded to the Chief Cashier of the Bank of England.

Resolved that Sir Thomas W. Arnold be appointed the pro tem secretary of the Trustees of the London Mosque Fund in the place of Mr C.A. Latif, resigned.

Confirmed: Ameer Ali 12 May 1926

[66]The letter from Khwaja Kamal-ud-Din corrects the figure of 2,000 recorded in the minutes of 31 October 1925 as reported in what seems to be the 25 October 1925 issue of the *Sunday Times*.

A meeting of the Trustees and of the Executive Committee of the London Mosque Fund was held at 4 o'clock on Wednesday 12 May 1926 at 2 Cadogan Place SW1

Present:

The Rt Hon Ameer Ali (chairman)
The Rt Hon Lord Lamington
Mr G. A Ardalani
Mr A.W. Azzam
Dr Saud S. Mohamedi[67] (as supervisor of 111 Campden Hill Road)
Sir T.W. Arnold (secretary)

The minutes of the last meeting were read and confirmed.

The Chairman raised the question whether the sum of £130 should continue to be paid for the Namaz-Gah at 111, Campden Hill Road. Resolved that a letter be sent to Kamal ud-Din enquiring whether he was prepared to take over this house and make himself responsible for the payment of the rent, and whether in this case he would let one large room to the London Mosque Fund and at what rent.

The purchase of a house for the purpose of a Mosque was considered by the meeting to be an infraction of the Trust, the purpose of which is the building of a mosque.

Resolved that it was not in accordance with the purpose of the Trust to devote any portion of the income of the Trust towards defraying the expenses of the burial of indigent Moslems dying in the neighbourhood of London.

Read a letter from Sir Abbas Ali Baig resigning his position as a Trustee of the London Mosque Fund and as a member of the Committee. His resignation was accepted accordingly.

Read letters from His Highness the Aga Khan and the Rt Hon Lord Ampthill, regretting their inability to attend the meeting.

Resolved that Mr Withers (of Withers, Bensons, Currie, Williams and Co.) 4, Arundel Street, W.C, be appointed to draw up a Trust Deed for the London Mosque Fund.

Draft notes for the preparation of the Trust Deed were read and accepted by the Committee.

[67] Member of the Moslem Society of Great Britain.

Resolved that Jaafar Pasha Askari, representative of the Iraq Government and Shuja ud-Daulah Khan, the Afghan Minister be invited to join the Committee.

The Treasurer submitted a statement of account which was accepted by the Committee.

Confirmed: Ameer Ali 6 November 1926

A Joint Meeting of the Trustees of the Executive Committee of the London Mosque Fund, held at 18 Sloane Street, S.W, on Saturday, 6 November 1926 at 4 pm

Present:

The Rt Hon Ameer Ali (Chairman)
The Rt Hon Lord Ampthill
Sir Mohammed Rafique
Sheikh Abdul Wahab-al-Azzam
Mr A.S.M. Anik (Hon Teasurer)
Mr G.A. Ardalani

1. The minutes of the previous meeting were read and duly confirmed.

2. The Chairman read a letter he had received from the Honorary treasurer dated 5 November regarding the mention in the Trust Deed[68] of the sums of £6,000 as on deposit at the Bank of England in the name of the London Mosque Fund. The Honorary Treasurer pointed out in his communication that the actual market value of the securities was only £5,511, the sum of £6,000 represented the "purchase value". The Chairman reported that on receipt of this letter he immediately sent an extract from it by special messenger to Mr Withers for his consideration before the meeting; and had just received Mr Withers'

[68]While monies were being collected and partly invested from 1910 onwards, it was not until 19 November 1926 that the LMF was officially registered as a trust for the purpose of building a mosque in London. The following were declared its trustees: Sir Sultan Mahomed Shah Aga Khan; C.A.N. Cochrane-Baillie, 2nd Baron Lamington, A.O.V. Russell, 2nd Baron Ampthill; Syed Ameer Ali; and Sir Mohamed Rafique. No copy of the Trust document was included with the Minutes but the 'Declaration of Trust' is available in the library at the ELM Archives.

reply[69] asking that the execution of the Trust Deed by the Trustees might be postponed so that an "accurate rental and description of the securities representing the funds collected, at the date of the Deed" might be included in a fresh engrossment which he would prepare after these particulars had been furnished by the Honorary Secretary.

3. After discussion the Committee was of opinion that no difference as to the "market value" and the "face" or "purchase" value of the securities should be introduced into the Trust Deed but a simple statement as to the details of the Fund which was forthwith furnished by the Honorary Treasurer, as follows:

Credit Account with the Bank of England in the name of the London Mosque Fund £284-15-3

Securities registered with the Bank of England in the names of the Rt Hon Lord Lamington and the Rt Hon Syed Ameer Ali, purchased for £6,857-11-4

India $3\frac{1}{2}$% Stock	£5,814-1-8
Loan 5% 1927/47	£1,500

4. It was agreed to leave Mr Withers to insert these particulars in the Fund Trust Deed in their proper phraseology and on Lord Ampthill's suggestion it was also agreed to request Mr Withers when he had prepared the fresh engrossment for execution, to send it round himself either by hand or through the post, to the various Trustees for execution as he (Mr Withers) would have the proper facilities for doing this expeditiously.

6. [*sic*] Rules for the Executive Committee The Chairman reported that he had received a letter from Lord Ampthill criticising the draft Rules which had been already circulated to the Trustees and the Executive Committee. This letter he had sent to Mr Withers for consideration together with a memorandum containing certain observations and suggestions as regards the amendment of the Rules, particularly nos. 7, 10, 19, and 23. Mr Withers had accordingly amended the Rules which were forthwith read and after discussion Rules 7, 10 and 23 as amended were approved, and Rule 19 was further amended by the meeting to read thus: "The Executive Committee shall have power to delegate the collecting of funds in furtherance of the objects of the Fund to any local committee or committees

[69]Mr Withers of the Trust's solicitors, Messrs. Withers, Bensons, Currie, Williams & Co., 4 Arundel Street, Strand, WC.

subject to any regulations that the Executive Committee may impose".[70]

6. It was unanimously agreed to delete Rule 22.

7. Burial of Indigent Moslems. The Chairman reported that another point had been raised by the Honorary Treasurer in his letter of the 3 November in regard to the burial of Indigent Moslems dying in London – to the grant of £105 made by the London Mosque Fund to the Necropolis Co., for the perpetual upkeep of a piece of ground in the Brookwood Cemetery for the burial of Mohammedans and for which an agreement was held between the Trustees of the London Mosque Fund and the London Necropolis Co. The grant was for keeping the burial ground in proper repair but as far as the actual burial of the Indigent Moslems was concerned, it was resolved at the meeting of the Trustees and the Executive Committee on the 12 May last that it was not in accordance with the purpose of the Trust to devote any portion of the income of the Trust towards the expenses of the burial of Indigent Moslems dying in the neighbourhood of London. The matter was fully discussed and it was resolved that the London Mosque Fund is not in a position to undertake any expense in connection with the burial of Indigent Moslems as it does not come within the Trust for the erection of a mosque.[71]

8. Subject no. 4 on the Agenda, viz. "the consideration of the share of the rent of 19 Sloane Street to be paid by the London Mosque Fund" was postponed.

Confirmed: Ameer Ali Chairman 31 December 1926

[70] The rules referred to are not attached to the Minutes. However, the Memorandum of Association (the document that regulates a company's activities) of the East London Mosque Trust Limited, dated 25 April 1949, is attached as Appendix II.

[71] Shortly afterwards, a fund was started for the provision of the burial of indigent Muslims in accordance with Islamic rites. The Aga Khan, the president of the Indigent Moslem Burial Fund, donated £200 and the chairman, Ameer Ali, 50 guineas (Lord Lamington became chairman in 1931). A.S.M. Anik, the honorary secretary and treasurer, contributed £100. A plot of ground was reserved for burial and Barclays Bank acted as trustees (see *The Times*, 14 April 1925). While the Nizam of Hyderabad contributed £1,000, it was thought that a minimum of £5,000 was necessary to generate sufficient income to provide indigent Muslims with a decent burial and to keep the ground in good order (see *The Times*, 3 April 1928). See below, p. 129, for a copy of the Deed of Declaration of 'The Indigent Moslems Burial Fund' Trust, dated 19 December 1927 and with Ameer Ali and A.S.M. Anik named as Trustees.

A meeting of the Trustees and the Executive Committee of the London Mosque Fund held at 2 Cadogan Place, S.W. on Friday 31 December 1926 at 4.30 pm

Present:

The Rt Hon Ameer Ali (in the chair)
The Rt Hon Lord Lamington G.C.I.E, G.C.M.G
The Rt Hon Lord Ampthill G.C.I.E, G.C.B
Sir Thomas Arnold, C.I.E, LL.D
Abdul Rahman Bey Fikry[72]
Dr Saud S. Mohamedi (as supervisor of the Namaz-gah at 111 Campden Hill Road)

1. The minutes of the last meeting were read and confirmed.

2. Mr Abdul Rahman Bey Fikry was formally introduced as a member of the Executive Committee.

3. A proposal made by the Honorary Treasurer to hire a safe at the Safe Deposit was discussed. Proposed by Lord Ampthill and seconded by Lord Lamington and carried without dissent that the Trust Fund be deposited with Messrs. Withers, the solicitors.

4. The location of the Namaz-gah in 111 Campden Hill Road was discussed. A letter from Mr J. W. Lovegrove* was read in which he stated that the best centre would be near Oxford Circus. The Chairman explained the circumstances under which the London Mosque Fund agreed to pay the rent for the Namaz-gah and supplied the furniture. After some discussion it was proposed by Lord Ampthill and seconded by Lord Lamington that the payment to Messrs. G.H. Watts Ltd. of £300 since 1920 and for the present year in respect of rent for the premises at 111 Campden Hill Road, should be and is hereby sanctioned. The motion was put to the vote and was carried without dissent.

5. Lord Ampthill then proposed and Lord Lamington seconded that the supervisor of the Namaz-gah be requested to look out for a more suitable and convenient place for a Namaz-gah at a rental not exceeding £150 per annum, and to submit a report in respect of

[72] Representative of the Royal Egyptian Legation in London.

any recommendation he may make. After discussion the motion was carried without dissent.

6. Lord Lamington proposed that the question of any change in the amount of the contribution from the London Mosque Fund towards the salary of the clerk-in-charge should be deferred and the Chairman be requested to formulate in consultation with the Honorary Treasurer, definite proposals. The proposal was carried unanimously.

Confirmed: Ampthill (Chairman) 3 November 1927

[Indigent Moslem Burial Fund Trust declaration]

Stamp 10/-

THIS DEED OF DECLARATION OF TRUST is made the nineteenth day of December one thousand nine hundred and twenty-seven [19 December 1927] BETWEEN the right honourable SYED AMEER ALI P.C, C.I.E., LL.D., of 2 Cadogan Place, London SW1 and ABDEALI SHAIKH MAHOMEDALI ANIK of Billiter Buildings Billiter Street London EC3 of the one part and BARCLAYS BANK LIMITED of 54 Lombard Street London (hereinafter referred to as "the Trustee") of the other part

WHEREAS:

1) It is desirable to make provision for the proper burial in accordance with the rites of the Moslem Religion of indigent Moslems dying in the neighbourhood of London and elsewhere in the United Kingdom including the providing of a plot of ground a coffin and the payment of interment and other expenses and to provide for the care and upkeep of the graves of indigent Moslems in the Mahomedan Cemetery at Brookwood reserved and allotted by the London Necropolis and National Mausoleum Company for the exclusive interment of Moslems under the terms of two Agreements dated the twenty-third day of June One thousand nine hundred and fourteen and the tenth day of October One thousand nine hundred and twenty-two respectively.

2) For the purposes aforesaid the Committee hereinafter mentioned of which the said Syed Ameer Ali is the Chairman

and the said Abdeali Shaikh Mahomedali Anik is the Honorary Treasurer and Secretary have raised a fund (to which they have themselves contributed) by public subscription and the contributions to the said fund which include the following sums of money contributed by the following persons that is to say Fifty-five Pounds by the said Right Honourable Syed Ameer Ali One Hundred Pounds by the said Abdeali Shaikh Mahomedali Anik One Thousand Pounds by His Exalted Highness Asaf Jah Nizam ul Mulk G.C.S.I., G.B.E., the Nizam of Hyderabad-Deccan One Hundred Pounds by His Highness Prince Omar Toussound Pacha of Alexandria and One Hundred Pounds by His Highness Sir Sultan Mahomed Shah Aga Khan G.C.V.O., G.C.I.E. together with other donations (after deducting amounts already paid for burials) now amount to the sum of One Thousand Four Hundred and Eighty-Seven Pounds Six Shillings and Nine Pence now standing to the credit of the account of the said Fund at the Head Office of the Trustee.

3) The said Committee have requested the Trustee to act as Trustee of the said Fund which the Trustee has consented to do.

4) It is intended that the said Fund and all other moneys hereafter to be contributed thereto shall be held and administered upon the trusts and subject to the provisions hereinafter declared and contained concerning the same.

NOW THIS DEED WITNESSETH And it is hereby declared as follows:–

Name:

1. THE said Fund and all additions thereto shall be called "the Indigent Moslems Burial Fund" and the same is hereinafter referred to as "the Fund".

Objects:

2. THE objects of the Fund are:

a) To provide for the burial of indigent Moslems dying in the neighbourhood of London.
b) Providing in special circumstances for the burial of indigent Moslems dying elsewhere in the United Kingdom but outside the neighbourhood of London.

c) Providing kerb stones or stone slabs for or erecting monuments on the graves of indigent Moslems in the said Moslem Cemetery at Brookwood or any other Moslem Cemetery that the Committee of Management may at any time and from time to time select and for the care and upkeep of such graves and of the Cemetery in which such graves shall be situate.

3. THE Fund shall be under the control and management of a Committee which shall consist of the Chairman Treasurer and Secretary and three or more ordinary members. The members of the Committee including the Chairman Treasurer and Secretary shall not (subject as hereinafter mentioned) exceed ten in number and shall not be less than three exclusive of the Chairman Treasurer and Secretary. The office of Secretary may be combined with that of Treasurer and the duties of both offices performed by one person.

The first members of the Committee shall be:

The Right Honourable Syed Ameer Ali P.C., C.I.E., LL.D. who shall be the first Chairman.

The Right Honourable Lord Lamington G.C.M.G., G.C.I.E.

Sir Muhammad Rafique Knight Member of the Council of the Secretary of State for India.

M. Abdul Rahman Bey Fikry representing the Egyptian Legation.

Mirza Ahmad Khan Ardeshir representing the Persian Legation.

John C. Nicholson Esquire J.P and

The said Abdeali Shaikh Mahomedali Anik who shall be the first Treasurer and Secretary.

Duration of the office of members of the Committee:

4. A member of the Committee shall hold office until he shall die or resign office or reside out of the United Kingdom for a period of more than twelve consecutive months.

Vacancies in the Committee:

5. THE Committee shall have power from time to time by resolution to fill up a vacancy among the members of the

Committee or to appoint additional members provided that the total number does not exceed ten members.

Appointment of Chairman Treasurer and Secretary:

6. THE Chairman Treasurer and secretary shall be appointed by the Committee from among their number and shall hold office for such period or periods as the Committee shall prescribe and shall be eligible for re-appointment and shall retain office until their successors are appointed. The Committee may by resolution remove any of them from office. A resolution passed by a majority of two-thirds of all the members of the Committee shall be necessary for the appointment or removal of a Chairman Treasurer or Secretary.

Meetings:

7 (i) There shall be at least one meeting of the Committee every year to consider the work of the past year and the duly audited accounts and other business.
(ii) The Secretary on instructions from the Chairman shall and any three or more members of the Committee may at any time call a meeting of the Committee.
(iii) There shall be a quorum when three members of the Committee are present.
(iv) The Chairman if present shall preside at meetings of the Committee and if at any meeting the Chairman is not present the members of the Committee present at the meeting shall appoint one of their number to act as Chairman for that meeting.
(v) At a meeting of the Committee every matter (other than the appointment of a new Chairman Treasurer or Secretary which shall require a resolution of a majority of two-thirds of all the members) shall be determined by a majority of the members of the Committee present at the meeting and voting on the question and in case of equality of votes the Chairman or acting Chairman shall have a second or casting vote. Votes may be given personally or by proxy appointed in writing but only a member of the Committee shall be entitled to act as proxy. The appointment of proxy shall be in such form as the Committee may from time to time prescribe.
(vi) Not less than seven days' notice of every meeting of the Committee shall be sent by post to every member of the Committee having an address in the United Kingdom.

The Treasurer:

8. THE Treasurer shall keep proper books and accounts and a balance sheet shall be drawn up each year to the thirty-first day of December and shall with a list of donations and interments be circulated to such persons as the Committee shall direct.

The Secretary:

9. THE Secretary shall keep minutes of meetings and records of interments and generally deal with all clerical work incident to the administration of the Fund.

All officers to be Honorary:

10. ALL officers i.e. the Chairmen and Treasurers and Secretary and other members of the Committee shall be appointed as honorary officers and shall perform their duties voluntarily but shall be entitled to be reimbursed all out-of-pocket expenses incurred by them in carrying out the work of the Fund.

Donations and Banking Account:

11. ALL legacies donations and subscriptions to the Fund shall be paid to the Treasurer (whose receipt shall be sufficient discharge for the same) and shall be paid by him into the capital account of the Fund. All cheques drawn on the banking or income account shall be signed by the Chairman and the Treasurer or by such other persons as the Committee shall from time to time appoint for that purpose.

The Trustee:

12. THE Trustee shall be the Trustee of the Fund.

Investments:

13. All moneys forming part of the Fund and requiring investment shall be invested by and in the name of the Trustee in any investment for the time being authorised by law for the investment of trust money and the Trustee shall at the request and in accordance with the directions of the Committee change such investments for others of a like nature. Such directions shall be given pursuant to resolutions from time to time passed by the Committee.

Trust of investments:

14. THE Trustee shall hold the investments for the time being forming part of or constituting the Fund and all additions thereto Upon trust to pay and apply and deal with the income thereof in accordance with the direction from time to time to be given to the Trustee by the Committee or of any member or members of the Committee empowered by the Committee. Such directions shall be given pursuant to resolutions from time to time passed by the Committee and the Trustee shall be entitled to act on any resolution on having a copy of the relevant resolutions purporting to be signed by the Chairman and a member of the Committee. Until otherwise directed the Trustee shall retain capital of the Fund that is the payments mentioned in Clause 11 hereof and shall pay the income derived from such investments into the banking account of the Fund.

Remuneration of the Trustee:

15. THE remuneration of the Trustee shall be at the rate of One per centum per annum of the gross annual income derived from the investments for the time being forming part of the Fund and standing in the name of the Trustee but so that the Trustee shall be entitled to a minimum fee of One Guinea per annum.

Urgent matters:

16. ALL matters regarding burial which are urgent may be dealt with by the Secretary in consultation with the Chairman and the Treasurer.

Rules:

17. SUBJECT to the provisions of this Deed the Committee may from time to time make alter and rescind rules for the administration and management of the Fund and the carrying of the objects of the Trust into full effect and in particular (but without limiting or restricting the generality of their powers in this respect) for the conduct of and arrangements for funerals in accordance with the Mahomedan rites and the powers and duties of the Secretary with regard thereto the amount so to be expended in each particular case whether or fixed or varying amounts and the keeping of accounts in relation thereto and the forms to be prescribed for applications for burials at the cost of the Fund.

IN WITNESS whereof the parties hereto of the first part have hereunto set their hands and seals and the Trustee has caused its Common Seal to be hereto affixed the day and year first above written.

SIGNED SEALED AND DELIVERED by the above-named The Right Honourable Syed Ameer Ali P.C., C.I.E., LL.D. in the presence of

(Miss) Ethel P. Holden
42 Chestnut Road Plumstead SE 18, Clerk in Charge.

SIGNED SEALED AND DELIVERED by Abdeali Shaikh Mahomedali Anik in the presence of

Henry Edward Davenport
Sheriff of City of London, Justice of the Peace.

THE COMMON SEAL of Barclays Bank Limited was hereto affixed in the presence of

W.S Gurney Director
Hugh Carroll Assistant Secretary 63492

[*Seal of Barclays Bank Limited*]

A meeting of the Trustees and of the Executive Committee of the London Mosque Fund was held at 3.45 p.m on Thursday 3 November 1927 at 2 Cadogan Place SW1

Present:

The Rt Hon Lord Ampthill (in the Chair)
The Rt Hon Ameer Ali
Mr A.S.M. Anik (Hon Treasurer)

1. The Minutes of the meeting held on the 31 December ~~1927~~ [*added in text:* 1926?] were read and confirmed.

2. In connection with the Minutes Mr Ameer Ali explained that the number of worshippers attending the Namaz-gah had become considerably fewer, and in consequence of the fall in their number it was considered by the Trustees desirable not to pay such heavy rent as was demanded by Messrs G.N. Watts Ltd for 111 Campden Hill Road. Notice was accordingly given to terminate the tenancy on

the 11 November 1927 with the final payment of a half-quarter's rent namely £16-5.

As the promoters of the Woking Muslim Mission desired to continue the tenancy for their own work, the Trustees had agreed to the payment of £60 per annum, payable quarterly, to the Pesh Imam for the maintenance of the Friday prayers on condition that he made proper arrangements for their performance and reported periodically to the Trustees as to the number of worshippers attending the Namaz-gah.

The payments of £16-5 and £15 were duly authorized.

3. A letter from Khwaja Kamal-uddin dated 30 August 1927 was read regarding the proposal put forward by him and Lord Headley for the collection of funds throughout India and other places for the London Mosque Fund, in conjunction with the funds of the Muslim Mission.[73] After a full discussion it was

Resolved:

that a reply be sent to Khwaja Kamal-uddin and Lord Headley to the effect that the Trustees thank them cordially for the offer to co-operate in the collection of funds for the London Mosque, but the Trustees greatly regret that they are precluded by their constitution from contributing to the expenses of the scheme proposed by Khwaja Kamal-uddin and Lord Headley.

Addendum

1. The following Resolution in regard to the furniture at 111 Campden Hill Rd was passed by correspondence:

Resolved:

That the Honorary Treasurer be instructed to write off the item of furniture at 111 Campden Hill Road now standing in the account at £60-14-1, and that the same be made over to the Woking Muslim Mission for the use of the worshippers at the Friday prayers etc.

18.11. 27 Ameer Ali

[73] In April 1927, Ameer Ali issued a fresh appeal to 'Moslem rulers, and the great and wealthy princes and magnates' to subscribe funds to endow 'a fitting place of worship in the capital of the British Empire'. In his view, 'The small mosque in Woking does not serve as the symbol of the dignity of the Moslem faith; it is also not available to Moslem residents in London for the daily prayers enjoined by their faith' (see *The Times*, 26 April 1927).

21. 11. 1927 [*unclear text*]

Confirmed: Ameer Ali 1 March 1928

Copy attached to the minutes:

Hyderabad Deccan

LCC Ameerali 2 Cadogan Place London

Nizam gives five lakhs[74] *to Lord Headley's London Nizamiah Mosque*[75] *will your trust cooperate with him and you now join him as trustees – Aminjung*

Copy reply sent:

8 February 1928

Sir Amin Jung Hyderabad Deccan

Apologise for delay due consultation with other Trustees. We offer respectful thanks to his Exalted Highness for munificent donation five lakhs for London Mosque Fund. Our appeal of 18th May 1927 to His Exalted Highness suggested name Nizamiah for London Mosque. We shall be glad to have Lord Headley as co-trustee we pray that donation be remitted direct to Bank of England to credit of London Mosque Fund

Ameerali

Copy:

Hyderabad Deccan

LCC Right Hon Ameer Ali 2 Cadogan Place London

Select Committee Nizam's council considered your cablegram etc. We propose new Trust with Lord Headley as chairman who has undertaken onerous task of going about personally to collect funds. Other Trustees, yourself, Lords Ampthill and

[74]One lakh = 100,000; thus 100,000 rupees in this context.

[75]The *Nizam* donated the money (£60,000) on the condition, it appears from the telegram, that a Trust, separate from the LMF, should be set up, and the name of the mosque be the Nizamiah Mosque. The Nizamiah Mosque Trust was duly formed and a trust deed was executed and registered in India as well as with the Charity Commissioners in Britain. In 1935 the surviving members were Lord Headley, the Aga Khan, Nawab Mehdi Yar Jung (Political Member of the Nizam's Government), and Dr S.S. Mohamedi (see *The Times*, 10 January 1935).

Lamington from your Trust, and Sir Abbas Ali Baig, Khwaja Kamaluddin from Lord Headley's trust and one Trustee representing Nizam. All three Trusts to co-operate cordially for attaining common object of erecting absolutely non-sectarian Nizamiah Mosque in London. Kindly cable reply – Amin Jung.

Copy reply sent 18 February 1928:

DLT Sir Amin Jung Hyderabad Deccan

Will gladly consider your proposal but request time as Trustees meeting immediate impossible owing to absence on continent principal members – Ameerali

A meeting of the Trustees of the London Mosque Fund was held at 3.45 p.m 2 Cadogan Place SW1 on Thursday 1 March 1928

Present:

The Rt Hon Ameer Ali (in the Chair)
The Rt Hon Lord Ampthill
The Rt Hon Lord Lamington
Sir Mohamed Rafique

1. The minutes of the meeting of the Trustees and Executive Committee held on 3 November 1927 were read and confirmed.

2. Read telegrams from Sir Amin Jung dated Hyderabad 6 February and 12 February 1928 and respective replies thereto dated 8 February and 18 February 1928.

3. Read copy of letter to His Exalted Highness the Nizam dated 18 May 1927 in which the Trustees of the London Mosque Fund suggested name "Nizamiah Mosque" and read also the reply of His Exalted Highness to it.

4. The Question of the reply to Sir Amin Jung's telegram was fully discussed and it was resolved that the following telegram be sent:

"Replying your telegram Trustee"
"London Mosque Fund glad to co-operate and to depute Ameerali and Lords Lamington and Ampthill to represent them on the new Trust His Exalted Highness proposes to form – Ameerali"

5. As Reuter's representative was seeking an interview in order to obtain information regarding the donation of five lakhs of rupees by His Exalted Highness for the Mosque in London, the following statement was drafted and unanimously agreed to:

"The Trustees of the London Mosque Fund have agreed to depute representatives to act with the Trustees for the Fund of five lakhs of rupees donated by His Exalted Highness the Nizam with a view to cordial co-operation for the common object of erecting an absolutely non-sectarian Mosque in London. That has always been the purpose of the London Mosque Fund. The Trustees of the London Mosque Fund have proposed to His Exalted Highness the Nizam that the Mosque should be styled the "Nizamiah Mosque."["]

6. The payment for the present in advance of the London Mosque Fund contribution of £15 (fifteen pounds) per quarter towards the maintenance of the Friday worship at 111 Campden Hill Road was agreed to.

Confirmed: Ampthill (Chairman) 9 October 1928

A meeting of the Trustees and of the Executive Committee of the London Mosque Fund held by kind permission of Lord Ampthill at his office 17 Piccadilly, W, on Friday 9 October 1928 at 5 pm

Present:

The Rt Hon Lord Ampthill (in the Chair)
Sir Mohamed Rafique
Sir Thomas Arnold (Hon Secretary)
Mr A.S.M. Anik (Hon Treasurer)
Mr Mirza Ahmad Khan Ardeshir

1. The minutes of the meeting of the Trustees held on 1 March 1928 were read and confirmed.

2. After discussions as to the future signing of cheques, it was resolved:

In view of the lamented death of the late Right Hon Ameer Ali the resolution of 7 June 1926 be modified as follows, viz: that all cheques and instructions be signed by any one of the following:

The Rt Hon Lord Lamington
The Rt Hon Lord Ampthill
Sir Mohammed Rafique

Being Trustees of the London Mosque Fund, and counter-signed by the Hon Treasurer, Mr A.S.M. Anik.

3. Instructions were given for a letter to be drafted for the bank of England embodying this resolution and sent to Lord Ampthill for his signature.

4. A cheque for £10 being the London Mosque Fund proportions of the rent of 18 Sloane Street for the September quarter was authorised to be drawn.

5. The Hon Treasurer explained that six months' notice had been given to the landlord of 18 Sloane Street by the British Red Crescent Society to vacate the front office of the suite rented by them, and that by arrangement all the future and effects had been moved into the Committee Room at the same address. The question of the London Mosque Fund proportion of the future rent was discussed, and it was resolved

to continue in occupation of the premises at 18 Sloane Street until the expiration of the six month's notice on the same conditions as hitherto, viz: one-third of the rent per annum, payable quarterly as heretofore.

6. Read letter from two English Muslims regarding the conduct of the Friday prayers at 111 Campden Hill Road, and attendance thereat. Following discussion as to the contribution towards the rent of the Namaz-gah of £15 per quarter, it was resolved

to discontinue contributions towards the holding of Friday prayers at 111 Campden Hill Road. And that the resolution passed at the meeting of the Trustees and Executive Committee on the 23 November 1927 be and is hereby cancelled.

The Hon Secretary was instructed to communicate with the Pesh-Imam of the Woking Mosque to this effect, and the Hon Secretary was instructed to make no further payments in respect of the contribution.

7. The Hon Treasurer enquired whether the Trust Deed executed last year had been registered at Somerset House, and the Hon Secretary was instructed to write to the solicitors Messrs Withers Co. about this, and if it had not been so registered to enquire whether such a formality was necessary.

8. As regards a Trustee to take the place of the lamented Rt Hon Ameer Ali, the Hon Secretary was instructed to write to His Highness the Aga Khan for his suggestions as to whom the Trustees might approach to join the Board.

9. The meeting closed at 6.15 pm

Confirmed: Aga Khan 9 January 1931

A meeting of the Trustees and of the Executive Committee of the London Mosque Fund was held on 9 January 1931 at 12.15 pm at the Ritz Hotel, Piccadilly, London, W1

Present:

H H the Aga Khan (Chairman)
The Rt Hon Lord Ampthill
The Rt Hon Lord Lamington
Col Nawab Malik Sir Umar Hayat Khan*[76]
Mr Waris Ameer Ali*
Mr M.K. Atabeki (1st Secretary Persian Legation)
Mr A.S.M. Anik (Hon Treasurer)

1. The Minutes of the last meeting held on 9 October 1928 were read and confirmed.

2. H H the Aga Khan expressed regret at the loss the Fund had sustained by the deaths of Mr Muhammad Rafique, one of the Trustees who had given valuable help, and Sir Thomas Arnold who had been Hon Secretary from the commencement of the Fund, and proposed that a record be made in the Minutes. The proposal was seconded by Lord Ampthill.

3. It was proposed by H H the Aga Khan and seconded by Lord Ampthill that Sir Umar Hayat Khan and Mr Waris Ameer Ali be appointed trustees in place of the late Rt Hon Syed Ameer Ali and the late Sir Muhammad Rafique. The same was unanimously approved and they were duly appointed.

[76] Sir Mahomed Umar Hayat Khan Tiwana.

4. In view of the fact that the Securities were standing in the Name of the sole survivor, Lord Lamington, it was proposed by him and seconded by Mr A.S.M Anik that they be transferred in the joint names of Lord Lamington, Sir Umar Hayat Khan and Mr Waris Ameer Ali, and the forms relative thereto were duly signed and completed.

5. Regarding the future singing of cheques, it was resolved

that in view of the lamented death of the late Sir Muhammad Rafique and the late Rt Hon Syed Ameer Ali, Col Nawab Malik Sir Umar Hayat Khan, Tiwana, K.C.I.E, C.B.B.E, M.V.O, A.D.C, and Mr Waris Ameer Ali, I.C.S, (Retd), be appointed Trustees in their place, therefore the Resolution of the 9 October 1928 be altered as follows, viz:

that all cheques and instructions be signed by any one of the following:

The Rt Hon Lord Ampthill
The Rt Hon Lord Lamington
Sir Umar Hayat Khan
Mr Waris Ameer Ali

Being Trustees of the London Mosque Fund and countersigned by the Hon Treasurer Mr A.S.M. Anik

6. A letter to the Bank of England embodying this Resolution was signed by the Chairman and also by the above mentioned four Trustees and Hon Treasurer.

7. Two specimen cards for the Bank of England were signed by the two new Trustees, Sir Umar Hayat Khan and Mr Waris Ameer Ali and witnessed by the Chairman.

8. The Account to 31 December 1930 was presented by the Hon Treasurer and passed.

9. It was proposed by the Chairman and seconded by Lord Lamington that in view of the fact that the value of the India 3 1/2% securities had considerably depreciated since their purchase before the War the investments be entered at the present value and the difference written off.

10. It was proposed by the Hon Treasurer and seconded by Lord Ampthill that a further £1200 face value India 3 1/2% be purchased.

11. The Report for the year 1930 was read and approved.

12. The [illegible] presented to the late Rt Hon Syed Ameer Ali was brought from the bank. After discussion as to the best means of using

the same it was proposed by H H the Aga Khan and seconded by Lord Ampthill that it be kept for the time being at the bank.

13. It was proposed by the Chairman and seconded by Lord Lamington that the question of utilization of the Fund be held over for a period of six months to give the new Trustees Sir Umar Hayat Khan and Mr Waris Ameer Ali an opportunity of investigating the matter and making proposals.

14. It was proposed by the Chairman and seconded by Lord Lamington that Mr A.S.M Anik combine the office of Hon Secretary with his present office of Hon Treasurer, and he was accordingly appointed Secretary for one year.

15. The meeting closed at 1.20 pm

Confirmed: Lamington 26 Feb 1931

HH the Aga Khan expressed the view that the funds of the London Mosque Fund should on no account be handed over to any other body. This was unanimously agreed to. L. 26 February 1931

A meeting of the Trustees and of the Executive Committee of the London Mosque Fund was held on Thursday 26 February 1931 at 12 noon at Lord Lamington's House, 3, Wilton Place, London S.W.1

Present:

The Rt Hon Lord Lamington (Chairman)
The Rt Hon Lord Ampthill
Col Nawab Malik Sir Umar Hayat Khan
Mr Waris Ameer Ali
Mr R.A Radi (2nd Scy. Egyptian Legation)
Mr A.S.M. Anik (Hon Treasurer)

1. The Minutes of the last meeting held on 9 January were read and confirmed.

2. The account to 31 January 1931 audited by Messrs Feasey, Hull and Hornsby, Chartered Accountants, was presented by the Hon Treasurer and passed for printing.

3. A report of the Fund's activities to date was presented and passed.

4. Letters received from Mr Syed Hashimi[77] dated London 13 August 1931 and Hyderabad 6 January 1931 addressed to the Hon Treasurer Mr A.S.M Anik were carefully considered. It was proposed by Sir Umar Hayat Khan and seconded by Lord Ampthill that the proposals made by Mr Hashimi be accepted and the same was unanimously agreed, viz:

I. The London Mosque Fund is only to provide a suitable small building as a Mosque and Religious School in the East End of London, to be named after the late Rt Hon Syed Ameer Ali.
II. The organisers at Hyderabad will make proper and permanent provision for the appointment of a good instructor and Imam and will also bear all other current expenses of the projected institution.

It was decided to send a letter and cable to Mr Hashimi as per copies attached. Mr Hashimi's original letters are also attached.

5. A telegram was received by the Hon Treasurer from H H the Aga Khan as follows: "Approve letter and cable drafts enclosed in your letter 23 February. Please proceed."

6. It was suggested by Mr A.S.M Anik that for the convenience of the Trustees and members of the Executive Committee, important matters should be circulated by letter and their views expressed in writing, and if absolutely necessary a meeting be called. This was unanimously agreed to.

7. The meeting closed at 1.15 pm.

Confirmed: Lamington 17 April 1931

786[78]

London Mosque Fund Report

The absence of a fitting Mosque in the Metropolis of the British Empire is felt acutely by all Moslems coming to England on business

[77] Syed Hashimi was the Nizam of Hyderabad's representative visiting London on a fact-finding trip.

[78] The number '786' is a numerological value for 'Bismillah ar Rahman ir Rahim'; it is used in this text as a heading. However, some Muslims think that the use of this number is an improper 'innovation' (*bidah* in Arabic) and therefore believe that it should not be used. Opinions remain divided on the issue.

or for pleasure. In order to supply this want the London Mosque Fund was organised in 1910 by H H the Aga Khan, the late Rt Hon Syed Ameer Ali and others. It received the support of many prominent Moslems throughout the Moslem world.

The Tripolitan War[79] which broke out in 1911, the Balkan War of 1912–13[80] and later the World War of 1914–18 interrupted the further prosecution of the Executive Committee's efforts to collect funds. The deaths of the Rt Hon Syed Ameer Ali, whose great wish it was to build a Mosque in London, Sir Muhammad Rafique another Trustee, and also Sir Thomas Arnold who acted as Secretary of the Fund from its commencement have delayed the fulfilment of the object.

With the income from the investments the Executive Committee maintained for Prayers a temporary place of worship for the followers of Islam.[81]

A meeting was held on the 9 January 1931 under the chairmanship of H H the Aga Khan, at which Col Nawab Malik Sir Umar Hayat Khan, Tiwana, and Mr Waris Ameer Ali were appointed Trustees in place of the late Rt Hon Syed Ameer Ali and Sir Muhammad Rafique. There are now five Trustees, viz:

H H the Aga Khan, G.C.S.I, G.C. I.E, G. C.V.O,
The Rt Hon Lord Ampthill, G.C.S.I, G.C.I.E,
The Rt Hon Lord Lamington, G.C.M.G, G.C.I.E,
Col Nawab Malik Sir Umar Hayat Khan, Tiwana, K.C.I.E, C.B.B.E, M.V.O, A.D.C,
Mr Waris Ameer Ali I.C.S (Retd)

It is hoped with the assistance of Moslems in India that the object of the Fund will be fulfilled.

The Accounts have been audited by the Charted Accountants and it will be observed that from the 9 November 1930 to 31 January 1931

[79]The Tripolitan War between the Ottoman Empire and the Kingdom of Italy began on 29 September 1911 and ended on 18 October 1912 with the signing of the Treaty of Lausanne, which awarded Italy control of the north African Ottoman provinces of Tripolitania, Fezzan, and Cyrenaica (present day Libya). See http://www.britannica.com/EBchecked/topic/297469/Italo-Turkish-War (accessed on 9 April 2010).

[80]The Balkan War was fought between the Ottoman Empire and the Balkan League, a coalition of Serbia, Bulgaria, Greece, and Montenegro. The defeated Ottoman state concluded the peace treaty in London on 30 May 1913, which resulted in the loss of almost all of its European territory. See http://www.britannica.com/EBchecked/topic/50300/Balkan-Wars (accessed on 9 April 2010).

[81]Premises had first rented been in 39 Upper Bedford Place and then in 111 Campden Hill Road.

the total donations received are £6069-3-4. This sum with part of the income has been invested in securities inscribed in the Bank of England, costing £7900-12-7. The India 3 ½% Securities which were bought before the War have considerably depreciated in value and the Trustees therefore passed a Resolution to write off the depreciation, £1895-9-3, from the surplus income, which is shown in the Balance Sheet. The total expenditure for holding prayers, etc. from November 1910 to March 1929 was £2362-5-9, which has also been paid out of income, and the donations received remain intact.

Lamington Chairman

A.S.M Anik Treasurer

London 26 February 1931

POST OFFICE TELEGRAPHS

184 Cannes 16309-20-20-1620

ANIK BILLITER BUILDINGS BILLITER STREET LONDON APPROVE LETTER AND CABLE DRAFTS ENCLOSED IN YOUR LETTER 23 FEBRUARY PLEASE PROCEED = AGA KHAN

LONDON MOSQUE FUND EXPENSES

As per Audited Account.

9th Nov 1910 to 31 Dec 1923	£ 1538 –	10 –	10
Less grant for Brookwood Cemetery	£ 105 –	10 –	10
1 Jan 1924 to 31 Dec 1926	£ 575 –	6 –	11
1 Jan 1927 to 31 Dec 1928	£ 340 –	12 –	6
1 Jan 1929 to March 1929	£ 12 –	15 –	6
	£ 2362 –	5 –	9

Registered

26 February 1931

Syed Hashimi Esq
Red Hill
Hyderabad-Deccan

Dear Sir

Your letters dated London 13 August 1930 and Hyderabad 6 January 1931 addressed to me (A.S.M Anik, Treasurer of the London Mosque Fund) have been placed before the Board of Trustees, H H the Aga Khan, the Rt Hon Lord Ampthill, the Rt Hon Lord Lamington, Col. Nawab Malik Sir Umar Hayat Khan, and Mr Waris Ameer Ali. They have carefully considered the contents and agree to the proposals made therein, viz:

1. The London Mosque Fund is only to provide a suitable small building as a Mosque and Religious School in the East End of London, to be named after the late Rt Hon Syed Ameer Ali.
2. The organisers at Hyderabad will make proper and permanent provision for appointment of a good instructor and Imam and will also bear all other current expenses of the projected institution.

On the part of the London Mosque Fund, a representative will occasionally visit the Institution and make such reports as may be necessary and desirable.

Any other assistance in this project will be gladly given except financial support, as our fund is not sufficient to do so.

We should like to know the names of the respective parties and full details of the arrangements made. As you are no doubt aware, in this country the majority of payments are made weekly therefore proper financial arrangements should be made on your side. The salary etc. of the Imam who will be engaged by you will be known to you but the current expenses in London cannot at present be estimated, until a test of about six months or a year's expenditure.

The Trustees of the London Mosque Fund hope that the proposed project will be successful and a permanent establishment.

Yours faithfully
For and on behalf of the LONDON MOSQUE FUND
A.S.M Anik Hon Treas. and Secy.

p.s the following cable has been sent to you today:

LONDON MOSQUE FUND TRUSTEES AGREE TO PROPOSALS IN YOUR LETTERS THIRTEENTH AUGUST SIXTH JANUARY NAMELY LONDON MOSQUE FUND TO PROVIDE SMALL BUILDING AS MOSQUE AND ALL OTHER FINANCIAL ARRANGMENTS INCLUDING IMAM TO BE PROVIDED BY THE ORGANISERS AT HYDERABAD TRUSTEES GLAD TO ASSIST IN EVERY POSSIBLE WAY DETAILED LETTER POSTED TODAY – ANIK.

26 February 1931

51

1 1 0

DLT SYED HASHIMI
REDHILL HYDERABAD-DECCAN

LONDON MOSQUE FUND TRUSTEES AGREE TO PROPOSALS IN YOUR LETTERS THIRTEENTH AUGUST SIXTH JANUARY NAMELY LONDON MOSQUE FUND TO PROVIDE SMALL BUILDING AS MOSQUE AND ALL OTHER FINANCIAL ARRANGMENTS INCLUDING IMAM TO BE PROVIDED BY THE ORGANISERS AT HYDERABAD TRUSTEES GLAD TO ASSIST IN EVERY POSSIBLE WAY DETAILED LETTER POSTED TODAY – ANIK.

c/o Haira Trading Co
66 Mark Lane
London E.C 3

13 August 1930

A.S.M. Anik Esquire:
Billiter Buildings
Billiter Street
E.C 3

My Dear Mr Anik

It is, as you know, the East End parts of London where a number of poor Muslims have permanently settled. They have married English wives and established different trades of their own[82] on something of

[82] For examples of such trades, see Appendix III.

a permanent basis. The number of such families is, so far as I am able to judge, not less that fifty, while there are always scores of Muslim Lhaskars[83] etc. employed by Navigation Companies temporarily staying in the same locality. These are the people who need most to have a Mosque and some provision for the religious instruction of their children who shall other wise inevitably drift towards ~~Christianity or~~[84] irreligion; and as a private Muslim I will on my return to India, try my best to persuade charitable trusts or individuals to interest themselves in the matter. But the first thing that strikes me as not altogether irrelevant in this connection is to approach you with the suggestion whether it will be possible for your London Mosque Committee, who I believe have considerable funds subscribed for building a Mosque in London, in their custody to undertake to establish a Mosque and school in the East End? The project of constructing a grand building[85] may now be left to the Nizamia Mosque Board and your funds might suitably be utilised in satisfying a real religious need of the poor but permanent Muslim Colony of London.

On making enquiries and visiting a number of houses I think it may be quite possible to get a building containing halls for congregation, instruction and other rooms that might bring in a small income to meet the maintenance charges of the Mosque, for a sum not exceeding £3,000. This amount, I imagine, you could easily devote for the purpose and commemorate the great services of the late Syed Amir Ali in the Cause of Islam by naming it the "Amir Ali Mosque", while it should not be difficult to find some Indian endowment or Mosque Trust to cooperate with you by undertaking to send an efficient Imam and Instructor at their own expense, acting in London under your Committee's supervision. The scheme appears to me worthy of your Mosque Fund Committee's consideration, as they, I venture to think,

[83]Usually spelt as 'lascar', this term (which comes from the Persian/Urdu *Lashkar*, meaning military camp or army, and *al-askar*, the Arabic word for a guard or soldier) was used to describe maritime manual workers, primarily from India, employed on British-owned ships on non-European contracts, with unfavourable conditions, and at a fraction of the wages of their British counterparts. Rozina Vizram's study, *Ayahs, Lascars and Princes: the story of Indians in Britain, 1700–1947* (London, 1987), explores the experiences of these migrant seamen in the nineteenth and early twentieth centuries.

[84]It is interesting that this was struck through, along with a few grammatical errors. It would appear that – to the writer of this Minute at that time – 'irreligion' represented a threat, but 'Christianity' *per se* did not.

[85]Even at this stage, the 'Nizamia' mosque was viewed as something grand, while the East London Mosque, on the other hand, was perceived in a totally different light, a 'chapel' as opposed to a 'cathedral'. See Hassan Suhrawardy's comments as chairman of the LMF from the late 1930s, available in correspondence held at the ELM Archives.

would hardly prefer to keep the funds continue to lie idle rather than be serving the religious purpose they were subscribed for.

I shall feel much obliged to you if you could kindly communicate to me the official decision of your Committee as early as convenient to you on the subject.

With best regards
I remain
Yours Sincerely

Syed Hashimi

14 August 1930

Syed Hashimi Esq.
c/o Haira Trading Co.
66 Mark Lane
London E.C 3

Dear Mr Hashimi

I thank you for your letter of the 13 inst. and note the proposal contained therein. The Trustees of the London Mosque Fund are at present out of Town but I have sent copies of your letter to them for their consideration.

With kind regards
Yours Sincerely

A.S.M Anik

The Rt Hon Lord Lamington G.C.M.G, G.C.I.E
Lamington
Lanarkshire

London Mosque Fund

I enclose herewith copy of a letter received from Syed Hashimi and also copy of my reply. This gentleman has been to see me twice and I understand that he has come as a private representative of H.E.H the Nizam to investigate the matter of the proposed Nizamiah Mosque and the conditions of Muslims in London and other places in the United Kingdom and to report to His Exalted Highness.

The proposal contained in Mr Hashimi's letter practically coincided with the one I had in view as mentioned in my letter to your Lordship dated 6 December 1929.

I send a further copy of his letter and my reply as you may wish to send same to Lord Ampthill. If Your Lordship and Lord Ampthill favourably consider the proposal then H. H the Aga Khan will have to be approached, and a meeting of the Executive Committee, which includes representatives of the Persian and Egyptian Legations, called.

I have sent a copy of Mr Hashimi's letter to Sir Umar Hayat Khan who has great sympathy and interest with Muslim affairs. He has agreed to become one of the trustees and his co-operation will be useful.

With kind regards
I remain, My Lord,
Yours Sincerely

A.S.M Anik

Red Hill
Hyderabad (Deccan)
6 Jan 1931

Dear Mr Anik

I am sorry I was too busy to have written to you earlier though I safely arrived in my station toward the end of November. You will be, however, glad to learn that I have already succeeded here in receiving definite promises of support for the proposed establishment of a religious School and Mosque in the East End of London, and we are now only awaiting the safe return of the Hyderabad Delegation before taking any practical steps for the consummation of the project; particularly so, as we expect Sir Mohammed Akbar Hyderi might have a good occasion to study Islamic needs on the spot during his stay in London. In the meantime I shall very much welcome to receive the decision of your Mosque Fund Committee in this regard as promised by you in your letter to me dated 14 August 1930. If you were willing to devote even half of this fund to buy or construct a suitable small building for the afore-said purposes... possibly transferring the rest of the money to the Indigent Burial Fund which you have so philanthropically instituted, we on our part will have only to make proper and permanent provision for the appointment of a good instructor and Imam as well as other current expenses of the projected institution. Any other ways, of your cooperation that you may think fit to suggest we shall only too gladly consider, and I may directly write to your chairman of the Committee if you so advise. But in case we do not hear anything from you up to the end of March we shall naturally conclude you do not propose to take any action in the matter and that we should proceed with our scheme independently.

With best wishes for a happy New Year and kindest regards
I remain Yours Sincerely

Syed Hashimi

[*Letter date-stamped 26 Jan 1931*]

27 January 1931

Syed Hashimi Esq.
Red Hill
Hyderabad (Deccan)

Dear Mr Hashimi

I have received your letter dated Hyderabad 6 January 1931 and have sent a copy of the same to each of the Trustees of the London Mosque Fund, viz.

H.H the Aga Khan
The Rt Hon Lord Ampthill
The Rt Hon Lord Lamington
Sir Umar Hayat Khan, Tiwana
Mr Waris Ameer Ali

for their consideration, and I will communicate to you further in due course.

With kind regards
Yours Sincerely

Red Hill
Hyderabad (Deccan)
24 March 1931

Dear Mr Anik

I hasten to acknowledge with thanks the receipt of your official letter dated 26 February 1931, containing the decision of the London Mosque Fund Trustees in favour of providing from their own fund "a suitable small building as a mosque and Religious School in the East End of London, to be named after the late Rt Hon Syed Amir Ali".

Owing to some error of the local Post Office the letter was delayed a week in delivery and was received after your later communication of the 2 Instt. Hence the delay in my reply.

I am naturally happy to see my humble suggestion unanimously accepted by your Board of trustees, and though you do not specify the sum of money the Trustees would be willing to devote for the Mosque building, I venture to presume it will not be less than £3,000 as suggested in my first letter of 13 August 1930 to you.

On our part a strong Board of Management for Amir Ali Mosque, London, has already been formed consisting of the following:

1) Nawab Mehdi Yar Jang*
2) Nawab Fakhr Yar Jang*
3) Nawab Zulqadr Jang
4) Nawab Mohammed Yar Jang
5) Mr Marmaduke Pickthall*
6) Mr Syed Hashimi

All of them, with the exception of your humble correspondent happen to be some of the most prominent people in Hyderabad, while Mr Pickthall has kindly consented to act as Hon Secretary to the Board and will henceforward take charge of all correspondence &ct [*sic*] pertaining to the project.

A petition is being submitted to the Hyderabad Government for a grant of £600, estimated sufficient to provisionally cover the current expenses of the proposed Mosque and School for one year; but as soon as the scheme takes practical shape, steps will be taken to found a permanent Endowment Trust in London for the purpose.

Concluding, may I take the opportunity to express feelings of my personal indebtedness to you for kind interest you have throughout shown in regard to my humble proposal and beg to remain,

Very Sincerely Yours
Syed Hashimi

[*handwritten*] to A.S.M Anik Esq. Billiter Buildings, London E.C 3

A special meeting was held on Friday 17 April 1931 at 2.30 pm at the Waldorf Hotel, Aldwych, London W.C 2. The Rt Hon Lord Lamington, G.C.M.G, G.C.I.E presided

Present:

The Rt Hon Lord Lamington (Chairman)
The Rt Hon Lord Ampthill
Sir Umar Hayat Khan, Tiwana
Mr A.S.M. Anik (Hon Treasurer and Secretary)

1. The minutes of the last meeting held on 26 February 1931 were read and confirmed.
2. A letter from Mr Syed Hashimi, Hyderabad, attached herewith was discussed and it was decided to reply to him as per copy attached.
3. The meeting was closed at 3 pm.

Note: Mr Waris Ameer Ali arrived after the close of the meeting. Sir Umar Hayat Khan explained to him the decision of the meeting, to which he agreed. A copy of the minutes has been forwarded to him and to the other Trustees.

Confirmed: Lamington 7 April 1932

Copies sent to The Aga Khan, Lord Lamington, Lord Ampthill, Sir Umar Hayat Khan, Waris Ameer Ali. Also copy of Minutes

Letter registered 23 April 1931

21 April 1931

Syed Hashimi
Red Hill
Hyderabad-Deccan

Dear Mr Hashimi

London Mosque Fund

I thank you for your letter of the 24 March 1931 which I placed before the Board of Trustees at a special meeting held on Friday last 17 April.

We note with pleasure the distinguished names on your Board of Management for the proposed Amir Ali Mosque and Religious School in the East End of London, and that Mr Marmaduke Pickthall who is known to the undersigned and others will act as Secretary. His recent publication of a translation of the Koran[86] is a valuable work and we congratulate him.

We note that you have submitted a petition to the Hyderabad Government for a grant of £600 for a year's current expenses and that as soon as the scheme takes practical shape you will take steps to found a permanent Endowment Trust in London for the purpose.

On our part, as soon as the Grant of £600 is made a building will be rented for the purpose, and when the permanent Endowment Trust is founded in London the London Mosque Fund will allocate the sum of £3000 (three thousand pounds) for the Amir Ali Mosque and Religious School in the East End of London.

Our Board considers that the scheme should be established on a firm footing to ensure its permanence.

We hope to hear shortly what further arrangement you have made.

I remain, Yours Very Sincerely
Hon Treasurer and Secretary

Hyderabad
Deccan
16 June 1931

[*handwritten letter, stamped*: 6 July 1931]

Dear Mr Anik

I am sure you must be anxious to know what is happening here with regard to the Syed Ameer Ali Mosque project. A committee was formed and we put up a petition that part of the interest[87] on the Nizamia Mosque Fund money might be applied to this purpose. After considerable delay we have been told that there is some objection to such an arrangement and that we should apply to the government for a new grant altogether. This we are going to do as soon as our great ones, some of whom are members of the committee and others friendly members of the Government, have returned from the hills.

This is a city of delay. To you who have lived so long in London our inevitable habit of procrastination will seem exasperating, but I

[86] Marmaduke Pickthall's translation of the Qur'an was published in 1930.

[87] At this point in time there seems to have been no religious objection either to the taking of interest (*riba*) or to its use, both of which have been considered by many Muslim jurists to be prohibited under Islamic law.

believe that the intention is to do something, and that something will eventually be done in this case.

With very kind regards, believe me,

Yours Ever

M. Pickthall

9 July 1931

Marmaduke Pickthall Esq
Civil Service House
Hyderabad-Deccan

Dear Mr Pickthall

Mosque and Religious School in the East End of London

I have duly received your letter of the 16 June and have communicated the contents of same to the Trustees of the London Mosque Fund.

I quite understand the cause of the delay in this letter.

I note that you have made a fresh application to the Hyderabad Government for a grant and we shall be pleased to hear in due course what has been done. In our opinion it is advisable to keep this undertaking quite separate from the Nizamiah Mosque Project.

With Kind Regards
Yours Sincerely

Hon Treasurer
London Mosque Fund

24 November 1931

Syed Hashimi Esq
Red Hill
Hyderabad-Deccan

Dear Mr Hashimi

London Mosque Fund

I have before me your letter of the 24 March 1931 to which I replied on 21 April. Since then I have not heard from you.

Regarding the proposed Mosque and Religious school in the East End of London, no arrangements have been made and we are waiting to hear from your side.

The year is nearing its close and I shall have to submit a report to the Trustees. I shall be very pleased to hear from you so that I may place the matter before the Trustees.

I remain
Yours Very Sincerely

Hon Treasurer and Secretary

A.S.M Anik Esq
London E.C 3

Red Hill
Hyderabad Deccan
15 December 1931

My dear Mr Anik

I was glad to hear from you after so many weeks. The East End scheme looked on a fair way to success last April and, as intimated to you at the time, a regular Board was formed with Mr Pickthall as its Secretary to cooperate with your Committee and conduct the proposed Amir Ali Mosque and School at London—when some formalities caused delay and later the second session of the R.T. Conference[88] intervened to bring the matter to a standstill till now. But the Hyderabad Delegation is at last expected back at the end of this month and I presume their final decision with regards to your scheme should soon follow. At any rate it will be possible in a couple of months to inform you of the exact position, I trust; in the meanwhile, you may kindly recommend to your Committee to defer any reconsideration of their last resolution about the scheme till, say the end of February next.

With best wishes for a happy New Year
I remain
Yours Sincerely

[88]Second of the three Round Table Conferences that were held in London between 1930 and 1932 following the report of the Indian Statutory Commission on constitutional reform, and whose main objective was to move India towards Home Rule. The Nizam was represented by his Prime Minister (*Dewan*), Akbar Hydari. See Judith M. Brown, *Modern India: the origins of an Asian Democracy* (New Delhi, 1994).

1 January 1932

WLT SYED HASHIMI
REDHILL HYDERABAD-DECCAN
REGARDING PROPOSED EASTEND MOSQUE RELIGIOUS SCHOOL ANXIOUSLY AWAITING YOUR FINAL REPORT AND DEFINITE ARRANGEMENTS. ANIK

7 January 1932

Syed Hashimi Esq
Red Hill
Hyderabad-Deccan

Dear Syed Hashimi

I thank you for your letter of 15 December received on Monday 4 inst. and note that you will shortly know the exact position regarding the proposed Mosque and Religious School in the East End of London and you wish me to keep the matter pending till the end of February.

As we were rather anxious about the matter as it has been pending a long time and there will shortly be a meeting of the Trustees at which a report should be given, I sent you a cable on 1 January reading:

REGARDING PROPOSED EASTEND MOSQUE RELIGIOUS SCHOOL ANXIOUSLY AWAITING YOUR FINAL REPORT AND DEFINITE ARRANGEMENTS. ANIK

Although you ask in your letter for our Committee to defer any reconsideration till the end of February, I hope you will place my cable before your Committee for consideration as it may help to accelerate the matter.

With kind regards and hoping you are well
I remain
Yours Sincerely

A.S.M Anik

Syed Hashimi Esq
Red Hill
Hyderabad – Deccan
1 March 1932

Dear Syed Hashimi

London Mosque Fund

I sent you a cable on 1 January this year regarding the proposed Mosque and Religious School in the East End of London and just afterwards I received your letter dated 15 December 1931, which I acknowledge by my letter of the 7 January. From your letter of the 15 December it seemed that you would be able to arrange the matter at the end of last month (February). As I have heard nothing further from you I sent you the following cable yesterday:

HOPE DEFINITE ARRANGEMENTS NOW MADE REGARDING PROPOSED EASTEND MOSQUE RELIGIOUS SCHOOL PLEASE REPLY – ANIK

We shall shortly be having our annual General Meeting and this matter will have to be placed before the Trustees and Members, so I am anxious to know the result. I hope you have been successful in all your efforts and shall be pleased to hear from you.

With kind regards
I remain, dear Syed Hashimi
Yours Sincerely

[*A.S.M. Anik*]

13 April 1932

Marmaduke Pickthall Esq
Civil Service House
Hyderabad – Deccan

Dear Mr Pickthall

London Mosque Fund

I have received your letter of 3 March, and the same was placed before a meeting of the Trustees which was called on 7 April. They are all greatly disappointed to see the failure of our joint efforts to establish a Prayer House and Religious School in the East End of London.

You know that Nawab Mehdi Yar Jung paid only a flying visit with Dr Sheldrake* to the East End of London. Seeing the interest shown and the expressed desire to support this scheme, it is a pity that a person of his position changed his mind and did not place the application before H.E.H the Nizam's Government.

We all know the generosity of His Exalted Highness and the application for this small grant would no doubt have resulted in a liberal endowment to establish Allah's house and the teaching of Islam which would have called forth the gratitude of many poor Moslems.

Syed Hashimi visited every condition in the East End and passed several days in careful investigation of the need of poor Moslems and came to the conclusion that ours was the best scheme. You have lived in London and know the condition of the poor in the East End.

Our funds do not allow us to proceed with such a scheme without substantial help, as whatever is done must be done on a permanent basis.

We warmly appreciate your kind promise to continue your efforts to achieve the object and we hope to hear from you soon that you have been successful. On your Board of Management there are other distinguished gentlemen and if one of them will bring this matter to the notice of His Exalted Highness we are sure that his generous disposition will sanction the desired grant and the scheme will eventually be successful.

With Kind Regards
I remain,
Yours Sincerely

[*A.S.M. Anik*]

Hon Treasurer and Secretary
London Mosque Fund

13 April 1932

Syed Hashimi Esq
Redhill
Hyderabad-Deccan

Dear Syed Hashimi

London Mosque Fund

I have read with great regret and disappointment your letter regarding the failure of your efforts, on account of Nawab Mehdi

Yar Jung's refusal to place the application before H.E.H the Nizam's Government. I note that you will continue your efforts to gain ultimate success and we hope to hear further from you.

I have written to Mr Pickthall as per copy enclosed to which I have very little to add.

With very kind regards
I remain, dear Syed Hashimi
Yours Sincerely

[*A.S.M. Anik*]

Villa Jane Andree
Le Cap D'Antibes

11 April 1932

Dr Mr Anik

Thank you for your letter of 24 March which I would have answered sooner, but I have been to the Disarmament Conference at Geneva, where I represent India,[89] and it is only now, during a short holiday, that I am able to deal with my own personal affairs.

I am sorry to hear that you have not been well, and I do hope that now that the winter is over you will soon get better.

It is indeed disappointing to hear that the scheme for a Prayer House and Religious School in the East End of London has not materialised and very discouraging for those who have worked so hard. I regret that I was unable to be present at the meeting on April 7 but I see little likelihood of being in London this year as the Disarmament Conference may continue until mid-summer. I strongly approve of the nomination of Dr Sheldrake to the Committee of the London Mosque Fund. He is a devoted worker and has the welfare of Islam at heart. I am very sorry to hear of the death of Ali Abdulla Bay.

With all good wishes, and I hope most sincerely that you will soon be quite well again.

Yours very truly

Aga Khan

[89]The Aga Khan represented India at the Geneva Disarmament Conference in 1932.

A meeting of the Trustees was held on Thursday 7 April 1932 at the Waldorf Hotel, Aldwych, London W.C. 2 at 3 pm

Present:

The Rt Hon Lord Lamington (Chairman)
The Rt Hon Lord Ampthill
Col Nawab Malik Sir Umar Hayat Khan Tiwana
Mr Waris Ameer Ali
Mr A.S.M Anik (Hon Treasurer and Secretary)

1. The minutes of the last meeting, held on 17 April 1931 were read and confirmed.

2. Accounts: The Accounts to 31 December were presented and passed.

3. Auditors: It was proposed by Mr A.S.M Anik and seconded by Lord Ampthill that Messrs. Feasey Hull and Feasey be appointed auditors for the ensuing year. Agreed.

4. Report: A draft report was read by the Hon Secretary and with some slight amendments the same was adopted.

5. A letter from Mr Pickthall regarding the proposed scheme for a mosque and religious school in the East End of London was read. The Trustees regretted that the Committee of Management in Hyderabad had been unsuccessful in their efforts to obtain a grant from the Hyderabad Government, and a suitable reply to Mr Pickthall was drafted.

The scheme was further discussed and the Chairman, the Rt Hon Lord Lamington, offered to write a personal letter to the Financial Secretary to the Hyderabad Government and the offer was very gratefully accepted.

6. Mr Anik proposed that Mr Khalid Sheldrake be elected a member of the London Mosque Fund Committee. The matter was discussed and as Mr Waris Ameer Ali promised to give every assistance when the necessity should arise, it was decided not to increase the number on the Committee at present.[90]

[90] It is not clear why this decision was made.

7. Mr Anil proposed and Sir Umar Hayat Khan seconded a voted of thanks to the Chairman.

The meeting concluded at 3.45 pm.

Confirmed: Lamington 19 May 1933

[*These minutes were sent to and approved by Lord Lamington, Lord Ampthill and Mr Waris Ameer Ali.*]

Hyderabad-Deccan
22 March 1933

No. 2139
The Rt Hon the Earl of Lamington
3 Wilton Place
London S.W 1

Dear Lord Lamington

With reference to your letter dated 14 June 1932 addressed to His Exalted Highness the Nizam recommending financial help to the London Mosque Fund for the education of the poorer classes of Muslims in London, I am commanded by His Exalted Highness the Nizam to say that while fully sympathising with the objects you have in view, he greatly regrets his Government is unable to offer any pecuniary assistance towards the attainment of those objects owing to the present widespread financial depression[91] and the many demands on our resources within the State itself.

Yours Sincerely

Mahdi Yar Jung
Political Member of H.E.H the Nizam's Government

[91] The worldwide Great Depression, which began in the late 1920s and continued until the mid-1930s.

51 Princess Gate
S.W

15 May 1933

A.S.M Anik Esq
Billiter Buildings
Billiter Street
E.C.3

Dear Mr Anik

London Mosque Fund

I am much obliged to you for your letter of 11 May enclosing the audited accounts up to the 31 December 1932 and the draft report.

I am afraid that I shall not be in London on Friday 19 May and it would anyhow not be worth my while to come up for five minutes business. I hope, therefore, that Lord Lamington and the other Trustees will kindly hold me excused.

I suppose you have heard that another scheme for building not only a Mosque but also a Social Club for Moslems is on foot? The movement seems to be organized by a body called "the National League"[92] which has its office at 16 St James's Street, and the object is that this Club and Mosque should be a Memorial to the late Mary Adelaide Broadhurst[93] who was, I think, President of the National League.[94] As the plan is to have a "group of Moslem buildings in St. James's" it seems to me to be beyond the bounds of possibility that the money will ever be collected and I do not think this rival project need worry us although Miss Farquharson, the present President of the National League, tells me that the Moslem Leaders themselves are enthusiastic about the project.

I think you would do well just to mention this matter at the meetings of the British Red Crescent Society and the London Mosque Fund.

Yours Sincerely

Ampthill

[92] See Introduction, p. 15, n. 62.

[93] BL, IOR, P&J (S)/916, 1934, fo. 243, Lord Willingdon to Sir Samuel Hoare, 20 June 1933.

[94] See Introduction, p. 15, n. 62.

A meeting of the Trustees was held on Friday 19 May 1933 at 83 Carlisle Mansions, Victoria, London S.W 1 at 3.30 pm

Present:

The Rt Hon Lord Lamington (Chairman)
Col Nawab Malik Sir Umar Hayat Khan, Tiwana
Mr Waris Ameer Ali
Mr A.S.M Anik (Hon Treasurer and Secretary)

1. The Minutes of the last meeting held on 7 April 1932 were read, confirmed and signed.
2. The Accounts: The accounts to 31 December 1932 were presented and proposed by Sir Umar Hayat Khan, seconded by Mr Waris Ameer Ali and unanimously passed.
3. Report: A draft report was read and unanimously adopted. Agreed.
4. The ~~Treasurer~~ [*illegible*] It was resolved that the Treasurer is authorised that whenever there is surplus money not required for immediate need to be invested in Trustees Securities. Agreed.
5. Auditors: It was proposed by Mr A.S.M Anik and seconded by Mr Waris Ameer Ali that Messrs. Feasey Hull and Feasey be appointed auditors for the ensuing year. Agreed.
6. A communication from Hyderabad stating that no contribution will be made by the Hyderabad Government for the Prayer House and School in the East End.
7. A letter from Lord Ampthill was read by the Chairman regarding Miss Farquharson's scheme. The Trustees ~~did not consider to associate with the National League.~~ Decided to lay the letters on the table.[95]
8. It was proposed by Sir Umar Hayat Khan and seconded by Mr Waris Ameer Ali that efforts were to be made to secure a Moslem Preacher and Prayer Room in the East End of London.
9. A vote of thanks to the Chairman and to Mrs Ameer was unanimously passed.

Confirmed: Lamington

[95] Handwritten, after the previous words were crossed out.

The Annual General Meeting was held on Tuesday 2 April 1935 at the Waldorf Hotel, Aldwych, London WC2

There were present:

The Rt Hon Lord Lamington, G.C.M G, G. C.I. E, Chairman Trustee
The Rt Hon Lord Ampthill, G.C.I.E, G.C. S. I, Trustee
Mr Waris Ameer Ali, trustee
Gholam Ali Khan Ardalan, 1st Secretary to Iranian Legation
Mr A.S.M Anik, Treasurer and Secretary

1. The Minutes. The Minutes of the last meeting held on 19 May 1933 were read, confirmed and signed.
2. The Accounts. The accounts to 31 December 1931 were presented and passed.
3. Report. A draft report was read and unanimously adopted.
4. Auditors. Messrs. Feasey Hull and Feasey were re-appointed auditors for the ensuring year. Unanimously agreed.
5. Resignation of Sir Umar Hayat Khan as one of the Trustees and a member has been noted with regret.
6. Resolved to invite Sir Abdul Qadir* as a Trustee of the Board.
7. It was proposed by the Rt Hon Lord Ampthill and seconded by Waris Ameer Ali that an expenditure not exceeding £150 shall be incurred from the income of the trust for the purpose of Moslem public worship by congregations in the East End of London. Unanimously agreed.
8. It was proposed by Mr A.S.M Anik and seconded by Mr Ameer Ali that a contribution not exceeding £10 be paid for Ashura Celebration[96] on Sunday 14 April in the East End of London on the understanding that all Moslems participate.[97] This was unanimously agreed.

[96] Ashura is the tenth day of the Muslim month of Muharram. It is the day when the death of Hussain, son of the Caliph Ali (the Prophet Muhammad's son-in-law) is commemorated, in particular by Shias.

[97] 1 This inclusive approach to Ashura is significant, as the East London Mosque today is a Sunni Muslim place of worship.

9. It was suggested by Mr Ameer Ali that the opinion of the brokers to be taken to change investment from India $3^{1}/_{2}$% to any fixed trustee security.
10. A vote of thanks to the Chairman was unanimously agreed.

Confirmed: Lamington 13 May 1936

The auditors having pointed out that the depreciation written off the cost of the India 3 $^{1}/_{2}$% stock in 1931 amounting to £1895-9-3 had been more than recovered by the increase in the market value since that date, it was resolved that such depreciation be now written back on 31 December 1935.

Lamington – Trustee and Chairman
Ameer Ali – Trustee
A.S.M Anik – Treasurer

The Annual General Meeting was held on Wednesday 13 May 1936 at the Waldorf Hotel, Aldwych, London WC2. The Rt Hon Lord Lamington G.C.M G, G. C.A.E presided.

Present:

Lord Lamington Chairman
The Rt Hon Sir Frederick Hugh Sykes*
Khan Bahadur Shaikh Sir Abdul Qadir
Mr Waris Ameer Ali
Mr A.S.M Anik
Monsieur Ardalan the First Secretary of Imperial Iranian Legation

The Minutes The Minutes of the last meeting held on 2 April 1935 were read, confirmed and signed. The Chairman said:

"It is with the deepest regret that we record the death of the Rt Hon Lord Ampthill G.C.I.E, G. C. S.I, who died on 7 July 1935. He was one of the Trustees of the Fund from the commencement in 1910 and gave very valuable assistance and advice."

The Hon Treasurer informed the Committee that a letter of condolence had been sent by him on behalf of the Committee to

Lady Ampthill and was acknowledged by her. This was approved by the Committee.

It was unanimously resolved that Major Gen The Rt Hon Sir Frederick Hugh Sykes, P.C, G.C.S.I, and Khan Bahadur Shaikh Sir Abdul Qadir, member of the Council of the Secretary of State for India be appointed Trustees in the vacancies caused by the death of the Rt Hon Lord Ampthill and by the resignation of Major Gen Sir Umar Hayat Khan who had left for India. This was agreed to and they joined the meeting.

In view of the appointment of the Rt Hon Sir Frederick Hugh Sykes and Khan Bahadur Shaikh Sir Abdul Qadir as Trustees the resolution of 9 January was to be amended as follows:

Viz. that all cheques and instructions to be signed by any one of the following

The Rt Hon Lord Lamington
Mr Waris Ameer Ali
Major General Rt Hon Sir Frederick Hugh Sykes
Khan Bahadur Shaikh Sir Abdul Qadir

being Trustees of the London Mosque Fund and countersigned by the Hon Treasurer Mr A.S.M Anik.

Copy of the above resolution certified by the Chairman Lord Lamington and signed by Mr Waris Ameer Ali and Mr A.S.M Anik to be sent to the bankers The Bank of England.

Specimen signature cards were signed by Sir Frederick Sykes and Sir Abdul Qadir to be sent to the bankers The Bank of England.

The Accounts The audited accounts to 31 December 1935 were presented and passed.

Auditors It was proposed by Sir Abdul Qadir and seconded by Monsieur Abdalarn that Messrs Feasey Hull and Feasey be re-appointed auditors for the ensuing year. This was unanimously agreed.

Report A draft report for the year 1935 was read and unanimously adopted to get same printed and circulated.

It was unanimously agreed that a sum of £10 be paid to Jamait-ul-Muslimin [*sic*][98] for Moulud[99] and a further £5 as per letters of 26 May 1936.

Sir Abdul Qadir was requested to draft a letter to be sent to H.E.H the Nizam on the occasion of his Jubilee for a contribution towards a Mosque in the East End of London and to the employment of a permanent Moulvi to conduct prayers for Moslems in that part of London.

Appointment of a Secretary This matter has been kept in abeyance for further consideration.

A vote of thanks to the Chairman was proposed by Sir Abdul Qadir and seconded by Monsieur Ardalan and heartily passed.

Confirmed: Lamington 26 Feb 1937

[98]The Jamiat-ul-Muslimin (Muslim Association) was established as a charitable society in 1934 with an office in Canton Street in East London. Branches were soon opened in Birmingham, Manchester, Glasgow, and Newcastle. 'The first meeting was held in 222 High St Poplar E.14 on 29th March 1934 [... when] a provisional committee was formed', with I.I. Kazi* as President, Sheikh Rahim Bukhsh as Vice-President, Said Amir as Secretary, and Noor Mohamad Sangha as Treasurer. See ELM Archives, Jamiat-ul-Muslimin (Muslim Association), *Register Karrawai*. Its objectives included the creation of facilities for the observance of Islam, providing help to poor and needy Muslims, promoting 'social intercourse between resident Muslims and visitors' to Britain, and working 'for the moral, intellectual and economic advancement of Muslims throughout the world'. In its First Annual Report, 1934–1935 (ELM Archives), detailing its activities up to 28 February 1935, it noted the Association's efforts 'to bring about co-operation between the Nizamia Mosque and Amir Ali Mosque Trusts to construct a Mosque in a central place in London'. It urged the Nizamia Mosque Trust to dispose of its site near Kensington, since this location was 'far off from the Muslim population in London', and instead to build a mosque 'in the East End of London, the centre of Muslim population and the resort of seamen from abroad'. It established its office at 30 Church Lane, Commercial Road, London, E1. Between 1934 and 1938, its main activities consisted of organizing Friday congregations and the celebration of Muslim festivals in the East End of London. These events were held in rented premises, and the congregations were largely local, although distinguished guests were invited from other parts of London too. From 1938, the Jamiat became politically more vocal, and for the next few decades it actively represented sizeable sections of the East End's Muslim population: see BL, IOR, L/P&J/12/468, fos 71–74. For details of its protest against the writings of H.G. Wells, see the Introduction, pp. 19–21.

[99]Celebration of the birth of the Prophet Muhammad, also known as Milad-i-Nabi.

The Annual General Meeting of the London Mosque Fund was held on Friday 26 February 1937 at the Waldorf Hotel, Aldwych, London WC2. The Rt Hon Lord Lamington G.C.M.G, G.C.I.E Chairman presided. There were present:

The Rt Hon Lord Lamington G.C.M.G, G.C.I.E
Maj Gen The Rt Hon Sir Frederick Hugh Sykes P.C., G.C.S.I, G.C.I.E, G.B.E, K.C.B, C.M G.
Khan Bahadur Shaikh Sir Abdul Qadir
Mr Waris Ameer Ali
Mr A.S.M. Anik

The Minutes. The minutes of the last meeting held on 13 May 1936 were read, confirmed and signed.

Accounts. The audited accounts up to the 31 December 1936 were presented and passed. The resolution was proposed by Sir Abdul Qadir and seconded by Mr Waris Ameer Ali and carried unanimously.

Auditors. It was proposed by Sir Abdul Qadir and seconded by Mr Waris Ameer Ali that Messrs. Feasey Hull and Feasey were to be re-appointed auditors for the ensuring year. This was unanimously agreed.

Loan. It was agreed that a loan of £50 to Indigent Moslems Burial Fund be made from the balance at the Bank of England. Unanimously agreed.

Report. The report of the work of the Fund up to the 31 December 1936 was read and adopted. This was proposed by Sir Abdul Qadir and seconded by Mr Waris Ameer Ali.

The appointment of Sir Firozkhan Noon,*[100] the High Commissioner for India as a Trustee of the Fund was unanimously agreed to, subject to his concurrence.

Transfer of Securities. £7,400 India 3½% 1931 and £3,150 War Loan 1952 was made in the names of the following Trustees:

The Rt Hon Lord Lamington
The Rt Hon Sir Frederick Hugh Sykes, P.C
Khan Bahadur Shaikh Sir Abdul Qadir
Mr Waris Ameer Ali

[100] Malik Sir Firoz Khan Noon.

All the papers regarding this transfer and to inscribe as Book Stock in the Stock Books of Bank of England were signed by the above transferees and witnessed.

H.E.H The Nizam's Silver Jubilee. It was reported by Mr Anik that a cable was sent to H.E.H the Nizam of Hyderabad and Benar congratulating him on his Silver Jubilee and in reply a cable was received from His Exalted Highness reading "Thanks, greatly appreciate contents of your telegram. Nizam"

Vote of thanks to the Chairman was carried unanimously.

Sir Firozkhan Noon subsequently agreed to become a Trustee of the Fund. This has been duly notified to all the other Trustees, and the Bankers, the Bank of England sending his specimen signature for signing cheques and instructions.

Confirmed: Lamington 17 May 1938

The Annual General Meeting of the London Mosque Fund was held on Tuesday 17 May 1938 at India House, Aldwych, London WC2.[101] The Rt Hon Lord Lamington G.C.M.G, G.C.I.E Chairman presided. There were present:

The Rt Hon Lord Lamington G.C.M.G, G.C.I.E
Khan Bahadur Shaikh Sir Abdul Qadir
Mr Waris Ameer Ali
Sir Firozkhan Noon
Mr Arthur Bird* (on behalf of the Treasurer, Mr A.S. M. Anik)

A message of regret for absent was received from Sir F Hugh Sykes and Mr A.S.M. Anik

The Minutes. The minutes of the last meeting held on 26 February 1937 were read, confirmed and signed.

Accounts. The audited accounts up to 31 December were presented and passed. The resolution was proposed by Sir Abdul Qadir and seconded by Mr Waris Ameer Ali and carried unanimously.

[101] This meeting of the LMF was held at the Office of the High Commissioner for India, as were several of its subsequent meetings.

Loan. Mr Bird reported that the loan of £50 made to the Indigent Moslems Burial Fund was being repaid.

East End Prayer House. There was a long discussion regarding the building of a prayer house in the East End of London and it was agreed that the matter should be left to Sir Firoz Khan to make enquiries through his marine superintendent and make a report at a later date.

Sir Abdul Qadir raised the matter regarding the payment of an honorarium to Mr H. Izharul Hasan who was at present leading the Friday prayers in the East End of London.[102]

Sir Abdul Qadir said he had asked Mr Hasan to come along in case the other Trustees wished to interview him. This was agreed to. Mr Hasan was then called in and several questions were put to him regarding his qualifications.

It was proposed by Sir Abdul Qadir and seconded by Mr Waris Ameer Ali that an Honorarium of £1 per week be paid to Mr Hasan for leading Friday prayers etc in the East End of London.

One month's notice to be given by either side to terminate the arrangement. This was agreed to.

Hon Secretary. Lord Lamington said he had approached Ernest Hotson*[103] who had agreed to become Hon Secretary. His appointment was unanimously agreed to.

Assistant Hon Secretary. Sir Abdul Qadir proposed that Mr Arthur Bird be appointed assistant Hon Secretary and that he be paid an honorarium of £ 10 per annum. Seconded by Mr Waris Ameer Ali. His appointment unanimously agreed to, also the proposed honorarium.

Auditors. Proposed by Mr Waris Ameer Ali and seconded by Sir Abdul Qadir that Messrs Feasey Hull and Feasey be re-appointed auditors for the ensuing year. This was unanimously agreed to.

Proposed by Mr Waris Ameer Ali and seconded by Sir Abdul Qadir a vote of thanks to Sir Firoz Khan Noon for his kindness in allowing the

[102] Friday prayers were being organized by the Jamiat-ul-Muslimin, first in the Queen's Hall and then at the King's Hall on Commercial Road. Various other Muslim festivals were also regularly held there. The LMF provided some financial assistance. As we have already seen, the need for more permanent premises had been under discussion for some years. See also ELM Archives, Jamiat-ul-Muslimin papers.

[103] Sir John Ernest Buttery Hotson.

Trustees the use of his room for the meeting. Carried unanimously. A vote of thanks to the Chairman was carried unanimously.

Confirmed: Lamington 9 December 1938

A Meeting of the Trustees of London Mosque was held on Friday 9 December 1938 at 3 Wilton Place London SW. The Chairman the Rt Hon Lord Lamington G.C.M.G, G.C.I.E, Chairman presided. There were present:

The Rt Hon Lord Lamington G.C.M.G, G.C.I.E
Khan Bahadur Shaikh Sir Abdul Qadir
Mr Waris Ameer Ali
Sir Firoz Khan Noon
Sir Ernest Hotson (Hon Secretary)
Mr Arthur Bird (Assistant Hon Secretary)

A message of regret for absence was received from Sir Frederick H. Sykes

The Minutes of the last meeting held on 17 May 1938 were read, confirmed and signed by the Chairman.

Business remaining from the Minutes: Nil.

Purchase of a site for a Mosque. Sir Firoz Khan Noon reported that he and Sir Abdul Qadir had seen two possible sites both of which are now in the market. One, in Adler Street, leading out of Commercial Road, is not built on, so that building would have to be undertaken immediately. Further it is quite close to a Jewish place of worship. The other nos. 446 and 448 Commercial Road, has building which with some alteration would be suitable. The corner site No. 450 is also to let, but not for sale. The price asked for 446 and 448 is about £2,000. Some of the rooms could be converted into bedrooms for the use of sailors and other Moslems visiting London.

Some could be let out as shops. No 450 could also be used, if it were decided to take a lease of it. The purchase of No 446 and 448 was approved in principle and a sub Committee consisting of Sir Abdul Qadir, Mr Waris Ameer Ali and Sir Ernest Hotson was appointed to inspect the site and go fully into all details, and make estimates of expenditure, and if possible to secure an option on the site, and to report to the Committee as soon as possible.

Sir Ernest Hotson as Hon Secretary was asked to convene a meeting or meetings of the sub Committee. Sir Firoz Khan promised to send a surveyor to examine the site.

The Hon Sec was instructed to inform the Jamiat-ul-Muslimin in reply to its letter dated 25 November 1938 that the purchase of a site for a mosque is under consideration.

There was no other business. A vote of thanks to Lord Lamington for his hospitality and for providing was unanimously passed.

Confirmed: Lamington 10 March 1939

Minutes of the Meeting of the London Mosque Trustees at 3 Wilton Place at 11 am on Friday 10 March 1939. Lord Lamington took the chair. There were present:

Rt Hon Lord Lamington
Sir Abdul Qadir
Sir Frederick Sykes
Sir Firoz Khan Noon
Mr Waris Ameer Ali
Sir Edward Hotson (Hon Secretary)
Mr A. Bird (Assistant Hon Secretary)

Minutes. The minutes of the last meeting held on 9 December 1938 were read and approved and signed by the Chairman.

Business arising. The action taken by the sub-committee appointed at the last meeting to enquire further into the suitability of the site in the Commercial Road proposed for the Mosque was reported to the Trustees.

It was decided that the Adler Street site was to be preferred and the same sub-committee (Sir Abdul Qadir, Mr Waris Ameer Ali and Sir Ernest Hotson) was empowered to proceed with negotiation regarding its purchase. Sir Firoz Khan Noon having kindly agreed to interview the surveyor Messrs Cuthbert Lake & Sutton,[104] the Hon Secretary was instructed to write to Sir Firoz Khan Noon stating the points to be considered at the interview, in the first place the charge to be made by the surveyors for work already done and to be done in future,

[104] A London firm of surveyors, estate agents, and auctioneers, originally founded in 1761: see http://www.cuthbertlake.co.uk/ (accessed 10 January 2010).

and if these points are satisfactorily settled, the conditional offer to be made to the vendors of the Adler Street site, the offer not to exceed £3,000, and to depend on the arrangements of suitable conditions regarding the area to be covered by buildings and other matters with the [*illegible*].

Sir Firoz Khan Noon also kindly agreed to take up the question of these conditions with the L.C.C.[105]

The Trustees notice that the sum available for the construction and maintenance of the Mosque is, at present market rate for the securities, much less than £10,000.

They were of the opinion that a further sum of two lakhs of rupees[106] at least would be required and that an appeal to the public in this country and in India would have better chance of success after the purchase of the site.

They therefore postponed the drafting of an appeal, but welcome the proposal of individual Trustees to canvas their friends for support at once.

There being no other business the meeting closed with a vote of thanks to the Chairman for presiding and for his hospitality.

Confirmed: Lamington 8 June 1939

[*The following notes were typed up and attached to the minutes on a separate sheet*]

The Trustees notice that the sum available for the construction and maintenance of the Mosque is, at present market rate for the securities, much less than £10,000.

They were of the opinion that a further sum of two lakhs of rupees at least would be required and that an appeal to the public in this country and in India would have better chance of success after the purchase of the site.

[105] London County Council.

[106] In the late 1930s, a pound Sterling was worth approximately 9.00 Indian Rupees (Rs.). Hence, two lakhs of rupees equalled approximately £25,000 at this time.

A Meeting of the Trustees of The London Mosque Fund held on Thursday 8 June 1939 at India House. The Chairman, the Rt Hon Lord Lamington G.C.M.G, G.C.I.E presided. There were present:

Rt Hon Lord Lamington
Sir Abdul Qadir
Sir Frederick Sykes
Mr Waris Ameer Ali
Sir Edward Hotson (Hon Secretary)
Mr A. Bird (Assistant Hon Secretary)

Minutes. The minutes of the last meeting held on 17 May 1939 were confirmed and signed by the Chairman.

Business arising. None

Accounts. On the proposal of Sir Abdul Qadir, seconded by Sir F. Sykes the accounts for the year 1938 were approved and passed.

Auditors. On the proposal of Mr Waris Ameer Ali seconded by Sir Abdul Qadir the Auditors Messrs Feasey Hull and Feasey were re-appointed for the current year.

Mosque Site. Sir Abdul Qadir reported the action taken by the sub-committee regarding the purchase of a site for the Mosque. An offer was put in for the Adler Street site, but an earlier offer was under the consideration of the vendors, and the site has since been sold. It is understood that the price paid is substantially more than £3,000, the limit fixed by the Trustees.

A third site, in Back Church Lane was inspected by Sir Abdul Qadir and Sir Ernest Hotson, but as its price was expected to be over £5,000 it had to be dismissed from consideration. Although in some respects suitable, it seemed likely to be very noisy.

There remained therefore only the site in Commercial Road. Nos. 446, 448 and 450. All three houses are now available for purchase though vacant possession could only be obtained of one of them at once. The site has again been inspected by Messrs Cuthbert Lake and Sutton, whose report dated 2 June was read to the Trustees.

At the proposal of Sir Abdul Qadir seconded by Sir Frederick Sykes, the same sub-committee namely Sir Abdul Qadir, Mr Waris Ameer Ali and Sir Ernest Hotson was re-appointed to proceed with negotiation for the purchase of this site. They were empowered to make a conditional offer up to £3,000, beginning with £2,500, as suggested by Messrs Cuthbert Lake and Sutton, or £2,750 as might seem best to them, the price demanded by the vendors viz. £3,250.

The offer was to be subject to satisfactory information about the sites on which vacant possession of the two occupied houses could be named, and a further report by Messrs Cuthbert Lake and Sutton as to suitability of the site for the Trustees' purposes and the probable cost of demolition of buildings, and to the consent of the London County Council to the erection of a Mosque on the site, and such other matters as might seem proper to the sub-committee.

It was decided that when Sir Abdul Qadir returns to India his successor as Trustee Sir Hassan Suhrawardy* should, if willing, take his place on the sub-committee.

It was agreed that the account of Messrs Cuthbert Lake and Sutton for £21 for work already done should be paid.

A letter received by the Hon Secretary purporting to come from the Jamiat-ul-Muslimin was read. As it is unsigned, and only has typed signature "Jamiat-ul-Muslimin" it was decided to take no notice of it.[107]

A letter received by the Hon Secretary from Mr J.H. Mougy[108] was read. Mr Mougy asked for help to pay an account received from the City Hotel for the expense of a Tea Party to celebrate the Anniversary of the Birthday of the Prophet, Sir Abdul Qadir mentioned that help had from time to time been given to the Moslems of the East End towards the cost of parties on similar occasions but it was considered that the two cases were not parallel. The Hon Secretary was instructed to inform Mr Mougy that the Trustees regretted that they had no funds available for such functions.

[107]It is not clear why this letter was ignored. It has not been found so the contents are unknown.

[108]Ibrahim Mougy was 'an Egyptian Moslem' (see BL, IOR, P&J (S)/607/33, fo. 207). In 1938, having been resident in Britain for several years, he was hoping to become a naturalized British subject; he married Mary Straker-Wilson on 17 August 1939 (see *The Times*, 19 August 1939). Considered 'well-disposed and honest' by the Foreign Office (BL, IOR, L/P&J/12/468, fo. 213, letter dated 3 February 1938), he was engaged 'in translating the Authentic Traditions of Mahomet into English on behalf of the Al Hazar University of Cairo'. He was reported in *The Times* as the 'organizer of the Islamic Institute of London' and said to be collecting funds in 1938. The 'first public function in the form of Id prayers was held in February 1938 at the Essex Hall at which [. . .] the prince [Seif-ul-Islam Hussein,

Business. Regret was expressed on the impending return to India of Sir Abdul Qadir who has rendered such valuable assistance to the Fund during his stay in London.

According to the Trust Deed his place as Trustee will be taken by his successor as advisor to the Secretary of State for India, to which post Sir Hassan Suhrawardy has been appointed. The Hon Secretary was instructed to make the necessary arrangements for the transfer of securities in consultation with the Hon Treasurer.

It was agreed that the Bank of England be notified of the change and a fresh authority for the signing of cheques supplied to them.

The proceedings then terminated with a vote of thanks to the Chairman.

The Hon Secretary was also instructed to thank the High Commissioner for the loan of the room in which the Trustees met.

Confirmed: Lamington 8 December 1939

Meeting of the Trustees of The London Mosque Fund was held, at the kind invitation of Lord Lamington, at 3 Wilton Place on Friday 8 December 1939 at 10.30 a.m

There were present:

Lord Lamington
Sir Hassan Suhrawardy
Sir Frederick Sykes

to whom Mougy was acting as secretary] of Yemen was present' (*ibid.*, fo. 208). At an Eid-ul-Azha celebration at the Royal Egyptian Club, he spoke of the need for a Muslim centre in London, which his committee was seeking to provide (*The Times*, 31 January 1939). Dr Mougy, who was apparently studying at the University of London in 1937 (see his letter to *The Times*, 14 July 1937), corresponded with the Foreign Office regarding the proposed establishment of an Islamic Centre in London in 1938. He hoped that the British government would support his scheme, by, among other steps, putting at his disposal some suitable premises (BL, IOR, L/P&J/12/468, fos 216–219). However, the Foreign Office 'were not convinced that Mougy was the right person to run it', as he was thought to want to establish it in opposition to the Mosque in Woking, which – in Mougy's view – was controlled by the heterodox Ahmadi sect, but which, according to official reports, 'most Mohammedans have come to regard as a Sunni Mosque'. He was referred to the India Office (see BL, IOR, P&J (S)/513, 1938, fo. 203, letter dated 16 June 1938).

Mr Waris Ameer Ali
Sir Edward Hotson (Secretary)
Mr A. Bird (Assistant Secretary)

An apology for his absence was received from Sir Firoz-Khan Noon.

The Minutes of the previous meeting, held on 8 July 1939[109] were read and confirmed.

On the proposal of Sir Frederick Sykes, seconded by Mr Waris Ameer Ali, Sir Hassan Suhrawardy was appointed as Treasurer.

It was resolved that, owing to the resignation of Sir Abdul Qadir, on account of the expiration of his term of office as Advisor to the Secretary of State for India, his successor, Sir Hassan Suhrawardy, be appointed Trustee in his place, and be authorised to sign cheques and instructions of the London Mosque Fund, and he is hereby appointed and authorised. This resolution shall be signed by the Chairman and sent to the Bankers to take note.

It was further resolved that cheques shall be signed by the Hon Treasurer, Sir Hassan Suhrawardy, and any one of the Trustees (viz. Lord Lamington, H H Aga Khan, Sir Frederick Sykes, Sir Firozkhan Noon, Mr Waris Ameer Ali).

The Trustees expressed their deep regret at the death of Mr A S M Anik, who had served the Fund as Hon Treasurer for many years, and whose absolute honesty of purpose and undeviating efforts to do the best for everybody commanded their warm admiration, and resolved that a letter of condolence be sent to the members of his family. This resolution was passed by the Trustees standing in solemn silence.

The Sub-Committee, consisting of Sir Hassan Suhrawardy, Mr Waris Ameer Ali and Sir Ernest Hotson, was given renewed authority to proceed with arrangements for the purchase of the Commercial Road site, the limit of price being fixed at £3,000 as before. Sir Hassan Suhrawardy explained the action which had been taken since the last meeting, and showed the correspondence between himself and Messrs Cuthbert, Lake & Sutton and the plans prepared by them.

The Trustees expressed their appreciation of the work done for them by Mr A Bird, and learned with much regret that, owing to the probable closing down of the late Mr Anik's business in the near future, Mr Bird's connection with the Fund would be brought to an

[109] This appears to be a mistake as, according to the minutes of the meeting itself, the meeting had taken place on 8 June 1939.

end. They would be glad to make use of Mr Bird's services as long as they might still be available. Sir Hassan Suhrawardy undertook that either he or Sir Firozkhan Noon would take charge of the records when Mr Anik's office was closed and arrange for carrying on the work now done by Mr Bird, until permanent arrangements for both could be made.

The meeting closed with a vote of thanks to the Chairman.

Lamington 19 February 1940

A meeting of the Trustees of the London Mosque Fund was held at 3 Wilton Place at 10.30 am on 19 February 1940. There were present:

The Rt Hon Lord Lamington (in the Chair)
Major-General the Rt Hon Sir Frederick Sykes
Sir Hassan Suhrawardy
Mr Waris Ameer Ali (also representing Sir Firozkhan Noon)
Sir Ernest Hotson was absent for reasons of health

1. The Minutes of the last meeting were read, approved and signed by the Chairman.

2. The progress of the work of the Sub-Committee for the purchase of a site was reported by Sir Hassan Shurawardy. After discussion it was proposed by Sir Frederick Sykes and seconded by Mr Waris Ameer Ali that steps should be taken by Sir Hassan Suhrawardy to purchase the Commercial Road site for a maximum of £3,000 through Messrs Cuthbert, Lake & Sutton, subject to reports by a firm of solicitors approved by the Trustees, that the site is free of encumbrances, etc.

3. Mr Waris Ameer Ali, on his own behalf and on behalf of Sir Firozkhan Noon, commended the work done and the initiative taken by Sir Hassan Suhrawardy in forwarding the project of building a Mosque in the East End, but they thought that with regard to Sir Hassan's resolution, which formed item No 3 of the agenda of the meeting, they considered it advisable to go forward with great caution, and to find out whether a Committee or a Board of Trust were going to be appointed to administer the funds of the Scheme of His Excellency

the Egyptian Ambassador,[110] also to find out what funds there were. A discussion followed.

It was resolved that the project for amalgamating the assets of the fund with those of the Scheme of His Excellency the Egyptian Ambassador be deferred for further consideration, and that the Trustees should enquire from H E the Egyptian Ambassador what are his suggestions in regard to this matter.

4. The question of the appointment of Mr Charles Gordon Ross, M.C as Honorary Treasurer of the Fund was considered. Sir Frederick Sykes stated that the Trustees did not know Mr Ross, and suggested that the proposal of his appointment should be deferred for further investigation. Sir Hassan Suhrawardy pointed out that the name of Mr Ross was suggested to him by Sir Firozkhan Noon, and the firm of solicitors of which he was the senior partner was recommended to the High Commissioner by the Chief Justice of the Punjab, and this matter had been discussed and approved at a meeting of the Sub-Committee held on 18 January. The matter was deferred for consideration at a full meeting of the Trustees.

5. The question of the appointment of a firm of solicitors to act for the Society was raised, and Sir Hassan Suhrawardy said that the firm of Messrs. Cardew-Smith & Ross appeared to be suitable for this work. Sir Frederick Sykes suggested that the opinion of the solicitors to the High Commissioner should be taken, but Sir Hassan Suhrawardy said that as the firm of Messrs Cardew-Smith & Ross had been recommended to the High Commissioner by the Chief Justice

[110] In June 1939, the Egyptian Ambassador met the Conservative politician Lord Lloyd (1879–1941), and discussed with him a proposal for the erection of a mosque in central London. The Egyptians would take the chief share in arranging for its construction and staff, including arranging for teachers of the students to be housed in adjacent hostels. At that point he wished only to secure from the British government a general blessing for the idea, and was hopeful that sufficient funds could be raised from Islamic sources. In February 1940, at a dinner of the Royal Central Asian Society, the Ambassador announced that he had submitted proposals to King Farouk, who had accepted them and had agreed to give the project his patronage; he said that he would ask 'representatives of various Moslem nationalities to meet [...] for the purpose of drawing up a satisfactory scheme'. Lord Zetland, the Secretary of State for India, and Suhrawardy were also present – the former's approval and sympathy was enlisted (see extract from his private letter to Lord Linlithgow, dated 4/9 February 1940, IOR, BL, P&J (S)/713, 1940, fo. 123), and the latter said that he would be glad to assist in co-ordinating the various efforts being made in this regard. See *The Times*, 1 February 1940. Lloyd felt that the assets and funds of the LMF and the Nizamiah Mosque Trust could be merged with those of the Central London Mosque Trust and applied to the purchase and construction of a mosque on a suitable site. He asked for assistance from the government to donate the land. See BL, IOR, P&J (S)/713, 1940, fo. 115, George Lloyd to Marquess Linlithgow, Viceoroy in India, 8 February 1940.

of the Punjab, and all legal work is controlled by the Legal Advisers at the India Office, their opinion, if any, ought to be consulted.

It was resolved that the opinion of legal advisers at the India Office be taken in this matter.

The meeting closed with a vote of thanks to the Chair.

Confirmed: F Sykes 6 January 1941

Resolution

Resolved that His Excellency Dr Hassan Nachat Pasha,*[III] the Egyptian Ambassador, be requested to include in his scheme of building a central Mosque in London, the scheme of building a Mosque in the East End on the following condition:

1) That the cash, investments in Government securities or otherwise and immovable property standing to the credit of the London Mosque Fund Trust, and representing the total assets thereof, be amalgamated with the London Mosque Fund started by His Excellency Dr Hassan Nachat Pasha, the Egyptian Ambassador, and controlled by a Committee of management.

2) That in the London Mosque in the East End a tablet should be placed mentioning the total assets which have been transferred from the London Mosque Trust Fund. In this tablet should also appear the name of the late Rt Hon Syed Ameer Ali, the Life-Chairman and originator of the scheme, together with the names of the present Trustees, the Rt Hon H H the Aga Khan, P.C, G.C.S.I, C.C.I.E, G.C.V.O, LL.D, the Rt Hon Lord Lamington P.R, G.C.M.G, G.C.I.E, Major-Gen the Rt Hon Sir Frederick Sykes, P.C, G.C.I.E, G.B.E, K.C.B, Malik Sir Firozkhan Noon, K.C.I.E, Mr Waris Ameer Ali, I.C.S, (Retd), Al Haj Lt-Col Sir Hassan Suhrawardy, O.B.E, LL.D, D.Sc, and the Secretary, Sir Ernest Hotson, K.C.S.I.

[III] Dr Hassan Nachat Pasha (sometimes Pacha) set up a committee of distinguished Muslims in London in 1940 to prepare plans for the establishment of a mosque in central London. He became its chairman. Sir Firoz Khan Noon (treasurer), Sir Hassan Suhrawardy, Sheikh Hafiz Wahba, Ata Amin Beg (Iraqi Chargé d'Affaires), and Rauf Chadirji Beg (former Iraqi Minister in London) were appointed its members. Funds up to £100,000 were approved by Parliament for this purpose. See *The Times*, 14 November 1940.

3) That the responsibility for:

a) The maintenance and upkeep of the Mosque

b) The provision of muezzins,[112] imams and teachers with suitable accommodation for them

should be undertaken by His Excellency the Egyptian Ambassador, and his Committee.

4) This building scheme should include provision of a suitable place where dead bodies may be taken for performing religious rites before they are taken to the London Necropolis Station preparatory to interment at the Muslim burial ground at Brookwood Cemetery. A suitable hearse with appropriate inscription should also be provided.

The above resolution to be proposed by Sir Hassan Suhrawardy and seconded by Sir Firozkhan Noon.

The reasons in support of the above resolution are as follows:[113]

Minutes of a meeting of the Trustees of the London Mosque Fund held at 11 am on Friday 24 May 1940 at 3 Wilton Place, SW1 by kind invitation of Lord Lamington

Present:

Lord Lamington in the Chair
Mr Waris Ameer Ali
Sir Hassan Suhrawardy
Sir Ernest Hotson (Hon Secretary)

An apology for absence was received from Sir Firozkhan Noon

1. The meeting having been convened for a special purpose, the Minutes of the last meeting were not read.

2. Sir Hassan Suhrawardy having explained the present position as regards the purchase of the Commercial Road site, an authority to him to conclude the purchase, the price stated being £2,800, was signed by the Trustees present, and the Hon Secretary was instructed to obtain the signatures of Sir Frederick Sykes and, if possible, of H H the Aga Khan.

[112] A *muezzin* is mentioned here for the first time in the Minutes. This is the man who gives the call to prayer, usually, but not always, from a minaret.

[113] Not included in the Minutes.

3. The honorarium of £10 to be paid to Mr A Bird from the London Mosque Fund was sanctioned. A testimonial to be given to Mr Bird in recognition of the valuable work he had done for the Mosque Fund, along with the British Red Crescent Society and the Indigent Muslims Burial Fund, was approved and signed by the Trustees present.

4. The secretarial charges since the handing over of charge as Assistant Secretary by Mr A Bird having been met in the first place from Sir Hassan Suhrawardy's pocket, it was agreed to sanction the employment of a paid stenographer at 30/- [shillings] a week, with effect from the 1 January, 1940, the cost being met as one third (10/-) each by the London Mosque Fund and the other two associated Societies. It was decided that after 30 June the employment of the stenographer should be extended quarterly until other arrangement could be made.

5. There being no further business, the meeting closed with a vote of thanks to Lord Lamington.

Confirmed: F. Sykes 6 January 1941

Minutes of the Trustees of the London Mosque Fund held at 11 am on Monday 6 January 1941 at India House, Aldwych, WC2

Present:

The Rt Hon Major-Gen Sir Frederick Sykes (in the Chair)
Malik Sir Firozkhan Noon
Al-Haj Sir Hassan Suhrawardy

Apologies for absence were received from Sir Ernest Hotson and Mr Waris Ameer Ali.

1. The Minutes of the meetings dated 24 May and 19 July 1940 were read and confirmed.

2. The Trustees placed on record their deep sense of appreciation of the devoted services rendered by the late Lord Lamington in maintaining the activities of the London Mosque Fund, and they also recorded their condolences with the bereaved family. It was noted that a letter of condolence had been sent to Lady Lamington on 18

September, jointly by Sir Hassan Suhrawardy and Sir Ernest Hotson and a wreath was also sent on the day of the funeral.

3. It was resolved that the election of a Vice-President in place of the late Lord Lamington be postponed for consideration at a later date.

4. The question of the election of a Chairman of the Executive Committee was considered in the light of paragraph 11 of the Deed of Trust, to which attention had been drawn by the solicitors of the Fund.

Sir Hassan Suhrawardy proposed, and Sir Frederick Sykes seconded that, pending the amalgamation of the Fund with the bigger London Mosque (Jamea) Fund, Sir Firozkhan Noon be appointed Chairman. Sir Firozkhan pointed out certain difficulties in acceding to the proposal, and stated that he had consulted Mr Waris Ameer Ali on the subject and they considered that the election of Sir Hassan Suhrawardy would be most expedient. It was therefore unanimously resolved that Sir Hassan Suhrawardy be elected Chairman of the Executive Committee.

5. Sir Hassan Suhrawardy reported the purchase of properties Nos. 450/448/446 Commercial Road E1, which was completed by our solicitors, Messrs Cardew-Smith & Ross, in December 1940, at a total cost of £2,800 (No. 450 being purchased for £1,050, and Nos. 446/448 for £1,750).[114] This amount is £200 less than the stipulated amount of £3,000 for which Sir Hassan Suhrawardy was authorised to purchase the property (vide resolution dates 20 May 1940).

Legal disbursements in negotiating and purchasing the property amounted to £48.4.- and the cost of postage, telephone calls, etc. amounted to £2.2.- for which a statement has been received from our solicitors, and the amounts paid.

Under the Statutory Scale, Messrs Cardew-Smith & Ross were entitled to a fee of £25.6.8 for their professional services but they have made no charge.

Messrs Cuthbert, Lake & Sutton, surveyors, submitted a bill for £36.5.2 for professional services, which was duly paid.

[114]The purchase of 446 & 448 Commercial Road was completed on 20 December 1940. See ELM Archives, Trust's solicitors to Suhrawardy, 21 December 1940.

It was resolved that the thanks of the Trustees be conveyed to Messrs. Cardew-Smith & Ross for giving their honorary services to the Fund.

6. The Committee considered the following items:

a) Sir Hassan Suhrawardy's proposal to give up renting the dance hall at 85–87 Commercial Road for the holding of prayers and religious observances, and to utilise the newly-bought premises for these purposes.

b) The application made by our solicitors for exemption of rates and taxes in respect of the above properties as it was proposed to use them for religious purposes only.

c) The application of the Jamiat-ul-Muslimin dated 15 November to be allowed to lease one of the buildings, and the draft resolution drawn up by our solicitors giving the terms and conditions under which the property could be leased out.[115]

After discussion, the Committee authorised Sir Hassan Suhrawardy to take necessary steps to obtain exemption for all the properties for the period they lie vacant, over and above the application already made regarding the properties to be used for religious purposes. They also authorised him to take necessary action regarding alterations and repairs to convert the buildings to provide a temporary place of worship and Islamic culture centre.

7. The Committee considered the question as to whether any of the buildings could be utilised in any way for welfare work among Indian seamen for the period of the war. Sir Firozkhan Noon stated that, as he was a Member of the Trust, he could not take any action in the matter as High Commissioner for India. The matter was therefore dropped.

8. Sir Hassan Suhrawardy presented a report regarding the present financial position of the Fund, which was noted by the Committee.

There being no further business, the meeting adjourned with a vote of thanks to the Chairman Sir Frederick Sykes.

Confirmed: Frederick Sykes 20 January 1941, and Suhrawardy 23 July 1941

[115] The Jamiat-ul-Muslimin office was situated at 59 Canton Street, London E14, prior to moving to Commercial Road. For the proposed resolution granting the Jamiat-ul-Muslimin the lease of 450 Commercial Road for purely religious purposes for the consideration of the Trust's solicitors, see ELM Archives, draft enclosed with Suhrawardy's letter to the Trust's solicitors, 13 December 1940.

To Sir Hassan Suhrawardy

Re: Nos. 446, 448 & 450 Commercial Road E. 1

We the undersigned Trustees of the London Mosque Fund hereby authorise and request you as our agents and on our behalf to enter into Contracts to purchase for the above Trust Fund the above premises from the respective owners thereof.

Dated that 29 day of July 1940

Signed: Firozkhan Noon 20/5/40
Lamington 24/5/40
Waris Ameer Ali 24/5/40
F.H. Sykes
Aga Khan [*handwritten – the above signatures being printed*]
——— [*another signature, unclear*]

The original authority, signed by the other Trustees, is in safe custody with the Fund's Solicitors, Messrs, Cardew-Smith & Ross, 27 Ely Place, E1.

Minutes of a Meeting of the Trustees of the London Mosque Fund held on Wednesday 23 July 1941 in Sir Hassan Suhrawardy's room at the India Office, Whitehall SW1

Present:

Al-Hadj Sir Hassan Suhrawardy (in the Chair)
The Rt Hon Sir Frederick Sykes
Malik Sir Firozkhan Noon
Mr Waris Ameer Ali
Sir Ernest Hotson (Hon Secretary)
Colonel Stewart F Newcombe* and Mr Chisholm of Messrs Feasey Hull & Feasey, the Auditors of the Fund, were present as advisors.

1. The Minutes of the last regular meeting held on 6 January 1941 were read and confirmed.

2. The steps taken for the completion of the East London Mosque and the Islamic Culture Centre were reported, and Sir Hassan Suhrawardy, Colonel S.F Newcombe and His Excellency the Egyptian ambassador were appointed to examine the accounts of the expenditure incurred and to pass them for payment.

3. The audited accounts of the London Mosque Fund from 1 January 1940 to 31 March 1941 were presented and approved. A vote of thanks to the Auditors, who are auditing the accounts for only a nominal fee was passed.

4. It was decided that the cost of structural alterations should be met by the London Mosque Fund and that the cash grants approved by the Jamiat-ul-Muslimin, if finally accepted, should be applied towards the furniture and fittings and the expenditure on upkeep.

5. Regarding the appointment of the Jamiat-ul-Muslimin as Agents of the Funds for the arrangement of prayers and other religious observances, Mr Waris Ameer Ali asked if it was competent for the Trustees to delegate their powers. Sir Hassan Suhrawardy stated that the Charity Commissioners had examined the contract which was drawn up by our Solicitors, and have found no objection to it. It was pointed out that the scheme is in accordance with the terms of clause 9 of the Trust Deed.[116] The appointment of the Jamiat was approved.

6. Sir Hassan Suhrawardy reported that it is not intended to repair No. 450 Commercial Road, which was damaged by enemy action;[117] so long as this house is kept vacant and not used, no rates will be payable.

7. Sir Hassan Suhrawardy was asked to fix a date for the formal opening of the Mosque and Culture Centre with Mr Amery* and Lord Moyne,* and it was hoped that an early day could be arranged before the return of Sir Firozkhan Noon to India. It was thought that a Friday would be suitable, and the time should be in the early afternoon. H E the Egyptian Ambassador should be asked to preside.

[116]Clause 9 of the Trust Deed states: 'The Trustees may in carrying out the provisions of this Deed co-operate with any other body state community society or association having objects altogether or in part to those of the Fund'. See ELM Archives, *The London Mosque Fund Declaration of Trust*, 19 November 1926.

[117]These premises were damaged in late December 1940/early January 1941 by German bombing. The Trustees decided to carry out the necessary repairs and alterations required for the provision of suitable accommodation for congregational prayers; however, only the most essential repairs were sanctioned for No. 450, which had been leased out to the Jamiat-ul-Muslimin on a small rent. See ELM Archives, Suhrawardy's memorandum to Firozkhan Noon on the acquisition etc. of the premises, enclosed with his letter, 4 February 1941.

8. It was agreed to invite H E the Egyptian Ambassador and H E the Minister of Saudi Arabia to become Trustees of the Mosque Fund to fill the vacancy caused by the death of Lord Lamington and an existing vacancy. This will bring the number of Trustees to the figure of 7, authorised by the Trust Deed.

9. The constitution of the Working Committee for the London Mosque Fund was authorised to consist of the Chairman, the Hon Treasurer, the Hon Secretaries, the Egyptian Ambassador and a representative of the Jamiat-ul-Muslimin.

10. The correspondence with the British Council[118] was considered, and it was decided to accept with thanks the offer of a capital grant of £100 and a recurring grant of £75 for this year and if possible for subsequent years. It was hoped that the success of the Culture Centre would be such as to justify an increase in the recurring grant. The opening of a "B" account with the Bank of England for the Islamic Culture Centre Fund was approved, and the donors of certain subscriptions already received for this Fund were thanked.

11. The constitution of a Working Committee for the Culture Centre was authorised, the membership to be similar to that of the Working Committee of the London Mosque Fund, with the addition of a representative of the British Council. Sir Hassan Suhrawardy stated that Mr Martin Blake had been nominated for this purpose by the British Council.

12. The budget estimate for 1941–42 was examined and passed. It was decided that the grant from the Mosque Fund to the Culture Centre should be £1 a week, that is £52 instead of £50. Sir Hassan Suhrawardy reported that Miss Evans, who has been assisting him, would be leaving shortly for other work. Miss Evans was thanked for the work she has done, and good wishes for her success in her new career were expressed. The provision for the salary of a clerk was passed. Sir Hassan Suhrawardy stated that he hoped it would be possible, in view of the decrease in the amount of work, to effect some

[118]The British Council provided a grant and also a range of free publications for the Cultural Centre attached to the Mosque (see ELM Archives, British Council to the Secretary of the Cultural Centre of the East London Mosque, 17 March 1942). The India Office was supportive of the British Council's contribution to the running of the Cultural Centre because it was of the view that 'a cultural centre of the kind proposed run on the right lines would be a useful influence among Indians in the East End of London and that assistance from the British Council would give a good deal of satisfaction in Indian Moslem circles'. See BL, IOR, L/P&J/12/468, fo. 197, India Office to the Foreign Office, 4 June 1941.

economy on this head in the new arrangement which he proposed to make.

13. The Treasurer's report was read and approved. It was decided that it should be suitably abbreviated before printing as the combined report of the Mosque Fund and linked Societies because of the cost of printing and paper.

14. His Excellency the Egyptian Ambassador was elected Vice-President of the Board of Trustees, subject to his agreeing to serve. Sir John Woodhead, K.C.S.I, C.I.E,* was elected Hon Treasurer and his consent to give his services to the Fund was welcomed. It was resolved that the Bank of England should be notified of his appointment accordingly, and that the funds should be operated on his signature with that of one of the Trustees. Sir Ernest Hotson and Colonel Stewart F Newcombe, D.S.O. were elected Joint Hon Secretaries. The firm of Messrs Feasey, Hull & Feasey were reappointed as Auditors.

15. On the proposal of Sir Firozkhan Noon, seconded by Mr W. Ameer Ali, a vote of thanks was passed to Colonel Newcombe for the invaluable help he has given in the arrangements for the reconstruction of the Mosque premises.

16. On the proposal of Sir Firozkhan Noon, seconded by Mr W Ameer Ali, a warm vote of thanks was passed to Sir Hassan Suhrawardy for the energy which he has displayed on behalf of the Fund, and for presiding at the meeting.

Signed:

H Suhrawardy

W Ameer Ali approved the Minutes on 23 January 1942

Lieutenant Colonel
Sir Hassan Suhrawardy O.B.E
India Office
SW1
Dear Brother in Islam

3 November 1939

I am glad to enclose IDUL FITR[119] card and I wish to convey to you Jamiat-ul-Muslimin's desire to welcome you at the time of prayer.

Yours faithfully, for and on behalf of Jamiat-ul-Muslimin

Hon Joint Sec.

[119] This feast (I'd, alternative spellings 'Id/Eid) is the celebration that takes place at the end of the Muslim month of fasting, Ramadan.

Lieutenant Colonel
Sir Hassan Suhrawardy O.B.E
India Office
SW1

13 January 1941

Dear Sir[120]

I'd al Adha[121]

I beg to inform you that the Jamiat-ul-Muslimin usually receives from the London Mosque Fund the sum of £5/10/- on the occasion of the I'd al Adha for renting the Hall for prayers.

I shall be obliged if you will kindly forward your cheque for the above sum at your convenience.

Yours faithfully

Hon Secretary.

36 Whitechapel Lane
E1

20 January 1941

Lieutenant Colonel
Sir Hassan Suhrawardy O.B.E
India Office
SW1

Dear Sir

I have the honour to inform you that 10 Muharram-al-Harram falls on 4 February and as usual the Jamiat-ul-Muslimin desires to commemorate the Day of A'Ashura for which your London Mosque Fund sends a cheque for the sum of £15.[122]

[120] It is worth noting that, in the earlier letter, he was addressed as 'brother in Islam'. Now he is referred to as 'Sir', a much more formal and distant form of address.

[121] This is the 'festival of the sacrifice' and marks the conclusion of the Hajj (or annual pilgrimage to the Holy Places of Islam). It marks the end of the rites that take place at Mina and takes place on the tenth day of the Islamic month of Hijja.

[122] Muharram is the first month of the Islamic Hijri calendar. The tenth day of the month (Ashura) is commemorated by Shia Muslims as a day of mourning for the martyrdom of Imam Hussain (the Prophet Muhammad's grandson) and his seventy-two friends and relatives at the Battle of Karbala in 680 CE.

Please send this cheque at your earliest convenience and oblige.

Yours faithfully

Hon Secretary

India Office
Whitehall
SW1

The Hon Secretary
THE JAMIAT-UL-MUSLIMIN
36 Whitechapel Lane
E1

Dear Sir

With regard to my conversation on the telephone with Mr Allahdad Khan and Mr Qureshi regarding the donation for £15 to enable the Jamiat to observe the anniversary of the martyrdom of Syedana Hazrat Imam Hossein on Friday 7 February, I have consulted other members of the London Mosque Fund at present available in London, and other prominent Muslims, and they are of opinion that the Mosque Fund, which at present has become very small on account of the purchase of the properties Nos. 446/448/450 Commercial Road, cost of repairs, payment of taxes, etc. should not be diverted for any other purposes.

I am therefore herewith enclosing a cheque for £2.2s as my own personal contribution, and I am sure that if you approach other members of the Muslim community, they will also show their interest by making subscriptions for this purpose.

Yours faithfully

Sir Hassan Suhrawardy
Hon Treasurer & Trustee
LONDON MOSQUE FUND

India Office
Whitehall
SW1

2 April 1941

Sahibdad Khan, Esq*
JAMIAT-UL-MUSLIMIN
36 Whitechurch Lane
E1

My dear Khan

I wanted to get into touch with you over the telephone to tell you that the less the number of speeches in a function, the better it is. In order to make it representative, it is very good for you to ask Mr Zada*[123] to say a few words and also I shall try to get someone from the Egyptian Embassy to take part.

You should leave me out, both for reasons of my present health, and also as I have excused myself from other places it will not be nice for me to speak here. I am with you, and I am your friend, and I shall be very glad to be present and give all moral support. I trust that you will understand, and accept my suggestions.

Yours sincerely

Hassan Suhrawardy

The first joint meeting of the Sub-Committees of the East London Mosque and Islamic Culture Centre was held in the Committee Room at 446 Commercial Road, E1 on Thursday 14 August 1941

Present:

Sir Hassan Suhrawardy, in the Chair
Col S.F. Newcombe
Mr Said Amir Shah[124]
Mr Ahmaddin Qureshi

Dr A.J. Arberry* attended the meeting of the Islamic Culture Centre by invitation.

Apologies for absence were received from Sir Ernest Hotson, Mr Martin Blake, Mr W.D.H Danby, Mr A. Yusuf Ali, and Mr Mahmood R. Zada.

[123]Mahmood R. Zada.

[124]A secret British intelligence report described Amir Shah as one of the Shah brothers, silk merchants, warehousemen, and film agents from Amritsar, Punjab, who had also run 'somewhat doubtful' Indian boarding houses in London in the early 1930s. In 1940, he began to take considerable interest in cases in which Indian seamen figured and he acted as official court interpreter. While a passionate proponent of India's independence, he was staunchly opposed to Soviet communism. Amir Shah had initially come to notice as representing East End Indians on the Executive Committee of the London Branch of the Indian National Congress, as a supporter of the nationalist V.K. Krishna Menon's India League, and 'generally as an agitator amongst East End Indians [...] It may be said that up to the opening of the Mosque there were indications that the Jamiat was politically inclined [...] Shah has made every possible effort to turn it into a political weapon'. In August 1942, Amir Shah's political activities greatly increased, he taking part in meetings and collecting funds. While denounced as a pro-Fascist and a Black Marketeer by Menon, as a leading member of the Committee of Indian Congressmen in Great Britain he remained bitterly anti-Muslim League and condemned the Pakistan plan as a suicidal policy for Indian Moslems fostered by the enemies of Islam and India. See BL, IOR, L/P&J/12/468, fos 73–77.

1. The appointment of a Managing Committee. This is to consist of Muslim members only: Mr Said Amir Shah, Mr Ahmadddin Qureshi, nominees of the Jamiat-ul-Muslimin: Mr Mahmood R. Zada, Mr Kemal Lebbane* and Sir Hassan Suhrawardy, nominees of the London Mosque Trust, with powers to add to their number.

2. The programme of prayers and religious ceremonies was specified as follows: Prayers five times daily; Juma Prayers; 'Id Prayers; Ramadan Tarawi Prayers;[125] Milad-i-Nabi, Ashura and any other religious meeting.

3. The appointment of Mr Naqibullah Nairullah as resident caretaker was confirmed. His duties were to include the following: (a) to arrange for all Prayers and religious observances as listed above, under the supervision of the Jamiat-ul-Muslimin;[126] (b) to look after the furniture, etc. in each room, of which he will prepare an inventory, sending one copy to the Jamiat-ul-Muslimin, one copy to the Secretary of the London Mosque Fund, and one copy he will keep himself.

4. Mr N. Nairullah was asked to prepare a statement in detail of the cooking apparatus required to be placed in No. 450 in the basement, and then obtain an estimate and forward it to Colonel Newcombe for consideration by the Trustees of the London Mosque Fund.

5. That the Trustees of the London Mosque Fund be approached to sanction an honorarium of £4 per month for the *pesh namaz* of the Mosque. And that Al-Hadj Hafiz Muhammad el-Shami be recommended to them for this appointment.

6. In any matter requiring financial assistance, a joint meeting of the Managing Committee and the Sub-Committee of the London Mosque Fund will be convened. Otherwise the Managing Committee will function independently.

As regards the Islamic Culture Centre, the following resolutions were passed.

[125] 'Tarawi Prayer', also written *Tarawih*, is the special prayer performed only in the month of Ramadan. It takes place every night after the *isha* or nightly regular prayer. In many mosques, one-thirtieth of the Qur'an is recited during this prayer, so that over the month of Ramadan the whole Qur'an is recited. *Tarawi* is not compulsory, but is *Sunnah* – that is, a recommended activity – since it is believed that the Prophet Muhammad performed it himself.

[126] This Minute suggests that the Jamiat-ul-Muslimin were in charge of the service provided by the caretaker.

1. That Mr Mahmood R. Zada and Mr Kemal Lebbane be invited to take on the direction of the Islamic Culture Centre with Dr Arberry, Mr Amir Shah and Mr Ahmaddin Qureshi, representatives of the Jamiat-ul-Muslimin, to be members of a Managing Committee to assist them, with powers to add to their number.

2. Lectures on Islamic Culture (usually in English) would be arranged for monthly or bi-monthly meetings; lectures to be free, and no refreshment arranged for except by the Committee's decision. The subjects and lecturers are to be selected by the Managing Committee.

3. A letter to Sir Hassan Suhrawardy from Mr Ikbal Ali Shah was considered, in which it was proposed that the Centre could:

i) Interpret Islam as a Social Force
ii) Correct misconceptions about Islamic ideals and suggest methods to achieve these objectives.

These aims set forth by Mr Shah were substantially the same as those the Committee had decided to follow, and it was therefore resolved to thank him very much for his interest. As he is now living in Oxford, Dr Arberry was requested to consult him about the subject on which he could be invited by the Committee to lecture.

The other points raised in Mr Ikbal Ali Shah's letter will be considered by the Managing Committee at their next meeting.

4. That Al-Hadj Hafiz Muhammad el-Shami be asked to give one hour's lesson to adults and one hour to children on the religion of Islam on Thursdays (or other agreed day) and £12 per annum was suggested as his honorarium to begin with. A school for Muslim children can be considered after the Islamic Culture Centre is well established.

5. That a quarterly bulletin should be issued, called "The East London Mosque and Islamic Culture Centre News Bulletin" or any other suitable name to be decided upon by the Managing Committee.

6. The offer of "Great Britain & the East" to send a weekly copy of that journal was gratefully accepted.

Colonel Newcombe was requested to arrange with the British Council for the free supply of newspapers, periodicals and books. Dr Arberry was requested to arrange for a free supply of publications in Arabic, Urdu, Persian and other Oriental languages.

7. In any matter requiring financial assistance, a joint meeting of the Managing Committee and the Sub-Committee of the London

Mosque Fund will be convened, otherwise the Managing Committee will function independently.

There being no further business, the meeting closed with a vote of thanks to the Chair

Signed: H Suhrawardy 18 August 1941
Confirmed: A Yusuf Ali 28 November 1941

The London Mosque Fund

At the Meeting of the Trustees held on Wednesday 23 July 1941 at which Sir Hassan Suhrawardy took the Chair, the following was noted in the Minutes :

"Sir Hassan Suhrawardy reported that Miss Evans, who has been assisting him, would be leaving shortly for other work. Miss Evans was thanked for the work she has done, and good wishes for her success in her new career were expressed. The provision for the salary of a clerk was passed. Sir Hassan Suhrawardy stated that he hoped it would be possible, in view of the decrease in the amount of work, to effect some economy on this head in the new arrangement which he proposed to make".

With the establishment of the East London Mosque and Islamic Culture Centre, the correspondence and book-keeping which had been heavy during the last eighteen months, has now decreased considerably, and it is suggested that the honorarium of the new clerk should be fixed at £2 a month, of which £1 should be paid from the British Red Crescent Society, the funds of which have no recurring expenditure, but which will be re-organised and most of the work will be for this Society. The London Mosque Fund and the Indigent Muslims Burial Fund, the work has been reduced to such an extent that 10/- a month would be quite a reasonable honorarium from each of these funds at present. Mrs W Gatcombe, a part-time stenographer-clerk at the India Office, has been temporarily appointed, and Miss Evans has undertaken to show her the work.

It is requested that the Trustees should sign below if they approve of the above resolution.

Signatures:
Hassan Suhrawardy, Firozkhan Noon, Frederick Sykes, Waris Ameer Ali
19 August 1941

The London Mosque Fund

At the Annual General Meeting of the Fund held on Tuesday 17 May, 1938, at which Lord Lamington took the Chair, the following resolution was passed:

"It was proposed by Sir Abdul Qadir and seconded by Mr Waris Ameer Ali that an Honorarium of £1 per week be paid to Mr Hasan for leading Friday prayers etc in the East End of London. One month's notice to be given by either side to terminate the arrangement. This was agreed to".

Following the establishment of the East London Mosque and Islamic Culture Centre, the duties and responsibilities of the *Pesh Namaz*[127] who leads the prayers have increased very much, as instead of arranging only for Friday prayers once a week and 'Id prayers, we have in addition now arranged for prayers five times a day, and also for Tarawi prayers during the whole month of Ramadan.

It is therefore proposed that the honorarium of the *pesh namaz* should be fixed for £4 per month for the duties stated above, and the Jamiat-ul-Muslimin have been asked to persuade the *pesh namaz* – Al-Hadj Hafiz Muhammad el-Shami – not to ask for more at the present time.

At a meeting of the Sub-Committee held on 13 August, 1941, it was resolved that Al-Hadj Hafiz Muhammad el-Shami should be given an honorarium of £1 per month from the Islamic Culture Centre for giving religious instruction, and this would bring his total honorarium up to £5 per month.

It is requested that the Trustees should sign below if they approve of the above Resolution.

Signatures:

Hassan Suhrawardy, Firozkhan Noon, Frederick Sykes, Waris Ameer Ali
19 August 1941

[127] 'Prayer leader' (Persian).

Minutes of a meeting of the Trustees of the London Mosque Fund held at India House on Friday 12 September 1941 at 12 noon

Present:

Sir Frederick Sykes
Sir Firozkhan Noon
W. Ameer Ali

With Sir John Woodhead (Hon Treasurer)
And Sir Ernest Hotson (Hon Secretary)

1. In the absence of the Chairman, Sir Hassan Suhrawardy, Sir Frederick Sykes was asked to take the Chair.

2. The Confirmation of the Minutes of the last regular meeting was postponed until the next meeting, this being a special meeting and time available short.

3. Owing to difficulties arising from slowness of communication and to absence of H H the Aga Khan in Switzerland and Sir H Suhrawardy on leave in India, and the early departure of Sir Firozkhan Noon, who is not likely to be succeeded at once by another Moslem as High Commissioner, it was decided that the number of Trustees should be increased at least temporarily, so as to ensure the presence of a quorum of three at meetings. The usual number of ordinary Trustees is five, to whom the Moslem Advisor to the Secretary of State for India and the High Commissioner for India, when a Moslem, are added ex officio. Of these, Lord Lamington has died and Sir Frederick Sykes desires to resign owing to the pressure of his other duties. The following were therefore elected Trustees, subject to their acceptance of office – Subhi Bey Ozbekhan, Commercial Counsellor, Turkish Embassy; Hussain Said Bey, First Secretary and Counsellor, Egyptian Embassy; A. Yusuf Ali, C.B,E.; Lord Winterton, M.P.*

The Hon Secretary reported that Sir Hassan Suhrawardy had been in correspondence with the first three of these gentlemen before his departure for India, and that there was good reason to believe that they would accept. He himself had been in correspondence with Lord Winterton and hoped for a final and favourable reply within a few days. The Hon Secretary was instructed to write again to Mr Yusuf Ali and to arrange to call personally on Subhi Bey and Hussain Said Bey if their replies were further delayed.

4. The resignation of Sir Frederick Sykes was accepted with much regret and he was warmly thanked for all the assistance he has given the Fund. It was, however, agreed that his resignation should not take effect until a sufficient number of the newly elected Trustees have accepted office to ensure a quorum.

5. The Trustees approved of the sale of India 3½ % stock to the face value of £1515.7.1 which had been arranged by the Chairman through the Bank of England to furnish cash for the payment of charges incurred in the purchase and reconditioning of the Mosque site. The fact that these charges were due and that securities would have to be sold in order to pay them was mentioned at the last meeting of the Trustees, but a formal resolution was not then passed.

6. The Hon Treasurer reported that some other small accounts were still unpaid and he was authorised to pay them, provided that they were not of large amounts and that cash was available.

7. The Hon Treasurer was authorised to pay the Insurance premium on the Mosque premises to the Guardian Assurance Co. Ltd. after Col. Newcombe has examined and approved of the policy. The Hon Treasurer understood that the premium would be 13/6d in the first year and £2.6.6 in subsequent years.

8. The Hon Treasurer and Hon Secretary were instructed to look into the question of war Insurance. It was understood that the premises were subject to compulsory insurance and that the chattels belonging to the Mosque would probably fall under the voluntary insurance scheme. The Hon Treasurer and Hon Secretary were empowered to pay such premia as might be found due.

9. Sir Firozkhan Noon suggested that the Mosque should be named "The Ameer Ali Mosque", the name "East London Mosque" not being sufficiently distinctive. The Trustees regarded this proposal favourably and directed that it should be brought up again at a later meeting after steps had been taken to sound the opinion of the Jamiat-ul-Muslimin and others.

10. There being no other business, the meeting closed with a vote of thanks to the Chair and to Sir Firozkhan Noon for his hospitality and an expression of sincere regret at Sir Firozkhan's departure from London, with good wishes for his happiness and success in his future career.

Approved: 23 January 1942 W. Ameer Ali

The Trustees of the London Mosque Fund

The following gentlemen have accepted office as Trustees of the London Mosque Fund:

The Rt Hon Earl Winterton, M.P
A. Yusuf Ali, Esq, C.B.E
Husain Said Bey Esq (addressed as Monsieur H.M Said), Counsellor, the Royal Egyptian Embassy
Mahmood R. Zada Esq, Counsellor, Saudi Arabian Legation

Bey Ozbekhan, of the Turkish Embassy, who was elected a Trustee at the meeting held on 12 September 1941, having been unable to accept office, an invitation was sent, after consultation with those of the Trustees who were accessible, to Mr Mahmood R. Zada, who has been kind enough to agree to become a Trustee.

At the meeting on 12 September 1941 the resignation of Sir Frederick Sykes was accepted on the condition that it should not take effect until a sufficient number of the newly elected Trustees had consented to serve. That condition has now been fulfilled, and the resignation of Sir Frederick Sykes has therefore come into force. The Trustees have expressed their great regret that his manifold other duties have made it impossible for him to continue to assist the Trust.

There is at present no business requiring the immediate attention of the Trustees, but a meeting will be convened as soon as such business arises.

[*handwritten next to this page*]

Trustees as on 1 November [*writing unclear*] 1941

1. H H the Aga Khan (. . . . . Trustee)
2. Sir Hassan Suhrawardy (. . . . . . the Trust Deed)
3. Waris Ameer Ali (. . . . . dated 9/1/41)
4. Yusuf Ali
5. Lord Winterton (. . . . .)
6. Husain Said Bey, Counsellor, Royal Egyptian Embassy (. . .)
7. Mahmood R Zada, Counsellor, Saudi Arabian Legation (formally . . . .)

448 Commercial Road
22 October 1941

Stepney Green
1948

Dear Mr Ali

Assalam O alaikum.[128] Many thanks for your telegram and the money. We missed you very much yesterday. I am glad to inform you that nearly 500 people were present and the luncheon was provided by His Majesty, King Farouk of Egypt through the Egyptian Ambassador in London.

I am sorry you are away as there are not many people here now and all the work has to be done by few men available. There is such a lot to do in the new place.

I read your telegram to members of the Committee and I herewith send their fraternal greetings on the happy occasion of Bairam and their appreciation of your spirit of Khidmat.[129]

May You be spared many a years [*sic*] to do something for Din[130] al Baraka.[131]

Wasalam[132] and my personal regards to you and your family.

Yours fraternally

Hon Secretary

Proceedings of a Joint Meeting of the Working (Sub) Committee of the East London Mosque and the Islamic Culture Centre held at the India Office on Friday, 28 November 1941

Present:

Mr A Yusuf Ali (in the Chair)
Mr Mahmood R. Zada

[128] This was the first time an Islamic greeting entered correspondence included in the Minutes in this way.
[129] 'service'.
[130] 'religion'.
[131] 'blessing/the blessed' (i.e Islam).
[132] 'and peace' (also written *wa salam*).

Mr Kemal Lebbane
Mr Gray (representing the British Council)
Mr Said Amir Shah
Mr Ahmaddin Qureshi
Sir Ernest Hotson
Colonel Newcombe
Sir John Woodhead

Dr Arberry sent his apologies for being unable to attend.

1. The minutes of the meeting held on 14 August 1941 were confirmed.

2. The following items of expenditure were confirmed:

Item	Date of Cheque	Amount £. s. d
a) Commercial Gas Co.	23 July 1941	– . 11. 3
	22 Nov 1941	5. 14. 5
b) Electric Light Co.	14 Nov 1941	1. 16. 10
c) Telephone Charges	6 Oct 1941	3. 5. 3
	14 Nov 1941	2. 8. 5
d) Charges for water	20 Sept 1941	3. 17. 8
	18 Nov 1941	7. 10. 0
e) Miscellaneous expenses	21 Nov 1941	34. 1. 6
	21 Nov 1941	3. 4. 4 ½
f) Notepaper and dies for the Culture Centre	21 Nov 1941	1. 6. –

3. An estimate of £6.15.- d for the installation of two gas fires in the prayer room and one gas fire in the office of the Jamiat-ul-Muslimin was approved.

4. The Hon Treasurer informed the meeting that the annual expenditure on account of the Mosque would exceed by at least £65 the amount provided in the budget. This was due to a) No provision having been made for the sum of £48 payable to Al Hadj Hafiz Mohammed-el-Shami as *Pesh Namaz* of the Mosque, and, b) the expenditure on heating, lighting etc being nearer £40 than £20, the amount provided for in the budget. After

considerable discussion the following changes in the budget were approved–

i) the provision for religious observances and prayers to be reduced from £56 to £36 by omitting the sum of £15 for the Ramazan[133] and Tarawi prayers and reducing the sum for the Milud-e-Nabi from £20 to £15.

ii) The payment to Al Hadj Hafiz Mohammed-el-Shami to be reduced to £30 a year, the reduction being accompanied by an increase in the payment to this person from the funds of the Culture Centre from £12 to £30. The payment of £30 from the funds of the Mosque should be described as for "the teaching of the Koran" and not for "the leading of the prayers".

Mr Amir Shah informed the meeting that in view of the funds the Jamiat-ul-Muslimin had received for this year's Id-ul-Fitr, they would be in a position to refund the grant of £10.10.-d provided for in the budget for that festival. In order, however, to make it quite clear that this grant would in all probability be required in future years, he proposed that a cheque for the grant should issue this year which would be refunded by the Jamiat-ul-Muslimin. The meeting agreed to this and placed on record their appreciation of the action taken by the Jamiat-ul-Muslimin.

5. The Hon Treasurer mentioned that correspondence in regard to the registration of the buildings as a place of public worship was continuing and it was hoped that the registration would shortly be completed. This would entitle the Trustees to a reduction in the rates and taxes payable on the premises. This relief would however, only operate from the date of sanction and no refund of payments already made would be obtainable.

6. The question of the provision of a loud speaker was discussed. Mr Amir Shah explained that one was necessary on important festivals for on these occasions the number of persons attending the prayer was large and in addition to the prayer room the sheds at the back were used for prayers. The cost of a loud speaker is, however, considerable and it was accordingly decided that further enquiries should be made before expenditure on a loud speaker was incurred. Colonel Newcombe kindly promised to

[133] Alternative spelling of 'Ramadan'.

investigate the matter by getting into touch with experts as to the most economical means of solving the problem.

7. As regards further capital expenditure on the present buildings the Hon treasurer said that funds were not at present available for expenditure on improvements on the present buildings – Securities to the value of £1,500 were sold a few months ago in order to provide for alterations and decorations to the present buildings and when all the bills had been paid the unspent balance of this sum would be small. The question of further capital expenditure on the present buildings had therefore resolved itself. It was agreed that there was no possibility of the present buildings being replaced by new buildings till some time after the war.

8. As regards the expenditure of the grant of £75 by the British Council, Mr Gray (representing the Council) informed the meeting that

(1) the grant could be spent on:

  i) the teaching of English to Moslems
  ii) books and papers other than religious books and papers
  iii) films
  iv) gramophones and records
  v) lectures on subjects other than religious subjects
  vi) a reasonable amount on the remuneration of the person for looking after the reading room and library

(2) the Council would provide free of charge, that is over and above the grant of £75, periodicals and newspapers

(3) the Council might be able to provide lecturers. It was decided that:

  (a) Mr Yusuf Ali and Colonel Newcombe be requested to prepare a list of books and papers to be acquired under (i), (ii) and (2) above.
  (b) A teacher of English should be appointed provided a sufficient number of "scholars" were available. Colonel Newcombe said he was already in touch with the British Council in regard to this matter.
  (c) Mr Mahmood R. Zada and Mr Kemel Lebbane be requested to take in hand the matter of lectures in consultation with the British Council.

9. Some members of the Committee mentioned the need for printed prayer cards. The Committee was, however, informed that the Woking Mosque had printed a large number of these cards and in all probability would be able to supply them, probably free of charge.

10. In connection with the resolution framed at the meeting held on 14 August 1941, in regard to the aims of the Culture Centre the Meeting was of opinion that the main activities of the Centre would be the education and welfare of Moslems in East London. There are no opportunities of the Boy Scout Movement at present since nearly all the children have left London. On the question of the name of the Culture Centre, which some members considered inappropriate, the Committee were of opinion that it would be better to call it simply the "Islamic Centre".

Confirmed: H Suhrawardy 3 July 1942

Minutes of the meetings of the East London Mosque Trustees and Executive Committee held on Friday, 23 January 1942 at 11.30 a.m

Present:

Mr Waris Ameer Ali, C.I.E (in the chair)
Earl Winterton, M.P
Monsieur H.M.Said
Mr Mahmood R. Zada

with

Sir John Woodhead
Colonel S.F Newcombe
Sir Ernest Hotson

and

Mr K Lebbane

The minutes of the meetings of the Trustees held on 23 July and 12 September were read and confirmed.

The assumption of office as a Trustee by Mr A. Yusuf Ali was recorded.

A letter of apology for absence from Mr A. Yusuf Ali was read. In it he expressed a desire to resign his Trusteeship on the ground of ill-health. The Hon Secretary was directed to inform him that the Trustees were most anxious that he should not resign and hoped that his health would enable him to resume his duties very soon.

Lord Winterton and Monsieur Said were welcomed and their assumption of office as Trustees recorded.

On the proposal of Mr Ameer Ali, seconded by Lord Winterton, Mr Mahmood R. Zada was elected a Trustee.

The resignation of Sir Firoz Khan Noon on his return to India was recorded with regret. The resignation of Sir Frederick Sykes, reported at the meeting on 12 September but postponed at the request of the Trustees, was recorded with regret.

It was recorded with regret that their Excellencies the Egyptian Ambassador and the Saudi Arabian Minister had been unable to accept an invitation (vide the meeting of 23 July 1941) to become Trustees.

The Hon Treasurer pointed out that the Trust Deed vested the general administration of the income of the London Mosque Fund in an Executive Committee which, owing to recent changes in the personnel, had almost ceased to exist and had not held meetings for some time. Its place had temporarily been taken by a Working Committee (or Sub-Committee). It was agreed to re-establish the Executive Committee and to instruct it to take over the duties recently performed by the working (Sub) Committee. On the proposal of Lord Winterton, seconded by Monsieur Said, the following gentlemen were appointed to Executive Committee: –

a) Sir Hassan Suhrawardy (Chairman)
   Mr Yusuf Ali (Chairman during Sir Hassan's absence)
   Mr Ameer Ali
   Mr Mahmood Zada (Trustee)
b) Mr K. Lebanne
c) Messrs. Amir Shah and Ahmaddin Qureshi (representing the Jamiat-ul-Muslimin)
d) Dr Arberry
e) A representative of the British Council when business concerning the Council is under consideration.
f) Sir John Woodhead Sir Ernest Hotson and Colonel Newcombe.

The meeting of the Trustees was then suspended and a meeting of the Executive Committee took place.

An invitation to attend had been given to Messrs. Amir Shah and Ahmaddin Qureshi but they regretted that they were unable to be present because the hour coincided with that of Friday prayers at the Mosque.[134]

Sir Ernest Hotson and Colonel Newcombe were appointed Joint Hon Secretaries and Sir John Woodhead was appointed Hon Treasurer.

The Hon Treasurer reported that on 23 July 1941 the Trustees had decided that owing to difficulties of communication due to the war, cheques should be signed by the Hon Treasurer and one Trustee, whereas Rule 17 of the Executive Committee's body of rules required the signatures of the Hon Treasurer and two Trustees. On the proposal of Mr Mahmood R. Zada seconded by Mr Lebbane it was agreed to amend Rule 17 in accordance with the decision of the Trustees.

The Executive Committee was informed that under arrangements made by Sir Hassan Suhrawardy two Managing Committees had been formed to manage the affairs of the Mosque and of the Islamic Centre connected with the Mosque. It was agreed to continue this arrangement and that the Mosque Managing Committee should consist only of Moslems[135] with the assistance of the Hon Secretaries and Hon Treasurer. The following Managing Committees were appointed:

a) Mosque Managing Committee
Sir Hassan Suhrawardy (Chairman)
Mr Yusuf Ali (Acting Chairman during Sir Hassan Suhrawardy's absence)
Mr Mahmood R. Zada
Mr Lebbane
Mr Amir Shah
Mr Ahmaddin Qureshi

b) Islamic Centre Managing Committee
Mr Mahmood R. Zada
Mr Lebbane

[134]It is curious that the meeting was taking place at prayer time, when devout Muslims would not be able to attend. It would seem that the Jamiat-ul-Muslimin adhered to the rituals of Islam more stringently and literally than did the Trustees. This may indicate a degree of friction between the two groups.

[135]This was the first time that non-Muslims had been excluded from a committee, presumably for religious reasons.

Mr Amir Shah
Mr Ahmaddin Qureshi
Dr Arberry
A representative of the British Council
with the Joint Hon Secretaries
and the Hon Treasurer

The meeting of the Trustees was then resumed and on the proposal of Monsieur Said, seconded by Mr Mahmood R. Zada, the amendment of rule 17 which had been passed by the Executive Committee was approved so as to require the signature of cheques by the Hon Treasurer and one Trustee instead of two.

A joint meeting of the Trustees and the Executive Committee was then held.

The Hon Treasurer reported on the financial position (vide statements attached at the end of the minutes) and the following expenditure incurred between 1 April and 31 December 1941 was approved:

LONDON MOSQUE FUND

Wages	£ 51.17.-
Gas, Electricity & Telephone	£ 23.11. 2
Contribution to Islamic Centre	£ 52. - .
Insurance	£ 13. 6
Audit Fee	£ 1. 6. 3
Rates & Taxes	£ 11. 8. 1
Contribution for religious ceremonies	£ 21. - . -
Miscellaneous Expenditure	£ 47.10.7
Furniture and fittings	£ 155.15.5
Repairs and improvements to the property in Commercial Road	£ 1375.14.8

ISLAMIC CENTRE

Wages	£ 17. 5. –
Printing	£ 1. 6. –

The estimates of receipts and expenditure for the year 1941/2 were also approved on the motion of Mr Mahmood R. Zada, seconded by Monsieur Said. In this connection the Hon Treasurer pointed out that accurate estimates of expenditure under several heads could not be made without further experience of the actual cost.

On the proposal of Lord Winterton, seconded by Mr Mahmood R. Zada the transfer of £100 from the Islamic Centre to the Mosque Fund to cover expenditure already incurred by the latter on behalf of the former was approved.

The need for whitewashing the exterior of the premises was mentioned and admitted, but in view of the financial position it was decided to postpone the work for some months.

Mr Ameer Ali proposed and Monsieur Said seconded a vote of thanks to Sir John Woodhead, Col. Newcombe and Sir Ernest Hotson for work they had done on behalf of the Mosque, the great economies which had been effected by the personal attention of Col. Newcombe to the alterations and decoration of the Mosque and the premises being specially mentioned.

Col. Newcombe also reported steps which were being taken to provide for the welfare of Moslems in London and other cities in this country.

The proceedings then terminated with votes of thanks to Mr Ameer Ali for presiding and for his many labours on behalf of Moslem welfare and to Sir John Woodhead for having arranged for the meeting to take place in the India Office.

Confirmed: Suhrawardy [? *writing unclear*] 15 June 1942

Approved at the meeting of the Trustees and Executive Committee held on 23 January 1942

ISLAMIC CENTRE

	£	s	d
British Council	75	-	-
Sir Hassan Suhrawardy	15	-	-
Mr Yusuf Ali	15	-	-
Messrs Shah Bros	25	-	-
Contribution from London Mosque Fund	52	-	-
Amount collected up to 1928 for the library and lecture room fund	22.	10.	1
BALANCE	204.	10.	1

	£	s	d
Telephone, Electricity and Gas	11.	-	-
Water Rate	5.	-	-
Al Hadj Hafiz Mohammed-el-Shami for giving religious instruction	30.	-	-
Caretaker	44.	4.	-
Library and Reading Room expenses	100.	-	-
BALANCE	204.	10	1

[*handwritten at the top*]: The Treasurer's Report as placed before the Meeting of the Trustees and Executive Committee held on 23 January 1942

1. On 31 December 1941 the cash balances were—

(i) London Mosque Fund	£402.	19.	6
(ii) Islamic centre	£300.	19.	6

2. 3 ½% India Stock to face value of £1515.7.1d held by the Trustees of the London Mosque Fund was sold in August 1941 in order to wipe out a debit balance of nearly £400 and to provide funds for meeting the balance of the cost of repairs and improvements to the property in Commercial Road.

   The repairs have been completed and final bills paid.

3. The balance at the credit of the Islamic Centre includes £100 which was received as a grant from the British Council towards the non-recurring expenditure on the Reading Room and Library. The expenditure actually incurred has exceeded £100 and the British Council has agreed that the items included within the actual expenditure are correctly debitable against the grant. No part of this expenditure has been debited to the Islamic Centre Fund but has been met entirely out of the London Mosque Fund. It is now proposed to transfer £100 from the Islamic Centre Fund to the London Mosque Fund.

4. Statements are attached showing:

   i) the estimated annual receipts and expenditure of the London Mosque Fund

ii) the estimated receipts and expenditure in 1941/42 of the Islamic Centre

i) The estimated yearly receipts and expenditure of the London Mosque Fund:

The Expenditure side is incomplete because it does not include expenditure of a) rates and taxes, excluding Water Rate, and b) miscellaneous expenditure. It is hoped that the property will be exempted very largely, if not entirely, from rates and taxes (other than the Water Rate) but until the decision of the taxing authorities is known it is impossible to forecast the expenditure under this head.
As regards miscellaneous expenditure, it is impossible to forecast the amount – it will probably be considerable. Everything points to a considerable excess of expenditure over receipts but it is impossible at present to say what this excess will be.

ii) The estimated receipts and expenditure in 1941/2 of the Islamic Centre:

The only expenditure so far incurred against the estimated amount of £100 on the Library and Reading Room is £1.6. -.

The solvency of the Islamic Centre Fund depends upon a renewal of the grant by the British Council and the continuance of donations.

J. A Woodhead
28 January 1942

THE BUILDING OF A MOSQUE IS NOT ONLY THE REALISATION OF THE SAYING OF PROPHET MOHAMMAD BUT ALSO THE FULFILMENT OF THE ORDER OF GOD

Brothers in Islam

It was in 1934 that the JAMIAT-UL-MUSLIMIN was founded in the great Metropolex of London, and under this association has gathered together Muslims and sympathisers from different parts of the world, without distinction of cast, creed or religion, to celebrate such festivals as the Birthday of Prophet Mohammad, A'Ashura, Idan and Friday Prayers.

It has now been found necessary to erect a Mosque for daily prayers, including a reading room, hostel, free bath for the needy and classes for Islamic culture and education.

So far this work has been carried on by the initiative of the members only, it has been found inevitable that funds should be collected from all Muslims and sympathisers for the complete realisation of this noble cause.

Hon Sec Jamiat-ul-Muslimin
59 Canton Street
London E 14

[*Urdu text follows this note*]

National Liberal Club
Whitehall Place
SW 1

Tel: Whitehall 9871

26 January 1942

Dear Mr Khan

I have been away from London and have just got your letter of 12 January on my return.

I enclose the report of my speech, duly corrected. As my health is uncertain, I will not at present accept an engagement for East London.

Salaams to you and brethren.

Yours sincerely,

Yusuf Ali

Approved at the meeting of the Trustees and Executive Committee held on 23 January 1942:

LONDON MOSQUE FUND

Estimated annual receipts and expenditure:

	£	s	d
Interest on Securities in the hands of Trustees:	234.	16.	6
1. Audit Fee	1.	1.	-
2. Clerical assistance	6.	-.	-
3. Caretaker	52.	-.	-
4. Religious Observances and Prayers			
Id-ul-Fitr £10.10			
Id-ul-Adha £10.10			
Milud-e-Nabi £15.-	36.	-.	-
5. Al Hadj Hafiz Mohammed-el-Shami			
(teacher of the Koran)	30.	-.	-
6. Annual grant to Islamic Centre	52.	-.	-
7. Telephone, Electricity and Gas	23.	-.	-
8. Water Rate			
(the annual Rate is £15 of which two-thirds			
is debited to the Mosque)	10.	-.	-
Total:	210.	1.	-

Telephone – The only guide to the yearly expenditure is the bill for the quarter ending 30 September 1941. i.e £2.8.5d. This points to an expenditure of say £10, two-thirds of which is debited to the Mosque fund and one-third to the Islamic Centre.

Electricity – Here again the only guide is the bill for the second quarter of 1941/42 i.e. £1.16.10. This points to an expenditure of say £8, two-thirds of which is debited to the Mosque and one-third to the Islamic Centre.

Gas – The expenditure is roughly estimated at £16 – two-thirds to the Mosque and one-third to the Islamic Centre.

Minutes of the Meeting of the Trustees of the London Mosque Fund held on 15 June 1942 at the India Office

Present:

Sir Hassan Suhrawardy
Monsieur H.M. Said
Sir M. Azizul Huque*
On the proposal of Sir Hassan Suhrawardy, seconded by Monsieur H.M. Said, it was resolved that Sir M. Azizul Huque be appointed a Trustee.

Minutes of the Meeting of the Trustees of the London Mosque Fund and the members of the Executive Committee held on 15 June 1942 at the India Office

Present:

Sir Hassan Suhrawardy
Monsieur H.M. Said
Sir M. Azizul Huque
Mr Amir Shah
Mr Sahib Dad Khan
Sir John Woodhead, Hon Treasurer
Colonel Newcombe, Joint Hon. Secretary

Apologies for absence were received from Lord Winterton, Mr Waris Ameer Ali, Mr K. Lebanne, Mr Mahmood R. Zeda and Sir Ernest Hotson.

1. The Minutes of the meeting held on 23 January were confirmed.
2. On the proposal of Sir Hassan Suhrawardy, seconded by Mr S.D. Khan it was resolved that Sir Azizul Huque be elected a member of the Executive Committee.
3. On the proposal of Sir Azizul Huque, seconded by Monsieur H.M. Said, it was resolved that sanction be given to the expenditure of £5 incurred on entertaining the Indian Pioneer Corps on the occasion of the opening ceremony at the East London Mosque on 1 August 1941.
4. On the proposal of Sir Azizul Huque, seconded by Monsieur H.M. Said, formal approval was given to the grant of £52 to the Islamic Centre during the year ending the 31 March 1942 and the authority was given for a similar grant during the year ending 31 March 1943.
5. On the proposal of Sir Hassan Suhrawardy, seconded by Sir Azizul Huque, formal approval was given to the division in the proportion of 2 to 1 between the London Mosque Fund

main account and the B (Islamic Centre) account of the total recurring expenditure on:

i) Gas
ii) Electricity
iii) Telephone
iv) Water Rate
v) Rates and Taxes

6. On the proposal of Sir M. Azizul Huque, seconded by Monsieur H.M. Said, it was resolved that the audited accounts for a) the London Mosque Fund (main account) and b) the Islamic Centre (B account) be passed.

7. On the proposal of Sir Hassan Suhrawardy, seconded by M.S. Amir Shah, it was resolved that:

a) the Auditors, Messrs. Feasey, Hull & Feasey, be thanked for their services during the year ending 31 March 1942;

b) Messrs. Feasey, Hull & Feasey be appointed auditors for the year ending 31 March 1943.

8. Sanction was accorded to the payment of the Audit Fee of £1.6.3d for the period ending 31 March 1941.

9. Sanction was accorded to the following expenditure incurred between 1 January 1942 and 31 March 1942 (both dates inclusive):

LONDON MOSQUE FUND (main account)

Wages	£28	-	-
Gas, electricity, & Telephone	£26	9	2
Rates and Taxes	£32	19	10
Miscellaneous Expenditure	£ 2	14	2

ISLAMIC CENTRE (B account)

Wages	£23	12	-

10. It was reported that the position in regard to rates and taxes (other than the water rate) was as follows:–

a) No. 450 Commercial Road has not been assessed because it is unoccupied;

b) The ground floor and basement of Nos. 446 and 448 Commercial Road and the building at the rear of Nos. 446/448 and 448/450 Commercial Road have been exempted as used for religious purposes;

c) The 1st and 2nd floors of Nos. 446 and 448 Commercial Road have been assessed at £80 gross value per year and £60 net annual value

d) The rates at present payable work out at £47.10.- d a year.

11. It was reported that Sir Ernest Hotson had reluctantly felt compelled to resign from the position of Joint Hon. Secretary. It was resolved that Sir Ernest's resignation be accepted with great regret and that the thanks of the Trustees and the Executive Committee be conveyed to Sir Ernest for his services. Colonel Newcombe very kindly agreed to carry on for the time being as sole Hon Secretary.

12. Mr Waris Ameer Ali in his letter regretting that he would be unable to be present at today's meeting had put forward certain suggestions for reducing the expenditure so as to ensure that the receipts and expenditure balanced. It was decided that the consideration of these proposals be postponed till a later meeting at which Mr Waris Ameer Ali would be able to be present.

13. The note by Sir Hassan Suhrawardy[136] in regard to:–

a) the disposal of the balance of the gift of £150 given by His Majesty, King Faruk I of Egypt on the occasion of the Id-ul-Fitr;

b) the copies of the Holy Quran and prayer caps[137] given by the Shaikh of the Al Azhar University,[138] His Eminence, the Shaikh-ul-Maraghi for use at the East London Mosque.

The Trustees and the Members of the Executive Committee desired that Sir Hassan should convey, through the proper channels, their grateful thanks for the very generous gifts of money made by His Majesty, King Faruk and for the copies of the Holy Quran and prayer caps presented to the Mosque by His Eminence, Shaikh-ul-Maraghi.

The Trustees and Members of the Committee concurred in the proposals made by Sir Hassan for the expenditure of the unspent balance of the gift by His Majesty, King Faruk I.

14. A letter was considered which had been received from the Hon Secretary (Mr S. Khan) of the Islamic Council in Great Britain requesting that the Council be permitted to use the

[136] A copy of Sir Hassan Suhrawardy's note was attached as an annexure to these Minutes: see below, pp. 217–218.

[137] Prayer caps, contrary to popular belief, are not worn by all Muslim men during prayers.

[138] Al Azhar Mosque in Cairo, Egypt, is associated with Al Azhar University, one of the oldest Islamic institutions in the world, established around 971 CE.

room in the Trustees' premises in Commercial Road, now used by the Jamiat-ul-Muslimin under licence from the Trustees and as agents of the Trustees. It was resolved that this matter be postponed till a later meeting and that in the meantime the Islamic Council be asked to supply full information about the aims and objects of the Islamic Council in Great Britain, together with the names of its office bearers and affiliated Societies.

15. The proceedings terminated with a note of thanks to the Chair.

Confirmed: A Waris H Suhrawardy 20 August 1942

[*Sir Hassan Suhrawardy's note, as mentioned above*]

To the Trustees, London Mosque Fund

While at Cairo in October 1941, I had an audience with His Majesty, King Faruk I. His Majesty not only discussed details regarding the big Central London Mosque scheme, of which he is the patron, but he also showed much interest in the small East London Mosque, at the opening ceremony of which, he was graciously pleased to send a message to us. On my representation, His Majesty ordered £150.0.0 from his privy purse to be sent to His Excellency, the Egyptian Ambassador to be spent on the 'Id-ul-Fitr entertainment. The money was to be given to our agent the Jamiat-ul-Muslimin, the names of some of the members of which, I gave to the King's Chamberlain. This was done and I understand the function went off most successfully. His Excellency, Shaikh Hafiz Wahba conducted the prayers and over 800 people were in the congregation, including soldiers from the Indian contingent and the Pioneer Labour Corps.

The Egyptian Ambassador, Hasan Nachat Pasha, whom I have seen on his return to London from Egypt a few weeks ago, I understand has got a certain sum of money unspent with him.

With the concurrence of the Trustees, I would like to approach His Excellency to spend the money in the following manner:

1. In providing and getting microphones installed so that the KHUTBA (sermon)[139] and TAKBIR (Call to prayer)[140] may

[139] Also written as *khutbah*, this is a sermon that the Prophet Muhammad gave regularly at Medina. It is prescribed by all Sunni legal schools at the *zuhur* (noon) Friday congregation prayers. In addition, similar sermons are delivered at the two annual festivals, Id al-Fitr and Id al-Adha.

[140] *Takbir*, as distinct from *Adhan*, is literally the Arabic call 'Allahu Akbar' (God is Great).

be transmitted from the prayer hall to the lecture hall which is also used as an additional congregation hall during the 'Id prayers and other religious celebrations. Any money which may be left over after paying for the microphones and their installation –

2. To be spent in purchasing a number of suitable books which may be presented on behalf of His Majesty, the King of Egypt to the East London Mosque Islamic Culture Centre.

During my stay at Cairo, I also had several discussions with the Shaikh of Al Azhar University, His Eminence, the Shaikh ul Maraghi, and at my request he was pleased to make a contribution to the East London Mosque of 50 bound copies of the Holy Quran and of 50 washable caps to be used during prayers. I arranged with the authorities at the British embassy to send them on through Diplomatic channel to London and also arrange for their distribution to the East London Mosque, 446/448 Commercial Road, E1, one half through the Ministry of Information and the other half through the British Council, as both of these organisations have representative members on the Committee of Management of the Islamic Culture Centre of the East London Mosque.

I very much regret to report that I have been informed that some of the copies of the Quran were given to the Imam of Woking Mosque, in Surrey, for distribution. I had correspondence with Dr Arberry suggesting that the copies distributed obviously by mistake should be recalled and distributed to the East London Mosque, as they were specifically given to me for this purpose and forwarded to London by the British Embassy at my request. I also suggested that the copies should be sent to our Honorary Treasurer, Sir John Woodhead, at the India Office, so that they could be put on the inventory as property of the Mosque and then made over to our agents, the Jamiat-ul-Muslimin, for use there.

Sir Stephen Gaselee has addressed Sir John Woodhead in connection with this matter, and I hope it will not be long before this matter is satisfactorily settled.

India Office
Whitehall
SW1
8 June 1942

INDIA OFFICE
Whitehall SW1

27 July 1942

The Rt Hon L.S. Amery, P.C., M.P.
Secretary of State for India

I am glad to inform you that, on Thursday 23 instant, we had a meeting of the London Central Mosque (Jamea) Committee at the Egyptian Embassy. This meeting was the first one to be held after the meeting held on Friday 25 July 1941, which you, Lord Moyne and Lord Reith also attended. We were very glad indeed on the successful acquisition of a splendid site in Regents Park with a fine building called the Regent Lodge, which, with some alterations, can be put into use almost immediately as an Islamic Culture Centre and as a Mosque. It is a great achievement, and Hassan Nachat Pasha deserves all credit for his practical imagination.

In this connection, I would like to bring to your notice the fact that the cost will be well under the £100,000 sanctioned by His Majesty's Government. The surplus will be credited back to the Treasury.

As you know, the London Mosque Scheme sponsored by His Highness the Aga Khan and the late Rt Hon Syed Ameer Ali in 1910, had collected a sum of money, a considerable portion of which has been utilised in purchasing a small property in the East End of London for use as a Mosque and Islamic Culture Centre. This was done in view of the large Muslim population in the East End, and the large numbers of Muslim seamen who in normal times visit the Port of London. This small Mosque and Islamic Culture Centre (at 446/448/450 Commercial Road, E1) was publicly opened by His Excellency the Egyptian Ambassador on 1 August 1941 and was visited by you on 7 August of that year.

On behalf of the Trustees of the London Mosque fund, may I venture to approach you with the request to interest yourself in this matter, and consult the Colonial Secretary and the Foreign Secretary as to whether it would be possible, with the residual money from the grant to the Central Mosque Scheme, to acquire the land contiguous to the present East London Mosque and Islamic Centre (446.448.450 Commercial Road E1).

If this were done, the Trustees of the London Mosque Fund would possess a site on which it would be possible to erect buildings in every way suitable for a Mosque and Islamic Culture Centre after the war.

Yours Sincerely
Hassan Suhrawardy

Minutes of the Meeting of the Trustees of the London Mosque Fund held on 20 August 1942 at the India Office

Present:

Sir Hassan Suhrawardy
Mr Waris Ameer Ali, C.I.E
Earl Winterton, M.P

With

Sir John Woodhead, Hon Treasurer
Colonel S.F Newcombe, Hon Secretary

1. The minutes of the meeting of the Trustees held on 15 June 1942 were read and confirmed.
2. The resignation (vide his letter of 13 June 1942) of Mr A Yusuf Ali, C.B.E was recorded. The Trustees placed on record their appreciation of the services rendered by Mr Yusuf Ali.
3. Mr Waris Ameer Ali and Lord Winterton, who were unavoidably absent from last (15 June 1942) meeting, signified their concurrence in the appointment of Khan Bahadur Sir M. Azizul Huque, C.I.E, as a trustee with effect from 15 June 1942.
4. The Hon Treasurer reported that the 3½% India Stock (1931), to the face value of £2596.12.11, held by the Trustees had been sold and that in the place of this stock the Trustees had purchased 3 ½% Conversion Stock (1961) to the face value of £2,500. The details of the transactions were as follows:

a) Sold, £2,596.12.11 India 3½% Stock at 101 per cent ex interest July 1942
£2,624.8d

Less stamp 6s od and commission £1.12.5d
£1.18.5d

£2,622.6.3d

b) Purchased, £2,500 Conversion 3½% Stock at 108 ¼ cum interest October 1942
£2,706.5.od

Plus stamp 6s od and commission £6.5.od

£6.11.od
£2,712.16.od

The difference between the sale proceeds of the India Stock and the cost of Conversion Stock will be met from the current funds of the Trust Fund.

5. Sir Hassan Suhrawardy explained the position, so far as information is available, in regard to the grant of £100,000 which had been provided by His Majesty's Government for the purchase of a site in Central London for a Mosque, and said that although it was not yet certain that there would be a saving out of this grant, he had thought it desirable to address the Secretary of State for India at the earliest possible moment with a view to urging that any balance should be utilised in acquiring the land contiguous to the East London Mosque so that the Trustees would be in possession of a site in every way suitable for the erection of a Mosque (a copy of the letter forms an annexure to these minutes). It was decided that:

a) the action taken by Sir Hassan Suhrawardy be confirmed;
b) steps should be taken to explain to the Press, informally and in so far as appeared desirable, the position in regard to
   i) the Mosque which is to be built on the site acquired at the expense of His Majesty's Government in Regents Park; and
   ii) the East London Mosque

The points which it is desirable to bring out are that the Moslem population, particularly in peace time, in the East end of London is considerable, that the proposed Mosque in Regents Park cannot meet the need of this community for a regular place of worship, that this need is met by the East London Mosque, and that the Trustees of this Mosque are in need of funds for the purpose of enlarging the site on which the present "temporary" Mosque is situated in order to enable them to undertake the erection of a Mosque suitable in every way to the religious needs of the Moslem Community in the East End.

6. The position of the Jamiat-ul-Muslimin in relation to the East London Mosque and the Trustees of the London Mosque Fund was discussed.[141] It was pointed out that according to

[141] At the inauguration of the East London Mosque, it was already apparent that it would be an arena in which Indian Muslim politics would figure. For instance, British intelligence reported that a Pakistan Movement pamphlet was freely circulated there. Shah Abdul Majid Qureshi, reminiscing later, pointed to the political divisions between some of the Trustees and others belonging to Jamiat-ul-Muslimin: 'In my early days I used to be a Congressman. Sir Hassan Suhrawardy was a pious Muslim from a learned family. During the war [. . .] we were celebrating our Eid prayers at the East London Mosque, under the leadership of Suhrawardy. At the end he said in a loud voice, "Oh Allah, give victory to the Allies!"

the arrangement, to which the Jamiat agreed, made in 1941, the Jamiat-ul-Muslimin was appointed as the "Agents" of the Trustees in regard to the carrying out of the religious observances at the Mosque and works in connection with the Islamic Culture Centre. (A copy of the letter by which the Trustees appointed the Jamiat as agents is attached to these minutes). Lately, however, there have been indications that the Jamiat was failing to recognise the "Agency" position. It was agreed that it should be explained to the Jamiat that they were acting in regard to the affairs of the Mosque and the Islamic Culture Centre purely as agents of the Trustees and in particular that the room in the Mosque building which had been placed at their disposal should not be used for any purpose other than connected with the affairs of the Mosque and the Islamic Culture Centre.

7. It was also considered that the Jamiat-ul-Muslimin should make over to the Trustees any funds which they may collect towards the building of the Mosque.
8. The meeting terminated with a vote of thanks to the Chair.

Confirmed Hassan Suhrawardy 20 August 1943

Annexure to Minutes of the meeting held on 20 August 1942

20 May 1941

Dear Sir

446 and 448 Commercial Road

We have converted the two houses above mentioned into one building to be used for religious purposes and (subject to any necessary consent being obtained) are willing to appoint you our agent for such purposes.

Congress Muslims in the mosque protested after the prayers [. . .] "Why did you pray for the British?" They made him cry, poor fellow [. . .] Some of us being of a reasonable mind said [. . .] but victory of Allies means victory of the Muslims' (Caroline Adams, *Across Seven Seas and Thirteen Rivers* (London, 1986), p. 162).

1. As such agent:

i) You are to be responsible for arranging in accordance with the directions which we may from time to time give to you the carrying out in the above premises of prayers, religious ceremonies and works in connection with the Islamic Culture Centre and also funeral and requiem prayers.

ii) You are to make good any damage which may be done to the said premises and the furniture and fittings therein by any person or persons in your employ such damage to be made good at your own expense.

iii) You are to use your best endeavours to prevent any damage being done to the said premises and the furniture and fittings therein from any cause or by any person or persons (other than your own employees) who may visit the premises.

iv) You are to see that all prayers, religious ceremonies and works are carried out with all due solemnity and that the resident caretaker and other persons employed by us carry out their duties in a satisfactory manner and that the said premises are used only for the religious purposes aforesaid and for no other purpose and in particular you are not to allow any meeting or speeches of a political nature to be held or to take place on any of the premises.

v) You are to carry out on premises other than the above premises such of your aims and objects set forth in your rules and regulations for the time being which are not of a religious character.

vi) Any persons employed by you are not to be regarded as our servants but are to be your servants and are to be paid by you accordingly.

vii) You are to keep us and our registered proprietors for the time being of the above premises and our Trustees and Members of our executive Committee for the time being indemnified from all claims and demands which may be made against us or them or any of them by reason of any wrongful or unpermitted user of the said premises.

2. In consideration of the foregoing you are to have the use of one room (to be selected by us) in the said premises to be used by you free of rent as an office in connection with the religious purposes aforesaid and also in connection with any other religious purposes in which you are concerned and of which we approve together with the use of the telephone free

of charge for official calls in relation to those religious purposes for which you are acting as our agent and you are also to be at liberty on paying for calls to use such telephone in relation to any other religious purposes with which you are concerned and of which we approve.

3. This document is not to be construed in any way as conferring upon you any estate or interest whatsoever in the said premises but is to be regarded as a mere licence only.
4. The agency hereby created is not to be transferrable by you and is to be terminable at any time by either you or us on giving to the other one week's previous notice in writing in that behalf.[142]

Yours faithfully

(Sd) E. Hotson
Sir Ernest Hotson
Hon Secretary
LONDON MOSQUE FUND

Jamiat-ul-Muslimin

We, the undersigned the Chairman, the Hon Treasurer and the Hon General Secretary of the Jamiat-ul-Muslimin hereby agree to the above on behalf of the Jamiat-ul-Muslimin and (pursuant to its rules and regulations) hereby sign this document on its behalf.

(Sd) Gholam Muhammad[143]	(Sd) Ahmeddin Qureshi[144]	(Sd) S. Khan[145]
Hon President	Hon Treasurer	Hon Secretary

[142] These conditions appear to represent a tightening up on previous, lax, arrangements.

[143] A silk merchant in London's East End, married to a British white woman. See BL, IOR, P&J (S)/716, fo. 2, report of the Metropolitan Police (Special Branch), 17 August 1938.

[144] Born in 1910, he was a silk merchant from Jullandur, Punjab, living in Aldgate, London. *Ibid.*

[145] This is the same Sahibdad Khan who was a leading member of the Jamiat-ul-Muslimin. See biographical note in Appendix I and note in Appendix III.

Minutes of the Meeting of the Executive Committee held on Wednesday 26 August 1942

Present:

Sir Hassan Suhrawardy, Chairman
A. Yusuf Ali Esq
M. R. Zada Esq
Sahib Dad Khan Esq
S. Amir Shah Esq
K. Lebbane Esq
Hatim Attari Esq*
Dr Arberry
A Steel, Esq (Representing the British Council)

With Sir John Woodhead, Hon Treasurer
Colonel Newcombe, Hon Secretary

1. The minutes of the meeting held on 15 June 1942 were read and confirmed.
2. On the proposal of Sir Hassan Suhrawardy, seconded by Mr Yusuf Ali, Mr Hatim Attari of 41 Berkeley Square, W1 was elected a member of the Executive Committee.
3. On the proposal of Mr Waris Ameer seconded by Mr R. Zada, it was decided that

a) the Managing Committee appointed to deal with the affairs of the East London Mosque and the Islamic Culture Centre, vide meeting of 14 August 1941 and 23 January 1942, be dissolved. (Note: The effect of this is that there is no Committee other than the Executive Committee which is provided for by the Trust Deed).
b) As provided for in the letter of 20 May 1941 from the Trustees to the Jamiat-ul-Muslimin, to the terms of which the Jamiat-ul-Muslimin agreed, the Jamiat-ul-Muslimin of Great Britain in its capacity as representing the Congregation of the East London Mosque and the Muslim population of the East End of London, be entrusted with the duty of administering, as the agents of and subject to the general direction and control of the Executive Committee and the Trustees, the affairs of the East London Mosque and the Islamic Culture Centre.

4. With reference to item 14 of the meeting held on 15 June 1942, Mr Sahib Dad Khan informed the meeting that the Islamic Council in Great Britain had made other arrangements and did not now wish to be given permission to use the room in the Mosque premises for office purposes. The Trustees would be informed in writing accordingly in the near future.

5. A long discussion took place in regard to the items of expenditure which would be met directly by the Trustees and those for which the Jamiat-ul-Muslimin would accept responsibility, subject to any financial assistance the Trustees might be able to give. No decision had been reached on this matter when the meeting was adjourned to a subsequent date.

H Suhrawardy 7 October 1942

Minutes of the Meeting of the Executive Committee of the London Mosque Fund, held on Wednesday 7 October 1942

Present:

Sir Hassan Suhrawardy (Chairman)
A. Yusuf Ali, Esq, C.B.E., I.C.S., (Rtd)
Sir Azizul Haque, C.I.E
Waris Ameer Ali, Esq, C.I.E., I.C.S
Sahibdad Khan, Esq
Colonel Stewart F. Newcombe, D.S.O (Hon Secretary)
Sir John Woodhead, K.C.S.I (Hon Treasurer)

Apologies for absence were received from M.R. Zada, Esq, Hatim Attari, Esq, and A. Steele, Esq (of the British Council).

1. The minutes of the meeting held on 26 August 1942 were read and confirmed.

2. The subject referred to in paragraph 5 of the minutes of the meeting held on 26 August was further discussed. The following decisions were reached with the concurrence of all present: –

I. The Jamiat-ul-Muslimin, as provided in the letter of 20 May 1941 from the Trustees to the Jamiat-ul-Muslimin, is entrusted with the duty of administering, as agents of and subject to the general direction and control of the Executive Committee and

The Trustees, the affairs to the East London Mosque and the Islamic Culture Centre.

II. The following items of expenditure will be met by the Trustees and the Executive Committee direct:

a) the Mosque:	Estimated Expenditure
1. Clerical Assistance	£ 6. -.-
2. Water Rates (two thirds of £77)	£11. 6.8
3. Rates (two thirds of £47.10) say	£32
4. Audit Fee	£ 1. 1.-
5. Cost of annual repairs, external and internal, including repairs at five and seven years intervals	£65. -.-
6. Insurance and other miscellaneous expenditure on account of postage etc.	£15. -.-
b) The Culture Centre:	
1. Water Rates (one third of £17)	£ 5. 13.4
2. Rates (one third of £47.10) say	£15.10.-

NOTE: Out of the amount of £65 shown under 5 above £15 will be at the disposal of the Jamiat-ul-Muslimin for internal repairs.

III. Subject to the grants referred to in V below the Jamiat-ul-Muslimin will be responsible for all other expenditure incurred in connection with the Mosque and the Islamic Culture Centre.

IV. The power of appointing, dismissing and fixing the salaries of the caretaker of the property in Commercial Road and the teacher of the 'Kuran at the Mosque will lie with the Executive Committee.[146] In these matters the Executive Committee will consult the Jamiat-ul-Muslimin and in reaching their decisions will take into consideration the views expressed by the Jamiat-ul-Muslimin.

V. For the year beginning 1 December 1942 and ending 30 November 1943 the Executive Committee will make a grant of £102 to the Jamiat-ul-Muslimin toward the expenditure referred to in III above; out of the £102 the sum of £52 is earmarked for expenditure on the Islamic Culture Centre. This grant will be made quarterly in advance, £25.10.- on 1

[146] In effect this allowed the Executive Committee to keep control of the teaching taking place at the mosque.

December, £25.10.- on 1 March, £25.10.- on 1 June and £25.10.- on 1 September, 1943. At the end of each quarter the Jamiat-ul-Muslimin will supply the Executive Committee with a statement of expenditure incurred during the quarter, showing separately the expenditure on the Mosque and Islamic Culture Centre.

3. After Discussion Mr Waris Ameer Ali agreed not to press the points made in his letter of 12 September to Sir Hassan Suhrawardy.

4. The Executive Committee thanked the Jamiat-ul-Muslimin for sending them a copy of their Annual Report for the year 1941–42.[147] In discussion it was pointed out that the form of the report and account attached thereto might lead to misunderstanding because it did not specifically bring out that, in regard to the Mosque and the Islamic Culture Centre the Jamiat-ul-Muslimin was acting as agents to the Trustees and the Executive Committee, and in regard to the burial of indigent Muslims as agents of the Committee of the Indigent Muslim Burial Fund. It was also pointed out that it was not correct for the Jamiat to describe 448 Commercial Road as their Headquarters Offices, for it was made clear in the Trustees letter of 20 May 1941, vide paragraph 1 (v) and 2, that the room which had been placed at the disposal of the Jamiat free of rent was for the purposes of carrying on their work in connection with the Mosque and the Culture Centre as agents of the Trustees and for any other religious work with which the Jamiat are concerned and of which the Trustees have approved.[148]

5. The meeting closed with a vote of thanks to the Chairman.

Confirmed: H Suhrawardy 7 April 1943

Minutes of the Meeting of the Executive Committee of the London Mosque Fund held on Wednesday 7 April 1943

Present:

Sir Hassan Shurawardy (Chairman)
Waris Ameer Ali, Esq C.I.E., I.C.S. (Rtd)

[147] Copy of report is available at the ELM Archives.

[148] From this note, it would appear that the Executive Committee was anxious that the Jamiat-ul-Muslimin might be engaged in activities that fell outside its remit as the agent of the Trust.

Sahebdad Khan, Esq
Said Amir Shah, Esq
Hatim Attari Esq
Anthony Steel, Esq, of the British Council
Syed Mahomed Sayeed ullah, Esq
Colonel Steward F. Newcombe D.S.C
Sir John Woodhead

Apologies for absence were recorded from Sir Azizul Huque.

1. The Minutes of the meeting held on 7 October 1942 were read and subject to the correction of an arithmetical error, were confirmed.

2. On the proposal of Sir Hassan Suhrawardy, seconded by Mr Sahebdad Khan, Mr Syed Md. Sayeedullah was elected a member of the Executive Committee.

3. The appointment of Mr Ali Basha as Caretaker and teacher of the Koran was confirmed.

4. Considered the following bills by Messrs. Turner & Cooper Ltd for repairs to the property in Commercial Road:

Ordinary Repairs:	450 Commercial Road	£ 44. 3.10
	446 &448 Commercial Road	£ 32.15. 7
	Sub total	£ 76.19. 5
War Damage Repairs:	446 &448 Commercial Road	£ 80. 5. 3
	TOTAL	£157. 4. 8

It was decided that payments be made in accordance with the advice of the Architect, Mr MacDonald.

5. The letter dated 10 March 1943 from the British Council (copy annexed) in connection with the Islamic Culture Centre was considered. It was agreed that the Committee would not be justified in asking the British Council to renew the grant of £75.

Mr Steel said that as regards the grant of £75 already made the Council would be pleased if they could be supplied with an account showing how it had been spent. He explained that while the Council did not propose to renew the grant of £75 they would be glad to continue to assist the work of the Culture Centre by supplying books and newspapers and by paying the salary of Mr Hussein. He suggested that a list of the books required should be prepared and forwarded to the Council. The Council would then decide what assistance they could give either by supplying the books or by meeting the cost thereof. As regards newspapers he said the Council would continue to supply the Daily Telegraph and the Sunday Times.

There was some discussion as regards visits to factories. The view was that visits to food factories would be welcomed. Mr Steel though this could be arranged.

The Committee desired to take this opportunity of recording their appreciation of the assistance the British Council had given to the Culture Centre. They were very grateful for Mr Steel's assurance that in spite of the difficulties experienced in the past the Council were desirous of continuing to assist the Centre.

6. The Hon Treasurer explained the financial position. He said the accounts for the year ending 31 March had not yet been finally prepared and audited and so the figures he would now give were subject to correction.

Mosque Accounts

(1) Receipts. Dividends £ 233. 2.10
Donations £ 80. 7.11 (including a grant of £20 by H. H the Aga Khan for the year 1943–4)

Transfer from "B" Account £ 30. 6. 6

Total: £ 343.17. 3

(2) Expenditure exclusive of the grant of £52 for the Culture Centre – this grant has not been made in 1942–3. £ 341.18. 6

Culture Centre ("B" Account)

(1) Receipts £ 10.18. 0
(2) Expenditure including transfers to Mosque Account £ 114. 0. 0

The Hon Treasurer pointed out that the expenditure of £341 odd included nothing on account of repairs. There would be considerable expenditure of this nature in 1943/4. The excess of expenditure over receipts in the Culture Centre account had been net out of the previous year's surplus.

7. It was decided that in view of the expressed desire of Colonel Newcombe to resign, his resignation be accepted. The Committee placed on record their great appreciation of all that Colonel Newcombe had done for the Mosque and the Culture Centre. They were deeply grateful to him for the assistance he had so willingly given and hoped that he would remain a member of the Executive Committee.

On the proposal of Sir Hassan Suhrawardy, seconded by Mr Waris Ameer Ali, it was decided that Mr Hatim Attari and Mr Sayeedullah (of 46 Kingswood Court, West End Lane, NW6) be elected Joint Hon Secretaries in place of Sir Ernest Hotson and Colonel Newcombe. (Note: Sir Ernest Hotson's retirement was noted in the Minutes of the Meeting of 15 June 1942)

8. The meeting terminated with a vote of thanks to the Chair.

Confirmed: H Suhrawardy 2 July 1943

THE BRITISH COUNCIL
3 HANOVER STREET
LONDON W1

10 March 1943

Dear Sir Hassan

I am very glad to hear from Miss Whitehorn that the long delayed visit to the margarine factory by Moslems from the Islamic Cultural Centre is really going to take place today. As, however, this is, I believe, only the second event which we have been able to arrange for the Islamic Centre during the whole winter in view of their difficulties over finding a caretaker, and, I am afraid I must add, their somewhat non-co-operative attitude, I am in some doubt whether the renewal of our £75 a year grant at this Centre and the supply of daily papers etc., which it seems to me are seldom read, are really justified.

I have had some discussion with Colonel Newcombe on this subject, and he is inclined to agree with me that before the £75 grant is renewed during the coming financial year, the British Council should receive an audited statement of what has been done with the money. If, as I suspect, there is a considerable balance on the 1942/3 grant, we should be prepared to allocate this towards the cost of certain religious books, toward which Mr Khan asked me for a contribution the last time I was in the Centre, but Colonel Newcombe agrees with me that it would not be proper for the British Council to continue their grant into the future simply for this purpose. We shall of course continue to pay the salary of Mr Hussein on the same basis as before, so that should be some help with the religious teaching, which is, I know, an important part of his work.

Perhaps you would be kind enough to let us know the views of your Committee on the subject of the grant and proposed purchase of religious books, and I should also be grateful if you could obtain the audited statement for 1942–3.

Yours Sincerely

(Sd) Anthony Steel
London and Eastern
Regional Officer

Sir Hassan Suhrawardy C.B.E
India Office

Minutes of the Meeting of the Executive Committee of the London Mosque Fund, held at India House on Friday 2 July 1943 at 11.30 p.m

Present:

Sir Hassan Suhrawardy (Chairman)
Sir John Woodhead (Treasurer)
Colonel Stewart Newcombe
Mr Waris Ameer Ali
Mr Yusuf Ali
Mr Anthony Steel
Mr Kemal Lebbane
Mr Hatim Attari) Joint Secretaries
Mr S.M Sayeedulla)

Absent:

Sir Aziz-ul-Haque
Mr Zada

Both being out of the Country.

1. The Minutes of the last meeting held on 7 April were read. Mr Steel made certain observations in regard to the salary of Mr Hussein and the secretaries were instructed to enquire the total amount of salary Mr Hussein is drawing, by whom paid and a list of subjects he is teaching. Mr Steel informed the meeting that the British Council would be agreeable to continue to pay the salary and also arrange to supply books, journals and periodicals required for the Islamic Centre, on receipt by them of the details. Mr Steel further agreed to arrange excursions on receipt of application from the Islamic Centre. The Minutes of the meeting were then confirmed.

2. The Chairman read to the meeting the letter dated 15 April 1943 received from Jamiat-ul-Muslimin in the matter of the resignations of Mr Sahib Dad Khan and Mr Said Amir Shah, and after discussion it was decided that the consideration of letters of resignation and the letter from Jamiat-ul-Muslimin be postponed.[149] In the meantime, the Committee authorised Sir Hassan Suhrawardy, Mr K Lebbane and Mr Yusuf Ali to interview the officials of Jamiat-ul-Muslimin with a view to ascertain their views as regards the continuity of their acting as agents of the London Mosque Fund for managing the East London Mosque, and their attitude towards trustees and officials of the Moslem Mosque Fund. The committee felt it desirable that the consideration of the postponed items should not be very long delayed, and accordingly fixed a meeting for Wednesday 21 July at 3 o'clock to hear from Sir Hassan Suhrawardy, Mr Yusuf Ali and Mr K Lebbane the report of their interviews with the Jamiat-ul-Muslimin, which they hoped to conclude before the date of the meeting.

3. Mr S.M Sayeedeilla's letter to the Chairman and correspondence arising out of it was read by the Chairman and the committee appreciated Mr Sayeedeilla's observations and his promptness in reporting the matter to the Chairman.

4. The lay-out of the Memorial tablet proposed to be put in the East London Mosque was considered by the meeting, and after discussion as to the usefulness of the names of the trustees being embodied on

[149] According to an extract from a Metropolitan Police Report of 14 October 1943 (BL, IOR, L/P&J/12/468, fo. 267), 'a dispute, which threatens to precipitate a crisis among Muslims in the East End of London, has arisen between the Board of Trustees and Executive Committee of the London Mosque Fund and the local Muslim association, the Jamiat-ul-Muslimin, over the administration of the affairs of the East London Mosque, 446/450 Commercial Road, E.1'. This extract summarizes and contextualizes the development of the dispute, examining how the opposing sides managed it (*ibid.*, fos 268–272). For more information, see Appendix III.

the Tablet, further consideration of this matter was postponed until the next meeting.

5. Sir John Woodhead informed the meeting that the auditors were not able to complete the accounts, and the consideration of finance was postponed for the next meeting.

6. It was resolved that the Chairman should write to Sir Aziz-ul-Haque and Mr Zada thanking them for their useful services to the committee during their membership and requesting them to tender their resignations in view of their departure from the country.

7. The meeting terminated with a vote of thanks to the Chairman.

Confirmed: 21 July 1943

Minutes of the Adjourned Meeting of the Executive Committee of the London Mosque Fund, held at the India Office on Wednesday 21 July 1943

Present:

Sir Hassan Suhrawardy (Chairman)
Mr Yusuf Ali
Colonel S.F. Newcombe
Mr Hatim Attari) Joint Hon Secretaries
Mr S.M Sayeedulla)
Sir John Woodhead Hon Treasurer

1. The Report of the sub-committee appointed to interview the officials of Jamiat-ul-Muslimin was read to the committee and is recorded herewith.

2. The Executive Committee considered the Report and resolved to forward a copy of the Report to the trustees of the London Mosque Fund for their consideration and deferred any further action on the Report until the trustees' decision.

3. It was resolved that the resignations of Sahebdad Khan and Mr S.A. Shah as members of the Executive Committee be recorded. It was further resolved that the letter of Jamiat-ul-Muslimin dated 15 April 1943, arising out of the above resignations be also recorded for the present.

4. Sir Hassan Suhrawardy reported that the sub-committee appointed to consider the Memorial Tablet for the East London Mosque has decided upon the text of this both in English and Arabic, as per both proofs submitted, which are recorded herewith.

5. The Treasurer submitted the draft balance sheets of the London Mosque Fund and Islamic Culture Centre, which showed a combined deficit of over £120. The income from the investment showed as £233. It was resolved that the payment of £10.10.0 for the year ending 31 March 1942 and £5.5.0 for the year ending 31 March 1943 to Messrs. Feasey, Hull & Feasey, the auditors, be approved.

6. The meeting terminated with a vote of thanks to the Chairman.

Confirmed: H Suhrawardy 31 August 1943

Minutes of the Meeting of the Trustees of the London Mosque Fund held on 20 August 1943

Present:

Sir Hassan Suhrawardy (in the Chair)
Lord Winterton
Monsieur H.M. Said
Mr Waris Ameer Ali

With

Sir John Woodhead, Hon Treasurer

1. The minutes of the meeting held on 20 August 1942 were confirmed.

2. The Trustees had heard with deep regret of the sudden death of Mrs Ameer Ali,[150] the wife of their colleague Mr Waris Ameer Ali. The Trustees conveyed to Mr Waris Ameer Ali their deepest sympathy in his bereavement.

3. On the proposal of Lord Winterton, seconded by Monsieur H.M. Said, the audited accounts for the year ended the 31 March 1943 were approved.

[150] Waris Ameer Ali's wife, Anne Marguerite, died on 14 July 1943. Her funeral was held in Holy Trinity Church, Prince Consort Road, London SW7. See *The Times*, 16 July 1943.

4. On the proposal of Mr Waris Ameer Ali, seconded by Sir Hassan Suhrawardy, a vote of thanks to the Auditors, Messrs. Feasey, Hull & Feasey, for their services during the year ending 31 March 1943 was passed. Messrs. Feasey, Hull & Feasey were appointed auditors for the year ending 31 March 1944.

5. It was decided that His Excellency Sheik Hafiz Wahba[151] be invited to become a Trustee in place of Khan Bahadur Sir M. Azizul Huque who had returned to India.

6. Sir Hassan Surhawardy reported (vide Memorandum attached) that he had received a donation of £1,000 from His Highness the Nawab[...] of Bhawalpur [*handwriting unclear here*] towards the funds of the London Mosque. The Trustees placed on record their joint appreciation of the generous gift of His Highness and there and then signed an airgraph conveying to His Highness their most grateful thanks to Sir Hassan Suhrawardy who had been instrumental in obtaining this handsome donation.

7. It was resolved that the sum of £1,000 received as a donation from His Highness the Nawab[...] of Bhawalpur should be invested in Savings Bonds, 3%, 1960–70. The Hon Treasurer was instructed to take steps accordingly.

8. The matters referred to in the annexed note were considered fully. On the proposal of Lord Winterton, seconded by Mr Waris Ameer Ali, it was decided

a) that the investments should be in the names of the Trustees with the exception of His Highness the Aga Khan – this decision was reached because it was within the recollection of some Trustees that in view of the fact that he is often away from the United

[151] Sheikh Hafiz Wahba (1889–1967), a scholar of the Al-Azhar University of Cairo, was a close associate of Ibn Saud, the king of Hejaz and Nejd, who appointed him as the Governor of Mecca in 1925. In November 1930, he presented his credentials as the first Minister to represent his country at the Court of St James's. Later he was appointed Saudi Arabia's ambassador in London. Well versed in the Islamic science, he became a leading and respected member of the capital's Muslim community. He was invited to lead prayers at annual Islamic festivals at the Woking Mosque (*The Times*, 28 December 1935); he was a member of the committee of influential Muslims set up to plan the establishment of a mosque in London during the Second World War (*The Times*, 14 November 1940); and he gave the *khutba* (sermon) and led the *juma* (Friday congregational prayer) at the opening of the East London Mosque on 1 August 1941 (*The Times*, 2 August 1941). He died in Rome in 1967. For more biographical details, see *The Times*, 25 November 1967.

Kingdom His Highness the Agha Khan did not desire that the investments should be registered in his name.

b) that steps be taken to place the appointment of the Trustees on a strictly proper legal footing by the execution of the deed as settled by Counsel.

9. The Trustees considered the report (vide annexure to these minutes) of the Sub-Committee of the Executive Committee of the London Mosque Fund on the working of the arrangement by which the Jamiat-ul-Muslimin was appointed in July 1941 as the agents of the Trustees for the management of the Mosque and the Islamic Culture Centre. This report had been referred to them by the Executive Committee. The Trustees decided that the agreement should be terminated. They were of opinion that it is not necessary under any Islamic obligations to appoint an association as agents for managing the religious functions connected with the Mosque. At the same time they desired to make it quite clear that the Mosque is open to all Muslims for worship during the appointed hours and that if the Muslim Association or any other body or person desired to arrange a function after 'Id' prayers or the Prophet's Birthday celebrations, they would be very glad to give permission, if timely application is made. They hoped that the Muslim congregation, who would use the Mosque and the premises, would continue to take the interest which is expected from them as Muslims.

10. The meeting ended with a vote of thanks to the Chair.

Confirmed: Suhrawardy 8 October 1943

Minutes of the Meeting of the Executive Committee of the London Mosque Fund, held at the India Office on Tuesday 31 August 1943 at 3.30

Present:

Sir Hassan Suhrawardy (Chairman)
Mr Waris Ameer Ali
Mr Yusuf Ali
Mr Hatim Attari)
Mr S.M Sayeedulla) Joint Hon Secretaries
Sir John Woodhead)

1. The minutes of the meeting held on 31 July 1943 were read and confirmed.

2. With reference to Item 2 of the meeting of 21 July, the committee was informed of the decision of the Trustees, which is as follows:–

"The Trustees considered the report (vide annexure to these minutes) of the Sub-Committee of the Executive Committee of the London Mosque Fund on the working of the arrangement by which the Jamiat-ul-Muslimin was appointed in July 1941 as the agents of the Trustees for the management of the Mosque and the Islamic Culture Centre. This report had been referred to them by the Executive Committee. The Trustees decided that the agreement should be terminated.[152] They were of opinion that it is not necessary under any Islamic obligations to appoint an association as agents for managing the religious functions connected with the Mosque. At the same time they desired to make it quite clear that the Mosque is open to all Muslims for worship during the appointed hours and that if the Muslim Association or any other body or person desired to arrange a function after 'Id' prayers or the Prophet's Birthday celebrations, they would be very glad to give permission, if timely application is made. They hoped that the Muslim congregation who would use the Mosque and the premises, would continue to take the interest which is expected from them as Muslims."

To give effect to the above decision, the joint Hon Secretaries were asked to serve notice on the Jamiat-ul-Muslimin as follows:

"Under the terms of our Agreement, notice is hereby given cancelling the appointment of Jamiat-ul-Muslimin, the Muslim Association, as agents of the Trustees for managing the religious ceremonies and other duties connected with the East London Mosque."

The Trustees have decided that it is not necessary under any Islamic obligations to appoint an Association as an agent for managing the Religious functions connected with the Mosque. They are desirous of making it quite clear that the Mosque is open to all Muslims for worship during appointed hours. If timely application is made, the Trustees will be very glad to give permission to the

[152] According to British intelligence (BL, IOR, L/P&J/12/468, fo. 83), the Jamiat-ul-Muslimin rejected the notice of termination 'as it was contrary to the word and spirit of the Koran'. For more information on this dispute, see Appendix III.

Muslim Association or any other body or person who would like to arrange an entertainment of 'Id prayers, the Prophet's Birthday celebrations, Muharram, or on any such occasion when in the interest of the Mosque or of any spiritual and religious needs, a meeting or celebration could be appropriately held in the Mosque premises.

It is hoped that the Muslim congregation who would use the Mosque and the premises will continue to take interest which is expected from them as Muslims.

This notice is given with effect from Friday, 3 September 1943, and the seven days required by the Agreement will expire on 10 September 1943.

The Hon Secretary was asked to send for Mr Ali Basha, the caretaker, to see about his salary and insurance book, and the inventory of the Mosque furniture.

3. The letter of resignation of Mr Sahebdad Khan and Mr S.A Shah has already been recorded and as they were representing the Jamiat-ul-Muslimin, and it has been decided to serve them with notice of termination of their agency, there is no reason to ask the Jamiat to send the names of members to fill up the vacancies caused by the resignation of Mr S.A. Shah and Mr Sahebdad Khan.

4. The Hon Treasurer explained the financial position set out in Item 5 of the Minutes of the meeting on 21 July 1943, and it was resolved that every effort should be made to reduce expenditure under different items.

5. Sir Hassan Suhrawardy reported that he has the consent of Mr Shaikh Abdul Hamid that if elected, he will serve as a member of the Committee. It was resolved, on the proposal of Sir Hassan and seconded by Mr Waris Ameer Ali, that Mr Shaikh Abdul Hamid should be elected as a member of the Executive Committee.

6. The meeting terminated with a vote of thanks to the Chairman.

Approved at the meeting of the Trustees and Executive Committee held on 23 January 1942:

LONDON MOSQUE FUND

Estimated annual receipts and expenditure:–

	£	s	d
Interest on Securities in the hands of Trustees:	234.	16.	6
1. Audit Fee	1.	1.	-
2. Clerical assistance	6.	-.	-
3. Caretaker	52.	-.	-
4. Religious Observances and Prayers			
Id-ul-Fitr £10.10			
Id-ul-Adha £10.10			
Milud-e-Nabi £15.-	36.	-.	-
5. Al Hadj Hafiz Mohammed-el-Shami (teacher of the Koran)	30.	-.	-
6. Annual grant to Islamic Centre	52.	-.	-
7. Telephone, Electricity and Gas	23.	-.	-
8. Water Rate (the annual Rate is £15 of which two-thirds is is debited to the Mosque)	10.	-.	-
Total:	210.	1.	-

Telephone – The only guide to the yearly expenditure is the bill for the quarter ending 30 September 1941. i.e £2.8.5d. This points to an expenditure of say £10, two-thirds of which is debited to the Mosque fund and one-third to the Islamic Centre.

Electricity – Here again the only guide is the bill for the second quarter of 1941/42 i.e. £1.16.10. This points to an expenditure of say £8, two-thirds of which is debited to the Mosque and one-third to the Islamic Centre.

Gas – The expenditure is roughly estimated at £16 – two-thirds to the Mosque and one-third to the Islamic Centre.

Minutes of the Meeting of the Trustees of the London Mosque Fund, held at 83 Swan Court, Chelsea, on Friday 8 October 1943 at 12.30 pm

Present:

Sir Hassan Suhrawardy, Chairman
Earl Winterton

Husain Said Bey, Esq.
Waris Ameer Ali, Esq.

Sir John Woodhead was also present.

1. The minutes of the meeting held on 20 August 1943 were confirmed.

2. The bronze memorial tablet which was to be put up in the premises of the East London Mosque, was examined and approved by the Trustees. The Trustees authorised the Chairman to arrange with Mr Alistair MacDonald, the architect, to take charge of the tablet, insure it for £60, and select a suitable place in the wall of the Reading Room of the Islamic Culture Centre and take necessary action to fix it there.

To provide against mishaps the Chairman was authorised to arrange for a photograph to be taken at a cost of about £1.12.6. The Chairman was to take necessary action to raise funds towards meeting the cost of putting up the Memorial tablet and send copies of the photograph to such persons of whom financial help was expected.

The Chairman was authorised to pay bill No. BW 1037, on account of making and supplying all materials for the Bronze Memorial tablet with enamel lettering, amounting to £46.5.0. from Messrs. Osborne Company Limited, 117 Gower Street, London WC1.

Proposed by Sir Hassan Suhrawardy and agreed unanimously that the thanks of the Trustees be conveyed to Mr Alireza Shinjan, Secretary of the Turkish Halkevi, 14 Fitzhardinge Street, W1 for very kindly writing the Arabic inscription as an act of friendship; also to convey the thanks of the Trustees to Mons. Kamal Labbane, Attaché to the Egyptian Embassy for kindly drawing up the Arabic Text of the Memorial tablet. To Mr A. Yusuf Ali, the Trustees were indebted, for being responsible for the English inscription.

3. The Trustees considered the correspondence connected with the Notice of Termination of the Agreement with the Jamiat-ul-Muslimin as agents of the Trustees dated 3 September 1943, their reply dated 10 September and letter dated 1 October 1943, from Messrs. Cardew Smith & Sons, Solicitors on behalf of the Trustees to the Jamiat-ul-Muslimin.[153] It was decided that further legal action be postponed till

[153] Through their solicitors, the Trustees served the notice of termination on 3 September 1943, cancelling the Jamiat's authority to act as agents of the Trustees and requiring it to quit the premises of the East London Mosque. See BL, IOR, L/P&J/12/468, fo. 269.

after consideration of the reply received by Messrs. Cardew Smith & Sons, the solicitors.

4. (a) The Trustees approved the proposal made by the Chairman that Dr Hasan Nachat Pasha, the Egyptian Ambassador, should be elected a Trustee in place of Sir Azizul Huque who had resigned on his return to India, and that His Excellency should be invited to accept the position of Vice-President of the Trustees. It was unanimously resolved that subject to his consent His Excellency should be elected a Trustee.

(b) The Chairman was authorised to issue a statement on behalf of the Trustees to remove misleading impressions caused by the action taken by the Jamiat-ul-Muslimin.[154]

5. The Honorary Treasurer informed the Trustees that on account of investment of the donation of £1,000 received from H. H the Nawab Ruler of Bahawalpur, the income from investments now amounted to £260 per annum and the expenditure £325, not counting the expenditure for repairs and renewals. Sir Hassan Suhrawardy expressed the hope that by converting the telephone into a coin call box and installing the shilling-in-the-slot form of gas meters, there will be certain control in expenditure and other measure would be taken to reduce expenditures. Sir John Woodhead informed the Trustees that he hoped before Sir Hassan Suhrawardy left England it would be possible for him to secure the services of a suitable Muslim gentleman to take over the duties of Honorary Treasurer.[155] Sir John Woodhead will be glad to give all assistance to the person elected to the position, and on this clear understanding he would be agreeable to stay on a little longer.

[154]This probably refers to the widely advertised public protest meeting that the Jamiat-ul-Muslimin held on 10 October 1943, at which it protested against the Trustees' notice of termination and presented its case for its refusal to accept it. According to the Jamiat, 'the India Office ran the affairs of the mosque through its representatives, the Trustees', who were not 'good Muslims and put the interests of the British Government before their duty to Islam' (see BL, IOR, L/P&J/12/468, fos 270–271).

[155]It seems that the Jamiat-ul-Muslimin's point of having only Muslims on the committee was being taken up by the committee itself here. Waris Ameer Ali put it on record that he did not want Woodhead to resign. Woodhead, uncomfortable about the objections raised by the Jamiat with regard to his position as a non-Muslim Honorary Treasurer on the LMF Executive Committee, sought advice at the India Office. The India Office, suspicious of the Jamiat's political leanings, was reluctant to advise Woodhead's resignation as 'there will be no-one to keep an eye on developments from the official angle'. See Appendix III, and correspondence in the ELM Archives.

Mr Waris Ameer Ali expressed the hope that it would be possible for Sir John Woodhead not to resign.

Sir Hassan Suhrawardy mentioned the name of a suitable Muslim gentleman from the Persian Legation but his acceptance of the responsibilities of the office depended on certain provisions to be made in the absence of Sir Hassan Suhrawardy.

6. The Trustees agreed that the next meeting would be held at 26 South Street, W1, in the Committee Room attached to the office of Mons. Husain Said Bey and that he should be approached in time to arrange details. Mons. Husain Said Bey was also invited to discuss with Sir Hassan Suhrawardy the proposed arrangements regarding the management of the Mosque, and the contribution of the Executive Committee.

7. The meeting terminated with a vote of thanks to the Chairman.

Confirmed: H Nachat

A meeting of the Executive Committee of the London Mosque Fund will be held at 83, Swan Court, Chelsea Manor Street, SW3 on Friday, 8 October 1943 at 2.15 pm

AGENDA

1. To confirm the minutes of the last meeting.
2. The Chairman to report the acceptance by him of the resignation from the Hon Secretary, Mr Hatim Attari, and to place correspondence in connection with it.
3. To consider:
   a) Correspondence in connection with the notice of termination of agreement with the Jamiat-ul-Muslimin dated 3 September 1943
   b) Their reply dated 10 September
   c) Letter dated 1 October on behalf of the Trustees from Messrs. Cardew, Smith & Ross, Solicitors, to the Jamiat-ul-Muslimin
4. To place on record the action taken by the Chairman on behalf of the Trustees and Executive Committee.
5. Finances. Report by the Hon Treasurer.

6. To consider:
a) Re-constitution of the Executive Committee
b) The scheme for the management of the Mosque
c) Arrangements during the temporary absence of Sir Hassan Suhrawardy from England

7. Any other business.

Chairman

Minutes of the Meeting of the Executive Committee of the London Mosque Fund held at 83 Swan Court, Chelsea, on Friday 8 October 1943 at 2.15 pm

Present:

Sir Hassan Suhrawardy (Chairman)
Mr Waris Ameer Ali
Mr Yusuf Ali
Sir John Woodhead (Hon Treasurer)
Syed M. Syeedulla (Hon Secretary)
Apologies for absence were received from Mr Kamal Lebbane.

1. The minutes of the meeting held on August 31 were read and confirmed.

2. Correspondence in connection with the resignation of Honorary Secretary-ship by Mr Hatim Attari which had been circulated was considered and recorded.

3. The Executive Committee considered the correspondence connected with the Notice of Termination of the Agreement with the Jamiat-ul-Muslimin as agents of the Trustees dated 3 September 1943, their reply dated 10 September and letter dated 1 October 1943 from Messrs Cardew, Smith & Ross, Solicitors on behalf of the trustees to the Jamiat-ul-Muslimin. It was decided that further legal action be postponed till after consideration of the reply received by Messrs. Cardew Smith & Ross, the Solicitors.

4. The Executive Committee approved of the action taken by the Chairman on behalf of the Executive Committee.

5. The Hon Treasurer informed the Trustees that on account of investment of the donation of £1,000 received from H. H the Nawab Ruler of Bahawalpur, the income from investments now

amounted to £260 per annum and the expenditure £325, not counting the expenditure for repairs and renewals. Sir Hassan Suhrawardy expressed the hope that by converting the telephone into a coin call box and installing the shilling-in-the-slot form of gas meters, there will be a certain control in expenditure and other measures would also be taken to reduce expenditure.

Sir John Woodhead informed the Executive Committee that he hoped before Sir Hassan Suhrawardy left England it would be possible for him to secure the services of a suitable Muslim gentleman to take over the duties of Hon Treasurer. Sir John Woodhead will be glad to give all assistance to the person elected to the position and on this clear understanding he will be agreeable to staying on a little longer. Mr Waris Ameer Ali expressed the hope that it would be possible for Sir John Woodhead not to resign.

Sir Hassan Suhrawardy mentioned the name of a suitable Muslim gentleman from the Persian Legation but his acceptance of the responsibilities depended on certain provisions to be made in the absence of Sir Hassan Suhrawardy.

6. The Committee considered Item 6 (a) (b) and (c) and authorised the Chairman to take necessary action regarding the matter and interview the authority concerned.

The Chairman who was already authorised by the Trustees was also authorised by the Executive Committee to issue a statement to remove misleading impressions caused by the action taken by the Jamiat-ul-Muslimin.

The Executive Committee agreed that the next meeting would be held at 26 South Street, W1 in the Committee Room attached to the office of Mons Hussain Said Bey and that sufficient notice be given him to arrange details.

7. It was reported to the Executive Committee that the Trustees had authorized payment of bill No BW 1037 on account making and supplying all materials for the Bronze Memorial tablet with enamel lettering amounting to £46.5.0 from Messrs. Osborn Co. Ltd. 117 Gower Street, London WC1.

To provide against mishap the Chairman was authorised to arrange for a photograph to be taken at a cost of about £1.12.6. The Chairman was to take necessary action to raise funds towards meeting the cost of putting up the Memorial tablet and send copies of the photograph to such persons of whom financial help was expected.

The Bronze Memorial tablet which was to be put up in the premises of the East London Mosque, was examined and approved by the Executive Committee. The Chairman was authorised to arrange with Mr Alistair MacDonald, the Architect, to take charge of the Tablet, insure it for £60, and select a suitable place in the wall of the Reading Room of the Islamic Culture Centre and take necessary action to fix it there.

The Chairman was authorised to take necessary action to raise funds to meet the deficit. After discussion, it was agreed that the Muslim members of the Executive Committee would annually subscribe any sum convenient to them to the Mosque Fund.[156]

The Meeting terminated with a vote of thanks to the Chairman.

Minutes of a meeting of the Trustees of the London Mosque Fund held at the Royal Egyptian Embassy on Wednesday 1 December 1943 at 12.30 pm

Present:

H.E Dr Hassan Nachat Pasha (Egyptian Ambassador – Vice President)
The Rt Hon Earl Winterton
Judge Waris Ameer Ali
Mr Hussein Mohammed Said

The minutes of the last meeting held on Friday 8 October were read and approved.

Lord Winterton began by saying, on behalf of the Trustees how pleased they all were to see His Excellency the Egyptian Ambassador in the chair. He felt very strongly that His Excellency's presence would render valuable help to the Trustees in the direction of the affairs of the Mosque.

Dr Hassan Nachat Pasha thanked Lord Winterton and the Trustees for their kind sentiments and for having asked him to become one of their number. He hoped that they would soon be able to overcome all their difficulties.

[156] It appears that the Trustees had decided to follow the example of the Jamiat-ul-Muslimin, albeit flexibly, with regard to the meeting of the Trust's annual expenditure. The Jamiat was an organization with an annual membership subscription. See ELM Archives, Jamiat-ul-Muslimin membership records.

Dr Hassan Nachat Pasha went on to say that he had heard of the trouble there had been between Sir Hassan Suhrawardy and some of the Moslems in England and he wanted to make it quite clear that as far as the Trustees were concerned there was nothing against their being of any religion or nationality. There was a distinction to be made between the Trustees, who were entrusted with the administration of money and the people who were entrusted with the services carried out on the premises of the Mosque itself. This latter committee should definitely be Mohammedan.

His Excellency said that he also wished to clear up the question of their Treasurer. There was a great deal of work to be done and they would then know where they stood.

Lord Winterton said he wished to propose Sir John Woodhead to continue with his support. He had been up till now such a valuable Treasurer and they still needed the benefit of his experience.

The other Trustees supported Lord Winterton.

Sir John Woodhead thanked the Committee but said he thought that perhaps the Treasurer should be a Mohammedan.

Dr Nachat Pasha assured Sir John Woodhead that this was not necessary.

Sir John Woodhead explained that at the present he was carrying out the duties of Secretary and that unless he had some of this work taken off his shoulders he did not feel he could take on the work of Treasurer.

Dr Hassan Nachat Pasha said that one of the Trustees then present would be appointed as Secretary.

Sir John Woodhead said that in that case he would be glad to continue as Treasurer.

Dr Hassan Nachat Pasha said that the Trustees all knew that Sir Hassan Suhrawardy had been having difficulties with the Jamiat-ul-Muslimin who had been entrusted with the services in the Mosque.[157]

[157] According to a Metropolitan Police report, the Jamiat-ul-Muslimin had 'the support of most, if not all, of the Muslims living in this part of London. Certain of its members have worked hard in the interests of Islam and have helped in many ways indigent Muslims and others who have suffered misfortune.' The dispute with the Trustees of the LMF, which began soon after the inauguration of the East London Mosque in Commercial Road in August 1941, was over who would control the mosque's affairs – the Trustees or the leaders of the Jamiat. See BL, IOR, L/P&J/12/468, fo. 267, 'Extract from Metropolitan Police report', 14 October 1943.

Judge Waris Ameer Ali said that he had warned Sir Hassan a long time before that he would have trouble with these people.

Dr Hassan Nachat Pasha said that Sir Hassan Suhrawardy had seen the difficulty of dealing with a self-constituted body. Dr Nachat understood that there was another Committee between the Board of Trustees and the work of the Mosque, which was the managing Committee.

Sir John Woodhead said that as far as he knew the Managing Committee had only met once.

Dr Nachat went on to inform the Trustees of another big project. All the Moslems were uniting to found a moslem and oriental cultural centre in London. They had been given a big house in Regents Park for this purpose and for the purpose of building a mosque after the war. They had decided to form this cultural centre where all the different moslem countries would be represented. There would be a committee for the management of all the mosques in England both outside London and in it. Dr Nachat suggested that the Board of Trustees should ask this committee if they would undertake the management of the East London Mosque.

Sir John Woodhead said that from the legal point of view there should be no difficulty in this project.

Lord Winterton and Judge Ameer Ali said they thought the idea was excellent.

Dr Hassan Nachat Pasha said that when he heard of the difficulties the mosque was experiencing, he wrote to the King of Egypt to ask him if he would send an imam for this mosque and to ask if, as there was not enough money to pay an imam, he could be paid at least for the first year or so. Unfortunately His Majesty was in hospital and Dr Nachat had as yet received no reply, but he had every hope that the reply would be favourable.

Judge Ameer Ali said that he supposed it would be difficult to find someone suitable in the middle of the war.

Dr Hassan Nachat Pasha replied that fortunately the sea route from Egypt was re-established and there should be no difficulty in sending someone over.

Judge Ameer Ali said that it was very important that they should have someone who had a really good influence. The mosque was frequented by the poor and uneducated moslems and it was most desirable that their spiritual and moral needs should not be forgotten.

Dr Nachat replied that if an imam was sent from Cairo he would always feel responsible to this Embassy.

Dr Nachat then read a letter he had received from Sir Hassan Suhrawardy:

"I am however worried about the Mosque and shall be most grateful if you will very kindly let me know what has happened, since I left London on the 26 October. I wanted to see you before I left but on account of leaving at a moment's notice unexpectedly, I couldn't let you know that they were trying to arrange a deputation to wait on you consisting of persons who would apparently look like disinterested persons but were really emissaries trying to take possession of the Mosque by indirect methods. I have explained the situation to H.E. Hassanein Pasha and His Eminence Sheikh Al Maraghi. I have sent you all papers received up to date from the solicitors and also a copy of the Minutes of the Meeting of the Trustees held on Friday October 8 at which Your Excellency was elected a Trustee and the Vice President, and thus the future of the Mosque was put in your hands."

Sir John Woodhead said he was not happy at the thought of starting legal proceedings against the Jamiat-ul-Muslimin.

Dr Hassan Nachat Pasha said he did not think it would come to that. He intended to speak to some of them as Moslem to Moslem.

Lord Winterton said that he had been told that a meeting of protest had been held by the Jamiat-ul-Muslimin in North London.[158]

Sir John Woodhead said that there had been such a meeting but nothing had come of it.

Mr Hussein Mohammed Said then read cables exchanged between His Excellency the Egyptian Ambassador and the Chief of the Royal Cabinet, regarding the East London Mosque.

"Boustane London. Secretary Jamiat-ul-Muslimin cables following Trustees East London Mosque contemplate immediate handing over

[158] British intelligence reports noted this meeting, which took place at Conway Hall. Several hundred Muslims and a small number of non-Muslims, in particular those with Indian Nationalist sympathies, were present. Delegates had also arrived from the Jamiat-ul-Muslimin's Newcastle, Manchester, and Glasgow branches. See BL, IOR, L/P&J/12/468, fos 271–272.

management Mosque to non-Muslim control. Please enquire and forward all available information kind regards. Chief Royal Cabinet"

"Excellency Chief Royal Cabinet, Cairo. East London Mosque is established under trust fund 1910 president Aga Khan money collected from various sources. Since foundation fund two trustees were non-moslems now only one Lord Winterton. Trustees appointed executive committee for management of the mosque amongst who were two non-moslems now all members executive committee are moslems. The self-formed Jamiat ul Muslimin who were lately authorised by the executive committee to manage the mosque disagreed with Suhrawardy who is chairman of the executive Committee. Consequently executive committee put end to the delegation given to Jamiat ul Muslimin to manage the mosque wanting to place mosque under direct control. Allegations by El Jamiat are totally unfounded. Report follows by post best wishes Ambassador."

"Excellency Hassanein Pacha, Palais Abdine, Caro. Référence ma dépêche du 12 octobre concernant East London Mosque vous prie soumettre qu'afin prevenir dissention facheuse [*sic*] entre mussulmans residant [*sic*] ici ai accepté poste vice président Trustees dite mosque. Pour arriver cette fin il est nécessaire avoir un imam connaissant anglais pour diriger services religieux d'une manière digne. Fonds trust ne suffisent pas pour paiement salaire imam et si ces trais sont supportés par Wakfs[159] publiques ou royaux le geste serait très bien apprécié. Amitiés. Nachat."[160]

Dr Hassan Nachat Pasha then proposed that Mr Hussein Mohammed Said be appointed secretary.

The other Trustees seconded this proposal which was carried unanimously.

This concluded the business of the day.

[159] Also spelt *waqf*, this is an inalienable religious endowment in Islamic law, typically denoting a building or plot of land for Muslim religious or charitable purposes. The donated assets are held by a charitable trust.

[160] Translation of paragraph: 'Excellency Hassanein Pacha, Palais Abdine, Cairo. With reference to my letter of 12 October concerning the East London Mosque, may I ask you to agree, in order to prevent regrettable disagreement amongst Muslims resident here, I have accepted the post of vice president of the Trustees of the mosque. To meet this aim it is necessary to have an imam who speaks English to run the religious services in a worthy manner. The Trust funds are not enough to pay a salary for an imam and if these aspects could be supported by public or private Wakfs, the gesture would be very much appreciated. Best wishes. Nachat.'

India Office
Whitehall
SW1
7 July 1944

Dear Mr Levrane

I am sending you the papers about which I believe I spoke to you and in connection with which you will find a resolution of the Trustees at their meeting held, if my memory is correct, in December last. You will find a note which I wrote on the matter over a year ago.

The Trustees decided that no change should be made as regards the names in which the securities are held, but they decided that the appointment of the existing Trustees should be placed on a proper footing and that the Deed as settled by counsel should be executed.

The difficulty has been that His Highness the Aga Khan is in Switzerland. At one time I though that we could get the Deed executed by sending it to him in Switzerland, but finally came to the conclusion that this would be very difficult and so I have done nothing in the matter so far. Now that the war is drawing to a close I think the best course is to wait until peace has been declared and His Excellency the Aga Khan again comes to this country.

Another reason I did not proceed with the matter was that the Trustees were changing rather rapidly and indeed the Deed which was settled over a year ago would now have to be amended in view of the changes which have taken place in the Trustees during the last twelve months.

I have also mentioned this matter to M. Said, who, I think, is fairly acquainted with the matter.

Yours sincerely
J. Woodhead

Minutes of a meeting of the Trustees of the London Mosque Fund held at the Royal Egyptian Embassy on 22 June 1944

Present:

H.E Sr Hassan Nachat Pasha, Egyptian Ambassador and Vice-President

Judge Waris Ameer Ali
Monsieur Hussein Mohammed Said

Sir John Woodhead, Honorary Treasurer was also present

1. The minutes of the last meeting held on 1 December 1943 were approved and signed.

2. On the proposal of Mr Waris Ameer Ali and seconded by Monsieur Hussein Mohammed Said the Committee accounts for the year ended 31 March 1943 were approved and signed by His Excellency the Chairman and the Honorary Treasurer.

3. The Honorary Treasurer placed before the meeting, the accounts for the year ended 31 March 1944. They were approved. The accounts with the Auditors' certificate have not yet been received. On receipt they will be placed before the next meeting and formally approved.

4. The Honorary Treasurer reported that the caretaker at the Mosque is paid partly from the Indigent Moslems Burial Fund. The amount paid from this Fund is £1 per week. In view of the fact that the only work done by the caretaker for the Burial Fund is in connection with the preparation of bodies for burial, for which he is paid separately, it was decided that, with effect from the beginning of July the sum of £1 per week which is now paid from the Burial Fund should be paid from the London Mosque Fund.

5. It was recorded that Mr M.R. Zada has resigned from the position of Trustee.

6. Sir John Woodhead informed the meeting that he was leaving England and would be away for at least six months.[161] It was therefore necessary to appoint someone to carry on the work of Honorary Treasurer. It was proposed by Monsieur Hussein Mohammed Said and seconded by Mr Waris Ameer Ali that Monsieur Kamal El Labbane should be appointed Honorary Treasurer.

This concluded the business of the day.

[161] Woodhead had recently been appointed to chair the Bengal Famine Inquiry Commission and so was travelling to India. This Commission, established by the Government of India under Ordinance No. XXVIII of 1944, first met in July of that year. Its report, which was issued in April 1945, gave a comprehensive and detailed account of the events in Bengal and of related happenings elsewhere. For more detail, see Henry Knight, *Food Administration in India, 1939–1947* (Stanford, CA, 1954), ch. 8, 'The Bengal famine of 1943: background'.

[*Signature at the end is impossible to decipher – but is probably that of Said, the Chairman at the next meeting*]

[COPY]

LONDON MOSQUE FUND
Trust Deed

[*dated 1926*]

The Trust Deed provides for (i) Trustees; (ii) Executive Committee.

(i) The Trustees present are:

H.H the Aga Khan, F.C., G.C.S.I., G.C.I.E., etc.
c/c The Swiss Hotel
London E1 President

H.E. Hassan Nachat Pasha
Egyptian Ambassador
75 South Audley Street
London W1 Vice-President
The Rt Hon Earl Winterton M.P
61 Eccleston Square
London SW1

Judge W. Ameer Ali, C.I.E., I.C.S., (Retd)
India House
Aldwych
London WC2

Private address: 1 Alexandra Court, Queens Gate, London SW7

Monsieur H.M. Said
Egyptian Embassy
75 South Audley Street
London W1

Lt. Col. Sir Hassan Suhrawardy O.B.E
4 Tughlak Road
New Delhi
India

Mr Zada was a Trustee, but has resigned as he has now left England. His resignation should be formally accepted at the next meeting of the Trustees.

According to the Trust Deed, the Muslim Member of the Council of the Secretary of State for India is entitled to be appointed as a Trustee. Sir Hassan Suhrawardy is now the Muslim Member. His term of office as Adviser to the Secretary of State expires in July 1944. His successor, when appointed, should be appointed a Trustee. I believe that Sir Hassan Suhrawardy wishes to remain a Trustee although he has returned to India.

(ii) The Executive Committee consists of the following:

Lt. Col. Sir Hassan Suhrawardy O.B.E
4 Tughlak Road
New Delhi
India

Judge W. Ameer Ali, C.I.E., I.C.S., (Retd)
India House
Aldwych
London WC2

Mr Kemal Lebbane
Egyptian Embassy
75 South Audley Street
London W1
Private address: 26 South Street, Mayfair, London W1

[*handwritten next to this* 'now left England']

Mr A. Yusuf Ali C.B.E
3 Mansel Road
Wimbledon
SW19

Mr Hatim Attari
41 Berkeley Square
London W1

Sheikh Abdul Hamid
34A Buckingham Gate
London SW1

Mr Mohammed Syed Ullah
(Hon Secretary)
India House
Aldwych
London WC2

Private Address: 46 Kingswood Court, West End Lane, London NW6

Dr A.J. Arberry
Balliol College
Oxford

(When questions concerning the Culture Centre are under consideration)

b) Investments

The investments consist of:

£4,130	3 ½%	War Stock (1952)
£2,500	3 ½%	Conversion Stock (1961)
£1,000	3 %	Savings Bonds

The interest on these investments is credited automatically to the account of the London Mosque Fund at the Bank of England. The Dividends are paid free of Income Tax. The scrip is held in safe custody by the Bank of England.

c) Property

The Trustees own the premises at 446–450 Commercial Road, E1. The title deeds are with the Solicitors. The property is insured with The Guardian Assurance Co. against damage by fire. The premium is £3.3.-d a year.

d) Income Tax and Land Tax

No income tax or land tax is payable on the property in Commercial Road. Although the Income tax and Land Tax authorities have agreed to this, a demand was received for payment of these taxes in January 1944. I think this demand was made in error, as on receipt of the papers, I telephoned to the Income Tax authorities, told them the same thing had happened last year and said that if I did not hear from them again I would presume a mistake had been made this year also. I have heard nothing further and have paid no further attention to the demand note. The property in Commercial Road is entitled to exemption from Income Tax and Land Tax because it is owned by a charitable organisation (The London Mosque Fund) and used for "charitable" purposes. The property is also exempt from the payment of war Damage Insurance Premium.

e) Architect

The Architect is Mr Alaister C. MacDonald, F.R.I.B.A., F.R.I.A.S., 29 Avenue Road, London NW8. (Telephone: Primrose 1622). He supervises the carrying out of any repairs to the property. If any repairs are necessary he will arrange to carry them out.

f). Caretaker

The caretaker is Mr Ali Basha. His wages are as follows:

i) as caretaker, £1.17.0d per week less 1s/10d a week on account of insurance contributions
ii) As Teacher of Koran, £5 a month (nos. i and ii paid for by the London Mosque Fund)
iii) £1 per week paid from the Indigent Muslims Burial Fund.

The insurance books on account of Unemployment and Health are kept by the Trustees and are stamped periodically. The cost of the weekly stamps is 3s/8d of which 1s/10d, as indicated above, is recovered from Ali Basha and 1s/10d paid from the funds of the Trustees.

Ali Basha is provided with free quarters at the Mosque and also with electric light and gas free.

I have suggested, vide separate note attached, that the £1 a week at present paid from the Indigent Muslim Burial Fund should be paid from the Mosque Fund.

f) General Expenditure

Apart from Ali Basha's wages, the main items of expenditure are:

i) General Rates
ii) Water Rate
iii) Electricity
iv) Gas
v) Telephone
vi) Repairs
vii) Miscellaneous expenditure incurred by Ali Basha.

There are two telephones at the Mosque. One is a coin box telephone. This latter is used by the general public. Ali Basha has the key to the coin box and periodically opens it and remits the money to the Trustees.

It has been proposed that there should be a shilling-in-the-slot meter for gas, but this has not been introduced as yet.

There are two accounts at the Bank of England:

a) The London Mosque Fund account
b) The London Mosque Fund "B" account

The "B" account was opened with the object of keeping the expenditure and receipts of the Culture Centre separate. While the Culture Centre was functioning, or rather endeavouring to function,[162] the following items of expenditure used to be debited in part to the "B" account:

General Rate
Water Rate
Electricity
Gas
Telephone Account
Caretaker's wages

– one third to the "B" account.

Wages of Teacher of Koran – Half to the "B" account.

I have not made this division since October 1943 because the Culture Centre is not in existence.[163] For the present the "B" account is not being operated on and if the Culture Centre is not revived it might just as well be closed and its small balance transferred to the main account.

g) Audit

The audit is carried out by Messrs. Feasey, Hull and Feasey, 5 Norfolk Street, Strand, WC2. The audited accounts are approved at a meeting of the Trustees.

h) Solicitors

The Solicitors are Messrs. Cardew Smith and Ross, 27 Ely Place, EC1. They are very helpful in many matters. They are paid for the work they do.

i) Cheques

Cheques require to be signed by a Trustee and the Hon Treasurer. The Bank of England are the Trustees' Bankers.

j) The British Council

When the Mosque was opened it was hoped that in addition to being a place of worship it would be a Culture Centre. The British Council

[162] This suggests that the Islamic Culture Centre was no longer conducting any activities.
[163] Date of closure could not be established.

gave a capital grant of £100 towards the establishment of a library and for one year gave a grant of £75 towards the cost of running the Culture Centre.

Dr Arberry and also a representative of the British Council attended meetings of the Executive Committee when questions concerning the Culture Centre were under discussion.

The attempt to establish a Culture Centre has failed completely and at present the Centre is not operating.

k) Furniture

There is on the appropriate file a stock list showing the furniture etc. which is the property of the Trustees of the Mosque. The Jamiat-ul-Muslimin supplied chairs and tables for the large rooms at the back of the Mosque which, in addition to being used as Prayer rooms when the congregation is large, are also used for entertaining the worshippers on the occasions of the great festivals. The Jamiat-ul-Muslimin claim that these are their own; they have not been entered on the stock list.

LONDON MOSQUE FUND

The caretaker, Mr Ali Basha, is at present paid –

a) from the Mosque Fund
   i) as caretaker, £1.17.-d a week (Net £1.15.2d after deducting Unemployment and Health insurance
   ii) as Teacher of Koran, £5 a month

b) from the Indigent Muslims Burial Fund £1 a week

In view of the amount of work done by Mr Ali Basha for the Burial Fund a payment of £1 a week does not appear to be justified.

The Mosque Fund is now in a stronger financial position – vide the annexed Memo – and I suggest that as from 1 April 1944 the £1 a week now met out of the Burial Fund should be charged to the Mosque Fund.

J.A. Woodhead
Hon Treasurer

Estimate of Receipts and Expenditure of the London Mosque Fund

Expenditure

A. Actuals of 1942/3:

Water Rate	£ 18.	0.	4
General Rate	£ 47.	10.	0
Telephone	£ 8.	14.	2
Gas	£ 35.	0.	2
Electricity	£ 8.	10.	6
Insurance	£ 3.	3.	0
Fee for registering premises as place for the solemnization of marriages	£ 3.	0.	0
National Health Insce.	£ 11.	14.	4
Miscellaneous	£ 21.	16.	10
Total:	£ 156.	19.	4[164]

Estimated:

Clerical Assistance	£ 6.	0.	0
Caretaker and reader of Koran:			
1. caretaker at £1.15.2 a week	£ 91.	8.	0
2. reader of Koran £5 a month	£ 60.	0.	0
Audit fee	£ 5.	0.	0
Total:	£ 157.	8.	0[165]

Grand total: £316.7.4[166]

Receipts

Conversion Stock Dividends	£ 87.	10.	0
War Stock Dividends	£ 143.	19.	0
Savings Bonds Dividends	£ 30.	0.	0
H.H. the Aga Khan's Grant	£ 150.	0.	0
Total:	£ 411.	9.	0

Excess of receipts over expenditure: £ 97.1.10[167]

Note: This estimate takes no account of expenditure on repairs. It is difficult to say what this will amount to over a period of years. An average annual figure of £65 may be taken.

[164] This total should be £157.9.4.
[165] This appears not to include the audit fee.
[166] This total should be £314.17.4 (or £319.7.4 with the audit fee).
[167] This total should be £96.11.8 (or £91.11.8 if the audit fee is taken into account).

Minutes of the Meeting of the Trustees of the London Mosque Fund held at the Royal Egyptian Embassy 15 February 1946

Present:

Mons Hussein Mohammed Said (in the Chair)
Sir Torick Ameer Ali*
Waris Ameer Ali

Sir John Woodhead was also present.

A letter of apology of absence had been received from Earl Winterton.

1. The minutes of the last Meeting of the Trustees held on 22 June 1944 were read and confirmed.

2. Judge Waris Ameer Ali said that he was prepared to agree that his letter of resignation of 22 June 1945, from his Trusteeship, should be treated as withdrawn and cancelled. It was accordingly recorded that Judge Waris Ameer Ali was still a Trustee.

3. The Meeting was informed that Monsieur Kamal El Labbane had resigned the post of Hon Treasurer on his return to Egypt. It was proposed by Monsieur H.M. Said and seconded by Sir Torick Ameer Ali that Sir John Woodhead be appointed Honorary Treasurer and that he be authorized to sign (together with one of the Trustees) cheques drawn on the London Mosque Fund's account at the Bank of England.

4. It was placed on recorded that under Clause 6 of the declaration of Trust, Sir Torick Ameer Ali, the Moslem Adviser to the Secretary of State for India, had been appointed a Trustee in place of Sir Hassan Suhrawardy who vacated the office. This change dates from November, 1944.

5. The appointment of Md. Saiyid Abbas as caretaker of the East London Mosque from 25 July 1945 at a salary of £2.17.0d a week was confirmed.

6. It was decided that the Hon Treasurer should be authorized, in consultation with Mr Alister MacDonald, the architect, to carry out the necessary repairs to the Mosque building in Commercial Road.

7. The meeting concluded with a vote of thanks to the Chair.

I agree to the appointment of Mr John Woodhead as Hon Treasurer of the London Mosque Fund in succession to Monsieur Kamal El Labbane, who has resigned that office on his return to Egypt.
21 February 1946 [*signature unclear*]

Ref: CCO/1475 BANK OF ENGLAND
26 February 1946

Copy

The Honorary Treasurer
The London Mosque Fund
75 South Audley St. W1

Dear Sir

I write with reference to your three letters of the 16th instant in which the Bank are –

1. Requested to transfer the balance, viz. £57.8.0 of the London Mosque Fund "B" account to the Fund's ordinary account and subsequently to close the former account.
2. Notified of your appointment as Honorary Treasurer in place of M.K. El Labbane, supplied with a certified copy of the Resolution of 15 February making the appointment and given your confirmation of their action in paying certain cheques signed by two trustees.
3. Advised of the cancellation of the resignation, dated 22 June last, of Mr Waris Ameer Ali and given a list of the present trustees of the Fund.

With regard to 1. above, I would say that to be effective this letter must be signed by the Honorary Treasurer and one of the trustees. I shall be obliged, therefore, if you will kindly arrange for the Bank to receive confirmation of these instructions over the signature of one of the trustees.

With regard to 3. above, it is noted that although Sir Torick Ameer Ali seconds the resolution of 15 February his name does not appear in your list of the present trustees. In the circumstances perhaps you will be good enough to let me know whether Sir Torick continues to be a trustee.

I would also refer to the Bank's letter of 23 October last and draw your attention to the fact that the Bank still await the resolution appointing

H.E Hassan Nachat Pasha a trustee, together with a specimen of his signature.

A resolution is also required stating which officers may order the delivery of, or otherwise deal with, the securities which are now, or may hereafter be, held by the Bank on behalf of the Fund.

You will also notice from the Bank's letter of 23 October that the name of Lt. Col. Sir Hassan Suhrarwardy, O.B.E who is no longer a trustee, appears as one of the stockholders on the certificate for £1,000 3% savings bonds 1960/70 held by the Bank on behalf of the Fund.

Yours faithfully

(signed) Gwylm-Williams [*name illegible*]
For Chief Cashier.

27 February 1946

Sir John Woodhead
G.C.I.E., K.C.S.I
Woking

Dear Sir John

The enclosed letter arrived from the Bank of England this morning. As it is only possible to deal with a portion of the letter, I am sending you a copy. I have prepared the required confirmation for the transfer of the £57 and this can be signed when you come in, when all the queries can probably be answered together.

Statements of Accounts from the Banks are in: -

Barclays –	Credit	Balance	I.M.B.F …..	£662.19.6
B. of E. –	"	"	Ldn Mosque	£344.16.4

A chit has been received to the effect that £50 has been paid into Barclays (via Coutts) on behalf of the Aga Khan, dated 1 January 1946.

Yours sincerely

…………………….. [*signature unclear*]

Minutes of the Trustees of the London Mosque Fund held at the Royal Egyptian Embassy on 12 December 1946

Present:

Monsieur Hussein Mohammed Said (in the Chair)
Sir Torick Ameer Ali
Waris Ameer Ali Esq.
Sir John Woodhead Hon Treasurer

An apology of absence had been received from Lord Winterton

1. The minutes of the last meeting of the Trustees held on 15 February 1946 were read and confirmed.

2. The Audited Accounts for the years ended 31 March 1944; 31 March 1945 and 31 March 1946 were approved (and signed by the Chairman and the Hon Treasurer) on the proposal of Mr Waris Ameer Ali and seconded by Sir Torick Ameer Ali.

3. On the proposal of Monsieur H.M. Said and seconded by Sir Torick Ameer Ali a vote of thanks was passed to the Auditors, Messrs. Feasy, Hull and Feasy, for their services during the years 1943, 1944, 1945, & 1945–46. It was also decided that Messrs. Feasy, Hull and Feasy be appointed auditors for the [year] 1946–47.

4. On the proposal of Sir Torick Ameer Ali and seconded by Mr Waris Ameer Ali, approval was given to the appointment as caretaker at £2 17s a week of:

i) F.B Powell, from 25 June 1946 to 22 September 1946
ii) Kale Khan from 23 September 1946

5. On the proposal of Monsieur H.M Said, seconded by Sir Torick Ameer Ali, the Trustees recorded with deepest regret the death of Sir Hassan Suhrawardy, who had been a Trustee for some years and who had taken the keenest interest in the establishment of the Mosque in Commercial Road. It was decided that a letter of condolence be sent to his daughter, Mrs Ikramullah[168] in New Delhi.

6. The question of the appointment of an additional Trustee or Trustees was postponed for consideration at a later meeting. In the

[168] Sir Hassan Suhrawardy's daughter, Shaista (1915–2000), was married to Mohammad Ikramullah, who was appointed Pakistan's High Commissioner to the United Kingdom in the 1950s. For reminiscences about her father, see Shaista Suhrawardy Ikramullah, *From Purdah to Parliament* (London, 1963).

meantime Sir Torick Ameer Ali agreed to review the position of the Trustees of the Trust Fund with the assistance of the Hon Treasurer.

7. The Hon Treasurer reported that he had hoped to have for presentation to the Trustees at this meeting an estimate of the cost of repairs to the Mosque. Unfortunately, it had not been received. The Hon Treasurer was authorised to carry out the necessary repairs.

8. The financial position of the Trust Fund as shown in the attached sheet by the Hon Treasurer was reviewed. The Hon Treasurer pointed out that the grant of £150 a year from H. H the Aga Khan would cease in 1949. After that date additional revenue would be imperative.

9. The meeting concluded with a vote of thanks to the Hon Treasurer for the work he had done, and to Monsieur H.M Said for taking the Chair.

Confirmed: W. Ameer Ali 5 February 1948

EXPENDITURE

<u>Receipt</u>

3 ½% Conversion St. Dividends	£ 87.	10.	0
3 ½% War Stock Dividends	£ 143.	19.	0
Savings Bonds (3%)	£ 30.	0.	0
H.H. the Aga Khan's grant	£ 150.	0.	0

Total: £411.9.0

<u>Expenditure</u>

a) Actuals of 1945/6:			
General and Water Rates	£ 52.	15	
Gas and Electric Light	£ 30.	12.	8
Telephone	£ 27.	13.	9
Insurance	£ 3.	3.	0
Postage & Sundries	£ 2.	16.	8
b) Estimated:			
Caretaker (£2.17 per week)	£ 148.	4.	0
Clerical assistance	£ 26.	0.	0
Audit Fee	£ 5.	0.	0
National Health, Pension & Unemployment Insurance £2s 10d per week	£ 7.	7.	4

Total: £303.12.5

Excess of Receipts over Expenditure:	£ 107.	16.	7

This estimate takes no account of expenditure on repairs. Mr Macdonald is having an estimate prepared of the cost of repairs and it is roughly estimated that it will cost us £300 (exclusive of the amount paid by the War Damage) to put the buildings into good repair.

On 11 September 1946 the balance at the credit of the fund was about £600.

23 August 1947

My dear Sir John Woodhead

In reply to yours of 21 August I have much pleasure in returning the transfer deeds duly signed and witnessed.

I too have been wondering what happened to the papers about which we wanted legal opinion concerning the assignment of the London Mosque Trust to a new body. I asked my brother the other day and he said that he had forwarded a legal opinion with the papers to Hussein Bey to whom I am therefore also writing.

Perhaps you may be kind enough to remind him also if you see him at any time. I will convey the gist of Hussein Bey's reply to you when received unless you have got any information of him first.

The matter whether my brother's trusteeship has lapsed with the lapse of his function as Adviser to the S. of S. for India ought I think also to be considered, if it has, he might be copied as a Trustee to keep our numbers up until further arrangements are made.

Very sincerely
Waris Ameer Ali

[*handwritten letter*]

Pollingfold
Rudgwick, Sussex

31. 8. 47

Dear Sir John

I saw the solicitors Norton, Rose Greenwold 116 Old Bond St. who are doing the scheme for the Central Mosque in May, and they advised definitely in favour of a similar charitable corporation.

Hussein Said Pasha was I think of this opinion that it was best to wait until then.

Central Mosque Scheme was on its way, though.

I have proposed calling on him on 12 September to see what his position is and ascertain his views.

I rather think I was a Trustee in my official capacity [illegible] ceased to be so.

Yrs Sincerely

Torick Ameer Ali

I enclose the solicitor's letter. I did not yet receive [illegible] advice.

Metropolitan Water Board

New River Road
Rosebery Avenue
London EC1

24 July 1947
The Honorary Treasurer
London Mosque Fund
26 South Street
LONDON W1

Ref: F/RSRR/E.215630

Dear Sir

450 Commercial Road

It is understood that it is proposed to carry out alterations in the water supply arrangements at the above premises, and that a request has been addressed to the Board's Inspector with reference to the fixing of a tap on the upper floor.

I have to advise you that the Board do not carry out work of this nature on private premises, and that you should instruct your own plumber to carry out the desired alterations.

All work should satisfy the Board's requirements, and I shall be glad to learn when this has been done.

I am, yours faithfully,

....

Distribution Engineer

In the name of Allah the Beneficent, The Merciful.

JAMIAT-UL-MUSLIMIN

The Muslim Association

448 Commercial Road
London E1
Telephone – Stepney Green 1948

12 May 1947

To Sir John Woodhead, Esq.
Hon Treasurer
London Mosque Fund
26 South Street
London W1[169]

Dear Sir John Woodhead

I thank you for appointing me as caretaker for the London Mosque and I have the honour to send herewith the required unemployment and National Health Insurance cards.

As to the Income Tax Code No., and tax deductions I have to say that so far I have never been in a position to pay any such tax.

For your information I beg to say that I am married and have three children of 5, & 3½ years and 8 months ages.

Yours faithfully AM Khan

Minutes of a Meeting of the Trustees of the London Mosque Fund held at the Royal Egyptian Embassy on 5 February 1948

Present: Judge Waris Ameer Ali (In the Chair)
Lord Winterton
Sir Torick Ameer Ali
Sir John Woodhead (Hon Treasurer)

[169] The members of the Jamiat appear to have been using the address in Commercial Road, while the Trustees of the Mosque were based elsewhere.

1. The minutes of the last meeting of the Trustees held on 12 December 1946 were read and confirmed.

2. The audited accounts for the year ending 31 March 1947 were approved and signed by the Chairman of the meeting (Judge Waris Ameer Ali) and the Hon Treasurer.

3. A vote of thanks was passed to the Auditors, Messrs. Feasey, Hull & Feasey for their services during the year 1946–47. It was resolved that they be appointed Auditors for the year ending 31 March 1948.

4. On the proposal of Lord Winterton and seconded by Sir Torick Ameer Ali, the Trustees recorded with the deepest regret the sudden death of Mon. Hussein Mohammed Said Bey who had been a Trustee for some years and who had always taken a keen interest in the work of the Trust. It was decided that a letter of condolence be sent to his brother in Egypt.[170]

5. Considered a letter dated 26 March 1947 from Dr Hassan Nachat Pacha[171] in which he expressed a desire to resign from the Trust on the ground that he is now living in Egypt. It was resolved that Dr Hassan Nachat Pacha be asked to continue as a Trustee until 30 September 1948, by which time other persons will have been appointed as Trustees.

6. It was pointed out that Sir Torick Ameer Ali became a Trustee by virtue of the provision of the Deed of Trust which lays down that the Mohammedan Member of the Council of the Secretary of State for India shall be entitled to be appointed a Trustee so long as he continues to hold that Office. Owing to India having obtained its independence,[172] the Secretary of State of India ceased to exist with effect from 1 August 1947, and the posts of Members of the Council of the Secretary of State for India (called Advisers under the Government of India Act of 1935) ceased to exist from that date.

   Sir Torick desired to continue as a Trustee and on the proposal of Lord Winterton, seconded by Judge Waris Ameer Ali, it was decided to re-appoint Sir Torick Ameer Ali as a Trustee with effect from 15 August 1947.

[170] See ELM Archives, Woodhead to Hussein Mohamed Said's brother in Cairo, 14 January 1948.

[171] ELM Archives.

[172] India officially attained its independence on 15 August 1947, while Pakistan celebrated its establishment as a sovereign state on 14 August 1947.

7. On the proposal of Judge Waris Ameer Ali, seconded by Sir Torick Ameer Ali, it was resolved that the following gentlemen, provided they are agreeable, be appointed as Trustees:

Mr. Hatim Attari, 41, Berkeley Square, London W1
Mr Fazal Shah, 36, Whitchurch Lane, London E14
Mr Ghulam Mohammed, 59, Canton Street, London E14

8. Considered the Note (attached) by the Hon Treasurer suggesting, for the reasons given in that Note, that following the example of the London Central Mosque Fund, a Trust Corporation be formed: proposed by Lord Winterton and seconded by Judge Waris Ameer Ali, that this course be followed.

9. The Hon Treasurer stated that the receipts and expenditure for the year 1946–47 had been as follows:

Receipts		Expenditure
Dividends	£261	£394
Contribution		
From H H the Aga Khan	£150[173]	
Total	£411	£394

It was pointed out that without the contribution of £150 from H. H. the Aga Khan there would be a heavy deficit. It was resolved that H. H. the Aga Khan be requested to be so good as to renew his subscription of £150 a year for an additional period of three years, i.e. the years 1950, 1951 and 1952.[174]

10. It was reported that the cost of repairs had amounted to £651 inclusive of the Architects fees. The amount received from the War Damage Commission[175] was £605.14.0d, and so the cost to the Trust had been only approximately £45.[176]

11. It was reported by the Hon Treasurer that Mr A.M. Khan was appointed Caretaker with effect from 6 May 1947 with the usual salary of £2.17.0d a week.

[173]The Aga Khan's annual contribution of £150 began in 1943. See ELM Archives, Woodhead to the Aga Khan, 14 February 1948.

[174]Woodhead requested the Aga Khan to continue his annual donation (*ibid*).

[175]The War Damage Commission was set up by the government to deal with war damage compensation.

[176]The Jamiat-ul-Muslimin contributed £200 towards the repairs. See ELM Archives, Woodhead to S.M. Jetha, 25 February 1948.

With a vote of thanks to the Chairman and to the Hon Treasurer the meeting terminated.

Royal Egyptian Embassy
LONDON

1. I do hereby agree to the re-appointment of Sir Torick Ameer Ali as a Trustee to the London Mosque Fund with effect from 15 August 1947.
2. I do hereby agree to the appointment of the following persons as Trustees of the London Mosque Fund: –

Mr. Hatim Attari
Mr Fazal Shah[177]
Mr Ghulam Mohammed

Signed:

The Aga Khan

Royal Egyptian Embassy
LONDON

1. I do hereby agree to the re-appointment of Sir Torick Ameer Ali as a Trustee to the London Mosque Fund with effect from 15 August 1947.
2. I do hereby agree to the appointment of the following persons as Trustees of the London Mosque Fund: –

Mr. Hatim Attari
Mr Fazal Shah
Mr Ghulam Mohammed

Signed:

Hassan Nachat
Jumalek, Cairo
24 February 1948

Witness: J Baradon (Private Secretary)
3 Saidi Street, Soliman Pacha Sq, Cairo

[177] Syed Fazal Shah was the brother of Said Amir Shah (see above, p. 194) and one of the directors of their firm, Shah Bros. Ltd.

Minutes of the Meeting of the Trustees of the London Mosque Fund held on 23 September 1948 at the Royal Egyptian Embassy 75 South Audley Street London W1

Present:

Judge Waris Ameer Ali, C.I.E (in the Chair)
Sir Torick Ameer Ali
Hatim Attari Esq
Ghulam Mohammed Esq

An apology for absence was received from Lord Winterton.

1. The Minutes of the Meeting held on 5 February 1948 were confirmed.
2. On the proposal of Sir Torick Ameer Ali, seconded by Mr Hatim Attari, the audited accounts for the year ending 31 March 1948 were passed.
3. The appointment of Messrs. Feasey, Hull and Feasey as Auditors for the year 1948–49 was approved and the Hon Treasurer was asked to thank them for their services during the year 1947–48.
4. It was recorded that Dr Hassan Nachat Pacha would cease to be a Trustee with effect from 30 September 1948. Dr Hassan Nachat Pacha had expressed a desire to resign prior to the meeting held on 5 February 1948, but at the request of the Trustees had agreed to remain a Trustee until 30 September 1948.
5. It was recorded that His Highness the Aga Khan had very kindly agreed to continue his donation of £150 a year to the funds of the Trust during his lifetime.[178] The Trustees were extremely grateful to His Highness and noted that the Hon Treasurer had already conveyed to His Highness the thanks of the Trustees.
6. The appointment of Mr Yusuf Nazeer as Caretaker with effect from 26 April 1948 was confirmed. It was noted that Mr Nazeer had agreed to serve without a salary. He would however, like his predecessors, be provided with free quarters, electricity and gas.
7. The draft Memorandum and Articles of Association of the East London Mosque Trust Limited[179] were examined and generally

[178] See his note communicating his agreement to this effect, ELM Archives.
[179] Copy not kept with the Minutes.

approved. The following decisions were taken on the following points:

a) The proposed Trust Corporation should not include the Indigent Moslem Burial Fund. No difficulties had been experienced in the working of this fund and it was considered to be undesirable to complicate the formation of the Trust Corporation for the Mosque Fund by including the Indigent Moslem Burial Fund.

b) The first Members of the Trust:

i) Judge Waris Ameer Ali did not desire to be a Member, chiefly on the grounds of his health. This was reluctantly agreed to.
ii) It was felt that Lord Winterton would not desire to be a Member. At the meeting of 5 February 1948 he had expressed his desire not to be a Member.
iii) It was hoped that HH. the Aga Khan would agree to be a member.
iv) The first Members of the Trust would therefore be:[180]

The High Commissioner for Pakistan.

The Ambassadors of Egypt and Saudi-Arabia.

The President of The Jamiat-al-Muslimin

95 Avenue Road
Penge
SE20

9 October 1948

Dear Sir John Woodhead

I am indebted to you for your kind letter dated 6 October 1948. In reply, I confirm my agreement to serve under all the three heads mentioned in para "4" of your letter and hope to discharge my duties to the best of my ability.

Here allow me to point out that my surname and not title is Kazi.

To put it in Arab phraseology (by the by the people that introduced the custom of surnames in the west) Kazi is my surname and not a title. To obviate future confusion you will be pleased to address me as Imdad. I. Kazi.

[180] The ELM Archives contains details of names and dates.

As to the title, I have none; unless you graciously allow an antiquated one to pass current. Under the act 3 of Queen Elizabeth of blessed memory, all the members of the Inns of Court are entitled in their personal right to the address as Esquires.

You will pardon me mentioning this, because change of name will create confusion not only with my bankers, but my wife's and my publishers as well.

Apologising for a lengthy letter, I remain

Yours sincerely
I.I. Kazi*

Hotel Ritz
Place Vendome
Paris

11 October 1948

Dear Sir John

Thank you for your letter of 5 October.

I will be glad to become a member of the Trust Corporation.

Yours sincerely

Aga Khan

Shillinglee Park Chiddingfold

Hon Treasurer
London Mosque Fund
26 South Street
London W1

13 October 1948

Dear Sir John

I am sorry not to have answered your letter before owing to pressure of work.

In regard to the project for the re-organisation of the Fund, it seems to me to be excellent.

I presume that the change is quite legal or that, if there is any doubt about its legality, steps have been taken to have expert advice.

I only mention this because I should not like, as a Trustee of the present Fund, to be involved in any litigation over the matter.

Yours sincerely

[*signature not legible*][181]

L'Ambassadeur de S.M. le Roi D'Egypt
Londres

75 South Audley Street
W1

15 October 1948

Ref: 2933/21/18/13 B

Dear Sir John

I have received your letter dated 13th instant regarding the formation of a Trust Corporation of the East London Mosque at No. 446 Commercial road, E1.

I am writing to inform you that I shall be pleased to become, as Egyptian Ambassador, a member of the Trust and of the Council of Management of the said Trust, but, owing to pressure of work, Mr. A.L. Fahmy, Secretary of this Embassy, will represent me on the Council of Management whenever I am unable to attend.

As to the Chairmanship of the Council, I wish to say that I am in agreement with nominating the High Commissioner of Pakistan for that post, for the reasons put forward in your letter.

Yours sincerely

[*signature*]

Ambassador

[181] Shillinglee Park at Chiddingfold near Horsham in Sussex was the Winterton family seat (see http://www.horshamsociety.org/history/winterton.htm (accessed 19 January 2010)). It is therefore reasonable to conclude that this letter was from Lord Winterton, even though the signature is not legible.

Norton, Rose, Greenwell & Co
116 Old Broad Street
London EC2

13 December 1948

Sir John Woodhead G.C.E.E, K.C.S.I
Chevremont
Hockering Road
Woking
Surrey

Dear Sir John

Re: East London Mosque

Thank you for your letter of the 11th instant giving me the information in regard to the three officers of the Jamiat-ul-Muslimin. I will now put in hand the preparation of the proof prints of the Memorandum & Articles of Association.

Yours sincerely

[*signature*]

Norton, Rose, Greenwell & Co
116 Old Broad Street
London EC2

31 December 1948

Sir John Woodhead G.C.E.E, K.C.S.I
Chevremont
Hockering Road
Woking
Surrey

Dear Sir John

Re: East London Mosque Trust Ltd

I now enclose three proof prints of the Memorandum and Articles of Association of the above proposed Company[182] in order that you may go through the same yourself and may show it to the Trustees. Perhaps you would be good enough particularly to check the spelling

[182] See Appendix II for the text of this document.

of the various names and that the right persons are shown as being first members of the Trust and first members of the Council respectively.

You will note that there are certain typographical errors in the proof which have been altered in ink, and when you let me hear that the proof is otherwise in order, I will have clean prints made for signature by the subscribers.

With best wishes for the New Year

Yours Sincerely

[*signature*]

Pollingfold
Rudgwick
Suffolk

8 January 1950

Dear Sir

I shall not be able to attend the meeting on 10 January owing to being unwell. Please give my apologies to the chairman.

Yours

Torick Ameer Ali

Minutes of the Meeting of the Trustees of the London Mosque Fund held on 10 January 1950

Present:

Waris Ameer Ali Esq. C.I.E (in the Chair)
Hatim Attari Esq
Syed Fazal Shah Esq
Ghulam Mohammed Esq
Sir John Woodhead, Hon Treasurer

An apology for absence was received from Sir Torick Ameer Ali.

1. The minutes of the meeting held on 23 September 1948 were read and confirmed.

2. The appointment of Mr Jamil Fazaldin as Caretaker of the Mosque with effect from 20 October 1949 was confirmed. It was noted that Mr Fazaldin receives no salary but is provided with free quarters and gas and electricity free of charge.

3. The audited accounts for the year ending 31 March 1949 were approved and signed by the Chairman (Waris Ameer Ali Esq) and by the Hon Treasurer.

4. The appointment of Messrs Feasey, Hull and Feasey as Auditors for the year ending 31 March 1950 was approved.

5. Sanction was accorded to the expenditure during the years ending 31 March 1948 and 31 March 1949 amounting to £1245.2.4d., on repairs plus £72.12.0d for the Architect's fees. It was noted that £605.14.0d has been recovered from the War Damage Commission; this amount was made up of £575.14.0d on account of repairs and £30 for Architect's fees. The Jamiat-ul-Muslimin had also contributed £200 towards the expenditure. The Committee placed on record their great appreciation of the generous contribution made by the Jamiat-ul-Muslimin.

6. Approval was given to the approximate expenditure of £308 which had been incurred on repairs to the shop in 450 Commercial Road. The Hon Treasurer explained that the original estimate was £183 of which it was estimated £150 would be recoverable from the War Damage Commission. Unfortunately, when the work was started it was found that the old timber structure holding up the front basement wall and over the shop was rotten. The additional expenditure on this account has been estimated at £125 bringing that total to £308. The work had been carried out but the bills had not as yet been received from the Architect and payment had not therefore as yet been made.

7. Approval was given to the letting of the shop and back room in 450 Commercial Road to the Caretaker, Mr Jamil Fazaldin, at a weekly rental of 30/0d., plus the general rates payable on account of the shop and back room, with effect from 14 October 1949.

8. The Hon Treasurer reported that the premises 446–450 Commercial Road had been insured with the Guardian

Assurance Co. for a total value of £7400 plus £400 rent charge. The previous insured value was £5550 plus £400 rent charge. The value had been increased because of the general rise in the value of property. This increase in the insured value was approved.

9. The Hon Treasurer reported on the progress made in the re-organisation of the Trust by the promotion of the East London Mosque Trust Corporation Ltd. It was explained that when the Trust Corporation has been formed it was found that owing to a recital in the purchase deed of the property, it would be necessary to obtain the approval of the Charity Commissioners. It was hoped that this approval would shortly be received and it would then be possible to proceed with the execution of the documents for the transfer of the property and securities from the Trustees to the Trust Corporation. The re-organisation would then be complete.

10. Consideration was given to letter ACF/LMC of 4 January 1950 from the Auditors. It was decided to write off the two sums mentioned in that letter, viz:

a) an item of £17.10.0d. This is a book entry from the Mosque Fund and the Mosque and Culture Centre in Commercial Road
b) a small debt of 4/9d due to the Trustees which had been shown for many years as outstanding.

W. Ameer Ali 13 February 1951

Circular

The shop and back room at No 450 Commercial Road were let to Jamil Syed Aladin Fazaldin, the Caretaker, at a rent of £1.10.6 a week plus the rates, 15.5d. a week, with effect from 14 October 1949.

A shop takes some time to become established and I am satisfied that for the present, at any rate, the above rent is more than Fazaldin can afford to pay. I have visited the shop fairly regularly and formed the impression about six weeks ago that the rent was on the high side, but postponed a final conclusion until more experience had been gained. I am now convinced that the rent should be reduced.

I propose that the rent be reduced to £1.0.0d., a week, plus the rates (15/5d) a week, with effect from 14 October 1949 and that the reduced rent be fixed for twelve months, until 14 October 1950 when it will be brought under review.

It will be recalled that the Caretaker is not in receipt of any salary. It is convenient to have the shop let to the Caretaker, for it means that he is practically always available at the Mosque.

J. A. Woodhead
Hon Treasurer.

[*not dated but probably 4 April 1950*]

I556
Good Friday 1950

My dear Sir John Woodhead

Ref enclosed circular I agree entirely with your proposal to reduce the rent of the shop and back room to £1 a week plus rates. As you very rightly point out, if I may say so, the lessee works for the Mosque Fund as caretaker without a salary and his shop takings are probably precarious too. Furthermore we can review the rent as you say on 14 October. Do we have to vary an agreement or anything?

Can we job up the solicitors who are dealing with the new body for the Trust in any way? Let me wish you a Happy Easter, and believe me

Very sincerely
Waris Ameer Ali

Do pray let me know some time you are coming to London.

GHULAM MOHAMMED

59 Canton Street
London E14

Dear Sir

I agree with your proposal regarding the reduction of rent at No 450 Commercial Road from 30/- per week to £1, plus rates 15/5 which take effect from Oct 14 1949–Oct 14 1950.

Ghulam Mohammed (Trustee)

19 Berkeley Street
W1

HA/EP

Dear Sir John

Mr Wise sent me a notice as regards the rent of the shop at No. 450 Commercial Road, and I am in agreement with your proposal therein.

With kindest regards
Yours Sincerely
Hatim Attari

Pollingfold
Rudgwick, Sussex

London Mosque Fund

8.4.50

Dear Sir

Your letter of 4.4.50. I quite agreed to this proposal.

Yours

Torick Ameer Ali

244 Bilton Road
Perivale
Middlesex

21 April 1950

Sir John Woodhead
East London Mosque Trust
26 South Street
W1

Dear Sir

In the absence of Mr Syed Fazal Shah, who is in Pakistan at the present, I have opened your letter addressed to him dated 18 April.

Mr Shah will be pleased to reply to your letter as soon as he returns from Pakistan.

Yours Faithfully

B.H Shah

Minutes of a Meeting of the London Mosque Fund held on Tuesday February 13 1951 at the Royal Egyptian Consulate General, 26 South Street, London W1

Present:

Lord Winterton (in the Chair)
Judge Warish Ameer Ali
Mr Hattim Attari

Apologies for absence from Mr Ghulam Mohammed, Sir Torick Ameer Ali

1. The Minutes of the Meeting held on January 10 1950 were confirmed and signed.
2. The audited accounts for the year ending March 31 1950 were passed and signed by the Chairman and Hon Treasurer.
3. It was resolved that Messrs. Baker, Todman and Co., be appointed Auditors for the year ending March 31 1951.
4. The Hon Treasurer reported that the final bill for the repairs to the shop in 450 Commercial Road amounted to £320.12.9. against an estimate of £308.0.0. approved at the last Meeting. The small increase is accounted for by the cost of painting the internal walls which was not included in the original estimate. When the original estimate was prepared, the architect estimated that £150.0.0 would probably be recovered from the War Damage Commission. The final amount recovered is, however, only £92.0.0., the highest figure to which the approval of the War Damage Commission could be obtained. Sanction was given to the payment of the final bill less the amount received from the War Damage Commission.

5. The payment of the following amounts as fees to the architect, Mr Alister MacDonald were approved:

£30.6.0 on account of the work in connection with the shop
£25.0.0 on account of other work carried out to the premises 446/450 Commercial Road.

It was noted that of the sum of £30.6.0., the sum of £13.10.0 had been recovered from the War Damage Commission.

6. Sanction was given to the following expenditure on repairs to the property during the year 1950–51.

Aldgate Building Company

Bill dated April 15 1950 amounting to £26.10.0., for repairs to the roof.
Bill dated August 25 1950 amounting to £109.10.0 on account of internal decoration and miscellaneous repairs.
Bill dated February 2 1951 amounting to £28.0.0., on account of further repairs to the roof.

7. Sanction was given to the expenditure of £20.0.0 to be incurred on the installation of two power points and minor repairs to the electricity installation.

8. Approval was given to the installation in the caretaker's quarters of an Ascot gas heater at a cost of £16.16.0.

9. The Hon Treasurer reported that Mr Alladad Khan had agreed to take the four rooms on the first and second floors of 450 Commercial Road at a rent of 30s a week including rates. Sanction was given to the letting of these four rooms at the proposed rent and on the conditions in the Hon Treasurer's letter dated February 2 1951.

10. The Hon Treasurer reported on the progress made in the promotion of the Trust Corporation. He explained that the delay had been due to the long time taken by the Charity Commissioners in preparing a scheme. This scheme had been received towards the end of 1950 and the necessary notices had been issued. The solicitors were now awaiting the final scheme from the Charity Commissioners. When this had been received, it would be possible to proceed with the execution of the documents transferring the securities held by the present trustees and the property at 446–450 Commercial Road from the existing trustees to the Trust Corporation. Lord Winterton

proposed and the other trustees agreed that it would be desirable, when the re-organisation was complete, for the Solicitors to write a letter to the trustees informing them that their responsibility for the Trust Fund had ceased.

11. The Meeting closed with a vote of thanks to the Hon Treasurer and the Chairman.

The East London Mosque Trust Limited

Minutes of the First Meeting of the Council of Management held at 446/448 Commercial Road, London. E.1 on 21 December 1951

Present:

H.E Habib I Rahimtoola,* High Commissioner for Pakistan
Dr H.H. Bilgrami*
M.S Manawar Hossain*[183]
Sir John Woodhead, Secretary

1. The Certificate of Incorporation of the Company dated 11 May 1949, together with a print of the Memorandum and Articles of Association of the Company as registered were produced.

2. IT WAS RESOLVED that Sir John Woodhead, G.C.I.E, K.C.S.I. having acted as Secretary of the Company since its incorporation, his appointment be and it is hereby confirmed. It was reported that the necessary Notice of Sir John's appointment had been filed with the Registrar of Companies.

3. IT WAS RESOLVED that the situation of the Registered Office of the Company be at 446/448 Commercial Road, East 1, and it was reported that Messrs. Norton, Rose, Greenwell Co. had filed the necessary Notice with the Registrar of Companies together with Particulars of the Council of Management of the Company, being the Directors named in Article 18 (B) of the Company's Articles of Association. The Secretary was given instructions to have the name of the Company painted

[183]Mohammed Saiyid Manawar Hossain (sometimes spelt Hosain, Hussain).

or affixed on the outside of the Registered Office and to have the Certificate of Incorporation framed and hung up at the office.

4. IT WAS RESOLVED that Barclays Bank Ltd. (140–142 Commercial Road, E.1) be appointed Bankers of the Company. That the said Bank be and they are hereby authorised:

   1. To honour and comply with all Cheques Drafts Bills Promissory Notes Acceptances negotiable instruments and orders expressed to be drawn accepted made or given on behalf of this Company at any time or times whether the banking account or accounts of the Company are overdrawn by any payment thereof or in relation thereto or are in credit or otherwise.

   2. To honour and comply with all instructions to deliver or dispose of any securities or documents or property held by the Bank on behalf of the Company.

      Provided any such Cheques Drafts Bills Promissory Notes Acceptances negotiable instruments orders and instructions are signed by any one member of the Council of Management and countersigned by the Secretary.

   3. To treat all Cheques Drafts Bills Promissory Notes Acceptances negotiable instruments and orders as being endorsed on behalf of the Company and to discount or otherwise deal with them provided such endorsements purport to be signed by any one member of the Council of Management or by the Secretary.

   And that a copy of the forgoing Resolution be forwarded to the Bank by the Secretary, together with specimen signatures of the present Members of the Council and Secretary.

   IT WAS FURTHER RESOLVED that the Trustees of the London Mosque Fund be requested to transfer the balance standing to the credit of the account of that Fund with the Bank of England to the company's Account with Barclays Bank Limited.

5. IT WAS RESOLVED that Messrs. Baker, Todman and Co., of Canada House, Norfolk Street, London, W.C.2 be and they are hereby appointed Auditors of the Company and that until the Annual General Meeting of the Company to be held in

the year 1952 their remuneration should be arranged by the Board.

6. A Common Seal which had been prepared for the Company was produced and IT WAS RESOLVED that the same be and is hereby adopted as the Common Seal of the Company, and that an impression thereof be made in the margin of these Minutes in the presence of one of the Members of the Council.

7. IT WAS REPORTED that fifty prints of the Memorandum and Articles of Association of the Company, together with the necessary registers and books required by the Company, had been ordered and such orders were approved and confirmed.

8. IT WAS RESOLVED that all securities, stock and share Certificates and other documents of title from time to time belonging to the Company and not required for our rent purposes be deposited in the name of the Company with the Company's Bankers, and that all orders for delivery out by the Bankers be signed by any two Members of the Council, pursuant to a resolution of the Council to that effect.

9. It was reported that the Charity Commissioners, by an Order dated the 9 March 1951, had approved and established a Scheme whereby it was provided that the London Mosque Fund and the endowments thereof should be administered and managed by the Company, which should be the Trustee of the Charity and take the place of the Executive Committee and the Trustees. Such Order further provided that the land and buildings at 446, 448 and 450 Commercial Road should vest in the Company. It was further reported that in pursuance of such an Order the Company had been placed on the Register at the Land Registry in respect of the Commercial Road property.

10. There were produced transfers in favour of the Company of the under-mentioned securities held on behalf of the Fund by Syed Waris Ameer Ali, the Right Honourable Edward Earl Winterton, Sir Torick Ameer Ali, Hatim Attari, Syed Fazal Shah and Ghulam Mohammed:

£2,500	3 ½ Conversion Stock
£1,000	3% Savings Bonds, 1960–70
£4,113.3.7	3 ½ % War Stock

Such transfers being duly executed by all the above named gentlemen with the exception of Syed Fazal Shah who is now deceased.[184] IT WAS RESOLVED that the Seal of the Company be affixed accordingly. IT WAS FURTHER RESOLVED that such transfers be handed to Messrs. Norton Rose Greenwell & Co. in order that they could lodge the same with the Bank of England for registration and obtain new Certificates in the name of the Company. IT WAS FURTHER RESOLVED that Dividend Request Forms in favour of Barclays Bank, Commercial Road, E.1, be sealed by the Trust's Seal and the same be lodged with the Bank of England along with the transfers.

11. It was reported that the above formalities having been completed, the Company was now in a position to administer the trusts of the London Mosque Fund.

12. It was proposed by Dr Bilgrami and seconded by Mr Manawar Hosain that H.E.H.I. Rahimtoola be elected Chairman of the Council. Carried unanimously.

13. It was proposed that Dr H.H. Bilgrami and seconded by H.E.H.I. Rahimtoola that Mr S. Manawar Hossain be elected Vice Chairman of the Council. Carried unanimously.

14. It was proposed by H.E.H.I. Rahimtoola and seconded by Dr H.H. Bilgrami that Mr Suleman M. Jetha* be appointed a member of the Council in the vacancy caused by the death of Mr Syed Fazal Shah. Carried unanimously.

15. It was proposed by H.E.H.I. Rahimtoola and seconded by Dr H.H. Bilgrami that Mr Suleman N. Jetha be appointed Hon Treasurer. Carried unanimously.

16. IT WAS RESOLVED THAT Mr Sadiq Hassain Kazmi[185] having been proposed by Dr H.H. Bilgrami and seconded by Mr S. Manawar Hosain and having completed the prescribed application form be admitted a member of the East London Mosque Trust Ltd.

[184] Reported by the Trust's solicitors, Norton, Rose & Greenwell Co. in their letter of 28 August 1951, ELM Archives.

[185] Probably the nephew of Mohammed Saiyid Manawar Hossain.

Application for Membership of the East London Mosque Trust Ltd

(prescribed by the Council under Article 5 of the Articles of Association)

I ....of..
hereby apply to be admitted a member of the East London Mosque Trust Ltd. I declare that I am of the Moslem faith and am interested in and am willing to contribute to, or actively to further the objects of the Trust as set forth in the Memorandum of Association.

I undertake to further to the best of my ability, the objects and interests and influence of the Trust and at all times to observe the Regulations of the Trust.

I also undertake from time to time to notify to the Secretary of the Trust a place of business or residence to be registered as my place of address and the place so registered shall for the purpose of the Regulations of the Trust be deemed to be my place of address.

Sd. ....

The East London Mosque Trust Limited

Annual General Meeting held at 448 Commercial Road on 21 December 1951, at 3.45 pm

Present:

H.E.H. I. Rahimtoola (in the chair)
Dr H.H. Bilgrami
Mr Suleman M. Jetha
Mr S. Manawar Hosain
Mr Sadiq H. Kazmi

1. The Secretary read the notice convening the Meeting.
2. The Secretary reported that no Accounts were available for submission to the Members as, owing to various formalities having to be dealt with, it had only been possible for the Trust

Company to take over the Trusts of the London Mosque Fund that day.

3. The Secretary reported that, pursuant to the provisions of Article 18 (C) (iii) Sir Torick Ameer Ali, Mr Hatim Attari, Mr Ghulam Mohammed Khan, Mr Imdad Ali Imam Ali Kazi and Mr Suleman M. Jetha retire from their office as Members of the Council, but that Mr Hatim Attari, Mr Ghulam Mohammed Khan, Mr Imdad Ali Imam Ali Kazi and Mr Suleman Jetha, who had indicated their willingness to be re-elected were eligible for re-election.

4. It was resolved (i) on the proposal of Dr Bilgrami and seconded by H.E.H.I Rahimtoola that Mr Hatim Attari, Mr Imdad Ali Imam Ali Kazi, Mr Ghulam Mohammed Khan, Mr Suleman Mohomed Jetha be elected members and (ii) on the proposal of Mr S Manawar Hosain and seconded by Mr Suleman M Jetha that Mr Sadiq Hussein Kazmi be elected members [*sic*] of the Council of Management.

A hearty vote of thanks was passed to H.E.H.I. Rahimtoola for presiding at the meeting, to Sir John Woodhead for all the work he had done in connection with the reorganisation scheme and to Messrs. Norton, Rose, Greenwell & Co., the Solicitors, who had carried through so successfully the creation of the East London Mosque Trust Ltd.

APPENDIX I: INFORMATION ON KEY INDIVIDUALS MENTIONED IN 1910–1951 MINUTES

Information about some names that appear in the Minutes could not be traced, and there is very limited material available on other individuals. Much information has been drawn from the Internet, particularly *ODNB*, *The Times* archives, and Wikipedia.

Aga Khan, Sir Sultan Mahomed Shah (1877–1957); 48th Imam of the Shia Ismaili Muslims, and a prominent and strong supporter of various Muslim causes around the world. Based in India, he was appointed to the Council of the Viceroy of India in 1902. In 1906 he became one of the founders of the All-India Muslim League and was elected its first 'permanent' president. He was greatly respected by successive British governments and took a keen interest in the activities of Britain's Muslims, including those of the Muslim Mission established at Woking in 1912, giving generous financial assistance for the development of a number of Islamic institutions in England. See his autobiography, *The Memoirs of Aga Khan: world enough and time* (London, 1954).

Ali, Abdullah Yusuf (1872–1953); graduated from St John's College, Cambridge and called to the Bar at Lincoln's Inn in 1896; an officer of the Indian Civil Service, he served in various capacities, retiring in 1914. During the First World War he was a private in the West Kent Fencibles and president of the Indian Students' Prisoners of War Fund. Carried out much propaganda work for the government; represented Indian Muslims at the Paris Peace Conference in 1919; entered the service of the Nizam of Hyderabad, India, 1919; appointed as Revenue Member of the Council of the State 1921. In the early years of the School of Oriental Studies in London (later renamed the School of Oriental and African Studies) he was lecturer in Hindustani, Hindi, and Indian Religions, Manners, and Customs; an Arabic scholar, his recension in English of the Qur'an in 1935 is still acclaimed as a classic. Active supporter of the World Congress of Faiths and contributed learned lectures at meetings organized by the Woking Muslim Mission Trust and Literary Society, as well as writing books and articles on Islamic issues for various journals. See *The Times*, 15 December 1953.

Ali, Syed Ameer (1849–1928), Chairman of the ELM's Executive Committee, and a leading Muslim at the turn of the twentieth century. After an illustrious career as a high court judge in India, he settled in England in 1904, where he committed himself to several Muslim causes. Founded the London Muslim League in 1908, and the Red Crescent Society in 1912. In 1909, became the first Indian to be appointed Privy Councillor and to be given membership of its Judicial Committee. See Martin Forward, 'Syed Ameer Ali: a bridge builder', *Islam and Christian–Muslim Relations*, 6, no. 1 (1995), pp. 45–62.

Ali, Sir Torick Ameer (1891–1975); younger son of Syed Ameer Ali (q.v.) and brother of Waris Ameer Ali (q.v.); educated at Marlborough School and Christ Church, Oxford, before being called to the Bar in 1916; married Isabelle Ida; knighted. In November 1944, while acting as Chief Justice in Calcutta, he was appointed adviser to the Secretary of State for India in London and in this capacity later became the Chairman of the ELM Trustees.

Ali, Waris Ameer (1886–1975); elder son of Syed Ameer Ali (q.v.); educated at Wellington College, Berkshire and Balliol College, Oxford; entered the Indian Civil Service and retired as a Judge in 1929. During the Second World War served as the War Services Adviser to the High Commissioner of India in London. Well-versed in Islamic culture and history, and also conversant with a number of European languages. Fellow of the Royal Geographical Society and wrote small pieces for the *Geographical Journal*. See *The Times*, 9 April 1975; also the *Geographical Journal*, 141, no. 3 (November 1975), p. 515.

Ali Khan, Mirza Abdul (Sadigh-es-Sultaneh) (1876–?); Minister at the Persian Embassy in London; Imperial Commissioner to the Anglo-Persian Oil Company; Ambassador to Washington, DC, 1919–1921. See *The Times*, 27 March 1919.

Allanson-Winn, Rowland George Allanson, 5th Baron Headley (1855–1935); educated privately, save for a few months at Westminster School in 1868, and then at Trinity College, Cambridge; admitted to Bar at the Middle Temple, 1879. Spent two years as editor of the *Salisbury Journal* before studying at King's College London and becoming a civil engineer in 1896. In the autumn of 1913 he met Khwaja Kamal-ud-Din, and soon converted to Islam, taking the Muslim name Shaikh Saifurrahman Rahmatullah El-Farooq. Founded the British Muslim Society in 1914 and remained its president until 1935. In 1916 he unsuccessfully requested the Secretary of State for India to donate land for the construction of a mosque in London. In 1923, together with Kamal-ud-Din, he went on pilgrimage to Mecca and thereafter travelled to Egypt (1923), South Africa (1926), and India (1927 and 1928) to raise funds for a mosque in London. Died in a nursing home in June 1935 and was buried in the Brookwood Cemetery, near Woking.

Amery, Leopold Charles Maurice Stennett (1873–1955); Conservative politician and journalist noted for his interest and involvement in colonial and imperial affairs during the 1920s and 1930s, especially India, where he was born and where he learned to speak Hindustani. His mother was the sister of Gottlieb Wilhelm Leitner (q.v.). Educated at Harrow and Balliol College, Oxford. MP for Birmingham South (1911–1918) and for Birmingham Sparkbrook (1918–1945). Colonial Secretary 1924–1929; Secretary of State for India 1940–1945. Co-signatory with Lord Edward Halifax (the Foreign Secretary) and Lord Lloyd, to a memorandum sent to the Prime Minister and the Chancellor of the Exchequer proposing an allocation of funds for the purchase of a site for a mosque in London. See BL, IOR, P&J (S)/2033, fos 128–133, Halifax to Amery, 11 September 1940 and *ibid.*, fos 142–145, Amery to Lloyd, 26 September 1940. See also Amery's autobiography, *My Political Life*, 3 vols (London, 1953–1955).

Ampthill (*see* **Russell, (Arthur) Oliver Villiers, 2nd Baron Ampthill**)

Anik, Abdeali Shaikh Mahomedali (1860–1939); a Muslim from the Bohra community who operated as a merchant in London from 1901 onwards. Honorary treasurer of the Indigent Muslim Burial Fund, the British Red Crescent Society, and the London Mosque Fund; also a freemason, who was a member of a number of lodges.

Arberry, Arthur John (1905–1969); orientalist and prolific scholar of Arabic, Persian, and Islamic studies. Graduated from Pembroke College, Cambridge, 1929; research fellow 1931–1932. Head of Department of Classics at Cairo University 1932–1934; on returning to Britain he became the Assistant Librarian at the Library of the India Office, 1934–1939. During the Second World War, he served in the Ministry of Information. Professor of Persian, University of London, 1944–1947; Sir Thomas Adams's Professor of Arabic, University of Cambridge, 1947–1969.

Arnold, Professor Sir Thomas Walker (1864–1930); renowned scholar of Islam. Educated at the City of London School and Magdalene College, Cambridge. Teacher at the Mahommedan Anglo-Orient College, Aligarh, in the United Provinces, India, 1888–1898. Professor of Philosophy at Government College, Lahore, 1898–1904; later also Dean of the Oriental Faculty at Punjab University. Assistant Librarian, Indian Office, 1904–1909; appointed Educational Adviser to Indian students in Britain, 1909; Adviser to the Secretary of State for India, 1917–1920. Professor of Arabic and Islamic Studies at the School of Oriental Studies, University of London, 1921–1930. Companion of the Order of the Indian Empire, 1912; knighted, 1921. See Katherine Watt, 'Thomas Walker Arnold and the re-evaluation of Islam, 1864–1930', *Modern Asian Studies*, 36, no. 1 (Feb. 2002), pp. 1–98.

Attari, Hatim; successful businessman; in 1937, in partnership with Joseph Hobb and Alexander Tolmie, bought the Bruichladdich Distillery Co. (Islay) Ltd for a reported £23,000 (see http://www.bruichladdich.com/the_history_1881to2000.htm (accessed 19 January 2010)).

Baig, Mirza Abbas Ali (1855–1932); came from an old Mughal army family. Graduated from Bombay University, 1878. Inspector of Muslim Schools from 1882; held various other posts in the Indian Civil Service; Oriental Translator, 1893–1906. Member of the Council of the Secretary of State for India, 1910–1917. Knighted 1917. Awarded honorary LL.D. by the University of Glasgow. In England, he was an energetic supporter of the rights of the Muslim community and was instrumental in rescuing the Woking Mosque from being turned into a factory. In 1923 he was a member of the National Liberal Club. See the *Islamic Review*, March 1933, pp. 62–63; *The Times*, 3 June 1932.

Beg, Mirza Zulqadar; Sunni Muslim official and son of Nawab Sarwar-ul-Mulk. Judge of the High Court, then secretary to the Nizam of Hyderabad's government in the Judicial, Political, and General departments; finally Secretary in the Military and Medical departments. See *Hyderabad State List of Leading Officers, Nobles and Personages* (Potter Press reprint, 2007), p. 35.

Begum, Sultan Kaikhusrau Jahan (1858–1930); only surviving daughter of Sultan (Begum) Shah Jahan. Ruled the princely state of Bhopal, India from 1901 to 1926, when she abdicated in favour of her son. Her mother's donation had helped to construct the first purpose-built mosque in England, in Woking in 1889, which she visited in 1925 wearing a *burqa*. An energetic supporter of educational reform, she was the founding (and so far the only woman) Chancellor of Aligarh Muslim University, 1920–1930. Her prolific writing included several books on education and health. See Shaharyar M. Khan, *The Begums of Bhopal: a dynasty of women rulers in Raj India* (London, 2000).

Bey, Halil Halid (1869–1931), also written in the Minutes as Khalil Khalid (to convey the Turkish pronunciation, when writing in English, the letter *h* instead of *kh* was sometimes used). Graduated in law from the University of Istanbul in 1893 and came to England in 1894; Vice-Consul at the Ottoman Embassy from 1897. Teacher of Turkish at the University of Cambridge, 1902–1911. Halid was one of the Muslims who initiated the movement for a mosque in London (see *The Times*, 18 January 1911). Among his many publications, *The Diary of a Turk* (London, 1903), *A Study of Turcophobia* (1904), and *The Cross Versus the Crescent* (London, 1907) are especially noteworthy. See S. Tanvir Wasti, 'Halil Halid: anti-imperialist Muslim intellectual', *Middle Eastern Studies*, 29, no. 3 (July 1993), pp. 559–579.

Bey, Mundji Fikri (*c.*1869–?); Turkish Jew, whose father was a governor of several Ottoman provinces. Entered the Ottoman Sultan's service in 1887; served as a Consul in Greece and New York, before being appointed Consul-General in London before the First World War. See 'Turkish Jews in Westerbork', http://www.bevrijdinginterculltureel.nl/eng/turksjood.html (accessed 25 November 2009).

Bilgrami, Dr Hamid Hasan (1908–?); lecturer in Urdu at the School of Oriental and African Studies, London. President of the Jamiat-ul-Muslimin. He left London in 1953 and settled in Pakistan. See *The Times*, 15 August 1951; also ELM Archives, letter from Bilgrami to Sir John Woodhead, dated 25 January 1951.

Bilgrami, Syed Hassan; in the Indian Medical Service. His grandfather was the oriental interpreter to Governor-General Lord Dalhousie and his father was a Deputy Collector and Magistrate in Bengal. Chairman of the Mahomedan Anglo-Oriental College Association, London, with branches in Oxford, Cambridge, and Edinburgh.

Bird, Arthur; first appears in the Minutes in 1938 when standing in for the then Treasurer, A.S.N. Anik. He became an Honorary

Assistant Secretary but, following Anik's death in 1939 and the closure of his business, Bird's connection with the Fund ended in 1940.

Bull, Sir William (1863–1931); student at Birkbeck Institute (later College, University of London); qualified as a solicitor, 1889. Elected to the London County Council, 1892; Conservative MP for Hammersmith (1900–1918) and for Hammersmith South (1918–1929). Privy Councillor, 1918; created Baronet, 1922. Served in many Parliamentary capacities and was a member of one of its Missions to India. Also supported the movement for extending voting rights for women. See 'The papers of Sir William Bull', http://janus.lib.cam.ac.uk/db/node.xsp?id=EAD%2FGBR%2F0014%2FBULL (accessed 25 November 2009).

Bullock, Willoughby; Secretary and Clerk to the Society of Knights Bachelor (from 1912 Imperial Society of Knights Bachelor), in which Sir William Bull (q.v.) played a leading role. Later Attorney-General of British Honduras (now Belize). See 'The Imperial Society of Knights Bachelor', http://www.iskb.co.uk/TODAY.htm (accessed 21 November 2010).

Cochrane-Baillie, Charles Wallace Alexander Napier Ross, 2nd Baron Lamington (1860–1940); educated at Eton College and at Christ Church, Oxford. Conservative MP for St Pancras North (1886–1890); succeeded to title, 1890. Governor of Bombay, 1903–1907. On his return to Britain he retained an interest in movements supporting greater understanding between the British government and so-called Eastern peoples, especially the Islamic world, as well as the welfare of subject peoples and minorities within the British Empire. Active member of a range of organizations working in this field, including the Royal Central Asian Society, the East India Association, the Middle Eastern Association, The Indigent Moslems Burial Fund, and the British Red Crescent Society.

Cornwall, Sir Edwin (1863–1953); coal merchant. Elected mayor of the Metropolitan Borough of Fulham, 1900. A member of the Progressive Party, he was elected chairman of the London County Council in 1904. Liberal MP for Bethnal Green North East (1906–1922). Knighted 1905; created baronet, 1918. See *The Times*, 2 March 1953.

Gomme, Sir (George) Laurence (1853–1916). Working his way up the administrative hierarchy, Gomme became Clerk to the London

County Council (chief administrative officer) in 1900. A historian, anthropologist, and folklorist, he wrote prolifically and was a fellow of several learned societies. See *ODNB*, http://www.oxforddnb.com/view/article/38353?docPos=5 (accessed 25 November 2009).

Guinness, Walter Edward, 1st Baron Moyne (1880–1944); Anglo-Irish politician and businessman. Deputy Resident Minister of State in Cairo, August 1942–January 1944; Resident Minister, January–November 1944. Assassinated November 1944 by two members of the militant Jewish Zionist group Lehi.

Headley (*see* **Allanson-Winn, Rowland George Allanson, 5th Baron Headley**)

Hossain (Husain, Hussain), Mohammed Saiyid Manawar (1909–?); Director of Veday Laboratories Ltd.; Secretary of the Jamiat-ul-Muslimin; Trustee of the East London Mosque Trust Limited in the early 1950s.

Hotson, Sir John Ernest Buttery (1877–1944); educated at Edinburgh Academy and Magdalen College, Oxford. Served as an administrator in Bombay Presidency, acting as its Governor in 1931. Here he did 'much valuable social work in regard to children's welfare and the rescue of fallen women'. After retirement he devoted himself to public service in Britain, particularly for the Prisoners of War Bureau and the Red Cross. See *The Times*, 15 May 1944.

Huque, Mohammad Azizul (1892–1947); lawyer, parliamentarian, social worker, and writer. Born in West Bengal; graduated from Presidency College, Calcutta, 1911; law degree from University Law College, 1914. Practised as a lawyer and in 1926 was appointed government pleader and public prosecutor of Nadia and also elected Vice-Chairman of the District Board and member of the Bengal Legislative Council; received the title *Khan Bahadur.* Selected as a member of the Indian Franchise Commission in 1931; Education Minister of Bengal, 1934–1937. First speaker of the Legislative Assembly constituted by the 1937 general election, 1937–1942; received the title of CIE (Companion, Order of the Indian Empire); knighted, 1941. High Commissioner for India in London, 1942–1943. Joined Viceroy of India's Executive Council, 1943; in charge of commerce, industries, civil supplies, food, and, later, the Textile Directorate under the Supply Department. Counsel for the Enquiry Commission constituted by the Central Government following the August 1946 riots in Calcutta. Supported the Muslim League protest against the Viceroy's actions, renouncing all his titles. See http://bpedia.org/H_0200.php (accessed 20 January 2011).

Isfahani (Ispahani), Mirza Hashim; merchant and financier with Pan-Islamic sympathies. Member of the London All-India Muslim League; President of the Central Islamic Society, 1917; active member of the Woking Mosque congregation. See http://www.wokingmuslim.org/books/mus-pales/mus-pales-t.pdf (accessed 28 November 2009).

Jang, Nawab Fakhr Yar; Sunni Muslim born in Jullundhur District, Punjab. Educated at Aligarh; MA, Oxford. Worked at the British Agency in Kabul, 1903; honorary attaché to Sir Henry McMahon during the tour of the Afghan ruler Amir Habibullah to India, 1907. Financial Department, Government of India, 1907–1910. Entered the service of the Nizam of Hyderabad, 1913; was Deputy Accountant General and Accountant General before being appointed Finance Secretary. Judicial Member of the Nizam's Executive Council, 1936–1937; later Finance Member of the Executive Council. See *Hyderabad State List of Leading Officers, Nobles and Personages* (Potter Press reprint, 2007), p. 13.

Jang, Nawab Mehdi Yar (also Sayyid Muhammad Hussain Bilgrami) (1881–?); Shia Muslim. Inspector of Schools in the United Provinces of Agra and Oudh. Entered the service of the Nizam of Hyderabad, 1907; Director of Public Instruction; Secretary in the Judicial, Political, and General departments; Political Secretary to the Nizam's government. During the 1930s he became Sadr-ul-Maham (Member) in charge of the Political Department. See *Hyderabad State List of Leading Officers, Nobles and Personages* (Potter Press reprint, 2007), p. 21.

Jetha, Suleman Mohamed (1906–1996); came to London in 1933 where he set up a firm importing spices from India and supplying them to businesses in Aldgate East. An Ismaili, he converted to the Sunni tradition; married a Jewish woman. Active and leading member of the Jamiat-ul-Muslimin from the 1940s and represented it on the East London Mosque Trust; Chairman of the Trust from the 1970s; also ran the Indigent Moslems Burial Fund. He was deeply involved in the management of the mosque and gave much of his time and energy to raising funds that contributed enormously towards the construction of the mosque that was finally inaugurated in Whitechapel Road in 1985.

Jeevanjee, Alibhoy Mulla (1856–1936); leading Indian merchant, from a Daudi Bohra (Shia) family from Karachi; made his considerable fortune in East Africa. First Indian member of the Legislative Assembly of British East Africa, 1909 (sole Indian member until 1919).

Kaderbhoy, M.T.; barrister. Honorary Secretary of the London All-India Muslim League; resigned from the LMF in 1911, and returned to India.

Kamal-ud-Din, Khwaja (1870–1932); born in India; qualified as a lawyer in the 1890s. In 1912 he came to England to present a case before the Privy Council. While in London he learned of the existence of the Woking Mosque, which had been used for worship on only a small number of occasions. After visiting the mosque in 1913, he succeeded in having it re-opened and, with the help of Mirza Abbas Ali Baig (q.v.) in particular, persuaded the court to establish its status as a Muslim place of worship under a Trust. Established the Woking Muslim Mission and Literary Trust at the mosque, which constituted the centre of Islam in England from 1913 to the mid-1960s. Began editing a monthly journal, *The Islamic Review*, 1915, which for over fifty-five years was the main Islamic journal in Britain. While Kamal-ud-Din himself was affiliated to the Lahore Ahmadiyya Movement (a splinter from a heterodox sect founded by Mirza Ghulam Ahmed of Qadian (Punjab, India) in the late nineteenth century), the Islam that he (and later imams) presented at Woking was ecumenical, not promoting any particular sect or movement within Islam.

Kazi, Imdadali Imamali (1886–1968); venerated scholar from the province of Sindh in British India (after 1947 part of Pakistan). Came to England for higher education, 1907; remained until 1919, studying economics and psychology at the London School of Economics and King's College London respectively. Married Elsa Gertrude Loesch, daughter of a German composer, 1910; called to the Bar, 1911. Returned to India, 1919, but came back to England, 1931. Elected first president of the Jamiat-ul-Muslimin, 1934. In India from 1938; returned to England, 1947–1951. First Vice-Chancellor of the University of Sindh, 1951.

Khan, Habibullah (1872–1919); Amir of Afghanistan from 1901 until his assassination in 1919. Maintained strict neutrality during the First World War, despite coming under immense pressure from the Ottoman Emperor to support him.

Khan, Sahibdad (1896–?); from Jhelum, Punjab; came to United Kingdom, 1923. In 1927, on his return from the USA, he opened a perfumery business, which he ran for many years. Reported by British intelligence to be politically motivated from 1935 onwards, sympathetic to the Indian National Congress, and closely connected with Amir Shah, as well as the Indian seamen's communist leader, Surat Ali. Advocated Muslim–Hindu unity and Indian independence. During the Second World War, he was alleged to be engaged in the black market and profiteering, but was considered by the intelligence services to be a 'moderate man and a conscientious Moslem' (BL, IOR, P&J/12/468, fos 78–79).

Khan, Sahibzada Aftab Ahmad (1867–1930); educated at Christ's College, Cambridge; called to the Bar at the Inner Temple, 1894. Trustee of the Mahomedan Anglo-Oriental College, Aligarh; President of the Mahomedan Educational Association of Calcutta, 1911. Member of the Council of the Secretary of State for India in succession to Sir Abbas Ali Baig, 1917; represented Indian Muslims at the Paris Peace Conference, 1919. While in England he took interest in Muslim affairs, including those at the Woking Mosque, until his return to India in 1923.

Labbane (Lebanne, Lebbane), Kamal El; attaché to the Egyptian Embassy in London during the Second World War; active ELM Trustee until he returned to Egypt in 1944.

Lamington (*see* Cochrane-Baillie, Charles Wallace Alexander Napier Ross, 2nd Baron Lamington)

Latif, Camrudin Amirudin (1856–?); partner in a firm and agency for the sale of pearls and precious stones in Holborn, London, until its dissolution in 1914. Vice-President of the London branch of the All-India Muslim League. See http://www.london-gazette.co.uk/issues/28846/pages/5227/page.pdf (accessed 18 January 2010); *The Times*, 20 September 1912.

Leitner, Gottleib Wilhelm (1840–1899); born in Budapest; interpreter (mainly in Arabic, Turkish, and Russian) to the British

Commissariat in Constantinople, 1855. Studied at King's College London, 1858–1859; lecturer in Arabic, Turkish, and Modern Greek, 1859; Professor in Arabic and Muslim Law, 1861. Principal of Government College at Lahore (now Pakistan), 1864; helped raise its status to the University of the Punjab, of which he was the Registrar. Founder of a number of schools, literary associations, free public libraries, and academic journals. Author of comprehensive two-volume history of Islam (in Urdu). Returned to England, 1881; purchased the site of the Royal Dramatic College in Woking and established the Oriental Institute, for the purpose of educating students, especially from India, in 'oriental' languages, cultures, and religions. Established the Woking Mosque, 1889, to cater for the religious needs of these students. The Oriental Institute closed down at his death, but the Mosque was re-opened in 1913 by Khwaja Kamal-ud-Din (q.v.). See http://www.oxforddnb.com/view/article/51109 (accessed 3 February 2011).

Lovegrove, J.W. (Habibullah) (1867–1940); master tailor. Lived and worked in London, 1890s–1930s; active member of the Woking Muslim Mission. Converted to Islam and wrote the book *What is Islam?* (2nd edn, Woking, 1934). See http://www.lovegrove.co.uk/habibullah/index.htm (accessed 19 January 2010).

Mehmed V. Reshad (1844–1918); 35th Ottoman Sultan and 99th Caliph of Prophet Muhammad. Began his rule 27 April 1909. Attempting to rule as a constitutional monarch, he surrendered all authority to the Committee of Union and Progress, the liberal–nationalist organization of the Young Turk movement. Turkey entered the First World War on the side of Germany and Austria-Hungary, and, as caliph, he declared *jihad* (holy war) on his enemies, inviting all Muslims, especially those under the rule of the Allies, to rally to the support of the Ottomans. By the time of Mehmed's death, most of the empire had fallen to the Allies, and six months later Constantinople was under military occupation. See http://www.britannica.com/EBchecked/topic/373194/Mehmed-V (accessed 26 November 2009).

Moid-ul-Mulk, Sir Sayed Ali Imam (1869–1932); called to the Bar by the Middle Temple, 1890. President of the All-India Muslim League, 1908. First Muslim member of the Viceroy of India's Executive Council, 1910. Appointed President of the Executive Council of the Nizam of Hyderabad, 1919; resigned, 1922. Leading member of the National Moslem Conference, 1931. See *The Times*, 31 October 1932.

Morison, Sir Theodore (1863–1936); highly-respected educationalist and writer. Member of the Viceroy of India's Administrative Council, 1903–1904; member of the Council of India, 1906–1916; knighted 1910; member of the Commission on the Public Services of India, 1913–1915.

Morley, John, Viscount Morley of Blackburn (1838–1923); British Liberal politician, writer, and newspaper editor. Editor of the *Fortnightly Review*, 1869–1882 and the *Pall Mall Gazette*, 1880–1883. MP for Newcastle upon Tyne (1883–1895) and for Montrose Burghs (1896–1908). Secretary of State for India, 1905–1910, 1911. Together with the Viceroy, the Earl of Minto, he was responsible for the Indian Councils Act of 1909 (known as the Morley–Minto reforms), which allotted Indian Muslims reserved seats in the Municipal and District Boards, in the Provincial Councils, and in the Imperial Legislature in excess of their relative proportion of the population. Created Viscount Morley, 1908.

Moyne (*see* **Guinness, Walter Edward, 1st Baron Moyne**)

Newcombe, Colonel Stewart F. (1878–1956); soldier, explorer, surveyor, adventurer; a close friend of T.E. Lawrence. Awarded DSO 1915. Appointed Joint Honorary Secretary to the ELM Trust, 23 July 1941; resigned 7 April 1943.

Noon, Malik Sir Firoz Khan (1893–1970); member of one of the biggest landowning families of the Punjab. Educated at Wadham College, Oxford; held a number of ministerial portfolios in the Punjab from 1927. High Commissioner of India to the United Kingdom, 1936–1941; returned to India as member of the Viceroy's Executive Council, 1941.

Pasha (Pacha), Dr Hassan Nachat (1888–1969); Director of King Fuad's Royal Cabinet. Founded the Ittehad (Unionist) Party and played an important part in Egyptian politics until 1925. Ambassador to the United Kingdom, 1938. Towards the end of his tenure, in October 1944, he married Australian-born Patricia May Marsh, thirty-two years his junior, in a wedding ceremony officiated by Sheikh Hafiz Wahba, an Egyptian cleric who worked for the then Saudi diplomatic service. See *The Times*, 16 April 1938; http://egy-plus.com/landmarks/95-02-04.php (accessed 20 January 2011).

Pickthall, Marmaduke William (1875–1936); Western Islamic scholar and novelist. Educated at Harrow. Son of a Church of England rector, he embraced Islam in 1917 and was also a freemason with Conservative views. Learned Arabic early in his life; supported the Ottoman Caliphate during the First World War. On several occasions acted as the imam at the Woking Mosque and delivered scholarly lectures on various aspects of Islam, which he considered to be a progressive faith. Edited *Bombay Chronicle*, 1920; thereafter in the service of the Hyderabad government for ten years; editor of the *Hyderabad Quarterly Review* and founded the journal *Islamic Culture*. Made a well-respected translation of the Qur'an, 1930. Died at St Ives but was buried, in fulfilment of his wishes, at Brookwood Cemetery. See Ann Freemantle, *Loyal Enemy* (London, 1938); Peter Clark, *Marmaduke Pickthall: British Muslim* (London, 1986); *The Times*, 20 May 1936.

Qadir, Shaikh Sir Abdul (1874–1950); journalist and politician. Joined the *Punjab Observer*, the first Muslim newspaper published in English, 1895; later its editor. In 1901, he launched the literary magazine *Makhzan*, an Urdu-language publication that went on to acquire a reputation for excellence. Came to England to study law, 1904; called to the Bar at Lincoln's Inn, 1907, after which he returned to India. First elected President of the Punjab Legislative Assembly. Knighted; replaced Sir Umar Hayat Khan Tiwana as a member of the Council of the Secretary of State for India, 1934–1939. While in England he was actively engaged in Muslim affairs. In 1937, at the foundation-stone-laying ceremony for the construction of a mosque in London, he gave the address of welcome to the chief guest, the Nizam of Hyderabad's heir-apparent, the Prince of Berar and his wife (copy available at the ELM Archives). Gave public lectures on Islam and attended a number of National League functions as well as the World Congress of Faiths in 1936. Returned to India, 1939.

Qajar, Ahmad Shah (1898–1930); last ruler of the Qajar dynasty of Persia (later Iran) in 1909, following the overthrow of his father. Deposed by an army officer, Reza Khan, in 1925, who proclaimed himself as shah and took the name of Reza Shah Pahlavi, Shah of Persia.

Rafique, Sir Mohamed (1863–?); lawyer. Called to the Bar by the Middle Temple, 26 January 1886. Enrolled in the High Court at Allahabad as an Advocate but was a member of the Oudh Bar and practised in Lucknow. Later entered Judicial Service and was appointed a Judge of the Allahabad High Court, 1912. Retired 1923, but was then appointed member of the Council of the Secretary of State for India, in recognition of his judicial acumen. Co-opted onto the Council of the East India Association, 1928; replaced 1929 by Colonel Sir Umar Hayat Khan Tiwana upon his arrival in England.

Rahimtoola, Habib Ibrahim (1912–1991). Canvassed for the Muslim League in the 1946 Indian provincial elections. Founder president of the Bombay Provincial Muslim Chamber of Commerce, 1944–1947. First High Commissioner of Pakistan to London, 1947–1952. See http://www.pakpost.gov.pk/philately/stamps2002/independence_day.html (accessed 7 January 2010).

Rasul, Raja Tassaduq; from the family of *taluqdars* (large landholders) of Jehangirabad, United Provinces, India. Member of the All-India Muslim League; involved in Muslim politics in India during the early decades of the twentieth century.

Reshad, Mehmed V (*see* **Mehmed V Reshad**)

Rothschild, Nathaniel de, Baron Rothschild (1840–1915); Cambridge-educated member of the prominent Jewish banking family; had a particular interest in housing in the East End of London.

Russell, (Arthur) Oliver Villiers, 2nd Baron Ampthill (1869–1935); educated at Eton and New College, Oxford; appointed Governor of Madras, 1900, and acted as pro tem Viceroy of India in 1904 when Lord Curzon went on leave. Returned to England in 1906; championed Indians in South Africa and was chair of an advisory committee on Indian students in Britain set up by Lord Morley. While proclaiming liberal views, he became increasingly opposed to the Morley–Minto proposals for Indian political reform and spoke out against the 1919 India Bill. On the Council of the Indian Empire Society and of the India Defence League. He was an active and leading freemason throughout his life. See *The Times*, 8 July 1935; *ODNB*, http://www.oxforddnb.com/view/article/35874?docPos=3 (accessed 27 November 2009).

Sadigh-es-Sultaneh (*see* **Ali Khan, Mirza Abdul**)

Sadrud Din (Sadruddin) Maulavi (*c.*1880–1981); Imam of Woking Mosque, 1914–1916. Leader of the Lahore Ahmadiyya Movement, 1951–1981.

Shairani, Hafiz Mahmud Khan (1880–1946); scholar, writer, and editor. Edited and published (with the help of other Muslim sponsors) Henry Stubbe's eighteenth-century polemical manuscript, *An Account of the Rise and Progress of Mahometanism: with the life of Mahomet, and a vindication of him and his religion from the calumnies of the Christians* (London, 1911).

Sheldrake, Bertram William (Khalid) (1888–1947); son of a pickle manufacturer from Forest Hill, London; converted to Islam at the beginning of the twentieth century. Actively contributed to the Pan-Islamic Society, describing its activities from 1904 in some detail in the *Islamic Review and Muslim India* of January 1914. First Honorary Secretary of Moslem Society of Britain, 1914. In 1919, and again in 1929–1930, visited South Shields with the objective of organizing local Yemeni seamen and residents, representing their concerns to the government. Went to India, early 1930s. Reported to have been offered the throne in the Muslim-majority Chinese province of Sinkiang. Later moved to Turkey and worked for the British Council in Ankara during the Second World War. See *New York Times*, 13 March 1934; *Washington Post*, 10 June 1934; *Los Angeles Times*, 5 August 1934; Max Everest-Phillips, 'The suburban king of Tartary', *Asian Affairs*, 21, no. 3 (1990), pp. 324–335.

Suhrawardy, Sir Hassan (1884–1946); member of a prominent Calcutta Muslim family. Qualified as a medical doctor, but also a religious man and an Islamic scholar; carried out postgraduate studies in Dublin, Edinburgh, and London. Knighted in 1932. Trustee of the Nizamiah Mosque Trust while in England. Adviser to the Council of the Secretary of State for India, 1939–1944. A staunch supporter of the All-India Muslim League, he was at odds with some leading members of the Jamiat-ul-Muslimin who supported the Indian National Congress.

Swettenham, Sir Frank (1850–1946), Governor of the Straits Colony (Malaya) and High Commissioner for the Federated Malay States; Joint Director of the Official Press Bureau in London.

Sykes, Sir Frederick (1877–1954); Air Vice-Marshall in the Royal Air Force, retired 1922. Knighted 1919. Conservative MP for Sheffield Hallam (1922–1928) and for Nottingham Central (1940–1945). Governor of Bombay, 1928–1931. Returned to Britain, 1931, becoming involved in a number of philanthropic concerns.

Tiwana, Major-General Nawab Malik Sir Mahomed Umar Hayat Khan (1874–1944); landowner, army officer, and member of the Punjab Legislature. Posted on the Western Front, 1914, and then in Mesopotamia. Took part in the Third Afghan War in 1919. Member of the Council of the Secretary of State for India, 1929–1934; prominent freemason. Helped recruit soldiers in the Punjab for the Second World War. See *The Times*, 5 April 1944.

Turnour, Edward, 6th Earl Winterton (1883–1962); Irish peer and British politician. Conservative MP for Horsham (1904–1918), for Horsham and Worthing (1918–1945), and for Horsham again (1945–1951). Achieved ministerial office in several Conservative governments, including that of Parliamentary Under-Secretary of State for India, 1922–1924. Increasingly sidelined after 1938.

Winterton (*see* **Turnour, Edward, 6th Earl Winterton**)

Woodhead, Sir John Ackroyd (1881–1973); civil servant. Officer in Indian Civil Service; acting Governor of Bengal, 10 August 1934–1 April 1937 and June–November 1939. Headed the Woodhead Commission established in 1938 to investigate the circumstances leading to the failure of the Peel Commission to achieve resolution of the Arab Revolt that had begun in 1936. See http://www.worldstatesmen.org/India_BrProvinces.htm (accessed 10 January 2010).

Zada, Mahmood R. Counsellor to Saudi Arabian Legation to London during the Second World War; ELM Fund Trustee, 1942–1944.

APPENDIX II: ARTICLES OF ASSOCIATION OF THE EAST LONDON MOSQUE TRUST LIMITED, 1948

THE COMPANIES ACT 1948

COMPANY LIMITED BY GUARANTEE AND NOT HAVING A SHARE CAPITAL

ARTICLES OF ASSOCIATION OF THE EAST LONDON MOSQUE TRUST LIMITED

PRELIMINARY

1. In these Articles, unless there be something in the subject or context inconsistent therewith:

"Memorandum of Association" means the Memorandum of Association to which these Articles are annexed.

"The Trust" means THE EAST LONDON MOSQUE TRUST LIIMITED.

"Regulations of the Trust" means the Memorandum and Articles of Association and the other Regulations (if any) including by-laws for the management of the Trust for the time being.

"Member" means Member of the Trust.

"Council" means the members for the time being of the Council herein constituted.

"Secretary" and "Auditor" means respectively those officers for the time being of the Trust.

"General Meeting" means General Meeting, whether Ordinary or Extraordinary, of the Trust held in accordance with the Regulations of the Trust.

"Extraordinary Resolution" and "Special Resolution" mean an Extraordinary or a Special Resolution of the Trust (as the case may be) as defined by Section 141 of the Companies Act 1948, or any subsisting statutory modification thereof.

"The Register" means the Register of Members to be kept pursuant to section 110 of the Companies Act 1948.

"Office of the Trust" means the Registered Office for the time being of the Trust.

"The Statutes" means the Companies Act 1948, and the other Statutes (if any) to which the Trust shall for the time being be subject.

"In writing" means written or printed, or partly written and partly printed.

"Person" includes a firm and also a corporation as well as an individual.

The singular includes the plural, and the masculine the feminine, and vice versa.

"Month" means calendar month.

"By-law" means any By-law of the Trust made under the Regulations of the Trust for the time being in force.

MEMBERSHIP

2. For the purpose of registration the number of Members of the Trust is declared to be fifty, but the Council may at any time register an increase of membership.

3. The Subscribers to the Memorandum of Association and the first Members of the Council (so far as they shall not be such subscribers or first Members of the Council) His Excellency Abdel Fattah Amr Pasha,[1] His Excellency Habib Ibrahim Rahimtoola, His Excellency Sheikh Hafez Wahba, Mr Allah Dad Khan, Mr Naqibullah Khan, Mr Suleman Mohamed Jetha, Sir Sultan Mohammed Shah Aga Khan, Sir Torick Ameer Ali, Mr Hatim Attari, Mr Syed Fazl Shah, Mr Ghulam Mohammed and Mr Imdad Ali Imam Ali Kazi, shall be the first members of the Trust. The foregoing persons and all the members of the Council from time to time, and such other persons as shall be admitted to membership in accordance

[1] Egyptian Ambassador to the United Kingdom.

with these Articles, and none other, shall be members of the Trust and entered in the Register accordingly.

4. Membership of the Trust shall be confined to persons of the Moslem faith who are interested in and willing to contribute to or actively to further the objects of the Trust, as set forth in the Memorandum of Association, and who accordingly shall (subject to the provisions of Article 3) be admitted to membership by the Council as hereinafter provided: Provided always that the Council may from time to time determine to make eligible for membership on such terms as may be determined by the Council any other person who in the opinion of the Council shall have rendered or be capable of rendering special service to the Trust.

5. No person other than the first members of the Trust and members of the Council shall be eligible for membership of the Trust unless such person shall be eligible for membership in accordance with Article 4 and shall have completed an application in such form as may from time to time be prescribed by the Council together with any form of certificate or declaration which the Council may prescribe and shall have satisfied the Council as to the correctness of the particulars furnished therein, and shall be proposed and seconded respectively in writing by two members of the Trust, who shall certify that such person is qualified and is in their opinion a fit and proper person to be a member of the Trust, or shall be admitted by the Council without application as a person coming within the provisions of the proviso to Article 4.

6. All members other than the first members of the Trust and members of the Council shall be elected by the Council. Such election shall be by a majority of votes and, in the case of an equality of votes, the Chairman of the Council shall have a casting vote, but the Council may without assigning any reason and in the exercise of its discretion refuse to elect any applicant for membership.

7. (A) Unless and until otherwise determined by the Council, no entrance fee or annual subscription shall be payable by members, but the Council shall be empowered at any time and from time to time determine the entrance fees and/or subscriptions shall be payable, and to fix the amount or rate of such entrance fee or subscription (as the case may be) and to suspend, waive or vary the same as it may at any time and from time to time consider desirable.

(B) All entrance fees and subscriptions (if any) received by the Trust shall (subject to the right of the Council to apply the same or any part thereof towards the expenses of the Trust) be applied for or towards such one or more of the objects of the Trust as the Council shall at any time and from time to time determine.

8. In the event that subscription shall at any time be payable then all such subscriptions shall be payable in advance on the 1st January in each year, but every member shall forward the amount of his first subscription with his application for membership, or in the case of any member elected as eligible in accordance with the provisions contained in Article 4 hereof, in respect of whom no application shall be required, on notification to him of his election. Such subscription shall be returned by the Trust to the applicant if he is not elected a member. Such subscription shall if the applicant is admitted to membership be for the then current year, except that in the case of members elected on or after the 31st October in any year, the first subscription shall cover the period dating from their election until the 31st December in the next succeeding year. The said subscriptions shall entitle the Member to one vote only at General Meetings of the Trust.

9. If in the event that subscriptions shall at any time be payable, any member fails to pay his subscription for any year within one month of the same becoming due, the Secretary shall notify him of the fact, and if any member fails to pay his subscription for any such year within one further month of being so notified, he shall, ipso facto, cease to be a Member of the Trust, but shall still be liable for his subscription so in arrear, and shall be eligible for re-admission upon payment of all arrears due from him while a member and of the amount of the subscriptions that would have been due from him if he had continued a member up to the time of re-admission. Provided always that the Council may in any case, if they think fit, suspect or waive the operation of any of the provisions of this Article on such terms as they may determine.

10. Any member may at any time withdraw from membership of the Trust by giving to the Secretary at its registered office one month's notice in writing (or such shorter notice as the Council may in any case determine to accept) of his intention so to do, and upon the expiration of such notice he shall cease to be a member. Provided that if in any case such notice is given after the 30th November of any year and subscription shall at that time be payable, the member shall be liable to and shall forthwith pay his subscription for the whole of the next ensuing year of the Trust.

11. Should any member commit any serious or persistent breach of any of the Regulations of the Trust, or be guilty of any act or conduct

which in the opinion of the Council is detrimental to the interests of the Trust, the Council may at their discretion expel such Member from the Trust by a resolution passed by a majority of not less than two-thirds of the members of the Council attending and voting at a Meeting specially convened to consider the question of his expulsion, and at which Meeting not less than three members of the Council are present. The member concerned shall be given not less than twenty-one clear days' notice in writing of the time, place and object of the Meeting of the Council and shall be given an opportunity of attending and being heard in his defence, or if he so desires, of being represented thereat by another Member, or by Solicitor or Counsel. The decision of the Council at any such Meeting shall be final, and any Member who shall be expelled shall thereupon cease to be a Member of the Trust.

12. None of the rights and privileges of a Member in relation to the Trust shall be chargeable, transferable or transmissible by his own act, or by operation of law or otherwise, except with the written consent of the Counsel.

13. Every Member shall undertake to further to the best of his ability the objects and interests and influence of the Trust, and shall at all times observe the Regulations of the Trust and shall from time to time notify the Secretary of the Trust a place of business or residence to be registered as his place of address, and the place so registered shall for the purpose of the Regulations of the Trust be deemed his place of address; all notices may be sent by the Trust to such place of address by ordinary post.

14. A register shall be kept by the Trust containing the names and addresses of all the Members, together with such other particulars as may be required by the Statutes.

15. In addition to the provisions for cesser of membership hereinbefore contained a Member shall forthwith cease to be a Member of the Trust upon the happening of any one of the following events:–

(A) If such Member shall abandon the Moslem faith.

(B) If such Member shall express an intention to reside permanently out of the United Kingdom, and the Council shall determine that it is in the interests of the Trust that he shall cease to be a Member.

(C) If such Member becomes of unsound mind.

(D) If such Member becomes bankrupt, or makes or agrees to any assignment for the benefit of his creditors, and shall pay or propose to pay any composition to his creditors, or execute any similar deed or agreement, or shall take or attempt to take the benefit of any statutory provision for arrangement with his creditors.

(E) If such Member shall in the opinion of the Council cease for any reason to be eligible for membership of the Trust and the Council shall so resolve.

(F) If the Trust exclude such Member in accordance with the Regulations.

Provided always that in the case of a person ceasing to be a Member under either of the paragraphs (C) or (D) of this Article, the Council shall be entitled (if it thinks fit) to reinstate any such person as a Member upon such terms as it may think fit.

16. In the event that subscriptions shall at any time be payable, then no Member shall be entitled to vote or otherwise participate in the benefit of membership while his subscription shall be unpaid and in arrear within the meaning of the provisions of Article 9 thereof.

17. Any Member who shall by any means cease to be a Member shall nevertheless remain liable for, and shall pay to the Trust, all moneys which at the time of his ceasing to be a Member may be due from him to the Trust, or which may become payable by him by virtue of his liability under the Memorandum of Association of the Trust.

COUNCIL OF MANAGEMENT

18. (A) The affairs and property of the Trust shall be managed by the Council who (subject as hereinafter provided) shall consist of the Diplomatic Representative for the time being to the Court of St. James, High Commissioner or other accredited Representative (or some other person to be nominated by each such Representative, High Commissioner or accredited Representative) of Egypt, Pakistan and Saudi Arabia, the President, Honorary Secretary and Honorary Treasurer for the time being of Jamiat-ul-Muslimin, and not more than six further members, who shall hold office on the terms and subject to the provisions hereinafter contained.

(B) The first Members of the Council shall be (1) His Excellency Abdel Fateh Amr Pasha, His Excellency Habib Ibrahim Rahimtoola, His Excellency Sheikh Hafez Wahba, Sir Torick Ameer Ali, Mr Hatim Attari, Mr Syed Fazal Shah, Mr Ghulam Mohammed and Mr Imdad Ali Kazi; and (2) the persons for the time being holding office as President, Honorary Secretary and Honorary Treasurer of Jamiat-ul-Muslimin, provided they shall give notice in writing to the Trust that they are willing to accept office as Members of the Council.

(C) Each Member of the Council shall hold office (subject to the retiring or otherwise ceasing to hold office pursuant to the provisions of Article 31 hereof) on the following terms, namely:–

(i) The Diplomatic Representative, High Commissioner or other accredited representative of Egypt, Pakistan and Saudi Arabia respectively (or any person nominated by any such Representative, High Commissioner or other accredited representative) shall each hold office for so long only as he remains the accredited representative in the United Kingdom of his Sovereign or his Country's Government (as the case may be) or shall remain the nominee of such accredited representative (as the case may be). Any vacancy resulting from the retirement of a Member of the Council pursuant to the provisions of this sub-paragraph shall be filled by the appointment to the Council of the accredited representative of the Court of St. James, High Commissioner or other accredited Representative who succeeds him or by the appointment of another person nominated by any such Diplomatic Representative, High Commissioner or other accredited representative (as the case may be), or at the option of the Council, if no successor is appointed, the vacancy may remain unfilled.

(ii) The President, Honorary Secretary and Honorary Treasurer of Jamiat-ul-Muslimin shall hold office for so long only as they remain such President, Honorary Secretary or Honorary Treasurer respectively. Any vacancy resulting from the retirement of a member of the Council pursuant to the provisions of this sub-paragraph shall be filled by the appointment to the Council of the person who succeeds him as such President, Honorary Secretary or Honorary Treasurer of Jamiat-ul-Muslimin as the case may be.

(iii) The remaining Members of the Council shall retire at the Annual General Meeting in each year but shall be eligible for re-election.

(iv) The Council shall have power to appoint any person whom they consider suitable to be an additional member of the Council (provided the maximum number referred to in paragraph (A) hereof is not exceeded) to hold office on such terms as the Council in its discretion may determine.

(D) The first Chairman of the Trust shall be His Excellency Habib Ibrahim Rahimtoola and the first Vice-Chairman shall be Mr Imdad Ali Imam Ali Kazi, who shall hold office until the first Council Meeting of the Trust held after the Annual General Meeting of the Trust to be held in 1950, when they shall retire and a new Chairman and Vice-Chairman shall be elected by the Council in manner hereinafter provided.

(E) The Council shall at the Council meeting referred to in sub-paragraph (D) hereof and at each Council Meeting held first after the Annual General Meeting to be held in 1951 and in each year thereafter elect from their own Members a new Chairman and Vice-Chairman. Any retiring Chairman in any year shall be eligible for re-election, and the election of the Vice-Chairman in any year shall be at the discretion of the Council, and any retiring Vice-Chairman shall be eligible for re-election.

19. Casual vacancies in the Council may, subject to the provisions of Article 18, be filled by the Council; any member of the Council so elected shall, subject to the provisions of Article 18, hold office until the next Annual General Meeting, when he shall retire but be eligible for re-election, and the Council may provide by By-laws the manner in which such appointments shall be made, but any such appointment, and any such By-laws if made, shall have regard to the provisions herein contained as to the constitution of the Council and the capacity in which any Member of the Council is so appointed shall correspond to the capacity of the Member whom he replaces.

20. Notwithstanding the provisions hereinbefore contained, the Council shall be empowered at any time and from time to time to co-opt as an additional member of the Council any person not being a Member, but who in the opinion of the Council is likely to be of help to the Trust and who shall act in an advisory capacity only and shall not be entitled to vote.

21. One of the members of the Council shall (unless otherwise determined by the Council) act as the Honorary Treasurer of the Trust, and shall be appointed at the first meeting of the Council held after the Annual General Meeting in each year. Any such Honorary Treasurer shall be eligible for re-election at the expiration of his year of office.

22. The Council shall have the entire supervision, control and disposition of the affairs and property of the Trust, and generally may exercise all such powers and do all such things as it may consider necessary for or conducive or incidental to the due management of the affairs and property, or for effecting the objects of the Trust, subject nevertheless to the Statutes and the Regulations of the Trust, but no regulations of the Trust shall invalidate any prior act of the Council which would have been valid if such regulation had not been made.

23. Without limiting the effect of the last preceding Article, or any other powers specifically given to the Council by these Regulations, it shall be lawful for the Council, in its absolute discretion, to exercise on behalf of and in the name of the Trust or otherwise, and from time to time, all or any of the following specific powers (that is to say):–

(A) To make Rules and By-laws for further regulating the affairs of the Trust, and to amend or rescind any such Rules and By-laws, and every Member, present or future, shall be bound by all such Rules and By-laws as may be for the time being in force, provided that no such Rules or By-laws shall be inconsistent with the objects of the Trust or these presents.

(B) To regulate and control the custody, investment, realisation and expenditure of the moneys, stocks, funds and securities of the Trust as the Council shall think fit.

(C) From time to time to borrow or raise or secure the payment of such sums for the purposes of the Trust as the Council thinks fit.

(D) To give receipts by any one or more of the Council or by any person or persons whom it shall authorise, which shall be effectual discharges on behalf of and against the Trust for the moneys or property which in such receipts shall be acknowledged to have been received.

(E) To appoint and employ for the purposes of the Trust any managers, bankers, solicitors, officers, analysts, librarians, custodians, clerks, agents, servants or other persons, upon such terms as to their duties, powers, duration of office, or employment, remuneration and otherwise, as the Council shall think fit, and in particular to make such arrangements as to them shall seem appropriate in respect of secretarial services and office accommodation for the Trust, and also to remove or discharge from the service of the Trust any person for the time being in that service.

(F) To appoint any member of the Council, Member of the Trust or other person to do or perform any work, duties and services expedient or necessary to be performed and done by or on behalf of the Trust in pursuance of its registered objects.

(G) To delegate, subject to such conditions as the Council may think fit, any of its powers and duties to such committees consisting of such member or members of the Council or other Members of the Trust as the Council may think fit, and to appoint such special Committees (if any), as may from time to time seem to be in the interests of the Trust and to determine the constitution and powers of any such special Committees, and to make such regulations as to the proceedings of such sub-committees and special committees as may seem expedient.

(H) To petition Parliament in the name of the Trust.

(I) To resolve that the Common Seal of the Trust be affixed to all deeds and documents requiring the same in the presence of one member of the Council and the Secretary.

PROCEEDINGS OF THE COUNCIL

24. Until otherwise determined by the Council, two members of the Council present in person shall be a quorum, and may exercise all the powers of the Council. Subject to this Article, the Council may act notwithstanding any vacancy or vacancies in its number. Provided always that if at any time the number of members of the Council shall be reduced to less than the minimum number authorised by these presents, the Council may act for the purpose of filling up vacancies in its body, as hereinbefore provided and subject to the provisions of Article 18, or of summoning a General Meeting, but for no other purpose.

25. The Council may meet together for the despatch of business, adjourn and otherwise regulate its meetings and the proceedings thereat as it thinks fit; but all questions arising at any meeting of the Council shall be determined by a majority of votes, and in case of equality of votes the Chairman of the Meeting shall have a casting vote in addition to his vote as a member of the Council.

26. In case at any meeting of the Council neither the Chairman nor the Vice-Chairman be present within ten minutes after the time appointed for holding the meeting, the members of the Council present may choose one of their number to be Chairman of such meeting.

27. All acts done by any meeting of the Council or by any person acting as a member of the Council shall, notwithstanding that it be afterwards discovered that there was some defect in the appointment of such Council or person acting as aforesaid, or that such Council or any of the members thereof or such person were or was disqualified, be as valid as if such Council and every member thereof or such person had been duly appointed and were or was duly qualified.

28. The Council shall cause minutes to be duly entered in books, to be provided for that purpose, of all appointments of officers made by the Council, and of all resolutions and proceedings of General Meetings of the Trust and meetings of the Council and of any sub-committees or special committees.

29. A resolution in writing signed by all the members of the Council shall be as valid and effectual as if it were a resolution passed at a duly convened Meeting of such Council.

ROTATION OF COUNCIL

30. Any member of the Council may resign by giving one month's notice in writing to the Secretary.

DISQUALIFICATION OF MEMBERS OF THE COUNCIL.

31. The office of a member of the Council shall be vacated in any of the following events, namely:

(A) If by notice in writing to the Trust he resigns his office;

(B) If he be found lunatic or of unsound mind;

(C) If he becomes bankrupt or insolvent, or compounds with his creditors;

(D) If he be absent otherwise than on the business of the Trust from meetings of the Council for more than six consecutive calendar months without leave, or is absent from the United Kingdom for not less than six consecutive calendar months, and the Council resolve that his office be vacated;

(E) If he is prohibited from acting as a member of the Council by reason of any Order made under section 188 of section 332 of the Companies Act 1948.

GENERAL MEETINGS

32. The first General Meeting shall be held at such time, not being more than twelve months after the registration of the Trust, and at such place as the Council shall determine. Subsequent General Meetings shall be held in each year on such day and at such time and place as the Council may from time to time determine, provided that each such General Meeting shall be held not more than fifteen months after the holding of the preceding meeting.

33. The above General Meetings shall be called Annual General Meetings, and all other General Meetings shall be called Extraordinary General Meetings.

34. The Council may, whenever it thinks fit, and it shall, on the requisition in writing of any fifteen or more Members of the Trust convene an Extraordinary General Meeting.

35. Any requisition made by the Members must state the object of the Meeting proposed to be called, and must be signed by the requisitionists and deposited at the Office of the Trust.

36. On receipt of the requisition, the Council shall forthwith proceed to convene a General Meeting. If it does not proceed to call a Meeting to be held within six weeks from the date of the requisition being so deposited, the requisitionists or any fifteen or more members may themselves convene a Meeting by advertisement in two London daily newspapers not more than twenty-one days nor less than fourteen days before the day which the meeting is to be convened, stating the time place and object of the Meeting, and a copy of such advertisement shall be delivered at the Office of the Trust not less than thirteen days prior to the Meeting.

37. Every General Meeting shall be held in London or such other place as may be decided by the Council.

38. An Annual General Meeting and a Meeting called for the passing of a Special Resolution shall be called by twenty-one days' notice in writing at the least, and a meeting of the Trust other than an Annual General Meeting or a meeting for the passing of a Special Resolution shall be called by fourteen day's notice in writing at the least. The notice shall in either case be exclusive of the day on which it is served or deemed to be served and of the day for which it is given, and shall specify the place, the day and hour of the meeting and, in case of special business, the general nature of that business and shall be given in manner hereinafter mentioned or in such other manner, if any, as may be prescribed by the Trust in General Meeting to such persons as are, under the Article of the Trust, entitled to receive such notices from the Trust.

Provided that a meeting of the Trust shall, notwithstanding that it is called by shorter notice than that specified in this Article, be deemed to have been duly called if it is so agreed:–

(A) In the case of a meeting called as the Annual General Meeting, by all the members entitled to attend and vote thereat;
and
(B) In the case of any other meeting, by a majority in number of the members having a right to attend and vote at the meeting, being a majority together representing not less than ninety-five per cent of the total voting rights at that meeting of all the members.

39. (A) All business shall be deemed special that is transacted at an Extraordinary General Meeting, and all business that is transacted at an Annual General Meeting shall be deemed special, with the exception of the consideration of the accounts and balance sheets, and the ordinary reports of the Council and the Auditors' Report and the election of Auditors.

(B) Any member entitled to vote at a General Meeting may submit any resolution provided that he shall have served notice in writing thereof at the office of the Trust, duly signed by him, not less than six weeks before the date on which the Meeting is to be held, stating his intention to submit the same, and upon receipt of any such notice the Secretary shall include it in the notice of such Meeting or otherwise give notice to all Members, that such resolution will be proposed. Provided that if, after such notice has been served at the office of the Trust, a General Meeting is called for a date six weeks or less after the notice has been served, the notice though not served within the time required by this sub-paragraph, shall be deemed to have been properly served for the purposes thereof.

40. No business shall be transacted at a General Meeting, except the election of a Chairman of such Meeting, and the adjournment of the meeting, unless a quorum of Members entitled to vote be present, at the time when the Meeting proceeds to business. Unless and until otherwise provided by any By-laws of the Trust or in General Meeting a Quorum shall be four Members present in person. If within fifteen minutes from the time appointed for the Meeting a quorum be not present, the meeting, if convened on the requisition of Members, shall be dissolved; in any other case it shall stand adjourned to the same day in the next following week, at the same time and place, and if at such adjourned Meeting a quorum be not present, the Members present shall form a quorum.

41. The Chairman, or in his absence, the Vice-Chairman of the Trust, or in the absence of both, a member of the Council, chosen by the Meeting shall preside as Chairman at every General Meeting.

42. If the Chairman, Vice-Chairman and no member of the Council be present within fifteen minutes from the time appointed for holding the Meeting, or in case of refusal of all the members of the Council present to take the chair, the Members present and entitled to vote shall choose some one of their number to be Chairman.

43. The Chairman may, with the consent of the Meeting, adjourn any Meeting from time to time and from place to place, but no business shall be transacted at any adjourned Meeting other than the business left unfinished at the Meeting from which the adjournment took place.

44. At any General Meeting, a resolution put to the vote of the Meeting shall be decided on a show of hands and all resolutions which do not require to be passed as Special Resolutions by Extraordinary Resolutions shall be carried if passed by a majority of the Members present in person, and entitled to vote. Provided always, that if a poll is (before or on the declaration of the result of the show of hands) demanded by at least five Members present in person and entitled to vote, a poll shall be taken in manner hereinafter provided. And in case there shall be an equality of votes whether on a show of hands or on a poll the Chairman of the Meeting at which the show of hands takes place or at which the poll is demanded, shall be entitled to a second or a casting vote.

45. If at any Meeting a poll is demanded as above mentioned in regard to any particular resolution, such demand shall not prevent the conclusion of any other business before the Meeting at which the demand is made, but such poll shall be taken at such time and place and in such manner as the Chairman of the Meeting shall direct; and in case on any such poll there shall be an equality of votes, the Chairman of the Meeting at which such poll have been demanded shall be entitled to a casting vote in addition to his vote as a Member. The result of every such poll shall be deemed to be the resolution of the Meeting at which the poll was demanded.

46. At any General Meeting, unless a poll is demanded as provided above, a declaration by the Chairman that a resolution has been carried or carried by a particular majority, or lost or not carried by a particular majority, and an entry to that effect in the book of proceedings of the Trust shall be conclusive evidence xxxxx of the fact, without proof of the number of proportion of the votes recorded in favour of or against the resolution.

47. Save as expressly otherwise provided herein, every Member shall have one vote, and no person other than a Member duly registered (and in the event that subscriptions shall at any time be payable, whose subscription is not in arrear), shall be entitled to receive notice of or to be present or vote at any General Meeting.

48. No proxies shall be permitted for use at any General Meeting, save that if any Incorporated Company is a Member of the Trust it may vote by its duly authorised representative as provided by section 139 of the Companies Act 1948.

49. Subject to the provisions of the Statutes a General Meeting may remove any Auditor of the Trust and fill any resulting vacancy in the office of Auditor, and may (subject as hereinbefore provided) vary the number of Auditors.

50. It shall be lawful for any General Meeting:–

(A) By Special Resolution, to make, and to alter, or rescind any By-law of the Trust whether made by the Council pursuant to the provisions of Article 23(A) or by Special Resolution passed at a General Meeting as aforesaid (so that every By-law made or altered be reduced to writing, sealed with the Common Seal of the Trust and a copy thereof, or in case of the rescission of a By-law, notice of the By-law rescinded be sent to every Member as notices are hereinafter directed to be served) and generally for any General Meeting to decide on all matters and questions relating to the management or the regulations of the Trust, and

(B) From time to time by Special Resolution, to alter and make new provisions in lieu of or in addition to any of the Regulations of the Trust, and especially any General Meeting may by Special Resolution from time to time exercise all powers which by the Statutes a company limited by guarantee may exercise if authorised so to do by its Articles of Association.

SECRETARY

51. The Secretary shall be appointed, may be removed, and his salary (if any) shall be fixed by the Council and an Honorary Secretary may if the Council consider it desirable be appointed by the Council either as sole Secretary or in addition to any paid Secretary and shall hold office on such terms as the Council may determine.

52. The Secretary shall, unless the Council otherwise direct, keep the records, books, accounts and other papers of the Trust.

ACCOUNTS

53. The Council shall cause true and complete accounts to be kept of the assets, credits and liabilities of the Trust and in particular of all sums of money received and expended by the Trust and the matters in respect of which the receipt and expenditure takes place. Subject to any restrictions that may be imposed by the Council from time to time as to the time and manner of inspecting the same all the books of account of the Trust shall be open to the inspection of any member during reasonable business hours.

54. A balance sheet and an income and expenditure account, both made up to a date not more than three months prior to the Annual General Meeting, shall be made out once in every year and laid before the Meeting containing such particulars and in such form as shall be required by Statutes.

55. Once at least in every year the accounts of the Trust shall be examined, and the correctness of the balance sheet and income and expenditure account ascertained by an Auditor or Auditors. A copy of such balance sheet including every document required by law to be annexed thereto shall twenty-one days previously to each Annual

General Meeting be forwarded to every Member, addressed to him at his place of address, as registered in accordance with Article 14.

The Companies Act 1948

COMPANY LIMITED BY GUARANTEE AND NOT HAVING A SHARE CAPITAL.

MEMORANDUM OF ASSOCIATION
OF
THE EAST LONDON MOSQUE TRUST LIMITED.

1. The name of the Company (hereinafter called "The Trust") is "THE EAST LONDON MOSQUE TRUST LIMITED."

2. The registered office of the Trust will be situated in England.

3. The objects for which the Trust is established are:–

(A) To act as Trustees of the trusts relating to the London Mosque Fund as contained in a Deed of Declaration of Trust dated the 19th November 1926 and executed by His Highness Sir Sultan Mohammed Shah Aga Khan of Bombay, The Right Honourable Charles Wallace Alexander Napier Cochrane-Baillie Baron Lamington. The Right Honourable Arthur Oliver Villiers Russell Baron Ampthill. The Right Honourable Syer Ameer Ali and Sir Mohammed Rafique (which trust was constituted for the purposes in the said Deed contained) and of the freehold property, known as the East London Mosque and Islamic Culture Centre at Nos. 446/448 Commercial Road in the Parish of Stepney in the County of London (Registered Title No. LN 244192) and the further property at No. 450 Commercial Road aforesaid (Registered Title No. 30706) (both of which properties are held under the trusts of the said Deed of the 19th November, 1926); to acquire the said trust properties from the present Trustees thereof, and to perform and execute the said trusts in accordance with the terms of the said trust Instruments; and to act as Trustees of any other trusts relating to matters concerned with the Moslem faith which in the opinion of the Council of Management of the Trust can be conveniently and properly undertaken by the Trust.

(B) So far as the law may from time to time allow, to purchase, take on lease, hire or otherwise acquire any real or personal property and any rights or privileges necessary or convenient for the purpose of the Trust.

(C) To construct, maintain and alter any houses or buildings necessary or convenient for the purposes of the Trust.

(D) To invest and deal with the moneys of the Trust not immediately required upon such securities and in such manners as may from time to time be determined, but so that moneys subject or representing property subject to the jurisdiction of the Charity Commissioners for England and Wales or any authority exercising corresponding jurisdiction outside England and Wales shall only be invested in such securities and with such sanction (if any) as may for the time being be prescribed by law.

(E) To make regulations and by-laws for the guidance and control of the affairs of the Trust, and to define and settle the manner in which compliance, with the decisions or directions of the Trust shall or may be secured or enforced, and to enforce any bye-laws and regulations of the Trust and any directions given by it.

(F) To take such steps, by personal or written appeals, or otherwise as may from time to time be deemed expedient to procure and to accept grants of money and (so far as the law may from time to time allow) of land, donations, gifts, subscriptions and other assistance in furtherance of the objects of the Trust, and to conform to any proper conditions upon which such grants and other payments may be made.

(G) To present Petitions to Parliaments in the territories of the British Empire and elsewhere and Memorials or other documents to the Governments and legislative and other Authorities in any of such territories with a view to the promotion of the Trust's objects.

(H) To establish and support or aid in the establishment and support of associations, institutions, funds, trusts and conveniences calculated to benefit employees or ex-employees of the Trust or the dependents or connections of such persons, and to grant pensions and allowances to and to make payments towards insurance of such persons.

4. The income and property of the Trust, whencesoever derived, shall be applied solely towards the promotion of the objects of the

Trust as set forth in this Memorandum of Association, and no portion thereof shall be paid or transferred directly or indirectly by way of dividend, bonus or otherwise, howsoever, by way of profit to the Members of the Trust: Provided that nothing herein shall prevent the payment in good faith of remuneration to any officers or servants of the Trust or to any Members of the Trust or other person in return for any services actually rendered to the Trust, nor prevent the payment of interest at a rate not exceeding £ 5 per cent on money borrowed from any Member of the Trust.

5. The liability of the Members is limited.

6. Every Member of the Trust undertakes to contribute to the assets of the Trust, in the event of the same being wound up during the time that he or she is a Member, or within one year afterwards, for payment of the debts and liabilities of the Trust contracted before the time at which he or she ceases to be a Member, and of the costs, charges and expenses of winding up the same, and for the adjustment of the rights of the contributories amongst themselves, such amount as may be required not exceeding £ 1.

7. If upon the winding up or dissolution of the Trust there remains after the satisfaction of all its debts and liabilities any property whatsoever, the same shall not be paid to or distributed among the Members of the Trust, but shall be given or transferred to some other institution or institutions having objects similar to the object of the Trust, to be determined by the Members of the Trust at or before the time of dissolution, or in default thereof by such Judge of the High Court of Justice as may have or acquire jurisdiction in the matter.

8. True accounts shall be kept of the sums of money received and expended by the Trust, and the matter in respect of which such receipt and expenditure takes place, and of the property, credits and liabilities of the Trust, and subject to any reasonable restrictions as to the time and manner of inspecting the same that may be imposed in accordance with the regulations of the Trust for the time being shall be open to the inspection of the Members. Once at least in every year the accounts of the Trust shall be examined and the correctness of the balance sheet ascertained by one or more properly qualified auditor or auditors.

We, the several persons whose names and addresses are subscribed, are desirous of being formed into a Company in pursuance of this Memorandum of Association.

Names, addresses and Descriptions of subscribers:

His Excellency Abdel Fateh Amr Pasha, The Egyptian Ambassador, 75 South Audley Street, W1

His Excellency Sheikh Hafez Wahba, The Saudi Arabian Ambassador, 30 Belgrave Square, SW1

His Excellency Habib Ibrahim Rahimtoola, High Commissioner for Pakistan, 56 Park Avenue NW

Mr Imdad Ali Kazi, Barrister-at-Law, 45, Avenue Road, Penge, SE20

Mr Allah Dad Khan, Director, 34, Pellers Road, W6

Mr Naqibullah Khan, Merchant, 7 Beccles Street, E14

Mr Syed Fazal Shah, Director, 244 Bilton Rd, Perivale, Middx

Mr Ghulam Mohammed, Export Agent, 59 Canton Street, E14

Mr Suleman Mohomed Jetha, Importer and Exporter, 18 Albert Street, NW1

Sir Torick Ameer Ali, Retired Judge of the High Court, Calcutta, Pollingfold, Rudgwick, Sussex

Dated this 25th Day of April 1949

Witness to the above Signatures:

J.A Woodhead
Chevremont
Hockering Road
Woking

TRUST CORPORATIONS
LAW OF PROPERTY (AMENDMENT) ACT, 1926

I, WILLIAM ALLEN VISCOUNT JOWITT, Lord High Chancellor of Great Britain, having read the statutory declaration of Bernard William Gould on behalf of THE EAST LONDON MOSQUE TRUST LIMITED dated the 20th day of May, 1949, am satisfied that the said Corporation fulfils those of the provisions of subsection 1 of section 3 of the Law of Property (Amendment) Act, 1926, which are applicable to the case of the said Corporation, and authorise the said Corporation accordingly to act in relation to charitable, ecclesiastical and public trusts as a trust corporation.

JOWITT C.

Dated the 21st Day of June 1949

APPENDIX III: SELECTED DOCUMENTS RELATING TO THE EAST LONDON MOSQUE, THE JAMIAT-UL-MUSLIMIN, AND RELATED DEVELOPMENTS IN THE LATE 1930s AND EARLY 1940s

Evidence relating to the events surrounding the establishment of the East London Mosque, the Jamiat-ul-Muslimin, and other related developments in the late 1930s and early 1940s is deposited in the British Library. This appendix contains transcripts of a selection of the most relevant of these records (BL, IOR, L/P&J/12/468). While these transcripts are not annotated, they provide useful additional information on various developments mentioned in the Minutes.

Report on schemes to build a Muslim centre in London (dated 29.5.1941)

BL, IOR, L/P&J/12/468, fos 186–189

There are three schemes in existence for Moslem centres in London. Each of them includes proposals for a Mosque and a cultural centre. These schemes are:–

(1) The London Mosque Fund. This fund was founded in 1926. Sir Ernest Hotson is the Honorary Secretary and Sir Hassan Suhrawardy is one of the Trustees. The present assets of the fund stand, according to Sir Hassan Suhrawardy's note of November 1940, at £10,664 of which £1,050 has been invested in property in Commercial Road, possession of which has been obtained. Sir Hassan Suhrawardy stated in his note that this fund could be amalgamated with the Egyptian Ambassador's London Mosque scheme by resolution of the Trustees and that a meeting was to be held at an early date to discuss this question. Sir Hassan had suggested that the Egyptian Ambassador should become Chairman of the Executive Committee.

I understand from Mr. Blake of the British Council that the premises in Commercial Road have now been opened as a Moslem meeting place for the purpose of worship and that what the Council have been asked to do is to supply a sum of about £100 to provide furniture for a cultural centre and also to provide an annual sum of about the same figure to finance the purchase of literature for the centre. The Council are disposed to consider this favourably especially as they understand that some oral undertaking that it would be done was given by the late Lord Lloyd, although they have no record of this. It would seem that as this centre is now a going concern, its funds can hardly be amalgamated with those of the Egyptian Ambassador's scheme except in the sense that the Commercial Road centre and organisation might become a branch of the centre contemplated by the Egyptian Ambassador and his Committee. The money, however, would not be available for the Egyptian project. Mr. Blake told me that he was satisfied after consulting Sir Ernest Hotson that the London Mosque funds could not provide money from its own sources for the purpose for which the British Council has been asked to contribute.

(2) The London Nizamiah Mosque Trust. This Trust was set up in April 1928. Its present assets are somewhere between £67,000 and £77,000; the first figure being given by Sir Hassan Suhrawardy in his note of November last and the second in the Hyderabad memorandum enclosed with Sir A. Hydari's letter of the 23rd February. Possibly the difference is due to the fact that Sir Hassan Suhrawardy took the cost price of the site, while the Hyderabad figure is the present value based on an offer known to have been made by the War Office. The original Board of Trustees consisted of Lord Headley, the Aga Khan and three other Moslem gentlemen, but has been entirely reconstituted and now consists of Sir H. Suhrawardy, H.E. Hafiz Wahaba, Nawab Sir Aqeel Jung, Mr. Mohammed Ali Zainal Aliraza and Dr. Saeed Mohamedi.

A site has been purchased in Mornington Avenue, West Kensington, and in 1937 H.H. the Prince of Berar laid the foundation stone. The project is at present held up by legal difficulties with an architect (Brumwell Thomas) with whom there have been legal proceedings which were settled by a compromise payment, one of the terms of which was that if the work of building the Mosque started within 10 years of the date of the decree (July, 1933) and if any of the Trustees against whom the decree was passed, were in office at that time, the work should be entrusted to Sir Brumwell. The complete change in the personnel of the Trustees has removed this obligation but it is thought desirable to postpone work until July 1943 to be on the safe side.

It is stated in the Hyderabad note that as the foundation stone has been laid, the site cannot now be used for any other purpose. This presumably refers to some religious requirement.

(3) The Egyptian Ambassador's Scheme. This is the scheme strongly supported by the late Lord Lloyd. It is a plan for a Mosque and cultural centre in the centre of London which will be a central place of worship for Moslems in the Empire equivalent to the Moslem centres in Paris, Rome and Berlin. The scheme appears first to have been mooted by a Mr. Mougy in 1938 and was taken up by the Egyptian Government after the Palestine Conference. The Cabinet has authorised expenditure of up to £100,000 to provide a site and made the Secretary of State for the Colonies responsible for carrying the matter through. The promoters of the scheme were informed that H.M.G. were prepared "to provide a site on which the construction of a Mosque could begin as soon as the necessary funds have been contributed and conditions in the building trade allow". Lord Halifax and Lord Lloyd were satisfied that about £250,000 would be forthcoming from Moslem sources.

I understand from Mr. Luke of the Colonial Office who deals with this matter, that enquiries are being pursued with the Ministry of Works and Buildings for a site. The original proposal was for a site opposite the Victoria and Albert Museum in South Kensington, but the latest idea is a site on the south side of the river as a part of the L.C.C. reconstruction scheme for that area. Not very much progress has been made but I understood that the Colonial Office were expecting to hear from us the result of the approach to the Nizam.

It seems quite clear that the Nizam is not prepared to merge his scheme in one which is primarily under Egyptian auspices. This bears out the opinion originally held by Sir Miles Lampson that the Egyptian Government would desire to collect all the credit for this proposal and I understand that the Egyptian idea is that an Egyptian Government architect shall design and erect the Mosque. India is represented on the Committee by the High Commissioner and Sir Hassan Suhrawardy. The other representatives are the Iraqi Ambassador and the Saudi Minister. The Viceroy is not prepared to apply any pressure to the Nizam and the Nizam appears to expect to be protected from Egyptian competition. It seems very doubtful whether without the Nizam's support, funds will be forthcoming to erect the centre which from our point of view may perhaps be fortunate.

As regards the Foreign Office letter of the 9th May my own view is that the objections raised to the British Council contributing to the Commercial Road centre are not very strong. Mr. Blake told me that the basis of their belief that the India Office supported the proposal was that Sir Hassan Suhrawardy was one of the Secretary of State's Advisers. There does not seem to me to be any great force in the argument that the Council may be asked to support other religious movements. If they are they can refuse unless they think there is a good case for doing so. The Hindus are the only comparable religious body within the Empire and a request from them is perhaps unlikely. It seems that the London Mosque Fund are in possession of sufficient assets to keep the centre going for some time and I would suggest that we tell the Foreign Office that while we do not feel very strongly in the matter we should be inclined to support the proposal that the British Council should contribute something provided that they are satisfied that the centre is a fairly flourishing affair and requires assistance. I have asked I.P.I. if he can contribute anything on this point but he says that he has no definite information on this point, but that there are very few Moslems in the East End now, as shipping is largely diverted to West Coast ports and lascars are not coming to London. Dock workers generally have tended to move with the work. He feels a good deal of doubt whether there is a case for a contribution at the moment.

I think that on this, we might well tell the Foreign Office that while we favour the idea in principle and do not think there is much force in their objections, we are doubtful if at the moment there is a case for financing a centre in the East End, when it is very liable to be bombed and where there are believed to be few Moslems at the moment, and feel that any assistance given should be on a much lower scale than is proposed in their letter. I suggest a draft.

Assessment of the position of Sir H. Suhrawardy (dated 31.5.1941)

BL, IOR, L/P&J/12/468, fos 190–191

The position of Sir H. Suhrawardy in this matter is a delicate one. In his capacity as Muslim Adviser he has perforce had to shoulder the mantle of his predecessors in the shape of Trusteeship of both the London Mosque and the Nizamiah Mosque Trusts, which has since been induced to become closely associated also with the Egyptian scheme. His assertion that Fund (1) could be amalgamated with Fund (3) and his efforts to persuade the Hyderabad authorities to pool Fund (2) may be unduly optimistic. I understand that he and his colleagues on Fund (2) will probably take legal advice about the interpretation of the Nizamiah Trust, in the matter of diverting its capital to another project.

It seems best to consider the Foreign Office reference in regard to assistance to Fund (1) independently of what may be done in the matter of Fund (3) and on its own merits. There is clearly something to be said for making the gesture of giving some small assistance to a Moslem religious enterprise already working in a poor quarter of London where poor Moslems are most likely to be found. But as at the moment they are said to be fewer than usual I would advise very limited assistance, [deleted], particularly if the late Lord Lloyd contemplated some such assistance. This corresponds with Mr. Turnbull's suggestions at A & B of his note, except that I would make the recurring grant £50 p.a.

As regards the relation between Funds (2) and (3), I do not think that any obligation has been contracted to tell the C.O. what the Nizam's Government have said to the Trustees of Fund (2). This would raise the question how far that Government is free to override the views of the Trustees who, according to Sir H. Suhrawardy, have here a majority in favour of merger with the Egyptian scheme (Fund (3)). It might be sufficient for Mr. Turnbull to tell Mr. Luke that according to our information the Hyderabad Government's attitude has been defined in a letter to the Trustees of the Nizamiah Mosque Fund here and that they will no doubt explain the position to the promoters of the Egyptian Mosque in due course. (Sir H. Suhrawardy has told me that in fact he will be holding a meeting with his co-trustees to determine precisely what is to be said to the Egyptian Ambassador, probably after taking legal advice).

Report on the Jamiat-ul-Muslimin in Great Britain (dated 30.10.1943)

BL, IOR, L/P&J/12/468, fos 71–74

The Jamiat-ul-Muslimin was founded in England in 1934, with an office at 59, Canton St, E.14. It was registered under the Charitable Societies Act and was stated to comply with all the requirements of a Charitable Society. Its declared objectives were: to serve the cause of Islam truly and practically by creating facilities for the observance of its Principles: to produce a weekly paper (the, the [*sic*] 'Muslim Standard'); to collect funds for a Mosque in the East End of London; to provide for the training and education of Muslims generally: to succour poor and needy Muslims: to promote social intercourse between resident Muslims and visitors to this country and generally to adopt all practical and legitimate means to work for the moral, intellectual and economic advancement of Muslims throughout the world.

1. The original President was Dr Mohammed BUKSH, Co. Secretaries, AHMAD DIN QUERESHI (Silk merchant, trading as Quereshi & Co., of 36, Church Lane, Aldgate)

and GHULAM MOHAMMED, who lived at the address of the Jamiat: Treasurer, ALLAH DAD KHAN, salesman of 530, Commercial Rd, E.1. The Committee consisted of four officials and twenty members.

2. In its early years the JAMIAT did not come to notice, in fact it was first heard of in 1938 when it organised a protest against the chapter on the Prophet in Mr H.G. Wells' "Short History of the World". (A deputation was interviewed by the High Commissioner and dispersed quietly). In September 1938 it appealed for funds to the Jamiat-ul-Ulema-i-Hind in Delhi. In April 1939 it protested against the invasion of Albania by the Italians and, in sending a copy of its protest to the Italian Embassy, demanded that Mussolini should renounce the title of "Protector of Islam" which he had assumed after the conquest of Abyssinia. At this time of its existence the Jamiat was described by SURAT ALI as a purely religious body, but of progressive outlook; he said it should not be taken that it had any connection with the organisation of the same name which had been formed by the Grand Mufti of Palestine.

3. In November, 1910, a fund was started in London by influential Muslims for the purpose of building a Mosque worthy of Islam and of the capital of the British Empire. In November 1926 a Deed of Trust was executed and the Fund, known thereafter as the London Mosque Fund, was vested in Trustees: a clause of the Deed provided that the majority of the Trustees and the Chairman of the Executive Committee must at all times be Muslim. The Trustees arranged for prayers to be held at various addresses in the West End of London, but when it became obvious that the majority of Muslims frequented or lived in the East End, the King's Hall, Commercial Rd, E.1, was rented for weekly prayers and other religious functions and the local Muslim association, i.e. the Jamiat, was entrusted with the arrangements. (1935). On 31.12.39, the Fund stood at £10,687 odd and in 1940 the Trustees purchased freehold property at 446/450 Commercial Rd, E.1, for the erection of the East London Mosque, which was formally opened on 1.8.41 by H.E. The Egyptian Ambassador. The Jamiat were appointed agents for the Trustees for managing the religious and other duties connected with the Mosque.

4. At this time, the Treasurer of the Jamiat-ul-Muslimin was, and still is, SAID AMIR SHAH, a silk merchant and film agent, who had already come to notice in political connections as a

supporter of the INDIA LEAGUE and generally as an agitator amongst East End Indians. SHAH has recently claimed that it was only through agitation by the Jamiat that the East London Mosque was built and that it was only after repeated representations to individual Trustees that the latter made any move to implement the objectives for which the London Mosque Fund was created. It may be said that up to the opening of the Mosque there were no indications that the Jamiat was politically inclined; from August 1941, however, SHAH has made every possible effort to turn it into a political weapon.

5. This became increasingly apparent after the arrests of the Congress leaders in 1942. By this time, SAID AMIR SHAH had more or less broken with V.K. KRISHNA MENON and the latter's India League and had transferred his allegiance to AMIYA NATH BOSE and the latter's Committee of Indian Congressmen. That organisation was founded to give unqualified support to the Indian National Congress which, it maintained, had in its celebrated resolution of August 1942, declared a state of Civil Disobedience, and to demand that all power should be handed over to the Congress, making no mention of the claims of the Minorities. SHAH next created Provincial branches of the JAMIAT and followed this up by creating under the auspices of the Committee of Indian Congressmen and with the full cooperation of Bose a "NATIONAL INDIAN MUSLIM COMMITTEE", which gave full support to Congress and disputed the claims of the Muslim League to represent the majority of the Muslims of India.

Provincial Branches of the Jamiat-ul-Muslimin

6. SHAH and his colleagues now began to move about the Provinces, notably the Midlands and Glasgow areas holding meetings, with the result that his activities on behalf of the Jamiat and those for his Indian National Muslim Committee became inextricably tangled. It was reliably reported that by the end of 1942 he was using his position as an official of the Jamiat to obtain recruits for his own Muslim Committee and it later became clear that he was using both to obtain a control of the East London Mosque and the Mosque Fund and to create for himself the position of uncrowned king of the Muslim Community in Britain. He does not appear at any time to have been actuated by religious motives. As his Muslim Committee was from the start violently opposed to the Muslim League and

the Pakistan Plan, for both of which some supporters must exist in the Jamiat, the disruptive quality of his activities needs no stressing.

7. It was claimed that a branch of the Jamiat had been established in Glasgow and that premises had been taken there; the precise date of the inauguration of this Branch is not clear, but SHAH was in the habit of talking of "our people" in Glasgow long before he formed his Muslim Committee at the end of August 1942. It was further claimed that a Branch of the Jamiat had been established at Newcastle on Tyne in August 1942, a Manchester Branch in October and a Birmingham Branch in November of the same year. Many of SHAH's relatives and business associates were installed as officials of the provincial branches, particularly in the Birmingham one. (The Birmingham Committee includes Jan MOHAMED, friend of S.A. Shah; ABBAS SHAH (relative), ZAMAN ALI (agent of Shah Bros and suspected of being involved in the Black Market) and SHABIR HUSSAIN SHAH (connected with Black Market Trade and an associate of Shah, Abbas Shah and of Zaman Ali; he is probably a relative of Shah)[)].

The position in Glasgow is confused. The Jamiat there is under the guidance of Ghulam Mohamed SHARIF, a Punjabi Mohammedan, who was also a leading light in the Hindustani Majlis. In May 1943 the Jamiat closed its premises – it was said on account of disunity amongst the members. In July it was stated that since the majority of the Mohammedans in Glasgow were seamen and hence, to some extent already catered for by the Indian Seamen's Welfare Centre run by the Majlis, there was not much point in the Jamiat indulging in welfare activities which would probably only add to the existing confusion. (The latter was doubtless due to the visits of S.A. Shah to Glasgow, coupled with the activities of SURAT ALI, who was endeavouring to attract the Majlis into his own orbit). It is certain that the Jamiat still owns premises in Glasgow and that plans are entertained for developing a branch there. (See para 8).

8. It has become regular routine for the Supreme Council of the Jamiat to meet periodically in one or other of the Provincial Towns and not regularly in London – following the pattern of Ali's Federation of Indian Associations in Great Britain, and doubtless to offset the activities of the latter, as well as to enable Shah to proselytise amongst Muslims outside London.

On 16.5.43, the Council met in Birmingham. On this occasion a resolution was passed that at all centres where the Jamiat had branches freehold property should be bought which during the war would serve as headquarters of the Muslim community and that after the war, if the Muslim community seemed inclined to settle there permanently, a Mosque should be built; otherwise the property would be sold and the proceeds put to a fund for building a Mosque primarily in Glasgow and thereafter in any other centre which needed one.

On 19.6.43, a report was given on the Jamiat to the Manchester Branch by SAHIBDAD KHAN. He stated that at that date the Jamiat had £1,000 in hand: of this amount £400 had been collected in Birmingham, £260 represented a credit balance from the previous year and the remainder had been collected in London for the "Mosque Fund" (vide above). At this meeting a further £312 was collected. Said Amir Shah and Sahibdad Khan claimed to have contributed £200 apiece to the total funds. It was stated that it was proposed to run the Jamiat on lines similar to the Indian Workers Union (an organisation affiliated to Ali's Federation), i.e. the Committee administering the affairs of the Jamiat would, in future, be composed of representatives from the London Centre and from each of the Provincial Branches. (It is interesting to note that Manchester Jamiat members have, however, expressed doubts as to whether the money collected would be used for the purposes indicated and as to how Shah had disposed of monies collected in the past; similar doubts appear to have been voiced in Glasgow.[)]

On August 1st 1943 the Supreme Court of the Jamiat met at Newcastle on Tyne – this venue having been selected because other Indian meetings were taking place there round about the same date. Shah later boasted to Amiya Nath Bose that over £500 had been collected.

9. The East London Mosque and Trust Fund Dispute

The trouble which has arisen over the East London Mosque with the Board of Trustees appears to be almost entirely due to the ambitions and activities of SHAH and the results of his mobilisation of supporters from the Provinces was seen on October 10th, at a public meeting of the Jamiat, friends and supporters, convened by Shah on October 10th with the assistance of Bose. (It was decided between them that this meeting must be convened under the auspices of the Jamiat and not under those of Shah's National Indian Muslim Committee). The object was to protest against the action of the Trustees, who had cancelled the authority of the Jamiat to act as their agents and had required the Jamiat to vacate the premises of the East London Mosque. Shah, and Sahibdad Khan to a lesser degree, appear to have brought the trouble to a head because it was not felt that they were in a position to acquire a Mosque of their own in London and as a result of their collection of funds, possibly elsewhere, and that they were therefore strong enough to throw off the supervision of the Board of Trustees and to use the Jamiat openly as a political organisation and not as a Charitable one. It is unfortunate that shortly after the opening of the East London Mosque in August 1941, these two should have been co-opted as additional members of the Executive Committee of the London Mosque Fund (they were the first members of the Jamiat to be so appointed); but it cannot be denied that their selection was practically inevitable owing to the large following they undeniably commanded in the East End. It was also unfortunate that the Board of Trustees was weakened by the absence from England of distinguished members such as Sir Aziz ul Haque and Sir Hassan Suhrawardhy, and by the inaccessibility of the Aga Khan. For a time after their co-option, things went smoothly, then under the increasing influence of Shah, the Jamiat started to press for changes in the Board of Trustees designed to give it the control of the East London Mosque. The Trustees resisted this pressure, the two Jamiat members resigned and finally on October 1st, as no reply had been received to their notice to vacate the premises, the Trustees instituted legal proceedings, or threatened them.

10. The protest meeting on October 10th was attended by about 400 persons, less than 20 of them Europeans and most of them Punjabi and Bengali Mahommedans. It was very significant that amongst the audience were sundry non-Mahommedans such as Amiya Nath BOSE (who frankly confessed that he was very much interested in "certain political aspects of the dispute"), and I.G.P. SINGH, K.S. SHELVANKAR and others, who presumably went to spy out the land for the benefit of the Communist Party, Swaraj House and the India League, all of which take a very meddlesome interest in the affairs of East End Indians. Sunder KABADI considered the meeting so important that he cut the relatively more spectacular Delegate Conference of the India League which took place on the same

day and went instead to the Jamiat meeting. The atmosphere seems to have been electric and apparently only the diplomatic handling of matters by the chairman (Sahibdad Khan) and some counsels of moderation from the Manchester delegate prevented an uproar. As it was, Sahibdad Khan succeeded in preventing any discussion after the speeches. SAID AMIR SHAH, however, has no intention of letting matters rest there; he proposes to bring out a pamphlet keeping off legal points and stressing emotional and religious aspects of the dispute best calculated to foster agitation. So far there is no indication that Shah has secured via Bose any "Parliamentary support" for his side, but as there is no doubt that he had the full collaboration of Bose in the running of the Jamiat meeting, this may be due to the fact that Bose has recently been too much occupied with his Famine campaign to tackle the Jamiat question at the highest levels accessible to him.

Miscellaneous

11. In May 1943, a paper called "MUSLIM NEWS" made its first appearance, issued from 36, Whitechurch Lane, the address of AHMAD DIN QUERESHI, one of the secretaries of the Jamiat; it was distributed in the Provinces. This issue was innocuous, but as in June 1943, S.A. SHAH was generally interesting himself in securing articles for forthcoming issues and also in securing from I.K. KAZI, (Karachi) an "Indian Letter", it is probable that subsequent issues were not so reputable. (None have so far been seen).

12. Reports of the activities of the Jamiat-ul-Muslimin in England have been sent by S.A. SHAH to I.I. Kazi, who has promised to despatch books for the use of the organisation which he has purchased on their account.

Statement issued by Sir Hassan Suhrawardhy (n.d.)

BL, IOR, L/P&J/12/468, fos 58–60

As a Trustee, and also as Chairman of the Executive Committee of the London Mosque Fund, I am making the following statement to remove the misleading impression caused by the matter published in the leaflet circulated by the Jamiat-ul-Muslimin.

1. The London Mosque Fund dates from 1910 when a meeting was held, under the Chairmanship of His Highness the Aga

Khan, of persons interested in the project for the erection and maintenance of a Mosque in London. As a result of that meeting a Committee was formed for the purpose of collecting funds and for the purpose of appointing Trustees of the Fund. In 1926 a Deed of Trust was drawn up. The Trustees at that time were H.H. the Aga Khan, the Rt. Hon. Syed Ameer Ali, Sir Muhammad Rafique, Lord Lamington and Lord Ampthill and these five persons, three Muslims and two Christians, were appointed Trustees under the Deed of Trust.

2. The Deed of Trust also provides for an Executive Committee. The first Chairman of this Committee was the Rt. Hon. Syed Ameer Ali, the Secretary was Sir Thomas Arnold and the Treasurer Mr A.S. Mahomed Ali Anik.

3. Although between 1910 and 1928 over £6,000 were subscribed by representative Muslims all over the world, including H.I.M. the Shah of Persia, H.I.M. the Sultan of Turkey, H.E.H. the Nizam of Hyderabad and the Sultan of Perak, the building of the Mosque was not proceeded with because the funds were considered inadequate. Arrangements were, however, made by the Trustees for the hiring of premises where Juma and Id prayers could be held. At first these premises were in the West End of London but as the number of persons attending was small it was decided in 1935 to make similar arrangements in the East End, where there is a considerable Muslim population. The Jamiat-ul-Muslimin, the local Muslim Association, was entrusted with the arrangements and King's Hall in Commercial Road E.1. was rented out of funds provided by the Trustees. In 1938, in view of the considerable number of persons attending prayers, the Trustees decided to purchase a site for a small Mosque and a Muslim hostel in the East End and a Sub-Committee consisting of two Trustees, Sir Abdul Qader (Chairman) and Mr Waris Ameer Ali, and the then Honorary Secretary, Sir Ernest Hotson, was constituted for the purpose. In 1939 Sir Hassan Suhrawardy succeeded Sir Abdul Qader as a Trustee and as Chairman of the Sub-Committee and in 1940 the premises at 446–450 Commercial Road were purchased. These premises, purchased, repaired and remodelled at a total cost of over £4,000, provide accommodation for (a) the Mosque, (b) the Islamic Culture Centre and (c) the caretaker's quarters. The Mosque and the Culture Centre were opened by His Excellency the Egyptian Ambassador in August 1941. This ceremony was attended by a large gathering. Sir Ernest Hotson, the then Honorary Secretary to the Trustees, read the

report and speeches were made by Mr. Amir Shah and Mr Ahmeddin Qureshi in which they, on behalf of the Jamiat-ul-Muslimin, thanked the Trustees of the London Mosque Fund for providing a Mosque and a Culture Centre. They made particular reference to the work done by Sir Hassan Suhrawardy and Sir Ernest Hotson.

4. At this time although two of the Trustees and the Honorary Secretary were Christians, the relations between the Trustees and the Executive Committee on the one hand and the Jamiat on the other were cordial. The Jamiat out of their own funds had provided furniture and other fittings for some of the rooms. In 1941 the Trustees decided to appoint the Jamiat as their agents for the management of the Mosque and the Culture Centre. This arrangement was made in agreement with the Jamiat by means of a letter from the Trustees which inter alia provided for the termination of the arrangements by seven days' notice by either party. Two members of the Jamiat were also appointed as members of the Executive Committee.

5. The income of the Trustees from invested funds is about £250 a year and it is from this income that the greater part of the expenditure on the maintenance of the Mosque and the Culture Centre has been met.

6. Unfortunately the relations between the Trustees and the Jamiat have deteriorated and about two months ago the Jamiat demanded that a majority of the Trustees and of the members of the Executive Committee should be composed of members of the Jamiat. This was a demand to which the Trustees could not agree and it was decided that the agency arrangements with the Jamiat should be terminated in accordance with the terms of the agreement by which that agency was established. Seven days notice of the termination of the agency arrangement was accordingly given. The termination of the agency agreement involves, of course, no change in the position of the Mosque as a place of Muslim worship. It is open to all Muslims for the purpose of prayer. Further in the notice which was sent to the Jamiat the Trustees explained that if the Jamiat or any other body of Muslims desired to arrange a function after Id prayers or on the occasion of the Prophet's Birthday, they would be only too glad to allow such functions to be held.

7. The Jamiat alleges that the notice given by the Trustees is illegal because a non-Muslim cannot be a Trustee of a Mosque Fund. As has been pointed out, the Deed of Trust of 1926 was drawn

up by H.H. the Aga Khan, the Rt. Hon. Syed Ameer Ali, (an eminent jurist and recognised authority on Muslim Law) and Sir Muhammad Rafique (a former Judge of the Allahabad High Court). They certainly were well acquainted with Muslim Law and would not have included two Christians (Lord Lamington and Lord Ampthill) as Trustees if such a course was in any way opposed to Islam. Again it is impossible to believe that His late Imperial Majesty the Sultan of Turkey, H.I.M. the Shah of Persia, H.R.H. the Nizam of Hyderabad, the Sultan of Perak and other representative Muslims would have subscribed to a Mosque Fund, the Trustees of which included Christians, if the inclusion of persons of the Christian faith on the Board of Trustees was in any way repugnant to Islam tenets. It should also be remembered that the Jamiat took no objection to the presence of Christians among the Trustees (i) during the years during which it (the Jamiat) received assistance from the Trustees towards the renting of King's Hall, (ii) at the time of the purchase of the property in Commercial Road in which the Mosque is situated, (iii) at the time of the opening ceremony of the Mosque and the Islam Culture Centre and (iv) at the time the arrangement was made by which the Jamiat was appointed the agent of the Trustees for the Mosque and the Culture Centre. It was only when the Trustees terminated this arrangement that the Jamiat discovered that according to the Holy Quran no non-Muslim can be a Trustee of a Mosque Fund or be in any way connected with it.

8. The Jamiat-ul-Muslimin also seeks to maintain that the "Board of Trustees" is non-Islamic because it runs counter to the words and spirit of the Holy Quran and the Surat-al-Baqra and the Surat-at-Tauba relating to Islamic tenets which govern the laws of the Wakf and the Mutwalli. The Jamiat is again wrong. The true facts are that the passages on which they rely apply to idolators, their confederates and the hypocrite Muslim who, under the pretext of promoting the cause of Islam opened a Mosque in the neighbourhood of Prophet's Mosque at Quba near Medina, and were circulating misleading lies. These allegations certainly do not apply to the Trustees as they have not started a new Mosque in opposition to an existing one in the East End of London. The Trustees are not idolators. The Trustees have made it quite clear in the notice cancelling the appointment of the Jamiat-ul-Muslimin as their agents that the East London Mosque remains open to all Muslims without restriction, and permission will be given to the

Jamiat-ul-Muslimin or any Muslim Association, or any other body or person who would like to arrange any function for Id, Prophet's birthday, or any other such occasion, when in the interests of the Muslim such a function could be properly held in the Muslim premises. (This para. has not been printed by the Jamiat in their leaflet).

9. At present all the Trustees are Muslim, except one, Earl Winterton, well-known for his sympathy and friendship for the Muslim cause. All the members of the Executive Committee of the London Mosque Fund are Muslims with the exception of the Hon. Treasurer, who is a Christian.

   A Managing Committee for the Mosque, composed entirely of Muslims, was appointed in 1941. However, so long as the Jamiat was the agent of the Trustees such a managing committee was not functioning. Now that the Jamiat has ceased to be the agents of the Trustees, the Managing Committee for the Mosque will resume its duties and members of the congregation will be invited to serve on it.

Information on two leading members of the Jamiat-ul-Muslimin (dated 1.11.1943)

BL, IOR, L/P&J/12/468, fos 75–79

SAID AMIR SHAH

b/o Fazal Shah and ? nephew of Akbar Shah.
Born: Ajwala, dist. Amritsar, Punjab.

Treasurer Jamiat-ul-Muslimin.
m/o firm of Shah Bros., Silk merchants and warehouseman, 8 Whitechurch Lane. Has in his time run Indian boarding houses in the East End and also had a shop at 36 Old Montague Street. Before the war he acted as a contractor to Film Companies in respect of Indian "crowds".

AMIR SHAH first came to notice as representing East End Indians on the Executive Committee of the London branch of the Indian National Congress. (This branch was later disaffiliated by the I.N.C.). His name cropped up now and again between 1930 and 1932 as the owner of somewhat doubtful Indian boarding houses, but he did not otherwise attract attention until 1939, when, with his brother Fazal Shah, he ran an employment agency for Indian film extras whom they recruited from lascars and hawkers in return for substantial commissions. In

November of that year Fazal Shah returned to India and there was good reason for thinking that he had done so because he was alarmed lest the authorities had become aware that he and Amir Shah had been falsifying their Income Tax returns.

In 1940 Amir SHAH was taking a good deal of interest in cases in which Indian seamen figured and actually acted as official Court interpreter. His contact with V.K. Krishna MENON began at this time, as the latter was similarly interested in cases of lascars. In this year he was said to be very anti-British and showed symptoms of defeatism: he certainly did not wish to invest his money in this country.

During 1941 and during the earlier part of 1942, Menon, who had himself no means of approach to East End Indians, cultivated SHAH and endeavoured to secure his influence in propagating the India League "line". Neither of the pair has any great opinion of the other, but there was, nevertheless, a certain amount of collaboration between them in regard to meetings and collection of funds for the India League and for various objectives sponsored by the latter. Shah, for instance, was responsible for calling an East End Indian Conference on 9.8.41, and attended the India League conference on 10.8.41.

In September 1941, with Professor G.S. DARA who acted as accountant to the firm of Shah Bros., he formed the Hindustani Majlis. This organisation, it was stated, had been originally formed to promote studies in Indian languages, but was extended in its scope to include "social and cultural" activities; it finally embarked on politics with the ambitious intention of co-ordinating the activities of East End and "West End" Indians. There is no evidence that anything concrete was achieved along these lines by the Hindustani Majlis.

In 1942 it was reported that Amir SHAH was encouraging anti-Soviet ideas in the East End and was maintaining that neither Britain nor Russia had the right to occupy any Moslim country. On Indian Independence Day he attended a meeting organised by the India League as representative from the East End and read the pledge of Independence in Urdu.

With John Kartar Singh, Sahibdad Khan and Ahmed Din Qureshi, he evinced a certain amount of interest in the affairs of the Hindustani Social Club; they did not wish to associate themselves unduly with it, since it was run by the Communist, Surat Ali, but thought that there was something to be said for joining it in order to oust Ali from the secretaryship. They were unable to agree on concerted action in this matter.

In July 1942 Amir SHAH founded the Shah Film Corporation, with himself as Managing Director, and Kartar Singh and Herbert Bundy as co-Directors. On 4.7.42 Kartar Singh had been fined £2,500 for exceeding a quota of razor blades and penalised to the further amount of £250. There were reports that both Amir Shah and Kartar Singh were engaged in Black Market activities. This allegation has been quite recently repeated in regard to Shah.

In August 1942 Amir SHAH's political activities greatly increased. He became, so to speak, the "Moslem member" of the Committee of Indian Congressmen in Great Britain, and has taken a very active part in this connection, both in the direction of addressing meetings and collecting funds. The C.I.C. was originally the creation of Amiya Nath Bose, nephew of Subhas Bose, and P.B. Seal, and the presence of these two amongst its Office Bearers led to the organisation being regarded as pro-Fascist and pro-Subhas Bose, and also to a number of splits amongst the membership. Nevertheless, Shah remains one of the leading figures in the organisation and clearly intends, by means of it, to increase his influence upon East End Indians who are useful to him for his various commercial enterprises (e.g. the recruitment of film crowds). The fact that he has contacts with the Indian working class, is, of course, a decided asset to the C.I.C. These activities on Shah's part have naturally led to a rift with Menon, who is now denouncing him in no uncertain terms as a pro-Fascist and a Black Marketeer.

Amir SHAH has for some time (possibly at the original instance of Menon) been bitterly anti-Moslem League and has characterised the League as a traitorous organisation in the pay of Great Britain "led by Jinnah who received a princely sum as the price of his services to the British". He went to the expense of having copies printed of a speech expounding these views made by him at a meeting of the C.I.C. held in the East End on 28.10.42.

It is now clear that from 1941 onwards, SHAH has been trying to work himself up to a position of leadership in Moslem circles in this country. It is highly improbable that he has any religious motives in the matter, but desires to strengthen his hand as uncrowned king amongst Indian merchants, peddlers and seamen in the East End and in Provincial towns. In October 1941, when the East London Mosque was opened, he commented to the effect that it was not the Mosque he wanted, but it would have its uses. Shortly afterwards he was one of two members of the Jamiat-ul-Muslimin co-opted onto the Board of Trustees of the Mosque and the Mosque Fund, and thereafter campaigned strenuously to obtain control, through the Jamiat-ul-Muslimin, of the Mosque and the Fund. He was particularly bitter against Sir Hassan Suhrawardhy, whom he regarded as pro-Moslem League.

In pursuance of these tactics, he formed Provincial branches of the Jamiat-ul-Muslimin, and staffed them to a great extent with persons who were either relations, friends or business associates, with the result that the non-political character of the Jamiat-ul-Muslimin altered in the course of a few months. Still with the same end in view, at the close of 1942, he founded an "Indian National Moslem Committee" with the aid of Amiya Nath Bose, and under the wing of the latter's Committee of Indian Congressmen. He used his position as an official of the Jamiat to recruit members for his new organisation and used the latter to foment the dispute between the Jamiat and the Board of Trustees of the East London Mosque, which came to a head in October 1943. (In this affair, which is still unsettled and has reached the hands of solicitors on both sides, he is undoubtedly the prime agitator). The aim of the Indian National Moslem Committee purports to be the union of all Indian Moslems in Great Britain in one organisation for the protection of their religious and political rights; its political aim is stated in its constitution to be the realisation of the complete and immediate independence of India. In the same publication it is announced that the Committee stands for joint electorates with reserved seats for Minorities, and condemns the Pakistan plan as a suicidal policy for Indian Moslems fostered by the enemies of Islam and India. The Constitution further stated that "the Committee stood for democracy, since that was the basic creed of Islam, and was therefore opposed to all forms of nomination and hereditary devolution of power, either in religious or political fields, which are against democratic procedure.[1]

Throughout the first half of 1943 SHAH collaborated very closely with Amiya Nath Bose and followed the fortunes of the latter's organisation, the Committee of Indian Congressmen. During these months, and also up to date, he has acted as a spy for Bose on the activities of other Indian organisations. Nevertheless, he cannot be said to have been loyal to Bose, for in June and July of this year he was attempting pourparlers with both the India League and Swaraj House, ostensibly to create unity amongst Indians – but the piece de resistance in all suggestions was that Bose and Seal should be eliminated from the C.I.C. It seems that these moves were really an attempt to ascertain whether there was any chance of creating an organisation to defeat

[1] There is no closing quotation mark in the original document.

Surat Ali, of whose influence in the East End and the Provinces he has become exceedingly nervous.

SHAH is at the moment supporting Bose's Famine Campaign, partly to enhance his own importance in the East End and the Province generally, and partly because he apparently wants Bose's assistance, or that of Bose's Press contacts, in regard to the East London Mosque dispute. Bose sent a telegram to the Mayor of Calcutta in Shah's name, and other telegrams in his own name, Seal's, and that of his Committee of Indian Congressmen. Replies have been received out of which much capital is being made, the one sent to Shah being specially useful to the latter for display to his following. This rather astute move on the part of Bose will make it difficult for Shah to wriggle away from the Committee of Indian Congressmen for the time being. Bose, like other Indian leaders in the UK, evidently mistrusts Shah but is forced to use him as a contact with the Indian working classes.

SHAH has spoken at numerous meetings under various auspices during the past year, including meetings of Surat Ali's Hindustani Social Club, which he desires to penetrate. For example, on 10.5.43, he spoke at a meeting to celebrate "Indian Martyrs' Days", lauded the Mutiny as a great event in Indian history, and blamed the "Lords of Whitehall" for initiating and encouraging the Pakistan movement, which, he said, permitted the Moslem landlords to suck the blood of the Moslem peasantry. It was, he said, the latest example of the "Divide and Rule Principle". He urged Indians to do something concrete for their country – to act.

It is interesting to note that he held one meeting under the auspices of the Indian National Moslem Committee to pray for Gandhi's health during the latter's fast, and to demand his release. In his speech on that occasion, he said that the Moslem community had undying faith in Gandhi as their leader and that, in spite of what was published in the British Press, every Moslem in India was behind Gandhi, who had been elected leader of Congress by all castes and creeds. These utterances, coming from the Treasurer of the Jamiat-ul-Muslimin, which presumably includes supporters of Jinnah, are not likely to make for peace within that organisation.

SAHIBDAD KHAN

Punjabi Mohammedan, s/o Abdulah Khan.
Born: Kal Kligri, dist. Jhelum, on 8.8.96
Passport no. 4080, issued Lahore 1920, renewed London 17.3.26, to enable him to visit France, Germany and the U.S.A.

Married to an Englishwoman; two children.
Address: 135 Benhurst Avenue, Elm Park, Romford, Essex
According to Police records, KHAN first came to the United Kingdom in 1923, lived in the Mornington Crescent district and was known by his clan name "CHUMA". In 1926 he went to the U.S.A. and returned the following year, since when he has been engaged in the perfumery business. In 1935 he commenced to trade at 9 Assam Street, E.1, under the name of the Egyptian Perfumery Company, but since 1938 has traded under his own name. He has one employee, Ghulam Mohammed Buta, a Punjabi aged 40, who has been with him since May 1942 and is paid £5 per week. He is reported to be a "conscientious Moslem and less interested in politics than Khan".

At one time Sahibdad Khan and Syed Akbar Shah (relative of Said Amir Shah) were associated in business; in October 1937 they were granted a license in respect of the Oriental Artistes Agency (Films), but this business has now ceased to function.

Sahibdad KHAN first came to notice as interested in politics in 1935, when he was one of those who signed an address of welcome to Nehru. In the same year he was reported to be associating with Surat Ali and to be treasurer of the Colonial Seamen's Association but information is limited on this point to one not very conclusive report.

In 1939 he was described as by no means extreme in his sentiments but as coming under the thumb of Said Amir SHAH and as acting as Secretary of the latter's organisation "Indian Residents in Great Britain" (now apparently defunct). Shah's idea in forming this organisation seems to have been to counter the effects in the East End of Surat Ali's Hindustani Social Club. (Said Amir Shah loathes Surat Ali).

In August 1941 he attended the India League meeting held in the East End (9.8.41) which was run with the aid of Sair [*sic*] Amir Shah; with the latter he was on the platform representing Moslem interests and was described as Joint Hon. Sec. of the Jamiat-ul-Muslimin. He announced that the purpose of the meeting was to appoint delegates to the India League Conference the following day and was himself elected as also was Said Amir Shah. Speaking in Hindustani, he made a moderate speech, advising unity and punctuality amongst Indians as likely to be conducive to a co-ordination of activities in the direction of securing freedom.

On 24.1.42 he attended an Indian Independence Day meeting staged by the India League and on the following day presided over one organised by the Hindustani Social Club. He appealed to Indians to sink their petty differences and unite.

In March 1942 he was showing some interest in the Hindustani Club. He considered it would be better to "penetrate" it, with a view to removing Surat Ali from the secretaryship, rather than to increase friction by starting a rival show to the Club.

In October 1942 he appeared to be taking a very mild and friendly interest in the affairs of the Indian Workers Association, and on 25th October is reported to have attended the first public meeting organised by the Committee of Indian Congressmen in Great Britain (Amiya Nath Bose's organisation).

On 31st January 1943 he attended and spoke at an Indian Independence Day meeting run by the Hindustani Social Club in the East End. He contended that there was no disunity between the Hindu and Moslem Committees, and that it was a myth created by the British Government and exploited by them for propaganda purposes and to justify denial of freedom to India.

He referred to the then impending battles in North Africa and said that the Allies should not attack Tunisia, a Moslem country, thereby endangering the lives of Tunisian Moslems. He added that Moslems in the Middle East and in India were anxiously awaiting developments.

In August 1943 it was reported that KHAN, who had a license to purchase spirits for use in perfumery manufacture, disposed of his purchase at a profit of over 200%. The informant added that there was rivalry between him and Said Amir Shah, who also dealt in the Black Market, but that they were careful not to tread on each other's toes.

On 14th October, after the meeting held by the Jamiat-ul-Muslimin to protest against the action of the Trustees of the London Mosque Fund, Said Amir SHAH, discussing the proceedings, described Khan as "mentally defective". This was because Khan had wanted to stick to points which were absolutely legal – whereas Shah and his supporters wanted to avoid them, because "in agitation, controversial points must be avoided". Bose is understood to have commented that it must indeed be difficult to conduct a meeting of the Executive Committee of Shah's Indian National Moslem organisation, if that was Khan's method of procedure. Apparently Shah was incensed because Khan had jibbed at the publication of a pamphlet on the East London Mosque question, written from the "agitation" point of view, and wanted him to confine himself to facts.

Scotland Yard officers who have known Khan for nearly four years consider him a moderate man and a conscientious Moslem who devotes much of his time to the affairs of the East London Mosque. He is reported to have balanced ideas on the subject of Indian Independence in spite of being a keen nationalist. He has, according to them, never been deeply involved in extremist politics although serious attempts have been made to persuade him to take a more active part in both the India League and the Committee of Indian Congressmen, and they considered that he went to political meetings only to avoid trouble with his friends and spoke mildly at them, if at all.

INDEX